Cornell Studies in Security Affairs

edited by Robert J. Art *and* Robert Jervis

Strategic Nuclear Targeting, edited by Desmond Ball and Jeffrey Richelson
Japan Prepares for Total War: The Search for Economic Security, 1919–1941, by Michael A. Barnhart
The German Nuclear Dilemma, by Jeffrey Boutwell
Citizens and Soldiers: The Dilemmas of Military Service, by Eliot A. Cohen
Great Power Politics and the Struggle over Austria, 1945–1955, by Audrey Kurth Cronin
Military Organizations, Complex Machines: Modernization in the U.S. Armed Services, by Chris C. Demchak
Nuclear Arguments: Understanding the Strategic Nuclear Arms and Arms Control Debate, edited by Lynn Eden and Steven E. Miller
Public Opinion and National Security in Western Europe, by Richard C. Eichenberg
Innovation and the Arms Race: How the United States and the Soviet Union Develop New Military Technologies, by Matthew Evangelista
Men, Money, and Diplomacy: The Evolution of British Strategic Foreign Policy, 1919–1926, by John Robert Ferris
A Substitute for Victory: The Politics of Peacekeeping at the Korean Armistice Talks, by Rosemary Foot
The Wrong War: American Policy and the Dimensions of the Korean Conflict, 1950–1953, by Rosemary Foot
The Soviet Union and the Politics of Nuclear Weapons in Europe, 1969–1987, by Jonathan Haslam
The Soviet Union and the Failure of Collective Security, 1934–1938, by Jiri Hochman
The Warsaw Pact: Alliance in Transition? edited by David Holloway and Jane M. O. Sharp
The Illogic of American Nuclear Strategy, by Robert Jervis
The Meaning of the Nuclear Revolution, by Robert Jervis
Nuclear Crisis Management: A Dangerous Illusion, by Richard Ned Lebow
The Search for Security in Space, edited by Kenneth N. Luongo and W. Thomas Wander
The Nuclear Future, by Michael Mandelbaum
Conventional Deterrence, by John J. Mearsheimer
Liddell Hart and the Weight of History, by John J. Mearsheimer.
Inadvertent Escalation: Conventional War and Nuclear Risks, by Barry R. Posen
The Sources of Military Doctrine: France, Britain, and Germany between the World Wars, by Barry R. Posen
Winning the Next War: Innovation and the Modern Military, by Stephen Peter Rosen
Israel and Conventional Deterrence: Border Warfare from 1953 to 1970, by Jonathan Shimshoni

Fighting to a Finish: The Politics of War Termination in the United States and Japan, 1945, by Leon V. Sigal

The Ideology of the Offensive: Military Decision Making and the Disasters of 1914, by Jack Snyder

Myths of Empire: Domestic Politics and International Ambition, by Jack Snyder

The Militarization of Space: U.S. Policy, 1945–1984, by Paul B. Stares

Making the Alliance Work: The United States and Western Europe, by Gregory F. Treverton

The Origins of Alliances, by Stephen M. Walt

The Ultimate Enemy: British Intelligence and Nazi Germany, 1933–1939, by Wesley K. Wark

The Tet Offensive: Intelligence Failure in War, by James J. Wirtz

Inadvertent Escalation

CONVENTIONAL WAR AND NUCLEAR RISKS

BARRY R. POSEN

Cornell University Press

ITHACA AND LONDON

First published 1991 by Cornell University Press.

Cornell Paperbacks edition, 2014

ISBN: 978-0-8014-7885-7

Library of Congress Catalog Card Number 91-55055
Printed in the United States of America
Librarians: Library of Congress cataloging information appears on the last page of the book.

♾ The paper in this book meets the minimum requirements of the American National Standard for Information Sciences—Permanence of Paper for Printed Library Materials, ANSI Z39.48-1984.

Contents

Tables

Figures

Preface

The purpose of this book is to show how the interplay between conventional military operations and nuclear forces can inadvertently produce pressures for nuclear escalation in conflicts among states armed with both conventional and nuclear weaponry. It is premised on the assumption that knowledge of these hidden pressures may aid some future decision maker to avoid a catastrophe. Thus, this book continues in the tradition of the limited-war literature of the late 1950s and early 1960s. In Bernard Brodie's words, "Today . . . we speak of limited war in a sense that connotes a deliberate hobbling of a tremendous power that is already mobilized (nuclear forces) and that must in any case be maintained at a very high pitch of effectiveness for the sake only of inducing the enemy to hobble himself to like degree. No conduct like this has ever been known before."[1]

I base the analysis on the peculiarities of the East-West military competition in Europe, and its surrounding oceans and seas, in the 1980s. I believe, however, that it is relevant to all military competitions between states armed with both conventional and nuclear weaponry. Thus, this book speaks to some of the problems that will attend the proliferation of nuclear weaponry—especially to ongoing regional conflicts.

A great many suggestions for ways to limit a superpower war grew out of the early limited-war literature. Only two have had any long-term impact. The first was to have an assured nuclear retaliatory capability; the second was to have limited-war forces, which is to say conventional forces. Almost no new analysis of the requirements of limited war has been undertaken since.[2] The most outstanding exception, Richard

[1]Bernard Brodie, *Strategy in the Missile Age* (Princeton, 1959; reprint, 1965), p. 311.

[2]Many studies and analyses have been written in the government and by government consultants on "limited" nuclear war, especially its force structure requirements. This

Smoke's *War: Controlling Escalation* (1977), received less attention than it should have.[3]

The early limited-war theorists were influenced by three important problems: the record of costly, unintended escalation in the Korean War; the overdependence on nuclear forces of the Eisenhower massive-retaliation strategy; and the apparent instability of the strategic nuclear balance. The memory of Korea was washed away by Vietnam, an altogether different kind of catastrophe; the United States and its allies have purchased conventional forces in abundance since 1960; and the strategic balance came to seem so stable by the early 1970s that attention turned from fear that nuclear escalation might be too rapid to fear that the Soviets would not be deterred from anything by U.S. threats to escalate. Indeed, U.S. strategic nuclear weapons policy since the early 1970s has tried to generate more "usable" strategic nuclear forces, which has had the effect of rendering the strategic nuclear balance less stable rather than more.

My interest in the problem of limited war was kindled by two alarming developments in the public debate on U.S. national security policy in the late 1970s: the tendency to talk about a NATO–Warsaw Pact conventional war as a replay of World War II, as if nuclear weapons did not exist; and the tendency to talk about nuclear war as if it were a conventional artillery duel. Since these images of East-West conflict seemed implausible to me, an examination of the special qualities of conventional warfare among nuclear powers struck me as essential.

Since the 1960s the United States has pursued a two-pronged, internally inconsistent approach to its military forces. Secure second-strike capabilities and large conventional forces were bought to try to reduce the necessity and the temptation for rapid escalation to nuclear war. On the other hand, strategic nuclear counterforce capabilities have been acquired in an attempt to increase the adversary's perception that nuclear escalation might indeed occur. The United States acquired offensively postured conventional forces to add extra uncertainty to the task of any Soviet military planner and extra risks in the event of war. What U.S. policy makers did not do was examine the possibility that in actual practice these objectives could have proved inconsistent. In

literature actually discusses controlled nuclear escalation, which is not the subject of this book. Although some limited-war theorists have considered inadvertent nuclear escalation, it was not the primary focus of the limited-war literature.

[3] I believe this book suffered in the defense policy community from its focus on pre-World War II historical cases at a time when history was out of favor and, more important, from its lack of a few clear-cut, policy-relevant conclusions. It presented a rich menu of informed hypotheses more suitable to an academic audience.

the event of war, NATO's offensive conventional operations would have damaged Soviet nuclear forces in ways that encourage nuclear escalation. Similar tensions existed in Soviet military strategy throughout the 1980s.

With the lessening of great-power political hostility at the end of the decade, both parties to the competition seem disposed to reduce some of the offensive potential of both their nuclear and non-nuclear forces. But military doctrines and force postures tend to change slowly, and many of the problems outlined in this book will likely remain in some form for years to come. Even if these issues diminish in importance in the U.S.-Soviet military relationship, the spread of weapons of mass destruction to regional conflicts suggests that they will emerge in a slightly different, but arguably even more frightening guise.

From my perspective, the most important purpose of the book is to develop a sense of the hidden fundamental dynamics that would likely govern a large-scale conventional war between nuclear-armed adversaries. With three credible theories as our lenses, we are attempting to peer into a murky, horrible, possible future, the better to avoid it.

This effort has received generous support from the following institutions: the Carnegie Corporation of New York, the William and Flora Hewlett Foundation, and the Ford Foundation under the auspices of the Defense and Arms Control Studies Program at MIT; the Woodrow Wilson International Center for Scholars at the Smithsonian Institution; the Rockefeller Foundation; the Council on Foreign Relations; and the Center for International Affairs at Harvard University. John Mearsheimer, Jack Snyder, and Stephen Van Evera provided invaluable advice on the final rewrite of the manuscript. At various stages of the project, conversations with Bruce Blair, Joshua Epstein, Richard Kugler, and Steven Miller proved extremely useful. Robert Art, as usual, has far exceeded his responsibilities as an editor of this series. Laura H. Peters ably assisted in the editorial process. My wife, Cindy L. Williams, patiently supported my efforts to complete this project; although it often deprived me of my good humor, it never deprived her of hers.

BARRY R. POSEN

Cambridge, Massachusetts

Inadvertent Escalation

[1]

Introduction: A Model of Inadvertent Escalation

Can nuclear powers fight conventional wars with each other and avoid the use of nuclear weapons? Although this question has usually been raised in the context of the superpower competition, it is also relevant to future disputes in a world where nuclear weaponry has proliferated, including disputes among nuclear powers of every class, from the very great to the very small.

The most common view of how a conventional war could become a nuclear war stresses the initial stakes of the dispute. For example, had NATO found itself losing a conventional ground battle for control of Western Europe, the United States' most vital overseas interest, the United States might have reached for nuclear weapons in the hopes of salvaging its position. Alternatively, the Soviets would have expected such an event and preempted it with either a theater-wide or even an intercontinental attack. Although the issue is seldom discussed, this scenario has an analogue in terms of any dispute that would directly threaten the territory of a nuclear power. The French promise to employ nuclear weapons rather than see their territory violated by aggressor ground forces. Presumably, the United States or the Soviet Union would do the same, if either was threatened with conquest of its territory. These are quite standard views of the escalation process. They stem from the assumption that states are unlikely to leave such effective weapons unutilized in a struggle for vital political interests. This is a valid hypothesis and represents one plausible way that nuclear powers could move from conventional to nuclear conflict. Because of its simplicity, it is also a way that has been anticipated by political actors.

I propose in this book a second mechanism by which nuclear powers locked in conventional conflict might move to the use of nuclear weapons. Unpredicted by the political and military leaders who permit or order them, large-scale conventional operations may come into direct contact with the nuclear forces of an adversary and substantially affect the victim's confidence in his future ability to operate these forces in ways that he had counted upon. The most dangerous conventional attacks would be those that substantially degraded the basic nuclear retaliatory capability of the victim—his second-strike capability—for among nuclear powers this capability is the only insurance policy against nuclear coercion or annihilating attack. This fact suggests that the problems outlined herein will loom especially large for small and medium-sized nuclear powers, since they will have the most difficult time building nuclear forces that can survive. But lesser threats could also prove problematic, depending on peculiarities of each side's nuclear doctrine. For example, a series of non-nuclear attacks that degraded one side's ability to use its nuclear forces in discriminate ways for very limited attacks might be perceived as a major problem if that side had stressed this use of nuclear weapons in its prewar doctrine. Alternatively, if one side depended on a launch-on-warning or launch-under-attack posture, conventional damage to its early warning systems might be viewed as a major escalation.

I call this class of events "inadvertent nuclear escalation." It is a broad concept. I exclude from it occasional accidental conventional attacks on nuclear weapons—which are bound to happen in a conventional conflict. I also exclude from it deliberate and sustained conventional attacks on nuclear weapons that are explicitly developed and approved to alter a local or general nuclear-force relationship. In one short-lived incarnation the U.S. Navy's maritime strategy explicitly aimed to alter the nuclear "correlation of forces" through conventional attacks on Soviet ballistic missile submarines. During the 1980s the Soviet Union planned to attack NATO tactical nuclear forces with air-delivered conventional ordnance at the outset of any conflict in Europe for the purpose of reducing NATO's tactical nuclear capabilities. Neither of these scenarios ought to be viewed as inadvertent.

I would, however, include a rather broad range of events. For example, "incidental" conventional attacks on nuclear forces—conventional attacks that self-consciously threaten nuclear forces as a means to achieve a conventional mission—ought to be considered part of the problem of inadvertent escalation. The longer-lived incarnation of the U.S. Navy's maritime strategy, which deliberately threatened Soviet strategic missile submarines for the purpose of diverting to their defense Soviet attack submarines that might otherwise threaten the sea lines of communication (SLOC), would be an example of incidental attacks.

Since such operations were proposed and presumably approved on the basis of their contribution to a cherished conventional mission, I credit their advocates with lack of foresight, although some might argue they were simply disingenuous. Similarly, large-scale conventional operations conducted in a particularly sensitive area, which create the potential for multiple accidental encounters between conventional and nuclear forces, would also be included in the category of inadvertent escalation.

Thus, occasional encounters between conventional and nuclear units are not the main concern; rather, large-scale conventional operations that produce patterns of damage or threat to the major elements of a state's nuclear forces are the principal issue. Direct conventional attacks on critical nuclear forces, attacks that degrade strategic early warning or command and control systems, or even attacks on general-purpose forces that protect strategic nuclear forces, could all produce strong reactions from the party on the receiving end.

Large-scale conventional attacks on nuclear forces or their supporting structure are thus already a form of inadvertent nuclear escalation. The salience of nuclear forces for the conflict is raised inadvertently, before the imminent loss of the stakes that precipitated the conflict raises the nuclear specter. The threatened party could respond in many ways. It could ignore these attacks—a likely reaction if the state subscribed to a simple countervalue deterrence doctrine and the attacks really did not substantially erode the security of its retaliatory capability. If the state had not subscribed to a simple deterrent doctrine, it might suddenly be converted to such a doctrine—again ignoring these attacks unless they eroded the state's retaliatory capability. But if the attacks did erode the state's assured destruction capability, or the state subscribed to a strategy that called for the limited use of strategic nuclear weapons for purposes of bargaining or damage limitation and these capabilities were damaged by conventional attack, then stronger reactions from the threatened party are likely. And if its adversary was known to have a counterforce doctrine, a strong reaction seems even more likely. The most plausible response would be heightened preparations for nuclear operations, including the loosening of central civilian control over nuclear weapons and the dissemination of launch authority to military commanders. Among small nuclear powers this could be particularly dangerous, since their early warning and command and control apparatuses are likely to be less redundant and resilient than those found today in the medium-sized and great powers. More dangerous would be responses that actually employed nuclear weapons, ranging from limited demonstrative or tactical employment, through large-scale theater attacks, to full-scale counterforce exchanges.

Inadvertent nuclear escalation is clearly a difficult problem to study. We have no examples of such escalation so I cannot simply review multiple case studies and infer some lessons. Prospective analysis of plausible conventional wars among nuclear or near nuclear powers outside the superpower competition founders on an utter lack of data in most cases. The Israelis have told the world very little about their real military capabilities, and the Iraqis were equally reticent.

The NATO–Pact military competition—particularly in the 1980s—does provide useful material for this study. This period is notable for the extraordinary flow into the public domain of large amounts of data about both the military capabilities and the nuclear and conventional strategies of the East and West. Moreover, both sides had very large and very capable conventional and nuclear forces of tremendous range and striking power. Both stressed offensive operations of one type or another in both the conventional and nuclear realms.

U.S. and Soviet Nuclear Forces and Strategies in the 1980s

Aside from the loss of the stakes that precipitated war in the first place, the most long-lived and plausible hypothesized cause of nuclear escalation is perceived first-strike advantage. Standard criteria of strategic stability apply as much to escalation from conventional to nuclear war as they do to day-to-day strategic nuclear relationships. When both sides have large survivable retaliatory capabilities, nobody wants to move first. If one does and the other does not have a second-strike capability, then the dominant actor will be tempted to strike because he can thus save his country. Knowing this, the weaker, although he cannot save himself by striking first, may choose to operate his forces in ways that permit launch on warning or launch under attack in order to convince the dominant party not to try to exploit his capability. Some crisis instability may ensue.

The problem is, of course, much worse if both sides perceive that they have sizable first-strike advantages. Each will likely be tempted to strike first to exploit the advantage. If each also knows that the other perceives the world this way, they may both be tempted to strike first because of fear that the other will do so. Finally, there may even be "reciprocal fear of surprise attack." "I think that you will go first because you fear that I will go first, so I might as well go first."[1] When both sides perceive themselves and their adversary to have offensive advantages, it is very hard to imagine that serious, full-scale, conventional warfare could go on for long without one side or the other succumbing to the pressures and temptations of the situation and launching a nuclear preemption. Limited-war theorists of the late 1950s and early 1960s specified that secure second-strike capabilities were a precondition for sustained intense *conventional combat*.[2]

What would have induced either NATO or the Warsaw Pact to use nuclear weapons in the 1980s? Attitudes toward the first use of nuclear weapons among the western security elite were (and remain) contradictory. From one perspective, it came to be widely believed that neither the United States nor the Soviets have particularly itchy nuclear trigger fingers. Each side has deployed such massive nuclear forces, of such variety, that neither can generate a particularly plausible "theory of victory" for nuclear war.[3] Since the Cuban missile crisis, political leaders have shown great restraint whenever nuclear weapons were involved, and one suspects that the long-feared "clever briefer" would need powers of salesmanship that would put the most successful American used-car dealer to shame. Although mutual assured destruction (MAD), a purely punitive strategy based more or less exclusively on the ability to retaliate against adversary values, enjoyed no official political favor

[1]Stephen Van Evera suggests that reciprocal fear of surprise attack has been unusual in non-nuclear crises.

[2]William W. Kaufmann, "Limited Warfare," in *Military Policy and National Security*, ed. Kaufmann (Princeton, 1956), p. 119, observes of the Strategic Air Command, "Armed with nuclear weapons, it is not only the great instrument of last resort; it is also an absolute prerequisite to the conduct of limited war. It has the dual role of umpire and potential belligerent. As such it permits of military action on a lesser scale." Morton Halperin, *Limited War in the Nuclear Age* (New York, 1963), p. 98, observes: "Once both sides have invulnerable strategic forces the danger of preemption is low regardless of the strategies involved." See also p. 109. For similar views see Robert Osgood, *Limited War: The Challenge to American Strategy* (Chicago, 1957), pp. 125–130; Bernard Brodie, *Strategy in the Missile Age* (1959; reprint Princeton, 1965), pp. 331, 357; Thomas Schelling and Morton Halperin, *Strategy and Arms Control* (Washington, D.C., 1985), pp. 30–31, 62; Thomas Schelling, *Arms and Influence* (New Haven, 1966), pp. 105–116, 246–248.

[3]The most complete open-source technical analysis ever attempted is Michael Salman, Kevin Sullivan, and Stephen Van Evera, "Analysis or Propaganda? Measuring American Strategic Nuclear Capabilities, 1969–88," in *Nuclear Arguments*, ed. Lynn Eden and Steven E. Miller (Ithaca, 1989), tables 3.1 and 3.2, pp. 214–215, 222. The analysis suggests that had a war occurred "out of the blue" in 1987, after a surprise attack, 4436 U.S. strategic nuclear warheads, carrying 1411 equivalent megatons of explosive power, would have survived. After a similar attack by the United States against the Soviet Union, 847 warheads carrying 532 equivalent megatons would have survived. In either case, the residuals would have permitted not only utter destruction of the adversary's society but attacks against a large number of military targets, assuming that command and control survived.

in either the United States or the Soviet Union in the 1980s and continues to be unpopular, it appears that civilian decision makers have for a long time had very low confidence that any other nuclear war outcome is likely.[4] From the perspective of political leaders and their revealed propensity for risk, any first use of nuclear weapons has seemed quite improbable since the U.S. nuclear alert of the 1973 Arab-Israeli war, and even the heating up of Soviet-U.S. relations in the late 1970s and early 1980s did not increase the propensity for nuclear risk. Nevertheless, it is important to consider the potential energy for nuclear first use that has remained. On close inspection it seems to have been, and still is, surprisingly powerful. It is a worthwhile exercise to apply the most mature theories we have to try to predict the circumstances under which it might be released.

During the 1980s both superpowers organized their strategic nuclear forces to "wage" general thermonuclear war with objectives that were consistent with classical military thinking—the destruction of the adversary's forces.[5] Indeed, it is now clear that U.S. strategic nuclear forces have had a "warfighting" doctrine almost since their inception. Given the ineffectiveness of defenses against these forces, any possibility of unilaterally limiting damage to one's own country, should war come, depended on the strength of the offensive, the elimination of the adversary's nuclear weapons. Each side labored persistently and patiently in an effort to find ways to destroy the other's forces in the event of nuclear war. As of the period in question, each side had achieved only modest, and highly scenario dependent, success in this endeavor. For example, although the 1970s ended with a U.S. panic that predicted an imminent

[4] Raymond L. Garthoff, "Mutual Deterrence and Strategic Arms Limitation in Soviet Policy," *International Security* 3 (Summer 1978): 112–147, argues that this is the basic view of Soviet political and military leaders on the likely course of nuclear war. Western views on this matter are well known.

[5] David Holloway, *The Soviet Union and the Arms Race* (New Haven, 1983), chap. 3, pp. 29–64, presents the ambivalence of Soviet thinking about nuclear war; Michael MccGwire, *Military Objectives in Soviet Foreign Policy* (Washington, D.C., 1987), pp. 13–35, offers an evolutionary view of Soviet nuclear doctrine, positing a reversal in 1966 of previous Soviet assumptions about the inevitability of the escalation of any East-West conflict to an intercontinental nuclear exchange and an emerging belief that escalation could be deterred. Fritz Ermarth, "Contrasts in American and Soviet Strategic Thought," *International Security* 3 (Fall 1978): 138–155, presents a more unidimensional view of the classical military aspects of Soviet nuclear strategy. Aaron L. Friedberg, "A History of the US Strategic Doctrine, 1945–1980," *Journal of Strategic Studies* 3 (December 1980): 37–71, is one of several accounts that describe the long-standing commitment to counterforce operations in the U.S. strategic nuclear forces. For other descriptions of U.S. nuclear strategy see Barry R. Posen, *Sources of Military Doctrine: France, Britain, and Germany between the World Wars* (Ithaca, 1984), pp. 18–19, esp. n. 14.

Soviet first-strike capability against the U.S. ICBM force, the 1980s ended with a slightly less pessimistic assessment of Soviet capability. Official sources estimated that a Soviet ICBM attack could have destroyed, assuming no U.S. launch on warning or launch under attack, some 75 percent of the U.S. ICBMs.[6] This estimated outcome was hardly a splendid first-strike capability, but the Soviet capability it reflected scarcely seems unintended. The Soviet military was trying to target the ICBM force. For the most part, any success in these damage-limiting endeavors would have been dependent on beating the other side to the punch. The lethalness of the likely residuals ("secure second-strike capabilities") was very large and severely reduced the incentives of political leaders to permit soldiers to strike either "first" or early. All the same, the competition continued; political leaders may have been quite cautious about the first use of these weapons, but they were also quite unwilling to deny themselves the option to use them to reduce damage to their countries should some unforeseeable chain of circumstances have compelled it. This remains the situation as of publication.

In an effort to buy the time to track and kill the adversary's second-strike capability, military planners on both sides in the 1980s, perhaps earlier, turned their attention to the exploitation of the main potential weak link in the strategic nuclear forces—their command and control.[7] Modern communications systems are fragile, considering the damage that nuclear weapons can do. Nuclear command and control centers present a relatively small set of targets, partly as a natural consequence of bureaucratic hierarchy and partly as a consequence of the stress placed on the primacy of political control over these weapons.[8] It was

[6]Joshua Epstein, *The 1987 Defense Budget* (Washington, D.C., 1986), pp. 16–17, has done calculations that suggest this result. Lawrence Woodruff, deputy undersecretary of defense for strategic and theater nuclear forces, basically confirmed this estimate in March 1988. "The SS-18 Mod 4 force alone is capable of destroying well over ⅔ of all US ICBM silos while retaining over 1000 SS18 warheads in reserve." U.S. Congress, House, Committee on Armed Services, Subcommittee on Research and Development, *Statement on Nuclear Force Modernization*, 100th Cong., 2d sess., 1 March 1988 (mimeo), p. 6.

[7]Bruce G. Blair, *Strategic Command and Control: Redefining the Nuclear Threat* (Washington, D.C., 1985), esp. pp. 281–287, starkly summarizes the argument. See also Daniel Ford, "The Button," pts. I and II, *New Yorker*, 1 and 8 April 1985. He quotes Gen. Bruce Holloway, a former commander of the Strategic Air Command (1968–72): "Degradation of the over-all political and military control apparatus must be the primary targeting objective. Irrespective of whether we strike first or respond to a Soviet strike . . . it assumes the importance of absolute priority planning. Striking first would offer a tremendous advantage and would emphasize degrading the highest political and military control to the greatest possible degree" (pt. 2, p. 49). Although this quote is rather lurid, it should be understood that the Soviets have long been credited with the same thinking.

[8]John Steinbruner, "Launch under Attack," *Scientific American* 250 (January 1984): 43, argues that the U.S. command system "can be effectively destroyed by the direct blast

hoped that because of the destruction or temporary disablement of the "brain" of the adversary's strategic nuclear forces, those parts of the body that survive a first attack could be hacked up at leisure. There are, of course, grave risks associated with this strategy. The possibility that surviving forces will act with no, or partial, authorization cannot be denied. Given the destructiveness of single nuclear units (a lone bomber, ICBM squadron, or especially an SSBN at sea can wreak incredible havoc on urban targets), the consequences of such insubordination could be extraordinary. Nevertheless, attacks on command and control may be one of the few sources of leverage in a nuclear war.[9]

Thus the 1980s presented inherent contradictions in superpower attitudes toward nuclear weapons and nuclear war. Neither side showed any optimism about its ability to fare well in such a war. But both sides built their forces in the hopes of finding a way to do so. Any chance of faring well depended on getting the jump on the other side, but it is very hard to imagine circumstances in which the probability of success would have outweighed the risks of failure. The potential energy was there, however. In crisis, and especially in conventional war, the military commanders of the nuclear forces, at minimum, would have pointed out the costs of conceding the initiative to the other side. Military organizations on both sides would probably have pressed for ever higher levels of alert in order to better discourage preemption by the adversary, and better prepare for preemption themselves. Soviet and American nuclear commanders would have pointed out each other's preparations to their respective political masters in the hopes of eliciting still higher levels of alert. At some point recommendations for nuclear attacks were possible. These problems will remain with us so long as the strategic nuclear forces of both parties retain a commitment

---

effects of a few hundred weapons and very severely degraded by as few as 50 weapons." He notes that "although the Russian command system is thought to be more protected, the destructive effects of nuclear weapons appear to be so inherently damaging to any command network that differences in exposure between the U.S. and the U.S.S.R. are not likely to be significant given the scale of offensive firepower available."

[9]Of command and control attacks that aim to disrupt and delay the adversary's nuclear response in the hopes of buying the time to finish off his residual forces, John Steinbruner states," However heavily such a scheme might be discounted, it remains one of the few coherent methods of significantly reducing the damage suffered from retaliation, perhaps the only one, that cannot be dismissed on technical grounds." "Choices and Tradeoffs," in *Managing Nuclear Operations*, ed. Ashton B. Carter, John D. Steinbruner, and Charles A. Zraket (Washington, D.C., 1987), p. 545; Ashton Carter's essay in the same volume, "Assessing Command System Vulnerability," pp. 555–611, offers a thorough assessment of U.S. command system vulnerability in the mid-1980s. He is skeptical that a surgical decapitation could be performed by the strategic nuclear forces of the Soviet Union against U.S. command and control, but he does believe that such attacks could have caused U.S. forces some very serious problems.

to damage limitation; it is likely (for reasons discussed below) that they will want to preserve this commitment in the future and that they will persuade civilian authorities to let them do so.

Conventional operations that degrade second-strike capabilities were thus rendered especially dangerous by the ambivalent strategic nuclear doctrines of the two superpowers. If both superpowers had subscribed to the much criticized doctrine of MAD and postured their forces accordingly, it would have taken a great deal of conventional damage to provoke one side or the other to use some nuclear weapons as a vehicle for saving the rest.[10] In general, the greater the counterforce capabilities in Soviet and American strategic nuclear forces and the greater their commitment to counterforce strategies for nuclear warfighting, the greater the likelihood that the factors discussed in this book will lead to nuclear escalation. What might ordinarily seem an accidental or ambiguous conventional threat to one's strategic forces is more likely to be seen as deliberate and direct if one's adversary is believed to have a counterforce nuclear doctrine. What might seem a minor loss if one had a large, invulnerable second-strike capability could appear as a major loss if one's adversary were known to have many counterforce options. In this sense, large counterforce capabilities, which are often presented as a tool to control and limit damage in a superpower conflict, may become a cause of escalation from conventional to nuclear war.

If each superpower had dedicated its 1980s level of strategic nuclear resources to the simple task of assured retaliation, it would have been very difficult to do enough damage with conventional operations to produce a nuclear response. This was true for three reasons. The victim would easily have retained an imposing retaliatory capability for a very long time, so he would not have needed nuclear operations to save his deterrent. The victim would have known that the attacker had little incentive to attempt a nuclear counterforce attack to exploit his conventional successes, since the attacker's nuclear forces would have lacked the capability for effective counterforce operations; thus, the defender would not have needed to preempt the conventional attacker's possible

[10]Recent analysis confirms the widespread and long-standing belief that it does not take many nuclear weapons to do incredible damage to the social and economic fabric of a modern industrial power. William Daugherty, Barbara Levi, and Frank Von Hippel, "The Consequences of 'Limited' Nuclear Attacks on the United States," *International Security* 10 (Spring 1986), have carefully reviewed the possible casualties that might arise from a variety of Soviet nuclear attacks. A full-scale counterforce attack, with 2839 warheads, could kill between 20 million and 34 million Americans. An attack by 100 one-megaton warheads with the deliberate objective of killing U.S. population could produce between 25 million and 66 million fatalities. The same weapons targeted against the U.S. defense industry could kill between 11 million and 29 million Americans.

nuclear strike. Finally, the victim would have known that the attacker knew that the defender's retaliatory capability remained powerful. Escalation for the purpose of saving the remainder of one's nuclear forces was clearly not impossible in this situation, however. It is plausible that conventional operations could, over a very long time, succeed in taking away nearly all the defender's retaliatory capability. As the trend worsens, the defender might begin to fire nuclear weapons to indicate his fear and convince the attacker to desist. Nevertheless, in a self-consciously MAD world, *inadvertent* escalation from conventional to nuclear war seems unlikely. But the 1980s were not such a world, and we do not now live in such a world.

In spite of their continued attention to counterforce nuclear capabilities and doctrines, during the 1980s both superpowers gave some evidence of having developed the expectation that a very large conventional war might indeed be possible. U.S. views were clearer than Soviet and provide a good example.[11]

Since Secretary of Defense Robert McNamara began the review that culminated in NATO's 1967 adoption of MC 14/3, the strategy of flexible response, the achievement of a Western conventional force posture that would permit open-ended non-nuclear resistance has been a consistent U.S. objective.[12] Early in the Reagan administration decision makers embraced the idea of preparing for a long conventional war, as evidenced by its concern with the mobilization potential of the American defense industry.[13] Insufficient Western conventional capabilities were

[11]McCGwire, *Military Objectives*, offers perhaps the lengthiest treatment of Soviet military strategy for general war that suggests an expectation of protracted conventional conflict. For a summary and critique of Soviet conventional strategy for a European war, see Richard Ned Lebow, "The Soviet Offensive in Europe: The Schlieffen Plan Revisited?" *International Security* 9 (Spring 1985): 44–78.

[12]The United States and its European allies have disagreed about the extent of "conventionalization" that is either possible or desirable, with the United States a strong supporter. See Karsten Voigt, *Interim Report of the Sub-Committee on Conventional Defense in Europe* (Brussels, 1984), pp. 5–6, 27; William W. Kaufmann asserts that the U.S. objective in promulgating the shift to flexible response prior to its adoption in 1967 was "the acquisition of a nonnuclear deterrent fully capable of halting an all-out conventional attack by the Warsaw Pact." See his "Nuclear Deterrence in Central Europe," chap. 3, in *Alliance Security: NATO and the No-First-Use Question*, ed. John D. Steinbruner and Leon V. Sigal (Washington, D.C., 1983), p. 22. David Schwartz suggests that the United States and the allies disagreed about the meaning of flexible response: the United States wanted a conventional posture so strong that the Soviet Union would have to decide whether or not to use nuclear weapons first in the event of war, and the allies wanted to retain a threat of deliberate NATO first use. See *NATO's Nuclear Dilemmas* (Washington, D.C., 1983), pp. 176–177.

[13]See, e.g., the accounts of Secretary Caspar Weinberger's views in George Wilson, "Weinberger Order; Plan for Wider War," *Boston Globe*, 17 July 1981; and Richard Halloran, "Weinberger Tells of New Conventional-Force Strategy," *New York Times*, 7 May 1981. For further indications of the administration's views on this subject, see also Richard

often portrayed as the most probable cause of precipitate nuclear escalation. For example, in 1984 Gen. Bernard Rogers, then supreme allied commander in Europe, declared, "Because of our lack of sustainability—primarily ammunition, materials to replace losses on the battlefield, tanks, howitzers, trained manpower—I have to request the release of nuclear weapons fairly quickly after a conventional attack. And I'm talking about in terms of days, not in terms of weeks or months."[14] By 1987 Caspar Weinberger could declare that "US strategy seeks to limit the scope and intensity of any war, and confine it to conventional means. Our goal is to end hostilities on favorable terms to us by employing conventional forces that do not engender or risk escalation."[15] Underlying this policy was the belief that the United States should be prepared to fight a war that, in duration and character, would resemble World War II.[16] As of the date of publication many American strategists continue to seem optimistic about their chances of avoiding nuclear escalation in such a war if they so desire, providing they have sufficient quantities of conventional forces, weapons, and munitions to avoid conventional defeat.

Thus by virtue of data, forces, strategies, and beliefs, the East-West military competition in the 1980s seemed an ideal prospective case study. It also has the merit that much of the substantive information and insights developed from this period will have considerable relevance for the next decade and thus to current defense-policy debates. Political developments are calling into question some element of the 1980s case. Most notably, the conventional ground balance in Central Europe has

---

Halloran, "Needed: A Leader for the Joint Chiefs," *New York Times*, 1 February 1982; Richard Halloran, "Reagan Selling Navy Budget as Heart of Military Mission," *New York Times*, 11 April 1982; and U.S. Department of Defense, *Annual Report to Congress*, FY 1983 (Washington, D.C., 1983), pp. 1–13, 16–17, 28–29. Hereafter, U.S. Department of Defense, *Annual Report* and fiscal year.

[14]*Wall Street Journal*, 5 June 1984, p. 16.

[15]U.S. Department of Defense, *Annual Report*, FY 1988, p. 47; for additional evidence of "long-war" thinking, see pp. 45–47, 139–146, 221–226. It will be evident from the subsequent discussion that I do not believe that U.S. decision makers had a theory to guide the development or employment of conventional forces so that they would "not engender or risk escalation."

[16]A senior analyst of the Rand Corporation and veteran of the Department of Defense Office of Program Analysis and Evaluation recently declared that the Alliance should "develop stockpiles and production capability to sustain conventional conflict as long as necessary to thwart a Pact invasion." He also advises a reinterpretation of MC 14/3, the alliance document that lays out the strategy of flexible response to "require of the national partners development of stockpiles, production capability, and wartime distribution systems adequate to sustain NATO forces in a protracted conventional war." Paul K. Davis, *The Role of Uncertainty in Assessing the NATO–PACT Central-Region Balance* (Santa Monica, 1988), pp. 24–25. These observations were accompanied by the ritual declaration of the continuing importance of nuclear forces and the nuclear deterrent.

improved mightily by virtue of political changes in Eastern Europe that have all but eliminated the reliability of Eastern European forces as Soviet allies. But basic capabilities remain great, and it is unlikely that the offensive caste of military operational plans will change as quickly as public rhetoric.

THE MODEL OF INADVERTENT ESCALATION: THEORETICAL FOUNDATIONS

The causes of inadvertent escalation are derived from three bodies of theory: the work of Robert Jervis (and others) on the "security dilemma"; the application of organization theory to the behavior of military organizations; and Carl Von Clausewitz's analysis of the phenomenon of war itself, especially the concept of the "fog of war."

The Structure of the Situation: The Security Dilemma

The measures that one state takes to defend itself may seem offensive to the state against whom they are directed. Military resources acquired for the purpose of protecting national sovereignty often have the potential to threaten the security of others. Because international politics is a self-help system in which states have no recourse to higher authority if they are threatened, they tend to eye each other warily. When they perceive an increase in the offensive potential of others, they tend to assume the worst and initiate compensating political or military activity. This situation is called the security dilemma.[17] The state that initiates a particular improvement in its military resources *may have no choice* but to take such actions, even if its leaders understand that they threaten assets that others value highly. Sound political and military reasons may induce states to adopt explicitly offensive military strategies and to develop offensive military capabilities. But special dangers often arise because the leaders of states frequently do not understand how threatening their behavior, though defensively motivated, may seem to others. Thus, when those affected react, as is generally the case when vital interests are threatened, the initiator is surprised and may respond even more extremely.

The security dilemma is a concept generally employed to discuss peacetime spirals of increasing political hostility and military prepara-

[17] Robert Jervis, "Cooperation under the Security Dilemma," *World Politics* 30 (January 1978): 167–214.

tions—from arms races to crisis mobilizations and even preemptive war. To my knowledge, it has not been employed to examine the escalation of violence after military conflict begins.[18] But one of the critical aspects of the security dilemma is its "inadvertent" operation. The structure of the situation and the frequently amorphous nature of military capabilities permit states inadvertently to threaten each other and stumble into spirals of mutual hostility and competitive military preparations.[19]

Conventional war between nuclear powers involves elements of conflict and cooperation. If one or both states wanted to have a nuclear war, they could easily initiate hostilities with nuclear weapons. For analytic purposes, and consistent with the major defense policy assumptions of the NATO alliance for the past twenty-five years and with the evidence from Soviet military doctrine and practice, this analysis assumes that a war begins with conventional fighting. By the weapons they choose, the disputants indicate that they do not want the war to escalate to the use of nuclear weapons, even if they are willing to run the risks that it might. They have a shared interest in the avoidance of nuclear escalation. Thus, it is appropriate to examine the potential for nuclear escalation from the perspective of the security dilemma—duly adapted to the problem at hand.

Of course, no one can say with much certainty that what would induce a civilian or military leader to advocate, much less order, the use of nuclear weapons against an adversary so armed. It would surely be the most frightening decision any leader would ever have made. Nevertheless, we should be alert to the basic ingredients of the security dilemma as an engine of escalation in a conventional war among nuclear powers. These ingredients are as follows.

(1) Each side has nuclear forces that it values highly. Its nuclear forces are a core security asset, a vital interest. Threats to their integrity will be viewed with utmost seriousness. If the nuclear competition follows the pattern of the superpower arms race, in which each side tries deliberately to preserve a damage-limitation capability against the other, then the nuclear forces will be on high levels of alert, and nuclear planners will be looking for signs that the other side intends to operate its doctrine. Civilian cognizance of the delicacy of the situation may not be as high as is warranted since nuclear war plans are likely to be closely held by the military, and civilian leaders tend not to want to think about nuclear war in times of international quiet.

[18]John Mearsheimer called this point to my attention.

[19]Jervis employs the term *inadvertence* at least twice in his seminal article; see "Cooperation," pp. 170, 193.

(2) Conventional operations devised by either side to achieve success from the perspective of conventional warfare may nevertheless have deleterious consequences for nuclear forces. This is a subtle amendment to the basic assumption of the security dilemma—that states undertake military efforts that they perceive to be defensive. In this case, states may undertake conventional operations that an unbiased observer would concede were defensively motivated, and yet for reasons discussed below have offensive implications for nuclear warfare. Or states may undertake conventional operations that they know are offensive from a perspective of conventional war but that, unknown to the initiator, are also offensive from the perspective of nuclear warfare.

(3) The effects on the adversary's nuclear forces are sufficiently exotic, and the conventional plans themselves are sufficiently arcane, that political leaders are unlikely to have foreseen these consequences.

(4) Harsh reactions by the threatened party will thus probably be misconstrued as new indications of fresh malign intent, not reactions to one's own operations. Hence, new and more violent maneuvers may seem warranted, which when launched will be even more frightening to the other party.

(5) By virtue of the fact that conventional conflict is already under way, each side would be in a state of heightened competitiveness. Thus, the spiral of action and reaction is likely to be much more intense than it would be in time of peace.

In standard discussions of the security dilemma, both geography and technology can exert strong influences on whether or not offensive and defensive capabilities and actions are distinguishable.

In the case of the NATO–Pact competition, geography has been and will likely remain a particularly important contributor to this identification problem: territory necessary for defense may also facilitate offense. One geographic problem, for example, that would plague efforts to limit an east-west war is the proximity to Soviet borders of much of what the United States seeks to defend. The competition between the two alliances in Europe has created two major military asymmetries that substantially affect the relative security position of the two superpowers.[20] U.S. decision makers often seem to forget these asymmetries.

[20]This analysis in no way implies that the United States should have withdrawn from its alliance commitments on the Soviet periphery—or that it should do so now. The combination of the power and proximity of the Soviet Union, the repugnance inspired by its system of government, and the fear precipitated by its excessive military preparations and oftentimes belligerent foreign policy drove its neighbors into alliance with the United States. Fundamentally, the problems outlined in this book were exacerbated by the failure of both Soviet diplomacy and military strategy. Reforms in both areas assuaged the fears of Russia's neighbors. Understanding of how the Soviets might have perceived

The Soviet Union faces the possibility of very intense conventional military conflict close to its national boundaries; the United States does not. The Soviet Union faces an impressive array of nuclear forces based on its periphery and capable of penetrating deep into the Soviet Union. The United States faces a much smaller array of such forces, usually less than a half-dozen forward-deployed Soviet SSBNs. Most importantly, NATO's conventional and nuclear forces are all mixed together. They produce a special conventional war problem for the Soviet Union. Conventional war can become a cloak behind which a nuclear attack against the Soviet Union can be prepared and launched.[21]

A conventional conflict in Europe would involve large-scale military engagements near or over the Soviet Union which could be (or be perceived to be) threatening to Soviet strategic nuclear forces. Commanders of Soviet strategic forces may fear that surprise nuclear attacks could be camouflaged by the confusion and tumult of intense conventional combat. As Chapter 2 demonstrates, in an air battle over Central Europe thousands of planes would have been in the air in circumstances that could easily have made Soviet leaders nervous: Soviet air defenses would probably have been degraded, NATO would almost surely have had nuclear-capable aircraft in the air, and the Soviets might well have felt that important strategic assets such as command, control, communications, and intelligence facilities were threatened.

In short, what the West does conventionally to defend itself can produce an offensive threat against Soviet strategic nuclear forces. Because the United States does not now have an analogous geographical problem, it is difficult for American leaders to recognize the stress that conventional war might put on Soviet leaders concerned about the survivability of their strategic forces.

In conventional disputes among future nuclear competitors this problem could be much worse. With the exception of the rivalry between the Soviet Union and the People's Republic of China, we have had no

---

their military situation in the 1980s may provide insights into their current concerns and could be useful to the limitation of any great war that might still erupt in Europe.

[21]Maj. Gen. N. Vasendin and Col. N. Kuznetsov, "Modern Warfare and Surprise Attack," *Voyennaya Mysl* 6 (1968), reprinted and translated in *Selected Readings from Military Thought 1963–1973, USAF Studies in Communist Affairs* (Washington, D.C., 1982), vol. 5, pt. 1, pp. 226–233. "We cannot exclude attempts to achieve surprise by means of unleashing a local war. . . . The local war can be used by the aggressor for the additional mobilization of forces. In the guise of moving troops to the regions of the military conflict, a strike grouping of forces and means can be created for an attack. Such a war gives rise to an increase in the combat readiness of all armed forces of the aggressor, an intensification of strategic reconnaissance, the deployment of control points and communications centers in the territory of the dependent countries, and the carrying out of an entire series of other measures" (p. 230).

nuclear competition between states with a common border. And the USSR–PRC competition does not tell us much, in part because of poor data, in part because of the huge disparity in nuclear capabilities, but largely because of the long shadow on their conflict cast by the United States. But geography could be a critical problem among future competitors sharing common borders—especially if one or both has limited access to the sea for basing of its deterrent force.

Technology, like geography, can blur the line between offense and defense. Weapons useful for defense are often equally useful for attack. The United States, for example, maintains substantial antisubmarine warfare (ASW) forces to protect the sea lanes to Europe; many of those forces, however, could also attack Soviet ballistic missile submarines. Fighter aircraft of great range and payload can help defend Western Europe conventionally by interdicting the arrival of Soviet ground-force reinforcements. These same aircraft can carry nuclear weapons into the Soviet Union.

The Nature of Military Organizations: The Offensive Inclination and the Quest for Autonomy

Offensive military actions can cause, or require, hostile contact between conventional and strategic forces. For example, had war emerged in the mid-1980s, the offensive operations envisioned in the U.S. Navy's "maritime strategy" would have taken Western military forces close to the bases of Soviet strategic nuclear power on NATO's northern flank and in the Far East—with unpredictable consequences. This type of problem is hard to avoid because military organizations have both a proclivity for offensive operations and because they often resist civilian intervention in operational planning and execution.[22]

Planning. There is a generalized tendency for military organizations to prefer offensive doctrines and force postures long in advance of war. The Europe-wide cult of the offensive prior to World War I is the best example of military preferences for the offensive.[23] The Royal Air Force (RAF) in the 1930s was committed to the bombing of enemy

[22]The offensive and autonomy-seeking proclivities of military organizations can be deduced from organization theory, the civil-military relations literature, and from the instrumental problems of combat. See Posen, *The Sources of Military Doctrine.*

[23]See Stephen Van Evera, "The Cult of the Offensive and the Origins of the First World War," and Jack Snyder, "Civil-Military Relations and the Cult of the Offensive, 1914 and 1984," in *Military Strategy and the Origins of the First World War,* ed. Steven E. Miller (Princeton, 1985).

industry as their preferred military strategy, and considerable outside pressure was required to induce that service to plan carefully for the air defense of the country. Among the most influential and committed supporters of counterforce nuclear strategies in both superpowers today are the U.S. Strategic Air Command and the Soviet Strategic Rocket Forces.

Military organizations, like all large organizations, tend to seek autonomy from outside influences. Thus, in peacetime civilians are seldom exposed to the intricacies of military planning. As the editors of a recent monumental study of nuclear force operations have observed "the uniformed military views operations as its exclusive domain and does not welcome detailed involvement of even high ranking civilians in the Defense Department."[24]

Offensive Actions in Crisis or War. There are many historical examples of militaries striking out on offensive actions unbeknownst to their civilian superiors. In the immediate aftermath of the Soviet destruction of KAL Flight 007, unknown U.S. Air Force commanders, on their own authority, apparently ordered F-15 and AWACS operations close to the presumed crash area. The objective was unclear, and the operation was stopped when cooler heads prevailed. On 19 November 1985 two Israeli fighter pilots on their own initiative and without provocation shot down two Syrian MiGs in Syrian airspace, precipitating an unwanted extension of Syrian ground-based air defenses into Lebanon. Gen. John Lavelle conducted twenty unauthorized bombings of North Vietnam in 1971–72.[25] The U.S. Navy engaged in anti-submarine warfare operations against Soviet submarines during the Cuban missile crisis of an intensity and geographic scope unknown to the president or his advisers.[26]

Even when the intensity of a crisis or a conflict increases civilian efforts to intervene in the details of military policy, soldiers often interpret policymakers' injunctions in ways that allow them maximum operational discretion.

[24]Ashton B. Carter, John D. Steinbruner, and Charles A. Zraket, eds., *Managing Nuclear Operations* (Washington, D.C., 1987), p. 2.

[25]Seymour M. Hersh, *The Target Is Destroyed* (New York, 1986), pp. 74, 114. Thomas L. Friedman, "Israelis Wary on Striking at Missiles," *New York Times*, 17 December 1985; Richard K. Betts, *Soldiers, Statesmen, and Cold War Crises* (Cambridge, 1977), p. 49. British generals sent to protect the Abadan oil facilities at the outbreak of World War I decided to attempt the capture of Baghdad. Norman Dixon, *On the Psychology of Military Incompetence* (London, 1976), p. 96.

[26]Steinbruner, "Choices and Trade-offs," pp. 541–543; Scott D. Sagan, "Nuclear Alerts and Crisis Management," *International Security* 9 (Spring 1985): 112–117.

The 1982 Israeli invasion of Lebanon now appears to have gone far beyond the original objectives approved by the Israeli cabinet. Defense Minister Ariel Sharon (a retired general), Chief of Staff Rafael Eitan, and some other high-ranking officers orchestrated military operations in such a way as to elicit incremental cabinet approval for ever more extensive actions, especially against Syrian forces (although many high-ranking Israeli officers opposed these actions).[27]

During the Cuban missile crisis the U.S. Navy initially set its blockade line some 800 miles from Cuba. When President John F. Kennedy ordered it moved closer on the evening of 23 October (500 miles out from Cuba) to give the Russians more time, the navy resisted. This precipitated a short, sharp dispute that Kennedy and Robert McNamara seem to have won.[28] Yet the experience must have scared the president and his secretary of defense, since on the following day the secretary felt compelled to review aggressively the procedures for stopping a ship with the navy admiral responsible for coordinating operations.

On 5 November 1950 Gen. Douglas MacArthur ordered the Far East Air Force to bomb virtually anything usable to the communist logistical effort up to and including the Korean end of the Yalu River bridges. Even air force general George Stratemeyer understood that this order violated previous Joint Chiefs of Staff (JCS) directives that had been issued to help avoid bringing China into the war and passed the word to Washington where policymakers intervened to prevent the strikes on the bridges. Nevertheless, after considerable protestation by MacArthur, permission was finally granted to hit the bridges.[29]

During World War I the German chancellor endeavored to control the operations of German submarines so as not to antagonize the United States and risk its early entry into the war on the side of the Entente. Responding to public and naval pressure for submarine operations in response to the British blockade, he specified detailed and strict rules

[27]Ze'ev Schiff and Ehud Ya'ari, *Israel's Lebanon War*, ed. and trans. Ina Friedman (New York, 1984), pp. 43, 53, 301–304.

[28]Graham, Allison, *Essence of Decision* (Boston, 1971), pp. 129–130, argues that the navy evaded the order. But Dan Caldwell suggests that the original plan called for an 800-mile distance from Cuba, and that Kennedy successfully shifted in to a 500-mile distance. This version is better supported by the evidence. See Dan Caldwell, "A Research Note on the Quarantine of Cuba," *International Studies Quarterly* 22 (December 1978): 625–633. Sagan, "Nuclear Alerts," p. 110, n. 26, says that the commanding admiral's diary suggests that a 500-mile-distant destroyer picket line was the plan all along, and that Kennedy's intervention was probably meant to limit the discretion of the navy to intercept Soviet ships beyond 500 miles.

[29]Clay Blair, *The Forgotten War: America in Korea, 1950–1953* (New York, 1987), pp. 392–396.

of engagement against merchant ships for German submarines. The navy apparently made no effort to inform him that these were nearly impossible to follow. Instead, the potential for error within the rules was exacerbated by the unwillingness of German commanders even to try to follow them. In short order a crisis with the United States ensued.[30]

In an even earlier instance, prior to and during the Prussian war with France in 1870, the Prussian General Staff tried to prevent Bismarck from having any contact "with the operational aspects of the war."[31] These few examples suggest the difficulty that civilian leaders may have in exerting enough political control over military operations under way to have much influence on the risks of escalation.

Historically, offensive military strategies and operations have helped military organizations evade civilian control. The advocacy of offensive strategies has been a vehicle for the pursuit of organizational size, wealth, and autonomy in time of peace. In time of war the pursuit of offensive actions without seeking civilian concurrence, or in actual violation of civilian instructions, has been common. If a NATO–Pact war had broken out in the 1980s, this historical pattern suggests that American civilian policymakers would probably have had the least foreknowledge of, and influence over, the most escalatory operations. This, coupled with the geographical circumstances of the war, allows us to summarize the probable course of events with ease. Western conventional forces would have started the war close to the Soviet homeland and the strategic nuclear forces based there, and would probably have gotten closer. Civilians were unlikely to have grasped this fully before the outbreak of fighting, or to have understood the pattern of action and reaction that could have been set off. Once these operations were under way, military organizations would not have worked especially hard to explain the intricacies of the situation to civilian authorities. As of the date of publication, these risks remain.

The Fog of War

Inadvertent escalation may also result from the great difficulty of gathering and interpreting the most relevant information about a war in progress and using it to understand, control, and orchestrate the war. This is a problem that soldiers face, and they know something

[30]Karl E. Birnbaum, *Peace Moves and U-Boat Warfare* (Hamden, Conn., 1970), pp. 60–70; Ernest R. May, *The World War and American Isolation, 1914–1917* (Cambridge, Mass., 1966), pp. 248–252.

[31]Gordon Craig, *The Politics of the Prussian Army, 1640–1945* (London, 1955), p. 204.

about warfare; it would be worse for civilians. Not only might this difficulty help to cause inadvertent escalation but it may exacerbate potentially escalatory situations created by offensive operations or by the indistinguishability of offensive and defensive acts. The Fog of War works in two ways to increase the prospects of inadvertent escalation. First, it makes control of military operations under way difficult for high-level policymakers. Second, it creates conditions that heighten fears that an adversary can mount a successful surprise attack.

The disarray of command, control, communications, and intelligence, often called the "fog of war," would assume global proportions in an East-West war. Although modern technology may provide reams of intelligence data, it will not always be timely or accurate. Analysis is difficult under the pressure of intense conventional conflict. Communications to and from the theater of operations are likely to be uncertain and intermittent in any case. But critical links are often quite deliberately jammed or destroyed, as each side tries to gain a military advantage by reducing the other's understanding of events and control over its forces. Forces may end up in the wrong place, and events may be misreported. Civilians retaining the image of direct communication and control in the Cuban missile crisis or the Iran rescue mission may be shocked at how hard it is to follow, much less manage, a global war.

There are numerous examples of inaccurate or incomplete understanding by policymakers of ongoing military operations. General Lavelle's bombing of North Vietnam was apparently unknown to American leaders and damaged peace negotiations with North Vietnam.[32] During the Cuban missile crisis U-2 flights near the Soviet border were not authorized. But somehow a U-2 on a polar weather reconnaissance mission, which was permitted, strayed into Soviet airspace. U.S. fighters were launched without consultation with the national command authority to assist the U-2 in case it came under attack by Soviet fighters, which had scrambled. This intrusion may have hindered the negotiations to end the crisis, or it may have frightened the Soviets into a more cooperative attitude.[33] To this day we do not have an open-source accounting of why the intrusion occurred, nor do we know what were its real effects on the Russians.

The fog of war seems to have been one contributor to the entry of the People's Republic of China into the Korean War. The United States

[32] Betts, *Soldiers, Statesmen*, pp. 49–50.

[33] Allison, *Essence of Decision*, p. 141; Sagan, "Nuclear Alerts," pp. 118–121.

had three types of indicators that the Chinese intensely opposed the advance of U.N. forces to the Yalu River: diplomatic messages through third parties, propaganda declarations in the Chinese media, and limited military demonstrations in North Korea and along the Korean-Chinese border in late October and early November.[34] Although no indicators were missed entirely, the different channels by which the information was collected, the ambiguity of the meaning of Chinese military action, and a certain degree of self-deception all contributed to an underestimation of the risks.

Starting in the summer of 1940 the British and Germans both apparently misappraised the accuracy and reliability of the German bombing systems, especially at night.[35] The Germans were unaware of their initial accidental bombing of London on the night of August 24. This seemed a deliberate escalation to the British, who retaliated against Berlin with several feeble attacks. These attacks in turn enraged Hitler and, combined with a number of other motives, brought him to order a wholesale aerial assault on London, which became the Blitz. Even here, however, the Germans seem to have deluded themselves that military and industrial targets could be distinguished from residential areas.[36] Thus, the Blitz helped to further reduce any restraints the British might have been inclined to observe. The British, however, did cling to the illusion of discriminate bombing in the early phases of their aerial offensive, in order to make the action more palatable ethically.[37] In these examples the fog of war produced unintended military effects, obscured the meaning of adversary military actions, or both.

Modern conventional conflict in Central Europe would be characterized by large numbers, long range, and high lethality. Many of the longest ranged and most lethal weapons, tactical fighters, are capable of both conventional and nuclear operations. Central Region conflict

[34]Rosemary Foot, *The Wrong War: American Policy and the Dimensions of the Korean Conflict, 1950–1953* (Ithaca, 1985), pp. 79–80, 89; Blair, *Forgotten War*, pp. 340, 371–372, 382–384; James F. Schnabel, *United States Army in the Korean War, Policy and Direction: The First Year* (Washington, D.C., 1972), pp. 236–238. The traditional interpretation of the limited Chinese military actions during the last week of October and the first week of November is that they *were* meant as a warning. Whether or not the Chinese meant these operations as a warning, they should have been taken as such, especially in combination with explicit Chinese statements and against the background of other available intelligence.

[35]George Quester, *Deterrence before Hiroshima* (New York, 1955), pp. 115–122.

[36]F. M. Sallagar, *The Road to Total War: Escalation in World War II* (Santa Monica: Rand Corporation, 1969), pp. 89–93. Sallagar believes, however, that the Germans understood that their attacks on London would kill many people and would amount to mere terror warfare. His argument on this matter seems a bit convoluted.

[37]Ibid., pp. 128–131.

would also make greater use of radio, radar, electronic intelligence, and jamming than has ever occurred before in history. "Low observables" or "stealth" technology will create additional problems in any future conflict, as it will further reduce the ability of each side to keep track of the speediest and longest ranged platforms—aircraft and cruise missiles. In any conventional war in the 1980s NATO's conventional operations could easily have spilled across the borders of the Soviet Union, a possibility that will remain for some time to come. The result of this conventional war would have been to create a huge island of "fog" on the borders of the Soviet homeland. Hidden in this fog would have been nuclear weapons on such platforms as F-111 and Tornado fighter bombers with the range, yield, and accuracy to threaten a host of strategic targets from the Western Military Districts to Moscow. Lurking just offshore one would have found U.S. surface vessels and submarines armed with nuclear-tipped cruise missiles. In the mid-1980s ground-launched cruise missiles (GLCMs) and Pershing II missiles, both with the range to reach deep into the Soviet Union and the accuracy to attack very hard targets, were based on land in Europe.[38] If the Soviet strategy for very rapid conventional victory had failed, the Soviets might soon have found themselves in a dangerous strategic nuclear position. Soviet command and control facilities could have become vulnerable to nuclear attacks of which they would have had short warning or very ambiguous warning.[39]

In sum, the fog of war increases the likelihood of inadvertent escalation because misperceptions, misunderstandings, poor communications, and unauthorized or unrestrained offensive operations could reduce the ability of civilian authorities to influence the course of the war. It might also precipitate unexpected but powerful escalatory pressures due to the ever higher levels of uncertainty that would develop

[38]The successful conclusion of the negotiations for the elimination of Pershing II, GLCM, and SS20 eliminated what would have been a very potent source of the dynamics discussed in this essay. Problems of the kind discussed here and in the next chapter may be one of the reasons why the Soviets finally proved willing to accept the "zero option" proposal that they formerly rejected. It should be understood, however, that with some 1500–2000 nuclear bombs in Western Europe, NATO's tactical fighters, especially long-range aircraft such as F-111, Tornado, and the soon-to-be-deployed F-15E Strike Eagle, will continue to generate many of the uncertainties I have identified. The introduction of stealth fighters will further complicate matters.

[39]In effect, a Soviet decision to fight a conventional war would have automatically improved U.S. first-strike counterforce capability. This prospect might have strengthened NATO's ability to deter a Pact conventional attack, assuming that Soviet military planners understood how the war might have developed. I have not, however, found any evidence that NATO planners saw things this way. Thus, had *deterrence* failed and the Soviets attacked, these escalatory conventional operations would likely have been permitted to unfold, even though their deterrent power would have already disappeared.

about the status of the other side's strategic nuclear capabilities as intense conventional conflict unfolds.

Plan of the Book

The remainder of this book consists of two sections, each of two chapters. The first section deals with the possible course of combat on the Eurasian land mass, and the second with the war at sea. Each section has a chapter that addresses the potentially escalatory operations under consideration during the 1980s in that theater of war. Chapter 2 illustrates the complex, potentially escalatory interactions that might have arisen among NATO's conventional tactical air operations, Soviet strategic early-warning capabilities, NATO's long-range theater nuclear forces, and Soviet strategic nuclear command and control. Chapter 3 assesses the 1980s balance of conventional ground forces in Central Europe. The purpose of the chapter is twofold. First, it makes the case that conventional ground conflict could have unfolded favorably for NATO, still a somewhat controversial assessment of the conventional balance in that period. Therefore, other potential causes of nuclear escalation, aside from collapse, merited the attention of policymakers, attention that available evidence suggests was rarely paid. Second, because the assessment deliberately excludes consideration of the contribution of the air interdiction operations, discussed in Chapter 2, to NATO's ground effort, it shows that had NATO planners wanted to reduce the escalatory pressures set up by tactical air operations, they might have been able to do so without doing great damage to NATO's ability to resist successfully on the ground.

The second section addresses the maritime component of a NATO–Pact war. Chapter 4 discusses those aspects of the maritime strategy that were most escalatory, plans for attacks on Soviet nuclear-powered ballistic missile submarine (SSBN) bastions and naval bases ashore in the Barents Sea and the Kola Peninsula. I confine my remarks to the European theater of operations, but similar attacks would have unfolded in the Far East, with similar consequences. Because the U.S. Navy claimed that this strategy would be the only effective means of ensuring the supply of essential reinforcements to Europe across the Atlantic, Chapter 5 assesses the adequacy of a less escalatory defensive sea-control strategy for the successful completion of this mission with the forces then available. It makes the case that such an alternative was feasible, probably much more feasible than the maritime strategy. Indeed, the analysis suggests that the successful reinforcement of NATO by the United States would probably have been achieved in any case, lending further support to the argument advanced in Chapter 3 that NATO's forces on the ground would probably have held—much against the common expectations of the time. In combination, the analysis presented in Chapters 3 and 5 suggests that NATO might have sustained successful conventional resistance for quite a long time. This is important because the audacious air and naval operations discussed in Chapters 2 and 4 would likely have taken some time to affect Soviet strategic nuclear forces. But the analysis also shows that these operations could have been scaled back substantially, if not eliminated altogether, with little damage to NATO's power of conventional resistance.

Although each section illustrates the full range of potential escalatory pressures outlined above, they do so with different emphases. Tactical air operations in Central Europe place less direct pressure on Soviet strategic forces. Moreover, the pressures they create arise more from the pure indistinguishability of offensive and defensive acts, the security dilemma, and the fog of war than from organizational dynamics.[40] The maritime strategy, on the other hand, owed its origin more to the pressures of organizational interest and preferences than to accidents of technology, geography, and the normal course of warfare. These two cases are not exhaustive; they are meant to illustrate the kinds of trouble that could have arisen in a large-scale East-West conventional war during the 1980s.

These problems might have been exacerbated by peculiarities of both sides' strategic nuclear forces, which were probably not well designed to ride out a lengthy conventional war. In an intense crisis these would likely be brought to much higher states of alert than they normally maintain. By definition, this is an extraordinary effort, which is difficult to sustain for very long. As the ready forces of one side or the other begin to shrink because of wear and tear, windows of opportunity may open for one side or the other.

Together, the four case studies encompass the main conventional military activities that would have attended a NATO–Pact war in the 1980s. Such a war would likely have begun with a major Pact offensive air operation to try to ruin NATO's air forces and tactical nuclear capabilities. If they survived this onslaught, NATO's air forces would have

[40]This is a relative statement. A good deal of NATO's deep interdiction effort owes its impetus to the heritage of strategic bombing in the U.S. and Royal air forces, and the association of independent operations of this kind with the struggle to win and preserve autonomy from the other services.

launched a number of different operations. A large share of NATO's offensive air capability would have been committed to battlefield air interdiction. A smaller share would have attacked critical Pact airfields, and some would have engaged in deep interdiction. The mix among these missions would have varied with the situation. Chapter 2 deals with a small but critical piece of NATO's offensive air operations, the effort to suppress Pact surface-to-air missiles. The Pact air offensive would have been launched simultaneously with a large offensive armored operation along the old inter-German border. The Soviets and their Eastern European allies would have mustered about fifty ready divisions for the initial assault, to be followed some time later by about fifty more.[41] This is discussed largely in Chapter 3. U.S. (and perhaps British) nuclear attack submarines would have tried to insert themselves into the Barents Sea during the period of crisis leading up to the war. If not, they would have fought their way forward from the outset of hostilities. Two or three dozen nuclear-powered attack submarines (SSNs) would have been involved. They would have tried to sink any submarine they encountered. This is discussed in Chapter 4. Finally, the United States would have tried to reinforce its ground troops in Europe. Depending on the nature of the crisis that precipitated the war, much of this reinforcement might have had to await the outbreak of hostilities. Although Soviet naval strategy in this period placed sea lane interdiction at the bottom of its list of priorities, some Soviet submarines would probably have been committed to the harassment of U.S. reinforcements. Chapter 4 addresses this campaign from the perspective of a Soviet force allocation greater than that suggested by Soviet doctrine.

Several aspects of the war are not addressed in detail in the case chapters. Ground and tactical air operations in defense against a possible Soviet assault on northern Norway are omitted. There is no discussion of military operations on NATO's southern flank. Finally, the spread of the war around the world, quite likely in my estimation, is not directly addressed. These omissions are not critical with reference to the main argument. If anything, these events would intensify the phenomena in question.

Another set of activities is germane to the overall argument: the whole panoply of alert activities of both side's strategic nuclear forces, and the wartime activities of each side's intelligence-gathering organizations. I allude to some of this in the course of the case studies. Both are arcane

[41]From the vantage point of 1991, the assumption of enthusiastic East European participation in Soviet offensive operations, customarily made for planning purposes in the West in the late 1970s and much of the 1980s, appears to have been overly conservative.

fields. Alert activities, at least from the U.S. perspective, have received considerable attention from competent people in the past decade, but intelligence gathering has received little attention, probably because of the very high levels of classification that surround it. Nevertheless, it seems plausible that the kind of painstaking and creative research techniques employed by those who have written about strategic command and control (see below) and those who have written about the peacetime intelligence world might be applied to assess the interactions of intelligence-collection activities in wartime.[42]

Most of the work on nuclear command and control is consistent with my discussion above of the offensive caste of Soviet and U.S. nuclear doctrine during the 1980s. On this subject I particularly commend three sources, which I cite frequently: *Can Nuclear War Be Controlled?* by Desmond Ball; *Strategic Command and Control: Redefining the Nuclear Threat* by Bruce Blair; and the collection of essays edited by Ashton Carter, John Steinbruner, and Charles Zraket entitled *Managing Nuclear Operations*.

I have devoted my personal effort to the study of conventional operations because less attention has been paid to them, and conventional forces seem to me to be the most likely and the most lethal tools that statesmen will initially grasp should diplomacy fail.

The concluding chapter briefly recapitulates the argument, discusses its possible future ramifications for the East-West security competition, and suggests some of the implications for other possible conflicts among other nuclear powers.

The methodology employed in this study has been quite simple. The professional military literature, the open-source technical military press, U.S. Department of Defense publications, and U.S. congressional hearings have been the principal sources. The escalation model outlined above has been used as a lens to pull critical information out of a mass of inchoate, unorganized data and fit it into a meaningful pattern.

These sources have been supplemented with a small number of interviews in the United States and in other countries with civilian policymakers, soldiers, and knowledgeable academics. I have also benefited from participation in two defense policy study groups, a short stint as a Pentagon analyst, and reactions to numerous presentations I have given on this project.

Finally, to sharpen the analysis, I have developed some simple quantitative models of ground, air, and naval combat. These models draw

[42]Notable in the latter category are James Bamford, William E. Burrows, Duncan Campbell, and Jeffrey T. Richelson.

their inspiration from professional operations research but include little beyond addition, subtraction, multiplication, and division.[43] Yet, the application of personal computer spreadsheet packages permits a good deal of insight into military problems through repeated calculations with basic arithmetic. With the exception of Chapter 3, these models are confined largely to appendices.[44]

[43]The so-called whiz-kid systems analysts employed by Robert McNamara in the 1960s also relied largely on simple arithmetic. See Alain C. Enthoven and K. Wayne Smith, *How Much Is Enough?* (New York, 1971).

[44]Those attentive to national security issues during the 1980s are aware of several instances of espionage against U.S. forces, especially the compromise of some U.S. Army plans for war in Europe, and some U.S. Navy codes and encryption machines. Though initial reports of these incidents indicated that they had done major damage to U.S. wartime capabilities, I have not tried to infer their implications for my own work. First, I am not convinced that public accounts of these matters provide a complete picture of the damage done. Second, information about these compromises is in the nature of "one hand clapping." We do not know what Western espionage may have achieved versus the Warsaw Pact. Thus, my own assessments of the relative competitiveness of the two sides' conventional forces do not address these issues. Books on this subject tend to be of the popular variety. See Thomas B. Allen and Normal Polmar, *Merchants of Treason* (New York: Delacorte, 1988); John Barron, *Breaking the Ring* (Boston: Houghton Mifflin, 1987); Pete Earley, *Family of Spies* (New York: Bantam, 1988).

[2]

Air War and Inadvertent Nuclear Escalation

Conventional-Nuclear Linkage on the Soviet Periphery

The purpose of this chapter is to explore the possible ways that large-scale conventional conflict in Central Europe might have affected the Soviet political and military leadership's confidence in the survivability, and thus deterrent power, of their strategic nuclear forces in a war that might have occurred in the 1980s.

Large-scale conventional aerial warfare over Central Europe could have done sufficient damage to Warsaw Pact and Soviet air defenses, and created sufficient confusion for Soviet air defense commanders, to have permitted NATO's long-range theater nuclear forces to threaten a surprise attack against critical Soviet strategic nuclear early warning and command and control facilities. This threat could have developed over a period of weeks and would probably have elicited substantial attention from Soviet air defense commanders. Real pressures could have arisen to compensate for this developing NATO advantage, either by devolution of nuclear launch authority or actual nuclear attacks on threatening NATO systems.

The analysis that follows proceeds through three steps.

First, the vulnerability of key Soviet command, control, communications, and intelligence (C^3I) assets to short-warning, peripheral attacks by forward-based, nuclear-armed tactical aircraft and cruise missiles will be demonstrated. This vulnerability was modest in peacetime but would have grown quickly under conditions of intensive conventional air combat in Central Europe. The long-standing role of Soviet and Warsaw Pact air defenses in the defense of the Soviet homeland from attacks originating on the Soviet *periphery* will be demonstrated. The great resources assigned to this mission suggest that this threat was taken seriously by Soviet planners. Americans are accustomed to thinking of Soviet air defenses as enemies of the American bomber force attacking from over the North Pole. They are, but this oversimplifies their role and serves to obscure Soviet fear of attack from the west.

Second, the course of conventional air combat in Central Europe will be evaluated, including the full range of consequences that an intense Central Region air battle could have had for Soviet air defense and early warning capabilities. A very small piece of the overall air battle is examined in detail: NATO's planned effort to suppress the air defenses of the Warsaw Pact. A simple arithmetic model will be employed to illustrate the potential of this campaign to degrade air defenses over Eastern Europe. In effect, NATO's air-defense-suppression effort could have cut safe-passage corridors through Eastern Europe available for exploitation by NATO's nuclear-strike aircraft and ground-, sea-, or air-launched cruise missiles. This developing NATO capability would have attracted the attention of Soviet commanders, who in the event would have been unlikely to speculate on NATO's intentions.

Third, the pressures and temptations that could have arisen for the Soviet Union to employ nuclear weapons to reverse the course of this campaign are evaluated. Two subsidiary points are addressed. What does the analysis provided by Western specialists in Soviet theater nuclear doctrine tell us about when and how the Soviets might have employed nuclear weapons, and what inferences can we draw from their analysis for this specific situation? What targets could the Soviets have struck with limited numbers of nuclear weapons that might have reversed the success of the Western SEAD (suppression of enemy air defenses) campaign and degraded the surprise attack potential of NATO's theater nuclear forces?

Soviet "Strategic" Targets Vulnerable to Theater Surprise Attack

This section projects the worst fears of 1980s Soviet decision makers in the event of one plausible "worst case" contingency, a large-scale "first use" of forward-based NATO nuclear systems directed against key targets in the Soviet Union. To show that the Soviets did indeed take this contingency seriously, I show that they devoted substantial military resources to defend against it.

In the closing pages of his excellent and painstaking analysis of U.S. strategic command and control, Bruce Blair warns that because of their ability to avoid detection, cruise missiles are, in spite of their slow speed, useful assets for attacking C^3I. This is especially true if they can be "launched from delivery systems in close proximity to the targets." He advises the superpowers to agree "to prohibit close-in deployment of ships, submarines, aircraft, and ground bases armed with nuclear cruise missiles." Blair argues that forward-deployed cruise missiles "represent the most serious emerging threat to U.S. C^3I systems."[1] Since U.S. cruise missile programs remain technologically ahead of their Soviet counterparts, and since air- and sea-launched cruise missiles were already deployed in large numbers by the United States, it seems quite likely that if Blair was right about an emerg*ing* Soviet cruise missile threat to U.S. C^3I, then the threat of U.S. nuclear cruise missiles to Soviet C^3I had already emerg*ed* in the 1980s.

Regrettably, although we have excellent open-source "command analysis" of the U.S. strategic command and control system and its vulnerabilities, corresponding analysis of the Soviet system remains rather sparse.[2] The Soviets are certainly not going to be any more open about this subject than they are about any other security-related subject.[3] The American intelligence community, from which much open-source information on the Soviet military originates, is most unlikely to say much about Soviet C^3I, since the revelation of almost any detail about the system could compromise the very expensive intelligence asset that provided the detail. Moreover, since attacks on C^3I offer perhaps the last remaining source of leverage in a disarming, counterforce attack, such revelations could produce changes in the other side's structure that would negate these advantages. In general, then, "command analysis" of the Soviet C^3I system to assess its vulnerability to any kind of attack is exceedingly difficult. Nevertheless, the sources available do reveal a few fundamental facts that suggest dis-

[1] Blair, *Strategic Command and Control*, p. 301. See also Ashton Carter, "Assessing Command System Vulnerability," in Ashton Carter, John D. Steinbruner, and Charles A. Zraket, eds., *Managing Nuclear Operations* (Washington, D.C., 1987), p. 597.

[2] The term "command analysis" was coined by Bruce Blair.

[3] The most comprehensive recent survey of Soviet C^3I is Stephen M. Meyer, "Soviet Nuclear Operations," in *Managing Nuclear Operations*, ed. Carter, Steinbruner, and Zraket, pp. 470–531. Desmond Ball, *Can Nuclear War Be Controlled?*, Adelphi Paper 169 (London, 1981), remains very useful. U.S. Department of Defense, *Soviet Military Power, 1985* (Washington, D.C., April 1985), chap. 3, "Strategic Defense and Space Programs," pp. 43–59, provides useful detail. Subsequent editions provide additional information with *Soviet Military Power, 1988*, pp. 16–17, and chap. 4, "Soviet Strategic Programs and Space Forces," pp. 44–67, offering the most comprehensive discussion of the Soviet hard shelter program. Thomas K. Longstreth, John E. Pike, and John B. Rhinelander, *The Impact of US and Soviet Ballistic Missile Defense Programs on the ABM Treaty*, 3d ed. (Washington, D.C., 1985), pp. 37–41, and maps on pp. 70, 72, 74, offers information on the location of Soviet early warning radars.

turbing conclusions from the Soviet perspective—especially in the context of the long-standing shortcomings of the Soviet air defense system and its probable degradation in a NATO–Pact conventional war. Although we would be unwise to conclude from this information that Soviet nuclear forces could literally have been decapitated, it is plausible that relatively limited attacks could have seriously degraded the speed and comprehensiveness of a Soviet response, buying sufficient time for U.S. counterforce capabilities to attack silos, bomber bases, and SSBNs in port.

The center of the Soviet command and control apparatus is said to be concentrated in the Moscow area, in thirty to seventy-five hardened bunkers, some of which may be several hundred feet deep and hardened to withstand at least 1000 psi blast overpressure.[4] Early warning and attack assessment is the responsibility of the Soviet national air defense organization, the VPVO (Soviet Strategic Air Defense Forces). Its main command post is said to be in Moscow, and an alternate command post is reported to be not far away, in Kalinin. Standard calculations suggest that even bunkers hardened to withstand 2000 psi of overpressure would have stood little chance of surviving an attack by two U.S. ground-launched cruise missiles with 50-kiloton warheads.[5] The "Dog House" and "Cat House" phased array radars of the Moscow ABM system (and the Pushkino radar under construction) would have added little to this target set. Presumably, some critical communications transmitters in the Moscow area would have been

[4]Ball, *Can Nuclear War Be Controlled?*, p. 44, uses the figure of seventy-five hardened bunkers in the Moscow area. Meyer, "Soviet Nuclear Operations," pp. 482, 485, uses the same figure but also alludes to the lower number, thirty. U.S. Department of Defense, *Soviet Military Power, 1988*, pp. 59–62, offers a general discussion of the Soviet program for deep underground facilities to protect the political and military leadership, although it offers no estimate of the number of very hard facilities. The discussion also offers no estimate of the survivability of these facilities against a determined nuclear attack.

[5]Two sea-launched cruise missiles or air-launched cruise missiles would have had more than a 90 percent chance of destroying such a target, assuming 80 percent reliability and 95 percent penetration. Two ground-launched cruise missiles would have had about an 85 percent chance, under the same assumptions. See U.S. Congress, Congressional Budget Office, *Modernizing US Strategic Offensive Forces*, prepared by Bonita Dombey (Washington, D.C., November 1987), pp. 86–87, for air- and sea-launched cruise missile effectiveness. See Van Evera et al., "Appendix: How Our Simulations Were Performed," in *Nuclear Arguments*, ed. Eden and Miller, pp. 248–249, for probability formulae for single-shot kills. An 80 percent reliability is a number commonly used in back-of-the-envelope analysis for strategic and conventional weapons systems. A 95 percent penetration credits Soviet air defenses with an ability to shoot down 5 percent of the attacking cruise missiles, an effectiveness that Soviet air defense hardware has seldom achieved against tactical aircraft. I believe the two values to be conservative for these purposes. The overall kill probability (opk) for a single shot is thus reliability × penetration probability × single-shot kill probability. Two-shot kill probability is given by $1 - (1 - \text{opk})^2$.

targeted. One would also hypothesize that the Russian communications network of buried land lines must have had certain critical nodes in the Moscow area that could be struck. Finally, there is at least one airfield in the Moscow area where command and control aircraft were based, although it seems likely that any field close to Moscow with a runway of sufficient length to permit operations would be a plausible nuclear target.[6] I doubt that all seventy-five of the bunkers noted above would have merited attack. Target proximity might permit coverage of several targets by a single warhead, further reducing the requirement. Altogether, it seems unlikely that more than one hundred and perhaps fewer than fifty designated ground zeros, each targeted by two weapons, would have been required to do very serious damage to the heart of the Soviet system for strategic C^3I in the Moscow area in the period in question. A dedicated strategic nuclear command and control attack probably would not have stopped here, however. Official U.S. government publications reported the existence of "an elaborate system of emergency relocation facilities, many of which are bunkered . . . equipped with hardened communications equipment."[7] Moreover, there were numerous hardened military command and control installations of all kinds, as well as mobile vans, trains, and aircraft.[8] Nevertheless, it seems quite plausible that only a few installations could have been capable of taking over major command functions of the highest civilian and military echelons in Moscow.[9] If they could have been located by intelligence, a limited number of dispersed sites would also have been struck in a dedicated counter–command and control attack.

The issue, of course, is not whether Moscow or other Soviet strategic C^3I targets could have been struck by ground-, sea-, or air-launched cruise missiles, or even fighter bombers, launched from the European periphery. Such attacks were feasible. Nor is the issue whether the relevant targets could have been destroyed by the available weapons. There were sufficient weapons. As of 1987 the United States, the United

[6]Meyer, "Soviet Nuclear Operations," p. 502. The main airfield is Khodinka.

[7]U.S. Department of Defense, *Soviet Military Power, 1985*, p. 19. There are said to be 1500–2000 installations, some hardened to several thousand psi. Meyer, "Soviet Nuclear Operations," p. 502. (I suspect that as in the United States, the very hard facilities are ICBM launch-control-center command capsules.)

[8]Meyer, "Soviet Nuclear Operations," pp. 504–507. See also U.S. Department of Defense, *Soviet Military Power, 1986*, pp. 53, 60.

[9]From the attacker's perspective, a dedicated counter–command and control nuclear attack would probably aim at every center that could plausibly contain an individual with the legitimate authority to launch a nuclear weapon, or that could carry a critical message. On the other hand, if the attacker had intelligence indicating that operations were still being run out of Moscow, he would have an incentive to confine his attack to this area. There is a clear trade-off from the attacker's perspective between "surprise" and mass.

Kingdom, and West Germany deployed some 425 nuclear-capable F-111s and Tornados suitable for long-range attacks deep into the Soviet Union. There were 108 Pershing II missiles and 256 ground-launched cruise missiles based in Europe as well. Thus, an extraordinarily successful Soviet conventional preemption would have been necessary to degrade just the land-based elements of this capability. Moreover, the United States then planned to place nuclear cruise missiles on nearly all its attack submarines and many surface combatants, for a total of nearly two hundred platforms. Finally, the issue is not even whether or not the cruise missiles stood a high probability of reaching Moscow. Given the demonstrated flaws in the Soviet air defense system (see below), enough would have gotten through to do very serious damage. Under the right circumstances, even a dedicated force of U.S. Air Force F-111s or RAF Tornados flying from Britain with tanker support might successfully have mounted such an attack. A modern cruise missile force would have had even higher odds of success.

The main issue is whether Soviet decision makers could have come to believe that cruise missiles or aircraft could have reached Moscow or other critical targets and dropped their nuclear weapons before the Soviet leaders understood that a major nuclear attack was underway, *and that Western planners might also have come to this conclusion*. As many have pointed out, under day-to-day conditions, and probably even during a crisis, an undetected NATO attack should not have been a Soviet concern. As we shall see below, however, the situation could have changed rather drastically after two to four weeks of conventional aerial combat in Central and Northern Europe. Under such conditions cruise-missile-equipped nuclear-attack submarines and surface combatants would have been dispersed around the periphery of the European land mass, where Soviet intelligence would have had a very difficult time tracking their activities. (Many would have been deployed in the Barents Sea, perhaps more detectable than those elsewhere, but also closer. See chapter 4.) Western SEAD would have chewed many holes through the air defense and early warning systems in Eastern Europe. Some conventional air operations might have accidentally or intentionally spilled across the Polish border into the Western Military Districts of the Soviet Union. B-52 bombers configured for conventional operations, but similar to those committed to strategic nuclear missions, might have participated in conventional attacks on the Soviet periphery. Soviet intelligence-gathering assets would have been systematically attacked. The sheer noise of the battle could have overloaded those intelligence assets that remained intact. At this point the calculation would have changed. Cruise missile or tactical fighter time of flight from the Soviet-

Polish border, or the Barents Sea, to Moscow is a little over an hour. Given the slow and creaky performance of the VPVO against KAL flight 007 in 1983 and against a small Cessna aircraft in 1987—both under peacetime conditions, without jamming, and in a relatively uncluttered aerial environment—the Soviets' confidence in their ability to detect and classify this kind of cruise missile or even fighter-bomber attack might have deteriorated rapidly under conditions of large-scale conventional air war.[10] Indeed, an unidentified U.S. Air Force officer made the following observation to the *Economist* magazine on the KAL 007 incident:

> If this is the best they can do against a high-flying airliner, we should have no trouble in a war. A B-52 with all its decoys, jammers and other countermeasures could be over Moscow before they figured out what was going on.[11]

Soviet concerns about more limited or more exotic attacks should also not be discounted. Although the various sources are not entirely consistent, three ballistic missile early warning radars were situated relatively close to the Russian-Polish border, including radars near Riga (Skrunda), Minsk (Baranovichi), and Kiev.[12] A fourth radar was quite close to the Czech border, near Mukachevo. The Skrunda, Baranovichi, and Mukachevo sites were apparently all then equipped with Hen House radars but were undergoing modernization with "Pechora" type long-range phased array radars.[13] These sites are all less than thirty

[10]For a critical appraisal of Soviet performance in this episode, see William Durch and Peter Almquist, "East-West Military Balance," in *International Security Year Book, 1984–85*, ed. Barry M. Blechman and Edward N. Luttwak (Boulder, Colo., 1985), pp. 41–43.

[11]"Flight 007: A Glimpse of Chaos," *The Economist*, 24 September 1983. Another anonymous U.S. official observed, "This horrible incident not only points out Soviet disregard for loss of life, but it shows the inflexibility of the system and a lack of air defense technology capable of operating in near real time." See "US Says Soviets Knew Korean Air Lines 747 Was Commercial Flight," *Aviation Week and Space Technology*, September 12, 1983, pp. 18–21. Subsequent information showed the Soviets did not in fact know they were shooting at an airliner. See David Shribman, "Experts Say Soviets Had Failed Identifying Plane before Shooting," *New York Times*, 7 October 1983. Speaking of unidentified U.S. government sources, "The informants said the experts had reached general agreement that the Soviet air defense force had displayed a poor capacity to intercept aircraft in Soviet airspace, to distinguish between commercial and military aircraft and to identify a plane before shooting it down." In general, off-the-record observations of American intelligence experts quoted in journalistic accounts of this event echo these conclusions. As of late 1983, the Soviet homeland air defense organization suffered from very serious shortcomings.

[12]International Institute for Strategic Studies, *The Military Balance, 1984–85* (London, 1985), p. 155 (map). Hereafter, IISS, *Military Balance* and year.

[13]U.S. Department of Defense, *Soviet Military Power, 1987*, p. 48.

minutes from the Polish border for a cruise missile or a fighter plane. The Kiev radar was paired with another Over the Horizon (OTH) radar on the other side of the Soviet Union. In combination with the Soviet satellite early warning system, their purpose was to provide a *reliable* thirty-minute warning of a U.S. ICBM launch.[14] The Hen House radar sites seem to have been directed against submarine-launched ballistic missiles (SLBMs), from the Atlantic.[15] The Soviets might have had reason to fear an attack in which cruise missiles, or nuclear-armed fighter bombers, destroyed their ability to detect a Pershing II launch and SLBMs followed up with a rapid attack against the Moscow command complex.

Indeed, even conventionally armed fighter bombers might have been useful in such precursor attacks. As Desmond Ball points out, many strategic early warning assets are vulnerable to conventional weapons. This is especially true of radars and large radio transmitters.[16] Conventional air attacks on these assets close to the Soviet border would have created tremendous ambiguity for Soviet decision makers. In the absence of nuclear explosions, how easy would it be to make a launch-on-warning decision? But if the destruction of these large early warning radars could have even further reduced Soviet warning of an SLBM attack, how safe would it have been to allow the West to gain this opportunity, if the air battle went badly for the Warsaw Pact and NATO aircraft were regularly operating in proximity to these sites?

The Role of Soviet and East European Air Defenses

Observers of the Soviet military system have long been struck by the size and scope of the effort to defend the homeland from threats by aircraft, and now by cruise missiles. Although somewhat ambiguous as to what is being counted, the Pentagon's figures are the starting point for nearly all public discussions of the Soviet effort. According to *Soviet Military Power, 1985*, the Soviets deployed, as part of the strategic air defenses of their national territory, some "7000 radars of various types located at about 1200 sites."[17] These directed "nearly 10,000 SAM launchers at over 1200 sites for strategic defense" and "more than

[14]U.S. Department of Defense, *Soviet Military Power, 1985*, p. 45.

[15]These radars would presumably also have had a role to play in detecting a Pershing II launch from Germany. The Soviets complained about the ten-minute flight time of Pershing II, and insisted, in contrast to Western claims, that it could hit Moscow.

[16]Ball, *Can Nuclear War Be Controlled?*, p. 12.

[17]U.S. Department of Defense, Soviet Military Power, 1985, p. 45.

1200 interceptors."[18] According to the most recent open-source Central Intelligence Agency (CIA) analysis of Soviet defense spending, roughly half of all spending on Soviet strategic forces in the 1970s was allocated to these forces. Put another way, the Soviet Union spent more on these forces than the United States spent on *all* its strategic offensive forces during this period.[19]

Some 5000 tactical surface-to-air missile (SAM) launchers, associated mainly with the ground forces, 3000 radars, and 1800 interceptor aircraft associated with the tactical air forces should also be counted under the Soviet defensive effort for purposes of this analysis, since many of these assets would move into Eastern Europe in wartime, augmenting the barrier against intrusions from the West.[20] The efforts of the Eastern European allies are also important. Between them, Poland, East Germany, and Czechoslovakia deployed another 750-odd surface-to-air missiles on launchers, and 950 MiG-21 and MiG-23 interceptors in a strategic defense role.[21] East European ground forces were also equipped with mobile air defense missiles and radars.

It is quite common in official Western sources to view Soviet strategic defenses as oriented mainly against the U.S. strategic bomber force and its associated cruise missiles. For example, the unclassified summary of the 1985 national intelligence estimate of the Soviet strategic forces assesses the adequacy of Soviet defenses against a U.S. strategic bomber and cruise missile attack but says nothing about its vulnerability to attacks originating in Western Europe.[22] Similarly, the Department of

[18]Ibid., p. 48. *Soviet Military Power, 1988,* offers slightly different figures, 9000+ Sam launchers, and 2250 interceptors (p. 15). It offers no figure for total air defense radars but argues that the quality of Soviet air defense against low-altitude penetrators such as cruise missiles has improved (pp. 80–82). The 1988 document reports that the Soviets have since 1986 virtually reversed the reorganization of their air defenses attempted at the beginning of the decade (p. 80).

[19]U.S. Central Intelligence Agency, National Foreign Assessment Center, *Soviet and US Defense Activities, 1970–79: A Dollar Cost Comparison* (Washington, D.C., 1980), pp. 8–9. U.S. Department of Defense, *Soviet Military Power, 1987,* p. 5, observes that "since the late 1960s, the Soviets have greatly expanded and modernized their offensive nuclear forces and invested an approximately equal sum in strategic defenses."

[20]U.S. Department of Defense, *Soviet Military Power, 1988,* p. 80, for air defense aircraft; *Soviet Military Power, 1987,* p. 59, for SAM launchers. In the 1987 edition (p. 59), a figure of 10,000 was given for all air defense radars; in the 1985 edition a figure of 7000 was given for homeland air defense radars (p. 45). I deduce that subtracting the latter from the former gives us a figure of 3000 for tactical air defense radars. This figure probably does not count anti-aircraft gun engagement radars.

[21]IISS, *Military Balance, 1984–85,* pp. 24–27.

[22]Robert M. Gates, chairman, National Intelligence Council, and deputy director for intelligence, Central Intelligence Agency, and Lawrence K. Gershwin, national intelligence officer for strategic programs, National Intelligence Council, in U.S. Congress, Senate, Subcommittee on Strategic and Theater Nuclear Forces of the Senate Armed Services Committee and the Defense Subcommittee of the Senate Committee on Appro-

Defense is quick to compare directly the major air-defense efforts of the Soviet Union to the paltry effort of the United States, without any reference to the very different geographic and strategic circumstances of the two countries.[23] Hundreds of nuclear-armed enemy aircraft are not based in Canada, Mexico, or even Cuba. This "mirror imaging" obscures an important dimension of VPVO, that of opposing attacks originating on the Soviet periphery. Once this orientation is understood, the substantial resources allocated to the problem provide evidence of how large it looms in the minds of Soviet strategists.

Evidence for the proposition that Soviet air defenses have had a strong Western orientation can be found in a variety of sources. David R. Jones, a close observer of Soviet air-defense efforts for many years, has observed that in spite of its other missions, "the PVO continues to be concerned primarily with the threat from Western Europe."[24] Ironically, *Soviet Military Power, 1985*, contains the best evidence in support of this proposition. Its map, "Soviet Territorial Air Defense," shows the bulk of Soviet interceptor and SAM assets concentrated in the western part of the country.[25] This is consistent with the document's location of the Soviet Union's important strategic assets, including ammunition dumps, nuclear storage sites, petroleum stocks, air bases, strategic early warning radars, and even some intermediate and long-range nuclear offensive forces—all concentrated in the western part of the country.[26] The importance of these assets to the Soviet Union, as well as their vulnerability to aircraft attacks originating on the Soviet

priations, *Soviet Strategic Force Developments* . . . , 99th Cong., 1st sess., 1985 (Washington, D.C., June 26, 1985), p. 6. Hereafter, *Soviet Strategic Force Developments*, 1985.

[23]See U.S. Department of Defense, *Soviet Military Power, 1985*, pp. 48–54; and Organization of the Joint Chiefs of Staff, *United States Military Posture, FY 1986* (Washington, D.C., 1985), pp. 30–32.

[24]David R. Jones, "Air Defense Forces," in *Soviet Armed Forces Review Annual, Vol. 6*, ed. David R.Jones (Gulf Breeze, Fla. 1982), p. 173. His contributions to the 1980 and 1981 editions of the annual are also very informative. For a somewhat similar view see Gordon Macdonald, Jack Ruina, and Mark Balaschak, "Soviet Strategic Air Defense," in *Cruise Missiles: Technology, Strategy, Politics*, ed. Richard K. Betts (Washington, D.C., 1981), p. 65. "Not surprisingly, the Soviet air defense network seems primarily occupied with targets from the west and north. As noted earlier, the most modern aircraft are based in the western USSR and constitute roughly 30 percent of the active force; another 25 percent in the Baku and Moscow districts indicate Soviet concern with defending command centers. The Warsaw Pact countries' air defenses add depth to the western bastion. The first EW (early warning) radars were built overlooking the Baltic and Eastern Europe. Only recently has the Soviet Union begun reshaping its forces to get more complete coverage. As far as is known, there are very light air defenses or none, associated with the missile fields."

[25]U.S. Department of Defense, *Soviet Military Power, 1985*, p. 51.

[26]Ibid., pp. 8–9, 70–71, 84.

periphery, not only helps explain the size of the Soviet effort to defend the western part of the country but the fact that all air-defense assets of its Warsaw Pact allies were integrated into the Soviet air-defense organization, the VPVO.[27]

David Jones is skeptical that their efforts achieved much, noting that "the existing ABM complex is helpless against any major missile assault. In a similar manner, the PVO is only slightly more capable of combatting low-level penetration by US strategic or NATO's tactical aircraft that employ penetration and other devices. And this, it must be stressed is even without the cruise missile."[28] Somewhat obliquely, the CIA lends support to this judgment. "Against a combined attack of penetrating bombers and cruise missiles, Soviet air defenses during the next 10 years probably would not be capable of inflicting sufficient losses to prevent large-scale damage to the USSR."[29]

In late 1981 Gen. A. I. Koldunov gave evidence of the Soviet opinion that their efforts were not keeping up with the threat. He noted that new nuclear delivery systems "in the immediate vicinity of the frontier of the Soviet Union and the lands of the Socialist Commonwealth, make the threat of a *surprise* attack from the side of the imperialist aggressors even greater than before."[30] It would be tempting to dismiss these remarks as simply part of the propaganda campaign to oppose NATO's deployment of Pershing II and GLCM. Yet, Soviet air defenses were apparently reorganized twice in the 1980s; the Soviets seem to have perceived that they had a serious problem and tested different solutions.

A reorganization of Soviet air defenses that began in 1980 permitted the closer "integration of strategic and tactical SAM systems." Originally there seem to have been two aspects to this effort. First, administratively all air-defense assets, including SAMs associated with the ground forces, were placed under the general authority of the VPVO, the national air-defense organization. Presumably, the purpose was to ensure some kind of commonality and interoperability among all Soviet air-defense assets. Since the ground forces' air defenses are geared more toward operations at low altitude, their expertise and weapons

[27]Jones, "Air Defense Forces," pp. 173–174. See also U.S. Department of Defense, *Soviet Strategic Defense Programs* (October 1985), p. 19: "The Soviets maintain the world's most extensive early warning system for air defense, composed of a widespread network of ground based radars *linked operationally with those of their Warsaw Pact allies.*"

[28]David R. Jones, "National Air Defense Forces," in *Soviet Armed Forces Review Annual, Vol. 4*, ed. David R. Jones (Gulf Breeze, Fla. 1980), p. 147.

[29]Testimony of Gates and Gershwin, *Soviet Strategic Force Developments*, 1985, p. 6. They do expect, however, "an increasingly capable air defense" of certain point targets.

[30]Quoted in Jones, "Air Defense Forces," p. 133.

systems would have given the national air-defense forces enhanced capability against low-level attackers including the current B-52, the B-1, tactical fighters, and especially the cruise missile. The second element of the reorganization was the *operational* grouping of *all* available air-defense assets—strategic and tactical—in a given area—especially border areas—under the command of the relevant military district. This suggested an effort to further reinforce the air-defense bulwark to attacks from the West, by ensuring that anything useful for the defense of the Soviet homeland was capable of operating in that mission.[31] Jones observed in 1982, "While the outlines of the restructured service remain unclear, all generally are agreed that it results from the Soviets' renewed recognition of the failings of their already extensive and costly anti-air defensive system."[32]

Whatever the early 1980s reorganization was meant to achieve, Soviet authorities appear not to have been satisfied with the results. Operational control of homeland air-defense missiles and radars was returned to the independent national air-defense structure, the VPVO, as were many interceptor aircraft. Tactical SAMs returned to the control of the ground forces. It is not clear who got operational control over air-defense fighters associated with the military districts and the groups of forces, but it does not seem to be the VPVO.[33]

As further evidence that the Soviets were concerned about air-breathing threats to command and control, it is worth noting that the best new Soviet strategic SAM for countering targets with small radar cross-sections such as the cruise missile, the Sa-10, was disproportionately fielded in the Moscow area. As of 1988 one-third of the 150 completed launch units were in the Moscow area.[34] The Department of Defense (DOD) argued that this suggests "a first priority on terminal defense of wartime command and control."[35]

Finally, as further support of the proposition that the Soviet Union took NATO's theater nuclear weapons very seriously, it is useful to recall that most analysts of Soviet theater conventional strategy during this period posited the conventional suppression of NATO's theater nuclear capability as the fundamental mission of Soviet tactical air

[31]U.S. Department of Defense, *Soviet Military Power, 1985*, pp. 48–51, quotation from p. 50.

[32]Jones, "Air Defense Forces." On the reorganization and the possible reasoning behind it, pp. 133–144.

[33]U.S. Department of Defense, *Soviet Military Power, 1988*, pp. 79–82, presents details on the latest Soviet air-defense efforts, especially the latest reorganization.

[34]Ibid., p. 81.

[35]U.S. Department of Defense, *Soviet Military Power, 1987*, p. 61. As of 1987 more than half the completed sites were reported in the Moscow area.

power.[36] The Soviet military made substantial and rather expensive improvements in the conventional attack capability of its tactical air power to support this operation. This was often explained by a hypothesized Soviet belief that the elimination of these forces would permit a Pact conventional victory in the theater to unfold without nuclear escalation by NATO. This is one possible explanation, but the huge number of warheads still in U.S. hands in such a situation makes the hope of *no* NATO nuclear response seem a faint one. It seems equally plausible to me that it was the use of NATO theater nuclear forces for strategic nuclear attacks that the Soviets really feared—since under conditions of intense conventional combat these could have done a special kind of very threatening damage to Soviet command and control and early warning assets.

To summarize, the Soviet Union invested massive sums in an air-defense system designed to oppose attacks from the west, not just attacks from the north. Consistent with the western orientation, the air-defense organizations of the Eastern European Pact allies were integrated with that of the Soviet Union. Reorganizations of the VPVO tried to integrate more effectively the air-defense assets of the ground forces, and tactical air forces with the radars, missiles, and interceptors of the VPVO. These were likely to have been among the best defenses against low-level attacks, and the most densely distributed assets in Eastern Europe after mobilization. Finally, the Soviets themselves seemed conscious of the combined "surprise attack" potential of Western conventional and nuclear theater forces.[37]

A skeptical reader will be justified at this point for asking how much difference this sort of vulnerability could have made. How much more problematic was an "air-breathing" counter command and control at-

[36]See Chapter 1.

[37]On this point, in addition to Koldunov's 1981 statement, see Vasendin and Kuznetsov, "Modern Warfare and Surprise Attack," pp. 226–233. "We cannot exclude attempts to achieve surprise by means of unleashing a local war. . . . The local war can be used by the aggressor for the additional mobilization of forces. In the guise of moving troops to the regions of the military conflict, a strike grouping of forces and means can be created for an attack. Such a war gives rise to an increase in the combat readiness of all armed forces the aggressor, an intensification of strategic reconnaissance, the deployment of control points and communications centers in the territory of the dependent countries, and the carrying out of an entire series of other measures" (p. 230).

Joseph Douglas and Amoretta Hoeber, *Conventional War and Escalation: The Soviet View* (New York, 1981), interpret this essay as an example of what the Soviets intend to do to the United States. A reading of the English translation suggests that this essay may mean exactly what it explicitly says, that local war increases the West's ability strategically to surprise the Soviet Union. The geopolitical reasons for this are clear. There are many places where *large-scale* local war could break out on the Soviet periphery, and virtually nowhere that it could occur on the U.S. periphery.

tack than one mounted by sea-based ballistic missile or European-based Pershing II? This question is impossible to answer with any great confidence. If, as Stephen Meyer argues, roughly five to ten minutes would have been consumed simply in the collection, analysis, and communication of the data that early warning technology provided, then a Soviet leader would have had between five and ten minutes to decide whether or not to launch on warning.[38] This is obviously not a long time to make such a momentous decision, and an attacker sufficiently daring to mount any kind of major nuclear first strike might also be daring enough to count on five or ten minutes of indecision.

On the other hand, a serious missile attack, aimed at a combination of direct destruction and the generation of disruptive electronic effects, would probably have required quite a number of reentry vehicles—at least as many as the minimum number of designated ground zeros I have estimated in the Moscow area—plus a few additional ground zeros for dispersed command centers and a small number of high-altitude bursts—seventy five targets. Assuming a requirement for 2-on-1 attacks for reliability, perhaps nineteen Trident C-4 missiles with eight 100 kiloton warheads each could have covered the target set, although these would have been inadequate against the hardest targets.[39] If one discounts Western claims that the Pershing II lacked the range to reach Moscow, which the Soviets almost certainly did, then they would have counted these highly accurate theater weapons as a dangerous strategic threat, but the 108 deployed would have been insufficient to cover the target set reliably. Though these are relatively small numbers, the "good" side of such attacks from the Soviet perspective would have been the relatively uncluttered environment out of which they would have arisen. The "bad" side of such attacks is that they might have left only five or ten minutes of decision time available to political leaders. But under wartime conditions, and given multiple warning sources, this could have sufficed. More importantly, from the attacker's perspective, attacks of this kind must seem likely to capture the defender's full attention. This is not to make light of such a situation. It is merely to

[38]Meyer, "Soviet Nuclear Operations," p. 484.

[39]Assuming 80 percent reliability, two Trident I warheads (100 kilotons each) would have had no better than a 40 percent chance of destroying a bunker hardened to 2000 psi. The imminent deployment of the accurate Trident D-5 missile with a 400–500 kiloton warhead will make feasible SLBM attacks against hardened command and control targets. Again, if we assume 80 percent reliability, two warheads launched would have better than a 90 percent chance of destroying such a target. Perhaps twenty D-5 missiles at six to nine warheads each would be required to mount such an attack. See Jeffrey A. Merkley, *Trident II Missiles: Capability, Costs, and Alternatives* (Washington, D.C.: Congressional Budget Office, July 1986), pp. 3, 51.

suggest that an attack by air-breathing systems, under conditions of intense conventional combat, might have offered special advantages to the attacker and special problems for the defender, which would have made this problem a serious one for the Soviets.

An attack by air-breathing nuclear systems surrenders the possibility of using speed to get inside the defender's decision-making process for launch on warning or launch under attack. But, as I shall elaborate below, it offers the possibility of slowing this system down by reducing the clarity of the information provided to the Soviet defender. The cruise missile, and ultimately the stealth bomber and stealth cruise missile, are effectively based on this principle of information denial. The first has a small radar cross-section and a minimal heat signature, and it travels at such a low altitude that it is out of the line of sight of most radars until it is virtually on top of them. Moreover, the "ground clutter" at this altitude saturates the radar with false returns. The radar thus has great difficulty pulling out the real information that indicates the presence of an attacker. Stealth technology further reduces the signature of the cruise missile or aircraft. In effect, air-breathing counter command and control attacks would elevate these tactical advantages to a strategic principle. For a variety of reasons, such weapons would become even more lethal under conventional war conditions. The Soviets might have a very difficult time distinguishing that an attack was under way until it was too late.

I do not wish to seem cavalier about the prospects for success, or the wisdom, of the preceding strategy. But all forms of counter command and control attacks, indeed all major strategic nuclear counterforce attacks, have an unreal quality. Nevertheless, as discussed in Chapter 1, both superpowers had nuclear war plans and force postures to execute counterforce attacks in this period. The threat posed by air-breathing systems to command and control survivability, especially under the conditions of intense conventional conflict, was no less plausible than the threats posited in any of the other strategic nuclear first-use scenarios that have been proposed over the years. And the air-breathing threat to command and control is especially important for our purposes, because an intense conventional air battle makes this threat even more plausible. Given that both the Soviets and the United States took seriously the possibility of extended conventional conflict in the 1980s, it is advisable to examine in detail the special problems such conflict could have created.

In the next section we turn to the question of how NATO would have conducted the conventional air campaign, how successful the campaign might have been, and what consequences it could have had for Soviet strategic early warning capabilities.

The Air War

A comprehensive analysis of the NATO–Pact tactical air "balance" could require a book in its own right. Indeed, one author devoted an entire book largely to an analysis of Pact offensive air operations.[40] Here I will offer an encapsulated description of the conventional wisdom about the pattern (not the outcome) of the air war. This will put the subsequent discussion in some kind of context.

First, it is important to note the numbers of aircraft that would likely have been involved in such a battle. One plausible accounting pits approximately 4400 Pact aircraft against approximately 3200 NATO aircraft in Northern and Central Europe after reinforcement.[41] Though they reveal little about the true balance of aerial capabilities, these figures do give an idea of the magnitude of the battle. By comparison, the entire Israeli air force in the 1973 October War included roughly 300 combat aircraft, and a big U.S. raid during the 1972 "Christmas Bombing" of North Vietnam included perhaps 200 aircraft.

A plausible 1980s scenario looks something like this. The Pact would have gotten in the first blow, starting with an independent air operation in which hundreds, if not thousands of fighter bombers, fighter escorts, and bombers would have hurled themselves at NATO's airfields, nuclear storage sites, air-defense missiles and radars, and perhaps ports, railroads, and bridges.[42] The Pact might have had some tactical surprise advantage, although given the size of this operation and the time it would take to assemble the aircraft into mutually supporting packages, the surprise was unlikely to have been great.

During the initial hours of this attack (perhaps the first forty-eight hours) NATO air planners would not have expected to have authority to cross into Warsaw Pact airspace. Therefore, many multipurpose fighter-bomber aircraft such as F-16s and F-4s were likely to have been used in an air-defense role during this phase of the air battle, shifting to an offensive bombing role once political authorities gave the go-ahead. By my accounting of the available assets, this procedure could

[40]Joshua Epstein, *Measuring Military Power: The Soviet Air Threat to Europe* (Princeton, 1984).

[41]Lt. Col. D. J. Alberts, *Deterrence in the 1980s: Part II, The Role of Conventional Air Power*, Adelphi Paper 193 (London, 1984), p. 56. Like many official comparisons, this is probably somewhat generous to the Pact, counting some air-defense fighters likely to be held within the Soviet Union against the possibility of nuclear escalation. Additionally, it is my understanding that most published accounts of this kind tend to ignore the fact that there are several dedicated training aircraft in each Soviet air regiment that would probably not be available for combat.

[42]Epstein, *Measuring Military Power*. See also Stephen M. Meyer, *Soviet Theatre Nuclear Forces*, pts. 1 and 2, Adelphi Papers 187 and 188 (London, 1984), pt. 1, pp. 25–27, and pt. 2, pp. 22–24.

have added as many as 1200 defending aircraft to the 500-odd "interceptors" normally counted as NATO's defensive aerial strength in the Northern and Central regions.[43] Thus, by one estimate 2500 Pact attacking aircraft would have gone against 1700 NATO defenders.[44] It is worth noting that the overall 1.5:1 force ratio would not have been grossly unfavorable to NATO, and once surface gun and missile defenses are factored in, the Pact could not have counted on mass to guarantee decisive victory.[45] Indeed, a DOD analysis, which tried to account for the quality of each side's aircraft, suggested a 1:1 ratio of combat potential after thirty days of mobilization.[46]

During the initial phase of the battle the direct help that NATO's air forces could have provided to its ground forces would have come mainly from a relatively small number of close air support and shallow interdiction aircraft, perhaps 750 machines. Once the authority to cross the border was granted, however, and presuming that the "swing" aircraft could be freed from their defensive activities, NATO would have a whole list of missions on the other side of the border.

Battlefield air interdiction (BAI), much favored by the European air forces, delays the movement of tactical and operational reserves toward or in the immediate vicinity of the battlefield.

[43]NATO Information Service, *Nato and the Warsaw Pact: Force Comparisons* (Brussels, 1984), p. 21, provides the stock picture of the unreinforced air balance between NATO and the Pact in the Northern and Central regions. It credits NATO with 500 "Interceptors." Alberts, "Role of Conventional Air Power," p. 56, suggests that after reinforcement NATO would have 250 dedicated air-defense fighters in the United Kingdom and the Central Region, but 1524 "swing" aircraft capable of both bombing and air-defense missions. By my count, NATO had some 570 dedicated air-defense aircraft in the same region, and some 1225 "swing" aircraft. Our totals are nearly identical.

[44]Alberts, *Deterrence*, p. 22. This estimate seems a fair one. Alberts allocates roughly one-half of the Pact dedicated air-defense aircraft in Eastern Europe—Soviet, East German, Polish, and Czech—to escort missions and adds them to his estimate of the Soviet fighter bomber and bomber strength. His method seems sensible, but I suspect that the numbers he attributes to the other side are a little high.

[45]Epstein, *Measuring Military Power*, offers the only thorough analysis of this effort. See esp. Appendix C, pp. 243–245. He concludes that the Soviets will be unlikely to enjoy anything like complete success, even under the relatively favorable assumption that they are able to fly their whole force three times every day, and that the individual aircraft will enjoy rather astonishing accuracy in the delivery of their munitions. On the other side, however, Epstein does assign a perhaps unrealistically high lethality to NATO's air defenses. It would seem that these assumptions balance out. His conclusion is that even after the Pact has flown its force through some sixteen sorties, nearly six days of combat, it will complete only about 44 percent of its counterairfield, counternuclear missions. It thus seems most unlikely that the initial several sorties of the Pact forces will be able in any sense to "shut-down" NATO airfields, or "destroy" NATO's air forces, or win air superiority. Rather, the Pact air effort, depending on how it is allocated, will cause selective trouble in selective areas of NATO capability.

[46]U.S. Department of Defense, *Annual Report to the Congress, Fiscal Year 1989* (Washington, D.C., 1988), chart I.B.3, p. 31.

Offensive counter-air (OCA), favored by most NATO air forces, involves strikes against the airfields that support enemy air operations, especially offensive bombing operations.[47]

Air interdiction (AI), or "Deep Interdiction" as the Americans term it, seeks to delay the movement of large numbers of reinforcements and supplies to the battle area. This would involve strikes against railroads, bridges, and perhaps ports throughout Eastern Europe. For example, the gauge of the Soviet railroads differs from that of the East European and West European railroads. Thus, cargo must be transshipped in the vicinity of the border at special yards, some on the Soviet side and some on the Polish and Czech sides of the border. There are only four major lines going into Czechoslovakia and Poland from the Soviet Union.[48] There are about eight transshipment complexes along the Polish-Russian border.[49] An additional complex serves most traffic with Czechoslovakia and is located at Cierna just inside the Czech border.[50] It is less than fifty kilometers from Mukachevo, the site of a Soviet ballistic missile early warning radar. For fighter bombers traveling at speeds in excess of 1000 km per hour, this distance is insignificant and constitutes virtually no margin of safety. These transshipment points constituted huge bottlenecks in the Warsaw Pact logistics system, and under some circumstances they would have come under major conventional air attack. New attention focused on these areas in the early 1980s as an element in NATO's Follow-On-Forces-Attack (FOFA) initiative.[51] Large numbers of Soviet reserve divisions would have had to move through these yards, and in the event that hostilities had begun before such reinforcement were complete, it is unlikely that the U.S. Air Force, or indeed other NATO air forces, would have wanted to

[47]Federal Minister of Defense, Federal Republic of Germany, *White Paper 1985: The Situation and Development of the Federal Armed Forces* (Bonn, 1985), pp. 28–29. "The capability of attacking the enemy with firepower deep in his territory has long since been a part of the strategy of Flexible Response. This capability includes operations against the enemy's offensive air forces in their operating bases. NATO reserves part of its air forces for this mission."

[48]The major lines into Poland pass through Grodno, Brest, and Lvov in the Soviet Union. See "Thomas Cook Rail Map of Europe" (Peterborough, England, 1983).

[49]U.S. Congress, Office of Technology Assessment, *New Technology for NATO: Implementing Follow-On Forces Attack* (Washington, D.C., June 1987), p. 66, n. 27.

[50]*Jane's World Railways, 1984–1985* (London, 1984), p. 521.

[51]Boyd Sutton, et al., "Strategic and Doctrinal Implications of Deep Attack Concepts for the Defense of Central Europe," in *Military Strategy in Transition: Defense and Deterrence in the 1980s*, ed. Keith J. Dunn and William O. Staudenmaier (Boulder, Colo., 1984), p. 78. fig. 4-1, "Comparison of Air Interdiction Zones," prominently highlights a narrow strip along *both* sides of Polish-Russian and Czech-Russian borders, labeling the areas the "Follow-On Force Attack Interdiction Zone." See also U.S. Congress, OTA, *New Technology for NATO*, pp. 66, 80, 89.

leave these targets alone. It is important to note that this target system effectively straddles the Polish-Russian border and thus might have required conventional air attacks into the Soviet Union.[52] The U.S. Air Force seldom if ever indicated in public any plan or inclination to cross the borders of the Soviet Union during a conventional war. But testimony by the U.S. Navy indicated joint navy–air force planning for just such attacks, and many of the best interdiction targets were on the Soviet side of the border.[53]

To complicate matters further, it is entirely possible that bombers of the Strategic Air Command (SAC) would have been involved in conventional interdiction missions in Eastern Europe. Indeed, SAC's interest in conventional missions for strategic bombers grew in the mid-1980s.[54] "SAC has offices at USAFE and SHAPE to facilitate the tasking of these aircraft."[55] Training for such missions was reportedly under way.[56] The air force was also considering the possibility of attacking these interdiction targets along the Soviet-Polish border with conventional cruise missiles fired from B-52s flying out of bases in North America.[57] The Office of Technology Assessment (OTA) observed, how-

[52]In terms of FOFA plans for attacks against follow-on "fronts," a recent study observes that "the area of these attacks would range from about 17° east longitude to and perhaps across the Soviet border." U.S. Congress, OTA, *New Technology for NATO,* p. 80.

[53]U.S. Senate, Committee on Armed Services, *DOD Authorization for Appropriations for Fiscal Year 1985, Maritime Strategy, Part 8,* 98th Cong., 2d sess., 1984 (Washington, D.C., 1984), p. 3887. In response to questions about navy plans to attack the Soviet homeland with conventional weapons in the event of a conventional war, the former chief of naval operations, James Watkins, responded, "we simulate running strikes into the Crimea, low level strikes across the Black Sea using AWACs and F-15s and naval forces." He went on to discuss the possibility of early attacks against targets in the eastern Soviet Union. "We know where those weaknesses are up in Alekseyevka today. So we might put a carrier strike in there along with the Air Force. We know how to do that. We test that with the Air Force." The statement thus indicates that in principle, the air force, like the navy, does actively plan for conventional strikes into the Soviet Union in the event of war.

[54]See Gen. Bennie Davis, USAF, "Indivisible Airpower," *Air Force Magazine* 67 (March 1984): 46–50; and Edgar Ulsamer, "Bombers for the Battlefield," *Air Force Magazine* 70 (January 1987): 20–24. "SAC intends to allocate more of its heavy bomber fleet to theater operations. This will involve aircraft modifications, changes in training, and acquisition of precision-guided and stand-off weapons" (p. 12). Some allusions to conventional missions for stealth bombers have also appeared. See Richard Halloran, "Stealth Bomber Takes Shape: A Flying Wing and Crew of 2," *New York Times,* 16 May 1988.

[55]U.S. Congress, Office of Technology Assessment, *Technologies for Nato's Follow-On Forces Attack Concept* (Washington, D.C., July 1986), p. 15.

[56]U.S. Congress, OTA, *New Technology for NATO,* p. 138.

[57]Ibid. p. 8. Some seventy B-52s were already committed to conventional missions, but for the most part lacked sophisticated conventional ordnance, especially cruise missiles. See Stephen T. Hosmer and Glenn Kent, *The Military and Political Potential of Conventionally Armed Heavy Bombers* (Santa Monica, August 1987); U.S. Congress, Congressional Budget Office, *US Ground Forces and the Conventional Balance in Europe,* prepared by Frances M. Lussier (Washington, D.C., June 1988), pp. 58, 65–67.

ever, that "long range conventionally armed cruise missiles, like strategic bombers used for this mission, could raise a problem of confusion in wartime. Their use in the conventional role might appear to be escalatory, inducing the enemy to escalate to nuclear weapons."[58] Finally, one Pentagon publication indicated high-level political support for attacks on the Soviet homeland by very accurate long-range conventional weaponry that might be deployed in the 1990s.[59]

Although one cannot read NATO's war plans, it appears that BAI would have enjoyed a high priority, OCA a close second, and "deep" interdiction (AI) would have been of third priority, tied with close air support. In support of these offensive operations, NATO would have tried to suppress enemy air defenses (SEAD) in order to increase the effectiveness and lower the costs of these penetrations into Pact air space. SEAD involves both the destruction of enemy radars, air-defense missiles, and command and control, as well as the jamming of radars and communications within the air defense system. Below we shall return to a more detailed analysis of one aspect of this campaign.[60]

Effects on Soviet Strategic Air Defense

The NATO–Pact air battle could have influenced Soviet confidence in the ability of the VPVO to detect and classify potential strategic attacks in three basic ways. First, the act of waging this war would have

[58]U.S. Congress, OTA, *New Technology for NATO*, p. 96.

[59]The report is not particularly specific as to the exact type of weapon or when it could be deployed, but the general tenor suggests a stealth cruise missile with a conventional warhead. See Commission on Integrated Long-Term Strategy, *Discriminate Deterrence, Report of the Commission on Integrated Long-Term Strategy* (Washington, D.C., January 1988), pp. 29, 45–51. See esp. p. 50. "By the standards of a decade ago, the accuracies are extraordinary. Current technology makes it possible to attack fixed targets at any range with accuracies within one to three meters. These accuracies and modern munitions give us a high probability of destroying a wide variety of point and area targets with one or a few shots without using nuclear warheads. They make practical attacks on heavily defended military targets deep in enemy territory. *Airfields well inside the Soviet Union* [my emphasis] could be put out of commission with warheads designed to attack infrastructure (fuel and maintenance facilities, say) and command-and-control facilities. Bridges, surface-to-air missile sites, intelligence facilities, rail lines, electric generating plants, petroleum refineries—all are suddenly much more vulnerable in the emerging age of smart munitions." See also Carl Builder, *Strategic Conflict without Nuclear Weapons* (Santa Monica, April 1983), which takes an optimistic position on the technical effectiveness of such weapons, their strategic utility, and the unlikelihood that their use against targets in the Soviet Union would prove unduly escalatory. A team of Rand analysts subsequently further developed these ideas. See Carl Builder et al., *The Rand Winter Study on Nonnuclear Strategic Weapons: Executive Summary* (Santa Monica, December 1984).

[60]For a brief but extremely useful introduction to these missions and how they relate to each other, see Alberts, *Deterrence*, pp. 14–15, and pp. 48–49, nn. 12 and 13.

caused a tremendous amount of "noise." Extracting information from the noise would not have been easy. Second, the waging of war inevitably implies the compromise of technology and tactics. This is particularly true in the area of air defense and air attack. Third, NATO's prosecution of the air battle would inevitably have involved lethal and nonlethal attacks on the Pact's ability to detect and classify, as well as defend against, nuclear attacks by tactical aircraft and cruise missiles.

As outlined earlier, it is not unreasonable to suppose that some 6000 to 8000 NATO and Pact fixed-wing combat aircraft would have been engaged in the early stages of a NATO–Pact conflict. This would have created a tremendous amount of electronic noise. As additional sources of confusion, one must add flights by attack and transport helicopters, fixed-wing transport aviation, and reconnaissance aircraft. In the early stages of conflict every platform could conceivably fly twice a day, and some more often than that. As the conflict unfolds, wear and tear on the aircraft reduces sortie rates.

Hundreds of the Soviets' own aircraft would have transited from the Soviet Union into Eastern Europe, and perhaps as far as Western Europe, and back again each day. Their ability to track these aircraft and reliably distinguish friend from foe in this period is doubtful. For example, many analyses of the initial Soviet air operation assume that medium bombers (Backfire, Badger, and Blinder) and long-range fighter bombers (SU-24 Fencer) based in the Soviet Union make an important contribution to the Pact effort. These aircraft would be likely to fly from bases in the Soviet Union.[61] Similarly, Soviet transport aviation would fly many sorties from Soviet air space into Eastern Europe and back every day. Soviet air-defense fighters on the Soviet side of the Russian-Polish border would necessarily have been called upon to defend targets in Poland. Finally, the possibility that NATO aircraft would have crossed into Soviet airspace in small or large numbers cannot be ruled out. At minimum, the odd reconnaissance flight would have crossed the border. Maximally, NATO air commanders would have sought permission to strike the Russian bases out of which Soviet medium bombers and fighter bombers were flying sorties against the west, and the aforementioned transportation choke points. Thus, to improve their performance in the conventional air war, the Soviets would have had to create "fog" for themselves. They would probably have elicited NATO

[61]See, e.g., the Institute for Defense Analysis's briefing on its study "Nato Air Defense," U.S. Congress, House, Appropriations Committee, Subcommittee on Defense Appropriations, *Department of Defense Appropriations for Fiscal Year 1979*, pt. 4, 95th Cong., 2d sess., 1978 (Washington, D.C., 1978), pp. 283, 347. See also Meyer, *Soviet Theatre Nuclear Forces*, pt. 1, p. 26.

retaliation. They could have avoided these problems by limiting combat missions originating in their own territory, but only at some cost to their conventional capability.

The cumulative effect of all this aerial traffic would have rendered the task of classification in real time very difficult. This problem arises quite frequently when Soviet ground-based air defenses are deployed in actual combat. The Egyptians and Syrians had such a difficult time telling enemy from friendly aircraft in the 1973 war that they shot down large numbers of their own planes.[62] NATO planners are privately willing to admit that our own capability to do this is so poor that we shall inevitably shoot down large numbers of our own aircraft. Recall the argument above that strikes as small as 100 nuclear cruise missiles could have reduced the effectiveness of Soviet strategic C^{3}I to an important extent in this period.[63] It seems quite plausible that as the war unfolded this number would have been below the threshold of what the system as a whole was capable of identifying as "extraordinary."

Tactical and Technical Compromise

As a consequence of fighting the air war, NATO and the Pact would have learned a good bit about each other's hardware and tactics. The utility of this information depends a great deal on the speed with which it can be collected and exploited. The West has a demonstrated capability in this regard.[64]

The importance of capturing hardware is well known. The United States has long enjoyed, by way of Israel, and now Egypt, relatively privileged access to important items of Soviet equipment in good working order. For example, several Soviet fighter aircraft, including the MiG-23—the mainstay of Soviet air-defense fighters in Central Europe, are operated by the U.S. Air Force as training aircraft. Soviet air-defense missiles captured by Israel in 1973 were made available to the United

[62]Chaim Herzog, *The Arab-Israeli Wars: War and Peace in the Middle East* (New York: Vintage, 1984), p. 311.

[63]Here I am reasoning from the low end of the thirty to seventy-five bunkers estimated to be in the Moscow area. See n. 4 above.

[64]The U.S. Air Force was able to modify substantially its tactics and improve its performance in the eleven-day Linebacker Two bombing campaign against North Vietnam in 1982. See Brig. Gen. James R. McCarthy and Lt. Col. Robert E. Rayfield, *Linebacker Two: A View from the Rock*, USAF Southeast Asia Monograph Series, vol. VI, no. 8 (Maxwell Airforce Base, 1979), pp. 79–96. "ECM (electronic counter measure) tactics were changed significantly. Analyses of the ECM tests conducted in the States, plus additional reconnaissance information on enemy frequencies and techniques, gave the EWO's (electronic warfare officers) ideas on how their equipment could be used more effectively to degrade the defenses" (p. 121).

States for exploitation. In a NATO–Pact war important equipment is bound to fall into NATO's hands. Soviet fighter aircraft will crash in NATO territory, and it seems quite likely that their electronic equipment will prove of great interest to the United States. One can imagine, for example, how useful it would be to have a working Soviet IFF (identification friend or foe) device.[65]

Militarys do not like their best weapons to fall into enemy hands. During the 1982 Israeli war in Lebanon a Soviet Sa-8 surface-to-air missile apparently shot down an Israeli F-4 specially configured for attacking ground defenses. The Israeli Air Force wasted no time in ordering an immediate attack on the wreckage of the aircraft to prevent any of its electronic equipment falling into Soviet hands.[66] A critical feature of all modern Western electronic countermeasures equipment is "threat responsiveness." The devices are built in such a way that information gleaned from the battlefield can be quickly exploited tactically. According to one source, the United States began to install an "on-board active electronic countermeasures system" in its cruise missiles in 1982.[67]

Intense air combat in Central Europe would also provide tactical information to the West, not only on how air defenses work in Eastern Europe but about air defenses in the Soviet Union.[68] As the remarkably detailed accounts of its behavior during the KAL-007 incident show, Western intelligence means have the ability to extract a tremendous amount of information from an activated air-defense system. This one incident seems to have provided reams of useful information to the U.S. military.[69]

An air war over Eastern Europe would have activated the Soviet air

[65]In general, such systems do not work very well in any case, which is one reason why NATO officers believe that the Alliance would shoot down many of its own planes.

[66]"Soviets Order Sa-8s into Action in Bekaa after Israeli Successes," *Aviation Week and Space Technology*, 9 August 1982, pp. 18–19.

[67]"USAF Planning Stealth Cruise Missile," *Aviation Week and Space Technology*, 8 November 1982, pp. 18–21. A flurry of concern about the effectiveness of the cruise missile against developing Soviet air defenses erupted in 1982 and 1983. The upshot of this concern was the decision to add a countermeasures package to the forces deployed and to slow deployment of the current generation of cruise missiles in expectation of getting a "stealth" version soon. It is unclear whether this concern was warranted, how quickly stealth can be deployed, and whether it is needed. For a good discussion of these issues, see Michael Gordon, "Pentagon's Shift on Cruise Missiles Leaves Big Contractors Scrambling," *National Journal*, 26 March 1983, pp. 644–647. As the text of this essay indicates, I am skeptical that these weapons would have serious problems penetrating Soviet air space.

[68]Of course this cuts both ways; the Soviets will learn a lot about NATO's capabilities, but this would have fewer implications for U.S. strategic nuclear forces.

[69]See, e.g., Richard Halloran, "Soviet Air Defenses Rigid," *International Herald Tribune*, 19 September 1983; Shribman, "Experts Say Soviets Had Failed"; William Beecher,

defenses on a regular basis, under stressful conditions, in circumstances where the Soviets would have been more inclined to use everything they had out of fear that any given penetration could be particularly lethal. One practice that air-defense organizations like to pursue is to keep some of their radars mobile and some dormant so that the adversary lacks a complete picture of how well a given piece of terrain is surveyed. Constant "tickling" of Soviet air defenses would have forced these radars to emit, providing information that U.S. strike planners would have used to develop the best (which is to say, least defended) routes into the Soviet Union. The GLCM system was designed with the capability to plan strikes that exploit this kind of information.[70]

Of course, the effectiveness of NATO intelligence in gathering this information and the dispatch with which it may be exploited ought not to be overestimated. The fog of war would have had to affect NATO as well. Intelligence and deception operations in war are as competitive as the enterprise as a whole. One side may do better than the other in these efforts, and that side might not have been NATO. Nevertheless, the circumstantial evidence suggests that the United States was particularly well placed technically, organizationally, and geographically for an intelligence competition of this kind. The possible effects of U.S. success in this endeavor ought to be considered.

Direct Suppression of Enemy Air Defenses

To aid the offensive operations of its tactical air forces, NATO would have attacked Warsaw Pact air defenses, especially ground-based radars and missiles. This would include efforts to jam Pact radars and communications, and efforts to destroy Pact radars, surface-to-air missile launchers, and, perhaps, command and control installations.

Although it is difficult to extract the details of how these operations would have been conducted, it is probably fairer to view SEAD as actions taken to aid other offensive aircraft than as an independent campaign to win *theater* air dominance. Initial defense suppression operations within about one hundred kilometers of the forward edge of the battle area (FEBA) probably would have taken the form of a

"Tracking Flight 007: What Really Happened?" *Boston Globe*, 4 December 1983; "Flight 007," *The Economist*; and Clarence A. Robinson, Jr., "US Says Soviets Knew Korean Air Lines 747 Was Commercial Flight," *Aviation Week and Space Technology*, 12 September 1983, pp. 18–21.

[70]Both the Air Force GLCM and the Navy SLCM have this capability. On GLCM, see Walter Pincus, "Pershings Packed to Go," *Washington Post*, 16 October 1983; on the SLCM, see Miles Libbey III, "Tomahawk," *US Naval Institute Proceedings, Naval Review* (1984), pp. 150–163, esp. pp. 158–160.

deliberate, concentrated campaign to win at least local air superiority. SEAD operations deeper in Eastern Europe would have suppressed point defenses in support of particular attacks.

Weapons. The NATO alliance had a number of important weapons dedicated to or useful for the SEAD mission. The best-known weapon was the U.S. F-4G Wild Weasel aircraft, a variant of the F-4 specially configured for SAM hunting and killing. During most of the 1980s the main weapon of the F-4G was the Shrike antiradiation missile, which homes on radar emissions. This weapon demonstrated many shortcomings in Vietnam, and hence, toward the end of the decade, it began to be replaced by a combination of the new, and supposedly far more capable, HARM (high-speed antiradiation missile), and the imaging infra-red Maverick, which homes on the heat generated by SAM ground-control equipment. The United States has maintained a force of about one hundred Weasels since the end of the Vietnam war. Each Weasel tends to operate with a standard F-4 (or other tactical fighter, usually an F-16) as a partner, to facilitate the delivery of more ordnance (including standard bombs, cluster munitions, unguided rockets, and even precision-guided munitions) against the air defenses. Other NATO allies lack the F-4G but have the capability to configure some of their standard fighter aircraft to attack SAMs. I assume that 60 percent of the U.S. Weasel force, sixty F-4Gs and sixty accompanying F-4Es, would have been allocated to the central front, although given the high concentration of air-defense assets there, it is entirely plausible that nearly all would have been deployed to Europe. Thus this analysis is conservative.

Another possible air-defense suppression platform would have been the first F-117 stealth fighters, then in production at Lockheed, and first based at Nellis Air Force Base in Nevada.[71] Such aircraft are ideal air-defense suppression weapons, since they are far less detectable to Pact radars than the F-4G Weasel. Thus, the SAM operators might be unable to shut down their radars to avoid antiradiation missile lock-on until too late. Because of its smaller radar signature, a stealth Weasel would have more time to survey a given area for emitters and could conceivably take greater care in setting up an attack. Indeed, it seems plausible that stealth aircraft would not aim for radars at all, but for the launch-control

[71]John H. Cushman, "Air Force Lifts Curtain, a Bit, on Secret Plane," *New York Times*, 11 November 1988, p. A27. Fifty-two of fifty-nine planes scheduled had been delivered by late 1988, although two had crashed. According to the article, "the plane is designed to elude detection by radar, and its job is to penetrate enemy territory and destroy a few especially important targets, such as command posts, during a war."

vehicles or vans. These often have a high infrared signature and would be ideal targets for Imaging Infrared Maverick missiles. These vans are fragile and expensive and, when they are hit by the powerful armor-piercing warhead of the Maverick, will be much harder to repair or replace than radar antennae. Thus the overall effectiveness of stealth aircraft attacks may be higher than those of a standard Weasel with antiradiation missiles.

Circumstantial evidence supports the hypothesis that defense suppression is one mission of the stealth aircraft. The F-4G was already an aging platform in the 1980s, and the size of the force remained around one hundred for most of the period. (Indeed, as of publication there are still about one hundred F-4Gs.) In spite of constant worry about the lethality of Soviet air defenses in Eastern Europe during the 1980s, the U.S. Air Force put little impetus into finding a replacement for the F-4G. Both the F-15 and the F-16 could have been adapted to this mission had the air force cared to do so. I deduce that little effort went into a conventional aircraft upgrade because the stealth fighter was expected to conduct at least part of the defense-suppression mission.[72]

Many air-defense sites are either fixed or moveable only with some difficulty. It would not necessarily have required the real-time, on-board radar-detection capability of the Wild Weasel to attack them. Specialized low-level attack aircraft like the F-111 and the European Tornado would have been quite useful in these missions. The F-111 was used very effectively in this way in Vietnam.[73] By my count, NATO had about 430 such aircraft available in the Central Region by the second half of the decade.[74] I assume that 60 would have been allocated to SEAD activities.

[72]As this book goes to press, information on the employment of the F-117 stealth fighter in the U.S. air campaign against Iraq in January and February of 1991 is beginning to appear. The F-117s were generally operated in small groups, at night, against very high value targets, including those associated with the Iraqi air defense system. Gen. Merrill McPeak, Chief of Staff of the U.S. Air Force, summarized the F-117's contribution to the first night's air attacks: "Our stealth aircraft, low observable aircraft, which these Iraqi radars could not see, jumped off at H-Hour, actually slightly before H-Hour, and blinded the Iraqi early warning system by knocking out these radars, and then proceeded on into Iraq to begin to work on the rest of the strategic targets—principally the command and control apparatus, the fighter defense direction system, and so forth." Later he added, "They also attacked key parts of the air defense system throughout Iraq." See "The Air Campaign: Part of the Combined Arms Operation," DOD News Briefing, 15 March 1991, 2:00 P.M., transcript, p. 4.

[73]Gen. William W. Momyer, USAF, *Airpower in Three Wars* (Washington, D.C., 1978), pp. 239–241.

[74]My count: 140 U.S. Air Force F-111E/F, 108 RAF Tornados, 108 German Air Force Tornados, and 72 Germany Navy Tornados. See IISS, *Military Balance, 1987–1988*, country entries. I have counted only aircraft that appear to be in combat squadrons; training aircraft and attrition fillers would increase the total.

Finally, the United States deployed specialized electronic reconnaissance and electronic warfare aircraft. The TR-1 variant of the U-2 spy plane was equipped with devices to locate threat radars, as was the TEREC equipped RF-4 reconnaissance version of the F-4 fighter. Both of these aircraft had some real-time capability to communicate the information they gather. Compass Call, a C-130 transport loaded with electronic gear, was designed to jam enemy communications. Gen. Wilbur Creech, formerly commander of the U.S. Air Force Tactical Air Command, called this aircraft "the world's greatest force subtractor" because of its ability to break down the cohesion of the Soviet air defense network in Eastern Europe.[75] The EF-111, a jammer-equipped version of the F-111, was designed to degrade the performance of Pact early warning radars. Although contractor claims must be taken with a grain of salt, Grumman has repeatedly asserted that "a force of 5 EF-111As could radiate enough power to affect most of Warsaw Pact's air defense radars from the Baltic to the Adriatic."[76] The United States planned to buy forty-two of these aircraft, and some were deployed in Europe during the 1980s. EF-111s and Weasels work together. When early warning radars are jammed, SAM operators are forced to rely on the shorter ranged engagement radars at the battery level to acquire their targets. Once these are turned on, the Weasel knows where they are and has a much better chance of getting a "lock-on" with a Shrike or calling in a "dumb bomb" or precision guided munition (PGM) attack by another aircraft.

Tactics. As suggested above, NATO's defense suppression aircraft would not simply have been sent forth to destroy air defenses. Air-defense suppression would probably have been conducted in two different patterns. The bulk of the suppression assets would have opened corridors in Pact air defenses along the NATO–Pact border through which large numbers of attacking aircraft would penetrate and then fan out to conduct a variety of attacks. Pact ground defenses would have been densest where Pact divisions were concentrated, and in wartime this tends to be close to the border. Even here, SAMs are not distributed equally, and NATO planners would have looked for places where the

[75]"An exclusive AFJI interview with General Wilbur L. Creech," *Armed Forces Journal International*, January 1983, p. 32. "When it flies along on our side of the border and turns on all those jammers, he won't be able to talk Mig-to-Mig, Mig-to-ground, ground-to-Mig, and we even can jam some of his SAM links. This gets us into his C^3 nervous system. That disrupts anybody; it certainly gives us fits. It will do even more violence to him because he is so dependent on his rigid command and control system."

[76]Martin Streetly, *World Electronic Warfare Aircraft* (London, 1983), pp. 69–70.

adversary was thin on the ground, and where the terrain would help mask low-flying aircraft from ground-based radars. Rough terrain inhibits high concentrations of ground forces and also helps mask the attacker. Thus, a look at a map reveals some of the likely places that NATO might have conducted these operations. In the northern sector (Northag) the Harz Mountains look lucrative, although an end run across the Baltic also seems plausible. In the southern sector there is much rough terrain, although the East German–Czech border area appears to have been favored.[77]

These corridors could not be kept permanently open. Rather, they would be opened as needed. Once the adversary figured out the game, he might have strengthened his defenses in the exploited areas. NATO planners might have continued to view them as lucrative corridors and simply tried to destroy the reinforcing SAMs. Alternatively, NATO planners would have shifted to other corridors.

In a small number of cases suppression would have been conducted in direct support of offensive air attacks against particular high-value targets deep in the enemy rear. Some high-value targets such as bridges, railroad marshaling yards, and fighter bomber bases are often surrounded by dense defenses. Weasels and EF-111s might accompany a group of bombing aircraft into a particular target area, supplementing the self-protection electronic countermeasures customarily deployed on NATO's most modern aircraft. Direct suppression of local defenses not only lowers the attrition that attackers suffer but increases their effectiveness. For example, many modern precision-guided air munitions, including television-guided bombs and laser-guided bombs, require excessive exposure in the optimal engagement envelope of surface-to-air missiles in order to acquire and lock on to the chosen target. The presence of Weasels and EF-111s could buy a "window" for the effective delivery of these weapons.

Effectiveness of the Campaign

At the outset I argued that from the Soviet perspective cruise-missile flight times to critical targets may have to be measured from the Polish-Russian border, if the SEAD campaign is effective. To examine how effective the campaign might be, I have designed a simple model that

[77]U.S. Congress, House, Armed Services Committee, *Department of Defense Authorization of Appropriations for Fiscal Year 1984, Part 3, Statement of General Lawrence Skantze,* (98th Cong., 1st sess., 1983 (Washington, D.C., 1983), pp. 1088–1090, offers a series of maps to illustrate the pattern of Western air operations. Major penetrations are shown in the Czech–East German border area and from the Baltic.

can be run on a Lotus 1-2-3 or Symphony spreadsheet package. I have run excursions with the 180 standard aircraft enumerated above against a 2200-radar target set in East Germany, Poland, and Czechoslovakia. I have also run excursions with the addition of 50 stealth fighters. Appendix 1 explains how this target set was developed. I would argue that it is a conservative number for the period in question. A variety of assumptions about the effectiveness of Pact air defenses against NATO SEAD aircraft, and the effectiveness of the SEAD aircraft against the target set, are tested. The values employed are, again, conservative in my estimation. I run the force through sixty-two attacks against the target set. Enthusiasts are often willing to claim that NATO can fly three sorties a day in the initial stages of combat. Historically, two sorties a day has been achieved for as long as three weeks.[78] If one believes that initial Soviet air attacks would have done much damage to NATO air bases, then perhaps a sortie a day is more plausible. My personal judgment is that for the sophisticated aircraft involved in SEAD, and given some adversary success in airfield attack, two sorties a day is a good estimate.

For purposes of discussion, and consistent with my personal judgment, table 2.1 represents NATO's progress in the SEAD campaign after two and four weeks of combat. Even under *highly conservative* assumptions (see Appendix 1) of 5 percent attrition and a low .05 probability of kill (pk) per shot, nearly a quarter of the adversary's radars are destroyed in two weeks; nearly a third, in four weeks. Under the conditions that I personally find most plausible, 4–5 percent attrition and .1 pk, half the threat is destroyed in two weeks and nearly all of it in four. Figure 2.2 shows the effects of adding 50 stealth aircraft to this campaign, assigning each one four munitions with a .25 pk and subjecting that force to only 2 percent attrition per sortie. This boosts performance of the entire force to 60 percent destruction of the Soviet radar network in two weeks, and virtually all of it in four.

One must, of course, qualify the implications of this analysis. This is a model of combat, an abstraction from reality. It does not tell us exactly how things would have gone; it gives us a general idea of how they might have gone. This is a simplification, in that it does not fully capture the tactics outlined above; it does not account for destruction of ground-based SAM equipment other than radars; it does not include the effects of radar or communications jamming, either NATO's or the Pact's; it

[78]See Alberts, *Deterrence*, p. 52, n. 60, for sortie rate estimates. See Trevor N. Dupuy, *Elusive Victory: The Arab-Israeli Wars, 1947–74* (New York, 1978), pp. 549–550.

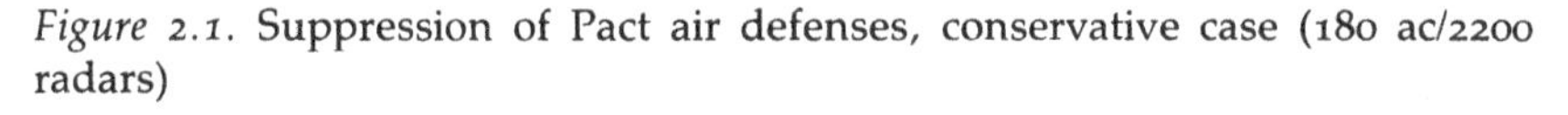

Figure 2.1. Suppression of Pact air defenses, conservative case (180 ac/2200 radars)

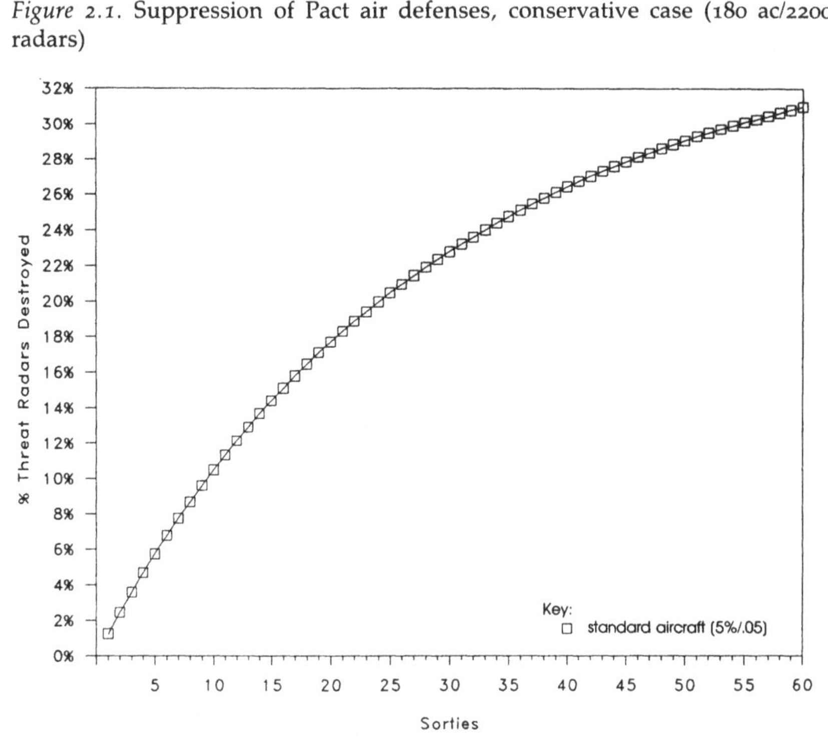

does not capture attacks against major command and control installations; it does not account for the very strong possibility that NATO would try to destroy surface-to-air missile stocks. Thus, the model "sheds light" rather than predicts outcomes. But these results are broadly consistent with other assessments of the probable course of a SEAD campaign. A 1987 OTA study suggested, "It is expected that Warsaw Pact SAMs and interceptors will be increasingly (but not completely) suppressed as a war progresses."[79]

Even given these caveats, however, the implications are striking. The application of a relatively small (albeit highly specialized) portion of NATO's tactical air capabilities against the Pact air-defense system could, in two to four weeks, have torn sizable holes in the air defenses of Eastern Europe and thus caused substantial worries for the Soviet

[79]U.S. Congress OTA, *New Technology for NATO*, p. 149.

Table 2.1. Model results: 180 SEAD aircraft

Percentage of threat radars destroyed after 28 sorties

	NATO aircraft attrition rate[a]		
NATO munitions effectiveness[b]	5	4	3
.05	22	24	27
.1	45	50	54
.15	71	77	83

Percentage of threat radars destroyed after 62 sorties

	NATO aircraft attrition rate[a]		
NATO munitions effectiveness[b]	5	4	3
.05	31	37	44
.1	70	82	96
.15	120[c]	138	157

[a]NATO's loss rate at the beginning of the campaign. The model reduces this loss rate as it destroys Pact radars on the assumption that the effectiveness of the whole system declines as pieces are lost. See Appendix 1.

[b]The probability of kill per shot. I assume that each aircraft that successfully penetrates takes four shots against the enemy. This obscures the fact that Tornados and F-111s on low-altitude sorties might simply drop an entire load of bombs on a single large fixed radar.

[c]Killing more than 100 percent of the threat is an artifact of the model, which continues to cycle the force showing its potential kills even after the notional threat is destroyed. I have included these numbers to show how much "insurance" there is in case the adversary diverts additional air-defense assets from other theaters.

air-defense planner.[80] These worries would have been magnified if, as suggested earlier, NATO air commanders were to receive permission to mount regular conventional attacks into the Soviet Union against high-value assets such as medium bomber and long-range fighter-bomber bases and railroad junctions and transshipment points.[81]

The "real" degradation in the hardware of the air-defense system of

[80]Surveillance radars and fire control radars are lumped together as a single target set in the model. But only early warning, height finder, and ground control intercept, and target acquisition radars, by my crude estimate only 600 surveillance radars, about a quarter of the total, can plausibly be assumed to be netted into the Soviet strategic air-defense system. Thus, their destruction would exert disproportionate effects on Soviet early warning capability. Similarly, NATO's jamming aircraft focus on the disruption of these systems, further exacerbating the strategic warning problem.

[81]Another possibility exists, which I hesitate to term "inadvertent" escalation. As discussed in a subsequent chapter, one of the many reasons the U.S. Navy has advanced to support its wish to attack Soviet SSBNs is "counterforce coercion," the alteration of the strategic nuclear "balance" by direct conventional attacks on Soviet strategic nuclear assets. One cannot ignore the possibility that plans exist, or that in the event of war the suggestion will be made, for deliberate conventional attacks on Soviet strategic nuclear

Figure 2.2. Suppression of Pact air defenses, stealth contribution

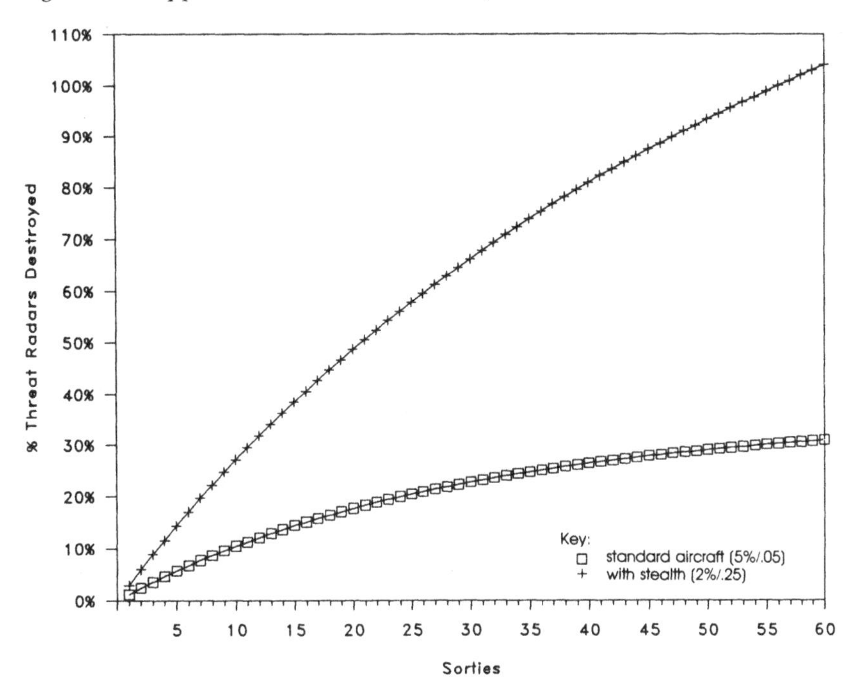

the Warsaw Pact must be combined with our understanding of the other problems discussed above to assess the overall position of Soviet air defenses after two to four weeks of combat. The confidence of the Soviet air-defense commander in his system's ability to detect and classify cruise-missile attacks of the kind outlined early in this essay is unlikely to have been high. Moreover, as he saw the West exploiting the knowledge gained in the course of the battle to lower the overall effectiveness of the Pact air-defense effort, his thoughts would have turned to NATO's assessment of the remaining Soviet early warning and defense potential. He would have wondered if the West perceived itself to have the capability to decapitate Soviet strategic forces. Finally, he would have been looking for signs and indicators that the West was moving in this direction. The tendency to give any ambiguous

assets. Soviet missile early warning radars on the Soviet periphery would be vulnerable to such attacks. The purpose would be to reshape Soviet calculations of the strategic nuclear balance to encourage them to "back down." This would be a high-risk strategy.

intelligence the benefit of the doubt, already lowered by the simple fact of open conflict, would have further deteriorated. What factors would have influenced how the Soviets interpreted this situation?

Soviet Attitudes toward Theater Nuclear War

The study of Soviet military thought is a specialized field. Here I make no pretense to expertise in this field. Rather, I draw extensively, if critically, on the reporting of those who are experts.[82] According to most students of Soviet military doctrine, its most striking feature through the 1980s was its emphasis on the offensive. This was true whether conventional or nuclear weapons are discussed. Soviet strategy for war against NATO was no exception.

The Soviets were keenly concerned over the threat that NATO's theater nuclear weapons posed to the Soviet armed forces and to the Soviet state. One could argue that this concern focused on two problems. First, in the event of war, the Soviets would have liked to destroy NATO's military power on the Eurasian land mass, and to do so without suffering the wholesale destruction of its own military forces.[83] Thus NATO's theater nuclear forces were an important obstacle to the achievement of their offensive military objectives.[84] Second, the Soviets were concerned that some NATO theater capabilities, especially the Pershing II, the GLCM, and the U.S. Navy sea-launched cruise missile (SLCM) provided NATO with important offensive options against the strategic nuclear forces of the Soviet Union.[85]

[82]It is necessary to proceed with some caution, however, because, as in any field, there are disputes among the experts. Moreover, because the experts have incomplete access to Soviet sources, because Soviet sources have their own peculiarities, and because nonexperts (especially the majority who do not read Russian) cannot always review the sources cited by the experts, one must maintain a healthy skepticism in reading this literature.

[83]Lebow, "Soviet Offensive in Europe."

[84]Meyer, *Soviet Theatre Nuclear Forces*, pt. 1, pp. 18–19.

[85]Though they must be understood as part of the public relations campaign against NATO's long-range theater nuclear forces (LRTNF) modernization, numerous statements to this effect can be found. See, e.g., the interview with Arbatov conducted by *Der Spiegel*, 24 October 1983, pp. 154–161, translated in Foreign Broadcast Information Service (FBIS), Daily Report, Soviet Union, 26 October 1983, esp. AA13-14, the article by Col. General Chesnokov, first deputy commander in chief of the USSR Air Defense Forces, "Preparedness in the Interest of Peace," Bratislava *Pravda* 1 April 1983 (FBIS, Daily Report, Soviet Union, 6 April 1983, p. v1); and the remarks of General Gribkov, chief of staff and first deputy commander in chief of the Warsaw Treaty Joint Armed Forces, in *Neues Deutschland*, 10 December 1983 (BBC Summary of World Broadcasts, EE/7514/A1/1, 12 December 1983). These and many other statements by Soviet soldiers and political officials stressed the first-strike potential of the Pershing II and GLCM. Remarks by military leaders also tended to stress the requirements for a huge increase in the readiness of Pact air-defense

The Soviet answer to NATO theater nuclear forces was the development of two major offensive options. First, the Soviets substantially improved their conventional air attack capability against NATO's theater nuclear infrastructure. The Soviets envisioned at least a phase of conventional conflict in any war, but they still seem to have viewed the probability of nuclear escalation as high and wanted to be in an advantageous military position should the occasion arise. Hence, they would try to destroy NATO's nuclear weapons without themselves using nuclear weapons.[86]

Although the Soviets hoped to destroy NATO's nuclear capability conventionally, they still seem seriously to have doubted their probability of success. They feared nuclear escalation, and they hoped to be the first to use nuclear weapons *decisively*. Here, analysts of current Soviet beliefs found real tensions.[87] On the one hand, the Soviets appeared to plan seriously on an extended conventional phase of conflict. At the same time, however, the Soviets thought it essential to get in the first telling nuclear blow. Stephen Meyer suggests that since NATO nuclear doctrine seems to have planned on an initial demonstrative use of nuclear weapons, the Soviets may have hoped to get in the first decisive blow, even if NATO used nuclear weapons first.[88] It seems unlikely, however, that after several days or weeks of intense conventional conflict, Soviet intelligence could easily distinguish between NATO preparations for a limited or for a general nuclear strike. If the Soviets believed what they said about the advantages of the first blow in a theater nuclear exchange and they believed that escalation was all but inevitable, it is unlikely that they could have fine-tuned their analysis of what kind of nuclear strike any disparate intelligence indicators suggested NATO had in preparation. Far more likely under these conditions is a tendency to assume the worst. It thus seems quite plausible that developments of the kind discussed earlier would have further exacerbated an already strong propensity for nuclear escalation. Moreover, the expectation of these kinds of developments might have been a key driver in the Soviet decision to launch its conventional preemption.

Finally, we are left with an unresolved tension in Soviet doctrine in this period. If they really expected nuclear escalation and they believed the first nuclear blow to be so decisive, then why engage in this elaborate

---

forces as a consequence of the new deployments. Of course, the nuclear SLCM causes similar kinds of problems, with the exception that it is harder to preempt.

[86]Meyer, *Soviet Theatre Nuclear Forces*, pt. 1, pp. 21–27; Phillip A. Peterson and John G. Hines, "The Conventional Offensive in Soviet Theater Strategy," *Orbis* 27 (Fall 1983): 695–739, esp. 705–711.

[87]Meyer, *Soviet Theatre Nuclear Forces*, pt. 2, pp. 32–38, lays out these issues very well.

[88]Ibid., pt. 1, pp. 27–30.

conventional phase at all? Does not the fact that they would devote so many resources to this effort indicate that they did not want to use nuclear weapons at all? These questions are difficult to answer. My own hypothesis is that the Soviet military tried to deal with a fundamental problem—Soviet civilians showed no sign of willingness to reach for nuclear weapons until they believed that all other options were closed to them. This development would parallel what has occurred in the West. At the same time, however, Soviet civilians and soldiers probably understood that a superpower conventional conflict does have a huge potential to escalate. Thus, their well-known caution in all superpower confrontations is explained. At the same time, however, should they be forced into war, they would have striven first for conventional victory. Failing that, they *hoped* to set the terms of the subsequent nuclear war. They did what they could in terms of planning and procurement to assure this. But, in the actual event, they would have had a very difficult time, and they probably knew it.

What Kind of Soviet Response?

Command and Control Adaptation?

Although, as discussed below, nuclear preemption was one possible Soviet reaction to the kinds of events I have outlined, there were other possible responses, not so immediately horrible but nevertheless creating the potential for subsequent catastrophe. If the Soviets had initiated any conventional attack, their nuclear forces would already have been brought to a high level of alert. They would have been on guard for any signs that NATO was "going nuclear." Indicators to that effect could have precipitated *even higher* levels of alert, which could have included limited and/or contingent diffusion of launch authority down the chain of command. Although the evidence suggests that the Soviet political leadership was firmly in control of its military and utterly committed to retaining the decision to use nuclear weapons in its own hands, we cannot know what kinds of procedures the Soviets may have worked out to govern circumstances like this one. Nor can we be sure that if and as stress were put on the Soviet early warning system, relatively clear delineations of authority would not have been muddied. Finally, we probably could not have maintained sufficient discrete control over our own military operations around the Soviet periphery, and over the Soviet ability to detect and interpret these operations, to have ensured that we did not inadvertently trigger a series of procedures that would temporarily place the authority to launch nuclear weapons in the hands of either a lower-level civilian official or a military officer frightened or angry enough to use the weapons.

Thus, the Soviets had options short of nuclear preemption that would have had the effect of substantially complicating a deliberate U.S. "decapitation" attack. But the options were risky in and of themselves, and it might have been in NATO's interest to forgo military operations that could prompt the Soviets to alter their apparently strict preference for firm civilian control over nuclear weapons.

A Theater Nuclear Operation?

The Soviets had two fundamental choices as to how to use nuclear forces to deal with the problems outlined above. Generally, students of Soviet nuclear doctrine and planning believed that the Russians would have used nuclear weapons in large numbers, to achieve decisive results.[89] Meyer suggests a NATO target set of roughly 285 air, naval, and army bases, nuclear storage sites, logistics installations, and C^3I.[90] Prior to the INF agreement of December 1987, SS20 intermediate-range ballistic missiles would have been the preferred weapon for such a strike. Once the INF agreement began to eliminate these weapons, the Soviets had a host of others to replace them. SLBMs or ICBMs could have been targeted against Europe, as could the new generations of Soviet air- and sea-launched nuclear cruise missiles. Others who tried to develop target sets for a Soviet conventional preemption, or who simply tried to track NATO's nuclear-related installations, came up with similarly large numbers.[91] Thus, from the perspective of Soviet doctrine, Soviet weapons, and NATO targets, the ingredients existed for a massive Soviet nuclear preemption.

It would be a mistake, however, to leave the argument at this point. States are not bound to do in war that which is revealed by their prewar military planning—much less their publicly stated military doctrine. And it is the latter source from which inferences about Soviet military

[89]See, e.g., Dennis Gormley, "Understanding Soviet Motivations for Deploying Long-Range Theater Nuclear Forces," *Military Review* 61 (September 1981): 20–34, esp. pp. 23, 33; also, Douglas and Hoeber, *Conventional War and Escalation*, p. 41; Meyer, *Soviet Theatre Nuclear Forces*, pt. 1, p. 30.

[90]Meyer, *Soviet Theatre Nuclear Forces*, pt. 2, p. 24.

[91]Epstein, *Measuring Military Power*, pp. 174, 191–201, comes up with 250 major command and control, nuclear storage, and airfield targets in Germany alone, plus numerous other targets. William Arkin has discovered what he believes to be "241 nuclear-related facilities" in Germany alone; William M. Arkin and Richard W. Fieldhouse, *Nuclear Battlefields: Global Links in the Nuclear Arms Race* (Cambridge, Mass., 1985), p. 236.

strategy were drawn. Before World War II the RAF preached a doctrine of massive city bombing. Yet civilians would not permit this activity in the early months of the war. Although we were fortunate to have no test cases, President Eisenhower generally displayed great caution whenever it appeared that his pledge to "treat nuclear weapons like any other" might be called into effect. The actual first use of nuclear weapons is going to be a big decision. This essay has argued that by the time the Soviets reach that decision, fear rather than greed may have been the primary motive. It is not utterly inconceivable that Soviet leaders would have looked for some compromise between their military's general commitment to "massive" use and a last hope of avoiding general thermonuclear war. Although the data is poor, it does suggest that a more "limited" (although still rather large) attack might have succeeded in pushing the perceived danger back from the Soviet border.

For example, the Soviets might have improved their position with the destruction of the bulk of NATO's most capable offensive tactical aircraft, and some associated command and control. The Soviets might even have found it advantageous not to run the risk of a British or French national nuclear response and avoided their territory. The strike might thus have been limited to major installations in Belgium, the Netherlands, and the Federal Republic of Germany; nine F-16, F-4 and Tornado bases where nuclear weapons appear to have been co-located with the aircraft, and perhaps two dozen command and control facilities associated with NATO's offensive air campaign and with the coordination of nuclear strikes originating in these three countries. Perhaps a dozen GLCM, Pershing I, and Pershing II base areas would also have been struck.[92] In all, it does not seem unreasonable to argue that the nuclear destruction of some thirty or forty targets would have bought the Soviets a cushion against the possibility of the kind of "surprise" attack discussed above. Much of the fog of air war could have been pushed back from the Soviet borders, and many, but by no means all, of the capabilities for launching the kind of nuclear attack discussed above could have been eliminated. Finally, if the war has gone on for several weeks, the Soviets might have been able to mount this attack with forward-deployed short-range missiles (SS-21, SCUD) or fighter bombers, such as the SU-24. A Soviet planner might have seen these

[92]See Arkin and Fieldhouse, *Nuclear Battlefields*, pp. 215–216, 227, 236–245 for GLCM, Pershing, and aircraft bases. Until the INF agreement entered full effect, three to four GLCM bases, and nine Pershing I and II facilities would likely have been included in this target set. Command and control targets are hard to estimate; one could include hundreds. Ibid., p. 104 (map) shows roughly two dozen in the three countries. Epstein, *Measuring Military Power*, p. 196, shows roughly three dozen major sites in the same area.

forces as safer to use than forces based in the Soviet Union, since they would have been less likely inadvertently to trigger U.S. strategic nuclear early warning systems. Finally, the use of these forces might have seemed to the Soviet planner to convey better the message of limited intentions than the use of Russian-based ICBMs or even SSBNs at sea. Again, it is important to point out that students of Soviet doctrine did not view the Soviets as likely to reason or operate in this fashion. The option was open to them, and under the circumstances likely to have prevailed, it might have seemed a good deal more attractive than a wholesale theater nuclear strike.

Conclusions

In this chapter I have explored some of the ways that aerial warfare that would attend a NATO–Pact conventional conflict in the Central Region could have affected Soviet strategic nuclear forces through the 1980s. Though detailed information on how the air war would have unfolded is sparse, a survey of the available information, combined with inferences from historical experience and a simple model of one important aspect of the campaign, indicates a strong probability that NATO's conventional air operations would have created substantial pressures on the Soviet strategic early warning system in a matter of several weeks.

Let us review the argument. First, a substantial number of important Soviet strategic targets, especially command, control, communications, and early warning installations, were vulnerable to attacks by nuclear-armed aircraft, and especially by nuclear-armed cruise missiles. The importance of this threat is indicated by the tremendous resources that the Soviets have devoted to meeting it. Nevertheless, Soviet air defenses still seemed inadequate to the task they had set for themselves.

Second, a combination of noise, technological and tactical compromise, and lethal and nonlethal suppression would have substantially degraded the Soviet air-defense network in Eastern Europe and, to an indeterminate extent, that of the Soviet Union proper.

Thus, it seems plausible that the capability of the Soviet system to detect and classify attacks by modest numbers of nuclear cruise missiles or nuclear-armed fighters would have been much reduced after two to three weeks of combat (and certainly after eight weeks.) The Soviet air-defense commanders might have begun to fear that U.S. confidence in its ability to mount a strategic counter–command and control attack, without fear of a Soviet launch-under-attack response, was growing.

While in and of itself such a possibility might not have been sufficient to provoke a decision to use nuclear weapons, it might have stimulated an erosion of tight central Soviet political control over the use of nuclear weapons. The fact that these developments would have occurred against the backdrop of a United States with the doctrine and capability for large-scale counterforce operations would have enhanced Soviet fears. And the Soviets' own counterforce doctrine and posture would have enhanced their own incentives to preempt. If, as suggested in Chapter 4, similar kinds of conventional "strategic" campaigns were under way elsewhere—for example counter-SSBN operations and conventional cruise-missile attacks against shore-based naval installations in both the Barents Sea and the northwest Pacific, the Soviet planner would have become even more nervous.

Finally, to the extent that we can infer anything from what the Soviets themselves have written about nuclear war, they had both a strong inclination and the developed capabilities to get in the first nuclear blow in the theater, as well as in intercontinental war. Ambiguous evidence in wartime suggesting that the United States could have beaten them to the punch could have been the spark that set off their nuclear offensive. Moreover, within their force structure, the Soviets had options well short of direct attack on the United States that could have strengthened their position by, at the very least, reducing the amount of noise they had to see through on a daily basis. In sum, the likely pattern of a NATO–Pact conventional air war did not bode well for the avoidance of nuclear escalation.

This analysis has implications for deterrence, for warfighting, and for our understanding of the Soviet Union.

First, the analysis suggests that on a normal day extended deterrence was probably quite strong. Soviet conventional aggression against NATO was unlikely to have occurred because a "clever briefer" made the risks out to be low, and the prospects for quick and easy victory high. A large-scale conventional war on the Soviet periphery would be very problematic for the Soviet Union. It seems quite likely that awareness of this fact was widespread in the Soviet national security elite in the 1980s and is even more so today.

Second, paradoxically, the stability of the East-West military relationship under serious crisis conditions was and remains much less certain. Here we are speaking of unforeseeable political events that create intense fears for regime survival in the Soviet Union, fears that are rightly or wrongly traced back to the West by the Soviet elite. In the early 1980s multiple political crises in Eastern Europe might have fallen into this category. Today, multiple crises within the Soviet Union proper or conflicts among East European countries that somehow would draw NATO forces toward the Soviet border might create such risks. Under such conditions, in which the West would already be identified as highly malevolent, the uncertainties that complicate the task of the clever briefer advocating preventive or preemptive war might enhance the persuasiveness of the earnest, prudent, military adviser suggesting preemptive escalation.

The analysis shows why the Soviets have a great deal to fear from an extended conventional war on their periphery. During the 1970s and early 1980s students of Soviet theater doctrine stressed its offensive inclinations. The development of Soviet conventional air-attack capabilities against NATO's nuclear weapons storage sites, missile bases, and air bases was especially noteworthy. The preceding analysis shows why the Soviets may have perceived it to be so important to destroy these forces before NATO's conventional tactical air campaign could cut holes in their early warning and air-defense systems. The analysis thus helps explain why the Soviets made this investment and also the intensity of their motivation in a serious crisis to get in an early, massive, conventional blow.

Finally, something can be learned by considering the tensions that seem to have been inherent to Soviet doctrine. Given the nuclear dangers that arise for the Soviet Union in a prolonged conventional war, one wonders why they abandoned their previous strategy of massive, theater-level nuclear preemption. Here it is hard to avoid the suspicion that, like the United States during the waning years of massive retaliation, the Soviet elite came to doubt its own willingness to use nuclear weapons except under the most extreme provocation. Although nuclear weapons would have been far more effective than conventional ones as agents of preemption against NATO's theater nuclear forces, the Soviets chose the conventional route. They chose to run a sizable risk that they would *not* be the ones to strike the first large-scale nuclear blow in the theater. By waiting to use nuclear weapons, they would have permitted many of NATO's nuclear forces to disperse and become difficult to target. This difficulty would have been exacerbated by the damage that Soviet intelligence, early warning, and defensive systems would have suffered in the initial weeks of conventional combat.

That the Soviets were willing to run such risks indicates that they were not in the least bit cavalier about nuclear war. They ran "higher" risks of "losing" such a war with their conventional strategy than with their previous nuclear strategy. They incurred a high cost for following the United States down the road of "flexible response." The implication, then, is that we may be able to have some influence over the Soviet inclination to use nuclear weapons if we are judicious in our choice of conventional operations.

[3]

The Balance of Ground Forces on the Central Front

This chapter argues that during the 1980s NATO's power of conventional resistance in a ground war in Central Europe was vastly underestimated. This position has two important implications for the argument of the book. First, rapid Western conventional collapse would not have been the main cause of nuclear escalation. But that would mean that the air attacks discussed in the previous chapter, and the attacks on Soviet SSBNs discussed in the next one, could have proceeded for quite some time—long enough to damage military assets important to Soviet strategic nuclear forces. These conventional attacks could thus have been an important cause of nuclear escalation.

The second implication lies in the fact that one of the pillars of the arguments advanced for offensive air and naval operations, NATO's weakness on the ground, was at least open to challenge. Given the high cost of preparing for those offensive operations, direct improvement of NATO's ground forces was at least a reasonable alternative. NATO's ground forces might have been rendered *confidently* competitive with those of the Pact at quite moderate peacetime costs. There were doubtless many possible reasons why this option was not pursued with much vigor. But the triumph of bold air and naval solutions lends some support to my general theoretical argument—that military organizations prefer the offensive, and that they have considerable latitude to pursue these solutions in peacetime.

The Problem

The distinctive characteristic of military competition in Central Europe during the 1980s was the large concentration of mechanized ground forces on both sides, supported by substantial numbers of attack helicopters and fighter aircraft. Most assessments gave the Warsaw Pact credit for quantitative superiority in these assets. These are the same kinds of forces that are associated with the major blitzkrieg operations of the past half-century: the German invasions of Poland, France, and the Soviet Union in World War II; the Israeli victory over the Arabs in 1967; and the Israeli counterattack across the Suez Canal in 1973. Western scholars and political leaders tended to fixate on the powerful offensive potential of Soviet armored forces, thus creating fears that a conventional war in Europe could end in a quick NATO defeat. As John Mearsheimer has pointed out, in the world of conventional deterrence it is confidence in quick, cheap, and decisive victory that tempts an aggressor to attack.[1]

In spite of the prevailing fears and perceptions, however, not all of the military history of the past fifty years confirms the hypothesis that armored forces enhance the offense's chances of success. Individual battles such as the Soviet defense at Kursk in 1943, perhaps the largest tank battle of World War II; the U.S. Army's defense against the surprise German armored offensive in the Ardennes in 1944, the Battle of the Bulge; and the Israeli defense of the Golan Heights in 1973 all suggest that armored assaults can be stopped—that mechanized defenders can also turn in impressive performances. Indeed, the German army's overall performance during the second half of World War II, when it was substantially outnumbered, is testimony to the defensive potential of even partially mechanized forces.

A survey of the history of armored warfare also suggests that the place to begin any assessment of the current NATO–Warsaw Pact military balance is the so-called breakthrough battle. Armored attackers customarily have concentrated their best resources on narrow sectors of their enemy's front, hoping to achieve a degree of quantitative superiority that could cause a serious rupture in the defense line. Such ruptures permit the deep exploitations associated with the classical German, and Israeli, practice of blitzkrieg, and the encirclements associated with German and Soviet operations on the Eastern Front during World War II. This essay, however, does not deal explicitly with the exploitation phase, but focuses on NATO's initial capability to keep it from arising.[2]

[1]John J. Mearsheimer, *Conventional Deterrence* (Ithaca, 1983), pp. 23–66.

[2]If breakthroughs do occur, operational reserves are necessary to combat the adversary's exploitation or encirclement efforts. Defenders should, therefore, to the extent that they can do so, maintain "operational reserves" to counterattack in the event that the adversary manages to achieve a clean breakthrough. This analysis cannot support a judgment as to the appropriate quantity of uncommitted operational reserves that NATO ought to have tried to maintain, although it does point to the size of the reserve NATO actually could

Most analyses of warfare in the Central Region of Europe correctly assumed a front of roughly 750 km and further assumed that the Soviets would have attempted to break through in a small number of areas where the terrain and the road net are particularly suitable for armored warfare. Figure 3.1, the map of the Central Region, shows the four most commonly discussed breakthrough sectors. Most analysts agreed that the Pact would have mounted at least one major attack in the north German plain, which is considered to be the best avenue of attack. One would almost surely have been launched in the Fulda Gap, if only to tie down the powerful U.S. V Corps. The Göttingen corridor running through the German III Corps sector just north of the Fulda Gap was more attractive as a third choice than the Hof corridor, which is a bit narrow. The first three corridors are roughly 50 km wide, the fourth perhaps 20 km.

In spite of the often cited Soviet numerical superiority in Europe, most analyses of potential Soviet attacks expected concentrated efforts on these three or four rather well-defined breakthrough sectors since the Pact's quantitative advantage over NATO was not great enough to permit it to greatly outnumber Western forces everywhere. (Indeed, the analysis I present below, and in Appendix 3, suggests that the Pact would not have found it advantageous to mount more than three breakthrough efforts.) Thus, the successful breakthrough battle was the first step to a quick Pact victory, and thwarting Pact breakthrough efforts was NATO's primary conventional military task. If NATO could achieve this in war, it ultimately could have mobilized its superior economic power against the Pact. If the Soviet Union believed that NATO could thwart the breakthrough effort, then overall deterrence was enhanced. This analysis, therefore, concentrates upon the relative ability of NATO and the Warsaw Pact to cope with the demands imposed by multiple breakthrough battles, had a war occurred in the 1980s.

NATO versus Pact Military Doctrine

How did the breakthrough battle figure in each side's general war plans? Every military organization, explicitly or implicitly, has a theory of victory, a notion of the combination of human and material resources

---

have maintained under a variety of stressful conditions. Nor do I know of any widely accepted rule of thumb that would provide reliable guidance. It is possible that a highly structured wargame, played a number of times with an assortment of players, with reference to the campaign of interest, could provide insight into the question.

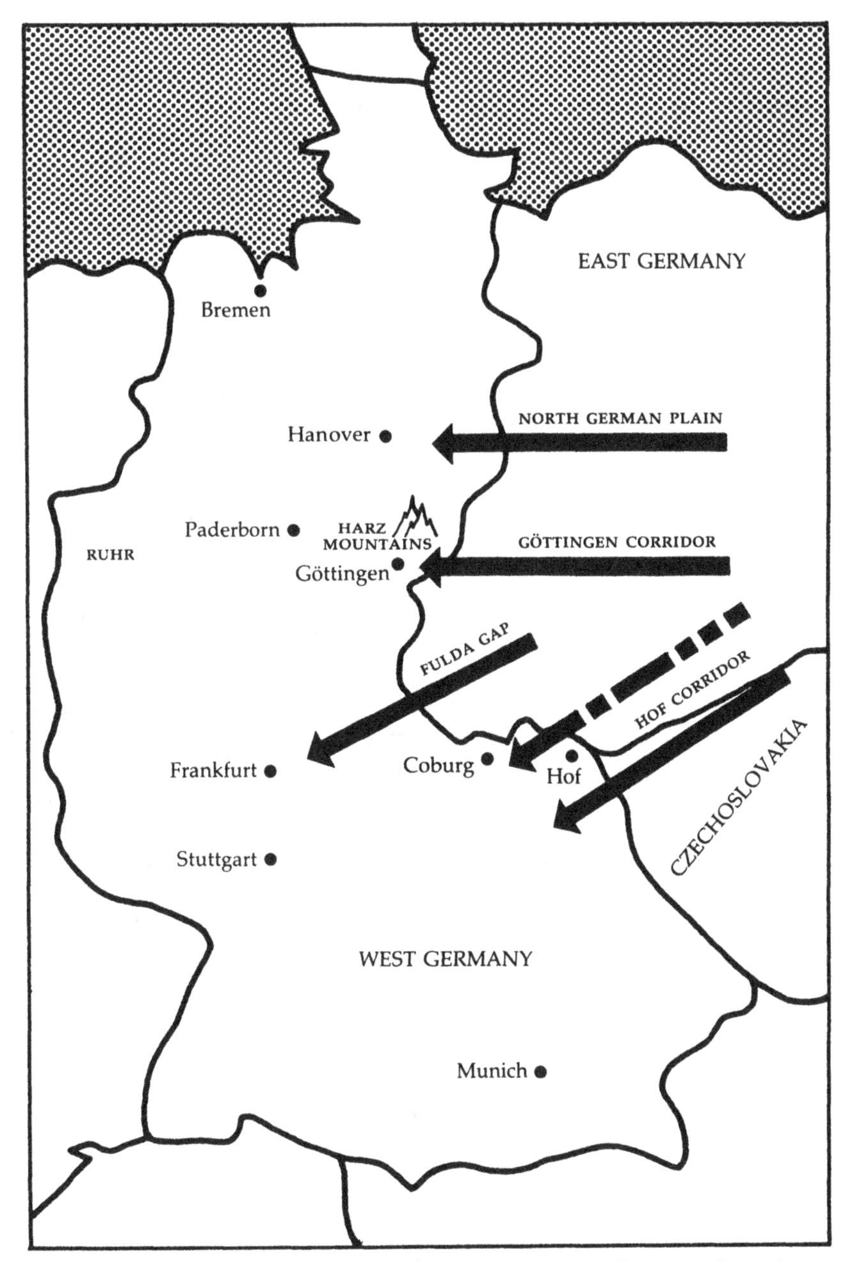

Figure 3.1. Most likely axes of advance in a Warsaw Pact attack against NATO. Reproduced from John Mearsheimer, "Why the Soviets Can't Win Quickly in Central Europe," *International Security* 7 (Summer 1982), by permission of the MIT Press.

and tactics that it believes is most likely to produce success on the battlefield. This theory of victory is the organization's military doctrine.

The Warsaw Pact's and NATO's military doctrines, which determined how each alliance built and organized its military forces, were quite different. At the most general level, the Pact preferred large numbers of major weapons and formations (often called "tooth") over training, the experience of military personnel, logistics, and the C^3I functions broadly defined. (Logistics and C^3I are often referred to as "tail.") Additionally, it preferred ground forces to tactical aviation, although the Soviet Union did have substantial tactical air capability. NATO, on the other hand, preferred a more balanced mix of tooth and tail, showed greater interest in the training and experience of its personnel, and placed greater emphasis on tactical airpower. Finally, even today, NATO continues to stress weapons quality to a greater extent than did the Pact.

In terms of military operations, Pact doctrine tended to extol the advantages of the offense. For years this was fairly explicit in Soviet military writings. Recently, the Soviet political leadership has begun to use the rhetoric of defensive specialization. This, coupled with some subtle developments in Soviet military literature and the planned withdrawal of its forces from Eastern Europe, suggest a possible change in the Soviet orientation. Nevertheless, even with these changes on the ground, Soviet ground forces are likely to retain impressive offensive capabilities. And given the basic proclivities of military organizations in general and the traditions of the Soviet military in particular, it is improbable that the Soviet Army will shed altogether its offensive tradition.

The Western alliance, on the other hand, partly as a function of its political orientation but also because of the lessons it has drawn from the school of military experience, tends toward a more balanced view of the relative advantages of defensive and offensive tactics. This view is more implicit than explicit in NATO doctrine, which as a whole tends to be less formal than that of the Pact. Particularly at the level of the small unit engagement, Western military thinkers have long held that the defense has a substantial advantage—one that can be turned into an overall strategic defensive advantage through careful planning and the skillful conduct of military operations.[3]

[3]On the defender's tactical advantage, see John J. Mearsheimer, "Why the Soviets Can't Win Quickly in Central Europe," *International Security* 7 (Summer 1982): 15–20, esp. n. 30. See his recent "Assessing the Conventional Balance: The 3:1 Rule and Its Critics," *International Security* 13 (Spring 1989): 54–89, for a lengthy discussion. The now superseded July 1976 version of the U.S. Army's basic field manual, *Operations* (FM 100-5), included some explicit statements on the extent of numerical inferiority that the defender could accept and still expect to hold successfully. In describing the tasks of a defending general,

The net result of these differences is that for many years the Warsaw Pact generated military forces that, at least at first glance, looked substantially more formidable than those of NATO. Although official comparisons of NATO and Warsaw Pact defense spending have consistently shown NATO outspending the Pact by varying degrees ($120 billion in 1985, according to one Department of Defense estimate), the tendency in both official and unofficial balance assessments has been to highlight Pact advantages in tanks, guns, planes, or divisions.[4] Moreover, official statistics suggested that the dollar value of NATO's military capital stock in the late 1980s was greater than that of the Warsaw Pact.[5] Finally, NATO had as much, if not more, military and civilian manpower directly associated with defense as the Warsaw Pact.[6] The

---

it asserts, "As a rule of thumb, they should seek not to be outweighed more than 3:1 in terms of combat power. With very heavy air and field artillery support on favorable terrain, it may be possible to defend at a numerical disadvantage of something like 5:1 for short periods of time" (p. 5-3). Somewhat ambiguously, these ratios are said to apply "at the point and time of decision" (p. 3-5). The document also holds that on the offense, U.S. generals should strive for "concentrated combat power of about 6:1 superiority" (p. 3-5). In general, then, the field manual seems to hold that defenders can fight successfully if outnumbered 3:1 and may be able to do so if outnumbered as much as 5:1. The new version of the field manual is silent on these numerical ratios. It does, however, seem to imply that given certain tactical advantages held by the defender, the attacker must muster numerical superiority at a small number of times and places of his choosing. See U.S. Army, *Operations*, FM 100-5 (1982), pp. 8-5, 8-6, 10-3, 10-4.

[4]These figures are from the statement by Richard DeLauer, undersecretary of defense for research and engineering, "Estimated Dollar Cost of NATO and Warsaw Pact Defense Activities, 1965–1985," in U.S. Department of Defense, *The FY 1987 DOD Program for Research and Development*, 99th Cong., 2d sess., 18 February 1986 (Washington, D.C., 1986), p. II-2, fig. II-2. All figures are in 1987 dollars.

[5]The military capital stock of the United States, plus the Federal Republic of Germany, the United Kingdom, and France, was roughly 25 percent larger than that of the Soviet Union, according to a Pentagon-sponsored study, Future Security Environment Working Group, *Sources of Change in the Future Security Environment*, Report to the Commission on Integrated Long Term Strategy (Washington, D.C., April 1988), fig. 6, "Military Capital Stock, Share of 7-Country Total," p. 8. It is implausible that the introduction of the remaining allies on both sides would alter the relationship in favor of the Pact.

[6]Summing the individual country entries from IISS, *The Military Balance, 1988–1989*, yields a maximum total for the Warsaw Pact of some 6.9 million men in military uniform, including 2 million internal security, construction, railroad, and administrative personnel in the Soviet Union. There were few civilian direct hires associated with the Warsaw Pact militaries, but one source suggests that there might have been as many as another million miscellaneous civilian and military personnel associated with the Soviet military. U.S. Congress, House, Appropriations Committee, Subcommittee on the Department of Defense, *DOD Appropriations for 1985, Part 1, Secretary of Defense and Chairman Joint Chiefs of Staff*, 98th Cong., 2d sess., 1984 (Washington, D.C., 1984), p. 546. Thus, the maximum number of individuals plausibly associated with the direct generation of peacetime military power in the Pact was roughly 7.9 million. The U.S. Department of Defense suggested that the total number of uniformed personnel and direct civilian hires associated with NATO's military effort was roughly 8.1 million. The authors chose the total uniformed and civilian military manpower of Alliance members as the appropriate metric for comparing relative military effort within NATO. I can see no reason why the same metric should not be applied across the two opposing alliances. Frank C. Carlucci, *Report on Allied*

possibility that NATO's higher spending might have generated less visible, but equally important, elements of military capability seldom received much consideration.[7] Instead, NATO's superiority in the spending comparisons and apparent equality in manpower were ignored, or explained away with relatively cursory arguments.[8]

Contributions to the Common Defense (Washington, D.C., April 1988), p. 30. Thus, there was at least military manpower parity between the two coalitions in the 1980s, and I suspect that NATO actually outmanned the Pact.

[7]Richard DeLauer argued that the Soviet Union somehow had a lower cost of doing business than the United States or NATO. This argument was probably based on the CIA dollar model that prices Soviet activities at the rate that it would cost the United States to accomplish them in exactly the same way that the Soviets do. Pact manpower was largely valued according to U.S. wages and maintenance costs for individuals of equal rank and experience. If Soviet manpower costs in dollars appeared lower than NATO's, it should have been a result of the relatively smaller professional noncommissioned officer and officer cadre in the mass conscription Pact militaries, not of greater Soviet efficiency. Moreover, Soviet maintenance practices were probably less efficient than those of the West. When priced according to the dollar model, these inefficiencies emerged as a higher cost of doing business, making the Pact effort appear to be greater than if it allocated its resources more efficiently. See U.S. Department of Defense, *The FY 1984 DOD Program for Research, Development and Acquisition* (Washington, D.C., 1983), pp. 1–9. On the CIA methodology, see U.S. Central Intelligence Agency, *Soviet and US Defense Activities, 1970–79*. I have dealt with this issue at greater length in "The Defense Resource Riddle," in *European Assertiveness: Is There a New Role for Europe in International Relations*, ed. Beverly Crawford (Berkeley, Calif., 1990).

[8]Although the investment (i.e., major procurement) spending of NATO compared with the Pact was only somewhat lower in the early 1980s (roughly $113 to $135 billion in 1981) and is probably greater today, the argument has often been advanced that NATO's procurement spending is less efficient than the Pact's. U.S. Department of Defense, *Annual Report*, FY1984, pp. 21–23. (I have crudely estimated Japan's investment spending and subtracted it from the "NATO plus Japan" figure offered by Weinberger.) These Pact investment figures are probably a little high, as the CIA subsequently concluded that its previous estimates in this area were wrong, and that Soviet procurement spending did not grow very much from 1976 to 1984. See "Soviets Seen Slowing Pace of Arming," *Washington Post*, 20 November 1983, p. A-14. The efficiency argument has an element of plausibility, since more Pact production is concentrated in big Soviet plants than NATO production is in any plants. Still, more than a sentence is required. The Pact, indeed the Soviet Union itself, tends to produce several different types of the same weapon simultaneously. For instance, somewhere in the Pact three or four medium tanks (T-55, 62, 64, and 72) were in production during the early 1980s. Finally, it has long been believed that the Soviet Union is less efficient than the West in most areas of industrial production. Why should the advantages of scale economies totally wipe out the West's historical advantages in managerial skills and production efficiency? U.S. Central Intelligence Agency, Directorate of Intelligence, *The Soviet Weapons Industry: An Overview* (Washington, D.C., September 1986). The study notes "distortions and inefficiencies in Soviet industry as managers seek to maintain output at the expense of quality" and that " 'Storming' to meet production targets—a practice in which as much as half of a plant's output is produced in the last 10 days of each month—requires extra shifts, raises labor costs, and often degrades the quality of output" (p. 17). See also pp. 29–33. If arguments to the effect that NATO's spending superiority is virtually irrelevant to the military balance, indeed that it produced a net military inferiority of substantial proportions, are to be taken seriously, then proponents must make their arguments more thoroughly than they have.

In effect, then, NATO bought its military forces on the basis of its own theory of victory, its own military doctrine. But official portrayals of the military balance often assessed it by criteria more appropriate to the Soviet theory of victory. Adopting Soviet criteria for measuring the balance would have always made the West look bad in comparison with the Pact, short of very substantial increases in NATO defense spending and manpower, because NATO organized and procured its forces by the quite different criteria outlined above. Indeed, if NATO had tried to build a military force to redress the numerical imbalances portrayed by its typical assessments, yet preserve the kind of personnel, training, support, and command structures that it prefers, it would have had to further increase its spending lead over the Pact and keep even more men under arms. Although the Reagan administration's substantial increases in defense spending permitted the army and the air force to modernize their weaponry and enhance the quality of their personnel, there was little effort to increase the number of combat units. Although concern about the number of Soviet weapons in combat units had helped provide the political support for the buildup, an increase in U.S. numbers was not viewed as the appropriate remedy.

NATO's political and military leaders consistently allocated scarce financial and human resources according to a particular military doctrine. In spite of assaults by dedicated military reformers, this pattern of resource allocation continues to this day.[9] The only conclusion that can be drawn from this situation is that NATO planners believed that their theory of military outcomes was correct. It was prudent planning to ask what could have happened if most of NATO's fundamental decisions about the allocation of its military resources proved to be wrong, in order to support the acquisition of some insurance against this possibility. Absent convincing arguments that most of NATO's military decisions were wrong (and I believe that the arguments made fell well short of this standard), these "worst-case" analytical exercises should never have been permitted to stand alone. Rather, they should have been accompanied by analyses that captured the expected positive

[9]Steven Canby, *The Alliance and Europe Part IV, Military Doctrine and Technology*, Adelphi Paper 109 (London, 1978), pp. 15–41, offers the clearest critique. Not much actually changed. In the mid-1970s Sen. Sam Nunn of Georgia succeeded in getting the Seventh Army in Europe to trade off some support for combat assets—creating two new combat brigades in Europe. Subsequently, the U.S. Army effectively reversed the senator's reforms. The "Division '86" reorganization reduced the number of maneuver battalions in the European-based divisions from eleven or twelve each, down to ten. The army disbanded one of the independent brigades based in Europe. The net loss was at least seven maneuver battalions, more than the six battalions contained in the Nunn brigades. Meanwhile, total army manpower in Germany increased by nearly 20,000 men.

military impact of the fundamental doctrinal assumptions that guided NATO's defense decisions. Failure to do so permitted political leaders and civilian strategists to focus on a single theory of nuclear escalation—NATO's conventional collapse, to the exclusion of other hypotheses that should have influenced other aspects of conventional military planning.

Factors in Thorough Balance Assessment

Public discussion of the conventional balance in Europe often focused on simple force comparisons that failed to include factors vital to the outcome of any real battle. The official NATO statement on the potential for conventional arms control in Central Europe stressed "the Warsaw Pact's superiority in key conventional weapons systems" and stated that the aim of conventional arms control was to "redress the conventional imbalance." This required "highly asymmetrical reduction by the East."[10] Such simplistic analysis represents only the beginning of a complete assessment of a military threat. At least six other variables must be taken into account before we arrive at a reasonable appraisal of relative battlefield capabilities. Analyses that exclude these factors are incomplete and unrevealing, and they provide no meaningful basis for military planning—in Europe or anywhere else. These variables are as follows:

Relative Reinforcement Rates. At what rate could both sides move military forces into the battle area along the inter-German and Czech–West German border? What was the likely combat capability of these forces when training, maintenance, command and control, leadership, and quantity and quality of weaponry was taken into account?[11]

The Effect of Tactical Air Forces on the Ground Battle. Most public assessments of the balance omitted a detailed treatment of the possible contribution of "tacair" (tactical air) to the ground battle, and official assessments often gave each side equal credit for tactical air effective-

[10]NATO, "Conventional Arms Control: The Way Ahead," statement issued under the authority of the heads of state and government participating in the meeting of the North Atlantic Council in Brussels (March 2–3, 1988), in *Conventional Forces in Europe: The Facts* (Brussels, 25 November 1988), p. 2, n. 2; pp. 5–6.

[11]Western tanks are a case in point. See Malcolm Chalmers and Lutz Unterseher, "Is There a Tank Gap? Comparing NATO and Warsaw Pact Tank Fleets," *International Security* 13 (Summer 1988): 5–49; see esp. pp. 23–45 on the qualitative advantages of NATO tanks.

ness.[12] In either case, possible advantages that NATO might have held in this area were omitted. In this analysis NATO and the Pact are assigned partial credit for their tactical air forces, although much more work remains to be done on the interaction between air and ground operations.

Force-to-Space (and hence Force-to-Force) Ratios. Implicitly, or explicitly, the Soviet Union and its allies were often given credit for an ability not only to move many divisions to the battle area quickly but to actually concentrate them on small segments of the front to achieve the very high local offense-to-defense force ratios that could produce breakthroughs. Yet, historically, armies have found that there is a limit to how much force can be concentrated in a given space. If NATO could achieve some level of density of its ground forces across the front, then it should have been very difficult for the Pact, even with more forces overall, to achieve very high ratios in selected breakthrough sectors.

Attrition Rates. At what "pace" or "level of violence" will the battle proceed? What kinds of casualties are attackers willing to take? Does "friction" place some limits on the pace at which the battle can be forced? Historically, short periods of very intense combat can be identified in which one side or both suffered 10 percent or worse attrition to armored fighting vehicles per day. On the other hand, rarely are battles of this intensity sustained for more than a few days.

Exchange Rates. How many destroyed armored fighting vehicles would NATO have had to pay to kill a Pact vehicle? Given the Pact superiority in numbers of major weapons, NATO needed favorable exchange rates in order to defeat the Pact.[13] Favorable exchange rates are not uncommon for defenders fighting on their own ground, particu-

[12]For an exception see U.S. Congress, CBO, *US Ground Forces*, pp. 26–28, where Frances Lussier offers a brief discussion of numerical ratios of total fighter aircraft, and the results of an enhanced air capability rating system called TASCFORM, which is somewhat similar in concept to WEI/WUV (see n. 24 for an explanation). But she offers no direct treatment of how each side's total air capabilities would effect the ground battle. She does, however, include close air support assets in her analysis, as do I. It is notable that the Congressional Budget Office has yet to publish an assessment of the overall "air-balance" in the context of a possible NATO–Pact war.

[13]In a pure attrition battle between two sides equal in every respect except numbers, the inferior side logically requires an exchange rate equal to the unfavorable force ratio if it is to stay the course. This is a highly idealized situation. Some of the analysis outlined below and in Appendix 3 suggests that NATO may be able to squeak out a stalemate with average exchange rates as low as 1.25:1.

larly if that ground has been prepared with field fortifications, obstacles, and mines. Indeed, an often quoted rule of thumb suggests that the defender can hold at an engaged force ratio of 3:1 in favor of the offense.[14] This would be consistent with a 3:1 exchange rate.

Advance Rates. Students of Soviet military doctrine, and analysts of the Central Region conventional balance, often assigned rapid advance rates to Pact forces, several tens of kilometers per day in some cases. Some of this tendency can be attributed to Soviet military literature, which called for very high advance rates. There was also a tendency simply to assume that the high advance rates characteristic of armored warfare's headier historical successes would be replicated by the Soviets. Finally, crediting the Pact with very large forces and very high force ratios in breakthrough sectors tends to produce very rapid destruction of outnumbered defending forces, according to some widely employed dynamic analytical techniques, such as the Lanchester square laws. Analysts have hypothesized that either high attrition, or its consequent diminishing force-to-space ratio, will soon produce rapid retreat for the defender.[15] On the other hand, even with armor pitted against armor, and often with favorable force ratios, modern mechanized armies have frequently found forward movement against determined defenders to be very difficult.

These six variables can be combined into a model that provides a

[14]Mearsheimer, "Assessing the Conventional Balance," pp. 54–89. Although one finds frequent allusions to this rule in field manuals, military history books, and the analytic literature, it suffers from considerable ambiguity in terms of the conditions under which it applies and the units of account, as the debate between Mearsheimer and Joshua Epstein suggests. Mearsheimer has done much to clarify the rule and to indicate the extent to which historical cases would lend it support. Epstein is unsatisfied with everything about the rule, as well as Mearsheimer's defense of it, with the exception that Epstein's other work indicates that he perceives a tactical advantage of substantial proportions for the defender—sufficient to generate exchange rates between 1.5 and 1.85:1. See Joshua Epstein, *Strategy and Force Planning: The Case of the Persian Gulf* (Washington, D.C., 1987), for the development of the 1.5:1 figure; see Joshua Epstein, "The 3:1 Rule, the Adaptive Dynamic Model, and the Future of Security Studies," *International Security* 13 (Spring 1989): 90–127, for his critique of the rule. (N. 57 seems to indicate some sympathy with the proposition that there is a defensive advantage.) In Mearsheimer's judgment (and in mine) the basic thrust of the rule is that the defender enjoys a substantial tactical advantage. Short of special qualitative advantages, markedly superior tactics, or a high degree of surprise, surmounting these advantages should require a substantial material superiority of 3:1 or better.

[15]It is not my purpose to write a general essay on military modeling. For a lucid discussion of the Lanchester Square Law, see John W. R. Lepingwell, "The Laws of Combat? Lanchester Reexamined," *International Security* 12 (Summer 1987): 89–134; Thomas F. Homer-Dixon, "A Common Misapplication of the Lanchester Square Law, A Research Note," in ibid., pp. 135–139. See also Epstein, *Strategy and Force Planning*, app. E, "Critique of Lanchester Theory," pp. 146–155.

more comprehensive approach to comparing forces, for it will include quantitative and other factors in precisely the way the one-dimensional comparisons do not. One such model, known as the "Attrition-FEBA Expansion Model," provides the framework for the subsequent analysis.[16]

This model assumes that at the outset of war NATO populates the front evenly at densities that experience suggests should permit a resilient defense and holds its remaining forces in reserve.[17] The Pact similarly populates the less important sectors of the front but concentrates as much force as is practical in the breakthrough sectors. As each side takes attrition in the breakthrough battles, it replaces losses with reserves. Also, it is assumed that, as the Pact's breakthrough effort begins to move in NATO's direction, each side tries to move forces into the flanks of the penetrating salient at a density equal to that achieved on the nonbreakthrough parts of the front (see figure 3.2).

The model tests the adequacy of each side's forces to meet the demands of these multiple breakthrough battles. Once some assumptions are made about attrition, exchange rates, the role of tacair, movement rates, and force-to-space ratios, a curve can be generated that shows each side's military requirements starting out with the first day of the war, then rising with the accumulated consequences of daily attrition and the need to populate a FEBA that expands as a function of the forward movement of the breakthrough salients. This requirements curve for each side can be compared with each side's mobilization curve to test the adequacy of its forces.

At some point, if the defending forces are inadequate to fulfill their requirements, the defense finds itself having to defend with an ever-shrinking force-to-space ratio—that is, fewer and fewer defensive forces are available to hold the line. The consequence is that the attacker can muster the large local force ratios in his favor that could produce a clean

[16]The Attrition-FEBA Expansion Model illustrates the stresses imposed on Pact and NATO forces, depending on the values assigned to these six variables. FEBA is an acronym for "Forward Edge of the Battle Area." I am deeply indebted to Dr. Richard Kugler, who devised this model, for introducing it to me. The uses to which it has been put in this essay are my responsibility alone.

[17]The Attrition–FEBA Expansion Model uses Armored Division Equivalents (ADEs) as the common basic measure of combat power: "The ADE is a relative measure of effectiveness of ground forces based on quantity and quality of major weapons. This measure—which is widely used within DOD for ground force comparisons—is an improvement over simple counts of combat units and weapons; however, it does not take into account such factors as ammunition availability, logistical support, training, communications, and morale." Caspar W. Weinberger, *Report on Allied Contributions to the Common Defense* (Washington, D.C., 1983), p. 36. The ADE scoring system used in this essay is summarized in William Mako, *US Ground Forces and the Defense of Central Europe* (Washington, D.C., 1983), app. A, pp. 105–125.

Figure 3.2. Simple model of a Warsaw Pact breakthrough effort

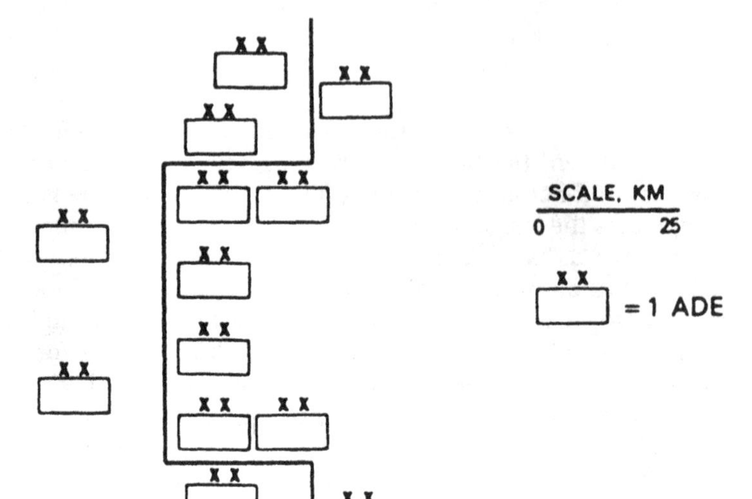

breakthrough. The defender's forces may shatter under the weight of the attack, or they may find themselves so thin on the ground that the offense can easily bypass and isolate centers of resistance. If the defender has not already ordered a general withdrawal to "shorten the front," he may soon suffer a catastrophic rupture of the line, followed by a classical armored exploitation. Since the defender's reserves have been exhausted by the requirement of defending an expanded FEBA, he is not in a position to combat the exploitation. The model does not address the actual process of defensive collapse; it simply indicates when, on the basis of a variety of assumptions, it becomes plausible that this process could commence.

The offense, on the other hand, may find its breakthrough effort stalling as a function of insufficient reserves to sustain high-intensity combat at the front of his penetrating salients or to defend the flanks of those salients from the defender's likely counterattacks.[18]

[18]The "Force Needs" curves are derived as follows. In figure 3.6, NATO needs 1 ADE per 25 km of front to establish a defensive line. The Pact needs 1 ADE per 25 km to tie down NATO's forces in the nonbreakthrough sectors. The Pact manages to concentrate

This model of hypothetical military confrontation in Central Europe will be used to illustrate the sensitivity of the outcome of such a battle to assumptions that are either consistent with the caricature of Soviet doctrine often used for balance assessments (referred to here as the "Soviet" doctrine) or with the very different military doctrine that appears to guide the way NATO builds its forces (referred to here as the "NATO" doctrine). This model highlights the interrelated effects of several aspects of combat between NATO and the Pact about which there is substantial uncertainty. If we resolve all these uncertainties in favor of the Pact's military doctrine, we can produce the pessimistic portrayal of the outcome of a conventional clash in Europe that was common during the last decade. On the other hand, if we resolve these uncertainties in favor of NATO's military doctrine, the Alliance appears to have been capable of preventing a successful Pact breakthrough.

Limitations of the Analysis

Before turning to a discussion of what we learn about the NATO–Warsaw Pact balance by employing the Attrition-FEBA Expansion Model, it is necessary to note the limitations of this or any modeling effort that attempts to approximate the vast and unpredictable complexities of the battlefield.

---

2 ADEs per 25 km in each of three 50-km breakthrough sectors for a total of 12 ADEs involved in breakthrough operations. Thus, for 750 km of front, NATO needs 30 ADEs to start; the Pact needs 36 to start. If 12 Pact ADEs on breakthrough sectors are willing to accept 10-percent attrition per day, they lose 1.2 ADEs. If the Pact-to-NATO exchange rate is 1.5:1, NATO loses 0.8 of an ADE to destroy the Pact forces. To generate the total demand for additional forces imposed by the day's action, the forces needed to populate the "expanding FEBA" must be calculated. Here, it is assumed that the Pact manages to advance 5 km per day, producing 30 km of additional FEBA (i.e., two flanks, 5 km long, for each of three penetrations). Both NATO and the Pact need another 1.2 ADEs to populate the flanks of the penetrating sectors. Thus, the Pact's total additional force requirement after a day of combat is 2.4 ADEs. NATO's is 2 ADEs. Each side's demand for forces rises at this daily rate whenever the Pact has a modest surplus of forces over its previous day's total requirements, producing the "Force Needs" curves. If the Pact has equal or fewer forces than it needed the previous day, it is not permitted to engage in intense combat. This same basic procedure is applied in figure 3.9. Aside from changing the attrition, exchange, and movement rates, the major change is the factoring in of armored vehicles killed by tacair. NATO's estimated number of tacair armored vehicle kills is converted to an ADE score and subtracted from the total daily attrition that the Pact is willing to accept. NATO must pay to kill the rest of the Pact's ground-force loss for the day in the coin of its own ground forces. The damage done by Pact tacair is added to this attrition to arrive at NATO's daily loss rate. For a more detailed discussion, please see Appendix 3.

Like all models, this one does not generate predictions for specific outcomes of a war in the Central Region. There are simply too many uncertainties for any model to capture, certainly too many for a model to capture with high confidence. This model tests the adequacy of forces of a given capability to cope with particular sets of military demands. The values assigned to the six variables discussed above determine the demands imposed and the amount of capability present to deal with those demands. Thus, the principal utility of the model is not a portrayal of a particular battlefield outcome in terms of forces destroyed or territory lost. Rather, it says, "Depending on how well Western and Eastern forces perform in combat in the likely breakthrough sectors, NATO should or should not be able to forestall a catastrophic rupture of its defense line with or without a major withdrawal across the front." The model tests NATO's forces against demands. These demands are determined by the analyst. The analyst employs the model to aid in the formation of judgments about the relative competitiveness of the two sides.

The Attrition-FEBA Expansion Model is a substantial abstraction from reality. Breakthrough sectors are not exactly 50 km wide; attrition does not occur at a steady rate; the offense does not move forward at a steady rate; all offensive efforts are not equally successful, or necessarily successful at all. Moreover, in real combat, divisions do not "fight to the finish" as assumed here; rather, they fight until they are down to 50–70 percent of their initial strength, and then they are pulled out of the line for rest and refitting. Additionally, not all the attrition is taken in breakthrough sectors; some occurs on "quiet" sectors of the front. Finally, this model does not make any complicated tactical assumptions. As any student of armored warfare knows, defenders and attackers do not merely attempt to populate the flanks of the penetration; the defender may counterattack to pinch off the salient, while the attacker tries to widen the hole in the enemy line.

The model also does not deal with the fluid warfare that would probably have characterized a Pact attack launched after only a few days of mobilization, one that would have caught most NATO forces before they were able to form a coherent defense line—in other words, a surprise attack. Such an attack would have pitted about three dozen Soviet and East German divisions against various U.S., West German, French, and other NATO forces, equivalent in strength to roughly two dozen U.S. mechanized divisions. This fighting would, at least initially, have taken the form of mobile warfare, in which NATO's small, ready, forward-deployed covering forces (equivalent to a few armored brigades), supported by some portion of NATO's tactical aircraft, would fight a running battle of delay to enable the rest of NATO's standing forces to form a rough defense line several tens of kilometers back from the inter-German border. The model would become useful only as an analytical tool if and when such a line were established. Under these circumstances NATO's forces might also try to mount some quick, sizable counterattacks during this covering force battle, in order to exploit some of the coordination and logistics problems that would surely attend the Pact's efforts to mount an attack with such little preparation time.

While it is true that, if Polish and Czech Category I divisions joined the Soviet and East German attack, the Pact could have outnumbered NATO in firepower assets (ADEs) by as much as 2:1, both sides would have experienced problems getting into action with only a few days of mobilization. To assess relative performance under these circumstances, one must do a thorough comparative assessment of the peacetime readiness for combat of each side's ground and tactical air forces, as well as an assessment of how many days would have been required for each to overcome its deficiencies. The circumstantial evidence is that NATO's standing forces were substantially readier for combat than those of the Pact, but data available in the public domain do not permit a high-confidence judgment. Skepticism emerged in the late 1980s regarding the Soviet ability to mount a short-preparation attack in Western Europe.[19] Subsequent political events cast doubt on the military reliability of the Soviet Union's Eastern European allies during this period, doubts that the Soviets themselves surely entertained.

Assigning Values in the Attrition-FEBA Expansion Model

These caveats aside, the Attrition-FEBA Expansion Model illustrates the effects of various assumptions about NATO–Warsaw Pact military

[19]See "A Soviet Attack Seen as Unlikely," *New York Times*, 5 December 1988, p. A-14. See U.S. Congress, House, Committee on Armed Services, *Soviet Readiness for War: Assessing One of the Major Sources of East-West Instability, Report of the Defense Policy Panel*, 100th Cong., 2d sess., 5 December 1988 (Washington, D.C., 1988). See also Stephen M. Meyer, "Soviets Can Make Cuts Be Major or Minor," *Los Angeles Times*, 11 December 1988, pt. V, p. 5. "There are now new intelligence findings that strongly suggest that forward deployed Soviet units in East Germany may be in a lower state of readiness than is commonly believed." Les Aspin, "The World after Zero INF," news release, House Armed Services Committee, 29 September 1987, p. 12. William W. Kaufmann, "Defense Policy," in *Setting National Priorities: Agenda for the 1980s*, ed. Joseph A. Pechman (Washington, D.C., 1980), p. 300; and William W. Kaufmann, "Nonnuclear Deterrence," in *Alliance Security: NATO and the No-First-Use Question*, ed. John D. Steinbruner and Leon V. Sigal (Washington, D.C., 1983), pp. 59, 70.

capabilities and the course of combat on NATO's ability to forestall a Pact breakthrough. But how are we to assign specific values to the variables captured by the model? In principle, one could assign values based upon a historical survey of many battles or upon an intensive examination of a few battles that one believes to be sufficiently similar to a NATO–Warsaw Pact clash to be instructive, or upon the use of military rules of thumb or planning factors. The analysis presented here relies upon all of these methods.

The values of the variables that determine the demands on military capabilities—tactical air attrition rates and kill rates, force-to-space ratios, ground force attrition rates, exchange rates, and advance rates—can be set to suit the user. The same is true of the mobilization schedules for each side's ground forces, the extent to which Western forces should receive "extra credit" for relatively greater resources allocated to the command and logistics functions, the quantity of available close air support forces, and their sortie rate.[20] *The only requirement is that the reasons for the user's judgments on these matters be explicit.* Below, I discuss my choices at length. Since these variables affect one another, the user should also work out plausible relationships among them.[21] For instance, it seems unlikely that low attrition rates and high offense-defense exchange rates would produce much retreat by the defender. In exploiting the model, I set variables at values that I judged to be within the broad range of those considered plausible by the conventional forces analysis community, and representative of the two different doctrines employed by the Alliance: the "Soviet" doctrine often used for balance assessment, and the "NATO" doctrine that in fact seems to drive NATO's force planning.

[20]The basic mobilization schedules for each side cannot be set by altering the values of particular variables in the Symphony version of the Attrition-FEBA Expansion Model. They include so many assumptions and estimates that I prefer to develop them directly and load them as data into the model. See Appendix 3.

[21]The most widely used dynamic analytical technique—the Lanchester Square law—assumes a relationship between force ratio and relative attrition, once some assumptions are made about the effectiveness of the forces engaged in a battle. An exchange rate can be derived from the calculation. Analysts have also attached movement equations to the laws, although they cannot be deduced theoretically from Lanchester's work. It is important to note, however, that those who use the equations must make several judgments about the values assigned to the key variables—particularly the forces included in the engagement, their effectiveness, and the relationship between the attrition suffered by the defender and his propensity to withdraw. Military analysis based upon the Lanchester Square law is thus nearly as dependent upon the analyst's "military judgment" as is the model suggested here. For a clear explanation of the Lanchester laws and how to use them, see William W. Kaufmann, "The Arithmetic of Force Planning," in *Alliance Security*, ed. Steinbruner and Sigal, pp. 208–216; Lepingwell, "The Laws of Combat?"; and Homer-Dixon, "A Common Misapplication."

Capabilities over Time

Assessments showing decisive Pact superiority in the 1980s shared certain questionable assumptions that reinforced their pessimistic conclusions. First, they stressed numbers of major weapons, without reference to quality. Second, they assumed that many Pact reserve units could be made combat ready in a matter of days and deployed quickly to combat zones; that Western reserve forces would have taken months to become combat ready and to reach the theater; and that France would have contributed less than she could have to NATO's defense. Third, they failed to estimate the contribution of NATO's greater efforts in command-and-support structures for ground forces.

By contrast, I employ a methodology for measuring firepower that effectively gives NATO some credit (although probably not enough) for the superior average quality of its weapons. This makes a marginal improvement in NATO's showing. Second, and more important, I more realistically assess the arrival times of Pact reserve divisions on the basis of their low peacetime readiness. I make similar assumptions (less pessimistic than the usual) regarding the readiness and arrival times of U.S. National Guard brigades and divisions. And I also include, rather than discount, most French ground forces as active participants in NATO's defense of West Germany. Third, and of great significance, is an increase in the basic firepower score of Western divisions to credit NATO's greater investment in command and logistics.[22]

I will discuss each of these three elements in turn and then demonstrate their effect on predictions of NATO's ability to meet the force needs of the opening phases of a Central European war, based upon very demanding combat assumptions.

The Pact and NATO ground force capabilities that could have been brought into Central Europe for a conventional confrontation (an estimate based on the improved weaponry and mobilization assumptions) are compared in figure 3.3 (showing force ratios in ADEs, explained below) and figure 3.4 (showing numbers of ADEs). Comparing only aggregated weapons quantity and quality, and assuming that NATO's mobilization decision lags the Pact's by seven days, one finds that the force ratio rises briefly to 1.6:1 in favor of the Pact in approximately ten days, but except for this brief peak, the Pact advantage is generally

[22]The principal differences between my mobilization estimates presented in Posen, "Measuring the European Conventional Balance: Coping with Complexity in Threat Assessment," *International Security* 9 (Winter 1984–85), and those presented here are an increase in estimated firepower to reflect equipment modernization and more favorable treatment of U.S. reserve units.

Figure 3.3. NATO–Pact mobilization—1987, force ratio–ADEs (WEI/WUV I)

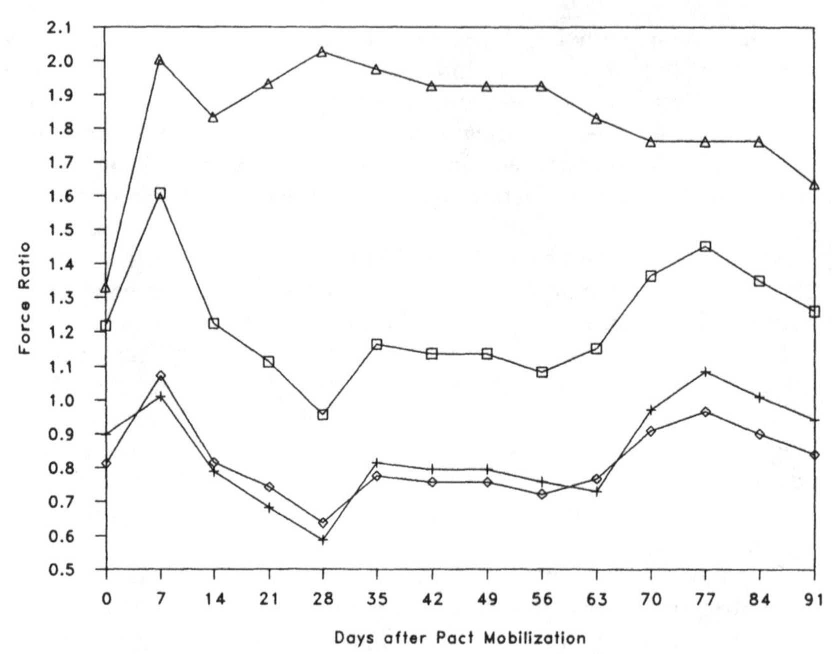

Key: Capability ratios over time:
- □ Pact:NATO—mobilization assumptions favorable to NATO
- ◇ Pact:NATO adjusted—NATO credit for command and logistics
- Δ Pact:NATO pessimistic—traditional mobilization assumptions, no NATO credit for command and logistics
- + Soviet Union:NATO—mobilization assumptions favorable to NATO; no credit for NATO command and logistics; East European allies fail to fight

These graphs do not reflect possible interdiction efforts, but Soviet reinforcement rates are constrained by railroad capacity, and U.S. reinforcements by hypothetical limits on convoy composition.

either non-existent or much lower, from 0.95:1 to 1.4:1 (see figure 3.3, "Pact:NATO" line). If NATO is given credit for its greater relative investments in command and logistics, then the *capabilities* ratio never exceeds 1.1:1 in favor of the Pact (figure 3.3, "Pact:NATO Adj" line) and is often much more favorable to NATO.[23] Below, I explain the reasons for this unusual view.

[23]No effort has been made in figures 3.3 and 3.4 to reflect possible interdiction of Eastern or Western reinforcements moving by land, sea, or air, but Soviet reinforcement rates are

Figure 3.4. NATO–Pact Central Region mobilization (WEI/WUV I, 1987)

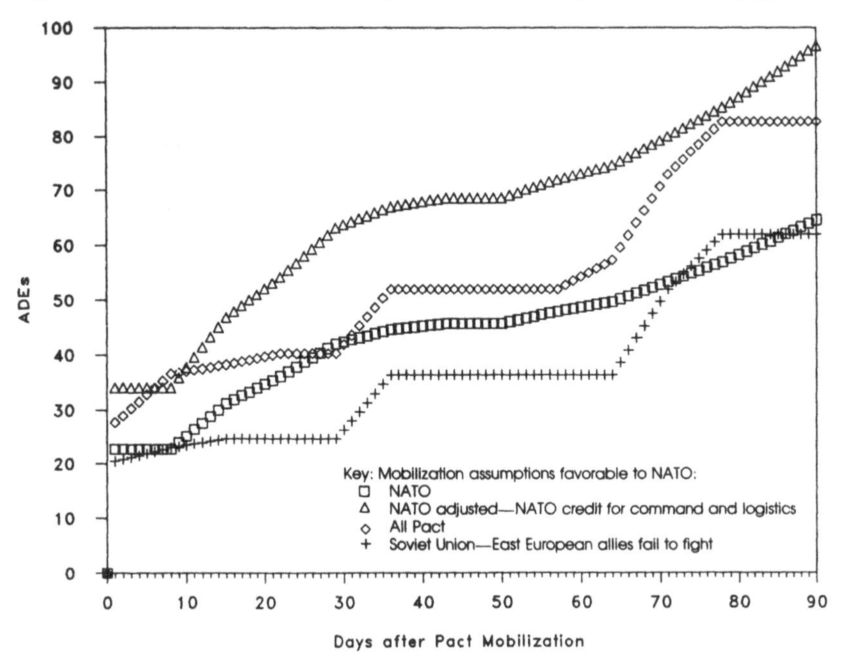

I employ a methodology, known as WEI/WUV, to measure the combat power of ground-force units in terms of ADEs. It was developed by the U.S. Army in the 1970s to compare the fighting power of divisions armed with different types and mixes of weapons (for example, a U.S. airborne division and a West German armored division can each be assigned an ADE score).[24] Using the methodology, I have recalculated

constrained by railroad capacity and U.S. reinforcements are constrained by hypothetical limits on convoy composition and departures. The reader should understand that the curves represented in the graphs are my best guess as to what is achievable. Real mobilization plans may deviate from those suggested here for any number of reasons.

[24]WEI/WUV stands for weapons effectiveness index/weighted unit value. The first component involves the qualitative assessment of individual weapons in terms of firepower, protection, and mobility. The second assesses the relative importance of different weapons classes (tanks, artillery, etc.) to battlefield success. Thus, every military unit can be given a score relative to the 1976 standard U.S. armored division, the ADE or Armored Division Equivalent. This methodology has since been supplanted by WEI/WUV II and III, and now by the DEF (division equivalent firepower) methodologies. The changes in methodology produce slightly different scores for identical divisions. The base division has of course changed and is probably now a fully modernized U.S. Army "Division

the ADE scores of active and reserve U.S. heavy divisions, and Category I Soviet heavy divisions to reflect modernization, and I have more crudely estimated the scores of other types of divisions and the major combat formations of other armies.[25]

In general, even pessimistic assessments of the conventional balance executed with ADE scores produce force ratios somewhat more favorable to NATO than those produced by simple weapons counts.[26] My assessment that deliberately favors the Soviets produces force ratios generally a little below 2:1 (see figure 3.3, "Pact:NATO, pessimistic" line). I believe that WEI/WUV gives NATO insufficient credit for weapons quality; by itself, WEI/WUV only modestly alters the impression that NATO is outgunned.[27]

86" formation. The DEF methodology is still secret, but it varies little from the ADE methodology as far as I have been able to discover, although it seems to provide greater credit for newer equipment. Given the uncertainties that govern open-source estimates of mobilization schedules, as well as the uncertainties of any firepower scoring methodology, the differences between WEI/WUV I and the current DEF methodology cannot be considered to be significant for our purposes. WEI/WUV III is declassified and circulates informally (if "unofficially") in the analytic community. I have chosen to employ WEI/WUV I in this analysis to preserve continuity with my personal databases and my previously published work, to preserve comparability with several official assessments of the balance that have appeared in the open literature over the years, and because the most accessible open-source comparison of NATO and Pact divisions in terms of ADEs was generated by the WEI/WUV I methodology. Mako, *US Ground Forces*, app. A, "Estimating Ground Combat Potential," pp. 105–125.

[25]See, e.g., table 3.1, which estimates total NATO firepower, and Mako's analysis, op. *US Ground Forces*.

[26]For example, two Congressional Budget Office monographs in the early 1980s suggested that the force ratio in ADEs for the first ninety days after mobilization would approach 2:1 in favor of the Pact for only a brief period and would stabilize at roughly 1.75:1. U.S. Congress, Congressional Budget Office, *U.S. Ground Forces: Design and Cost Alternatives for NATO and Non-NATO Contingencies*, prepared by Pat Hillier and Nora Slatkin (Washington, D.C., December 1980), p. 24; and *Army Ground Combat Modernization for the 1980's: Potential Costs and Effects for NATO*, prepared by Nora Slatkin (Washington, D.C., November 1982), p. 29.

[27]I believe that the WEI/WUV methodology does not go far enough in giving credit for NATO's qualitative superiority over the Warsaw Pact, and that estimates of NATO strength, based on WEI/WUV, are therefore unduly conservative. The tank provides the best example. WEI/WUV judges a U.S. M-1 battle tank to be roughly 10 to 15 percent better than a T-72. Yet it weighs 34 percent more and costs roughly 165 percent more. I have assembled these estimates from the following sources. For tank scores, see U.S. Congress, CBO, *Army Ground Combat Modernization*, pp. 61–67; and U.S. Army, *Weapon Effectiveness Index/Weighted Unit Values (WEI/WUV), Executive Summary*, War Gaming Directorate, U.S. Army Concepts Analysis Agency (April 1974, mimeo), p. 26; for tank weights see U.S. Department of Defense, *Soviet Military Power, 1987*, p. 73; for Soviet tank costs, see U.S. Congress, Joint Economic Committee, *Allocation of Resources in the Soviet Union and China—1985*, 99th Cong., 2d sess., 1986 (Washington, D.C., 1986), p. 160, suggesting a unit cost of $900,000 (1984 U.S. dollars) each for Soviet tanks procured from 1981 to 1985; and U.S. Department of Defense, *Annual Report*, FY 1984, p. 127, suggesting roughly $2.4 million (1984 dollars) as the price of an M-1 tank. Chalmers and

Relative Mobilization Rates: Reinforcements over Time

It has been common practice to assume that all Pact forces are ready for combat, and that Pact reserves could be deployed much more quickly than could NATO reserves.[28] This implausible, giving the Pact too much credit and NATO not enough, as I will show.

Soviet Reserves. Historically, it was often assumed that all 256 Soviet and Warsaw Pact divisions were quite ready for combat, and that Soviet Category II and III reserve divisions could mobilize and deploy in two to four weeks.[29] In fact, most Category III divisions normally lacked half or more of the men they need for combat and lacked anything like a full complement of logistics trucks. They would need to be filled out by mobilized reservists in wartime and would need to mobilize trucks out of the civilian economy. I estimate that, of 216 Soviet Army divisions of all types (plus 4 divisions amalgamated into two corps), only the 2 corps were manned at a notional 100 percent of the nominal 20,000-man division slice; and only 36 heavy divisions and their nondivisional support troops were manned at 80 percent of their wartime complement.[30] The rest were only partially manned: I estimate that there were 37 Category II ready reserve divisions and their support troops, manned at roughly 60 percent; 101 Category III divisions, manned at roughly 25 percent; 30 Category III divisions,

Unterseher, "Tank Gap," p. 46, judge on the basis of a thorough comparative treatment that the average NATO tank should be rated 1.5–2 times as effective as the average Pact tank.

[28]The standard Pact mobilization estimate under these assumptions that provided the basis for much pessimistic analysis was first published by the Department of Defense in 1976. U.S. Department of Defense, *A Report to Congress on U.S. Conventional Reinforcements to NATO* (Washington, D.C., 1976), Chart IV-1, p. IV-3, cited in Richard K. Betts, *Surprise Attack: Lessons for Defense Planning* (Washington, D.C., 1983), pp. 108–125. Although the published chart contained no actual numbers on its time and force axes, I used subsequently published information on the ADE scoring system to reconstruct those numbers in my 1984 essay, "Measuring the European Conventional Balance," fig. 3, p. 63. My estimate is quite close to that offered in the recently declassified Pentagon study: U.S. Department of Defense, Assistant Secretary of Defense for Program Analysis and Evaluation, *NATO Center Region Military Balance Study 1978–1984* (declassified, 13 July 1985), table I-11, p. I-19. Information on the ADE scoring system can be found in Mako, *US Ground Forces*, pp. 108–125.

[29]"Category I, II and III" refer to Soviet reserve divisions; divisions are, generally speaking, described as belonging to one category or another based upon percentage of full staffing and readiness for combat.

[30]The division slice includes the actual strength of the division, 11,000–13,000 people for Soviet tank and motor rifle divisions in the 1980s, and a prorated share of nondivisional combat support and combat service support elements.

manned at roughly 15 percent; and five unmanned sets of divisional equipment.[31]

Many Western experts believed that Category II divisions would need at least thirty days to mobilize and train; Category III divisions, at least sixty days. Additional time was needed for transit to the inter-German border.[32] Starting in 1985, DOD's *Soviet Military Power* began somewhat obliquely to corroborate this assessment, noting that the Soviets considered only 40 percent of their divisions to be "ready," with the rest requiring "up to 60 days to mobilize personnel and equipment, deploy to local dispersal areas, and train for offensive combat operations."[33] Other unofficial published estimates indicated that the Soviets (and their East European allies) would likely have subjected these mobilized divisions to intensive refresher training before committing them to combat: thirty to forty-five days for Category IIs, ninety days or more for Category IIIs.[34] There were two main reasons for such estimates. First, Soviet Category II and III divisions were manned at "cadre" strength, perhaps an average of 60 percent for the former and 25 percent for the latter. The cadre of these divisions were not all seasoned professionals. Perhaps one-half or more were themselves conscripts, serving their obligatory two-year term of service. Some were in their first six months of service and, like most Soviet conscripts (and unlike Western forces), received basic training in their combat units. Since these divisions had quite a bit of equip-

[31]This estimate is based on diverse sources and reflects late 1980s information. Most useful are IISS, *Military Balance, 1986–1987*, pp. 37–45; U.S. Department of Defense, *Soviet Military Power, 1988*, pp. 74–77, 89–91; U.S. Department of Defense, *Soviet Military Power, 1987*, pp. 70–71, 96–97. U.S. Department of Defense, *Soviet Military Power, 1982*, pp. 6–7, contains a map that lists the total Soviet divisional strength by region, and a percentage breakdown by readiness category. This indicates a total of 46 Category I divisions (7 of which were probably airborne units), 37 Category II divisions, and 97 Category III divisions. From year to year official and unofficial estimates of the makeup of the Soviet Army vary slightly and are often characterized by what seems to be deliberate ambiguity. Readers who have followed my work will note that this estimate varies marginally from those I have made in the past. Most estimates put the strength of the entire Soviet Army at roughly 2 million men. When a nominal 10 percent are subtracted for general headquarters and overhead, and an additional 70,000 subtracted for airborne and fortress infantry divisions, the breakout in the text consumes the remaining Soviet manpower.

[32]As far as I can tell, the International Institute for Strategic Studies (IISS) for the first time in 1986 added its voice to those who doubted the readiness of Soviet reserve divisions and estimated that Category II and III divisions would take one to two months to prepare for war. See IISS, *Military Balance, 1986–1987*, p. 37.

[33]See U.S. Department of Defense, *Soviet Military Power, 1985*, p. 66; *Soviet Military Power, 1986*, p. 98; *Soviet Military Power, 1987*, pp. 70–73.

[34]Irving Heymont and Melvin Rosen, "Foreign Army Reserve Systems," *Military Review* 53 (March 1973): 84–85; David C. Isby, *Weapons and Tactics of the Soviet Army* (London: Janes', 1981), p. 28; Jeffrey Record, *Sizing Up the Soviet Army* (Washington, D.C., 1975), pp. 21–22.

ment, much conscript time was spent in basic vehicle maintenance, not in field training. Similarly, because the divisions were only partially manned, thorough training of officers and enlisted men at all levels was not always possible.

Second, upon mobilization, these divisions would have been "fleshed out" with reservists who had completed their two-year term of service and returned to civilian life. Unlike U.S. National Guard or Israeli reservists, these people would not have known each other. Most received no annual refresher training. Because of the many generations of equipment in the Soviet inventory, mobilized reservists might have received equipment different from that with which they originally trained. Category II and III divisions seldom called up large numbers of conscripts for major exercises.[35] This was in sharp contrast to U.S. or Israeli reservists, who receive thirty to forty-five days of individual and unit training per year with the people and the units that they will accompany into battle. It is worth noting that, even given this level of annual activity, Israeli reservists did not perform as effectively as expected during the first few days of the 1973 war. Moreover, close observers of the U.S National Guard and U.S. Army Reserve suggest that a month or more of postmobilization refresher training is required.[36] The long postmobilization training periods suggested above reflect these shortcomings. Thus, as reflected by the upturns at thirty and sixty days shown in the mobilization curves on figure 3.4, Soviet and East European Category II divisions would not have been ready until after thirty days of postmobilization training, and Category III divisions would have been delayed sixty days. I suspect that even these figures are somewhat optimistic for the Pact.

NATO Forces. I treat U.S. National Guard brigades and divisions as equal in combat readiness to their Pact Category II and III counterparts. U.S. National Guard divisions have traditionally been expected to take a long time to mobilize, train, and reach Europe; few were expected to

[35]On the peacetime organization and training of low-readiness Category II and III divisions, see testimony of the Defense Intelligence Agency in U.S. Congress, Joint Economic Committee, Subcommittee on International Trade, Finance, and Security Economics, *Allocation of Resources in the Soviet Union and China—1981*, 97th Cong., 1st sess., pt. 7, 1982 (Washington, D.C., 1982), p. 199.

[36]Mako, *US Ground Forces*, p. 83, quotes Martin Binkin's estimate of fourteen weeks to prepare a U.S. reserve division for combat but judges this estimate to be pessimistic. U.S. National Guard combat brigades mobilized in early November 1990 in support of Operation Desert Shield were apparently considered much less capable than their regular army counterparts even after several months of intense training, since none were ever dispatched to the Persian Gulf.

arrive less than ninety days after NATO's decision to mobilize ("NATO M+90"). For three reasons, however, I assume that national guard and army reserve brigades, divisions, and combat support units would have reached Europe earlier than this. First, the guard and reserve received considerable infusions of money and personnel in the 1980s. By the second half of the decade guard units had a sizable full-time cadre.[37] In contrast to Warsaw Pact reserve formations, whose members seldom received refresher training and usually did not even know each other, the members of the U.S. reserve formations train together in units for at least two weeks a year and work together at least one weekend a month.[38] Second, there are suggestions in several sources that at least some large guard combat units were expected to arrive in Central Europe less than three months after mobilization, and that the transport shipping was available to get them there.[39] Third, a recently declassified high-level Pentagon study from July of 1979 projected that with then-planned infusions of resources, a mobilization schedule similar to the one I suggest here, would have been achievable by 1986. As the Reagan administration committed much greater resources to defense than then

[37]In general, more than 10 percent of the personnel associated with U.S. reserve units serve on a full-time basis. It is unlikely that the "long service cadre" of Soviet reserve units is much larger. See U.S. Department of Defense, *Annual Report*, FY 1988, p. 135, for the U.S. percentage.

[38]William W. Kaufmann compares the readiness of U.S. National Guard divisions favorably with that of Soviet Category II units but notes that the U.S. Army seems to believe that U.S. reserves require at least ninety days to ready themselves for combat. Thus he counts no U.S. reserve divisions as available in the first ninety days after mobilization. See William W. Kaufmann, "NonNuclear Deterrence," pp. 57, 62, 66–67, 70.

[39]U.S. Congress, Congressional Budget Office, *Improving the Army Reserves*, prepared by John Enns (Washington, D.C., November 1985), p. 24, suggests that even a reserve unit rated C-4 "not ready" by the Army could be made ready for combat in sixty days. This is roughly consistent with my estimate of when U.S. National Guard *divisions* would begin to arrive in Europe. The author seems to assume, however, that only three reserve divisions would have reached Europe by M+90 (p. 22). No reasons are offered for this constrained reinforcement. Adm. Wesley McDonald, then SACLANT, estimated that 8.5 million tons of equipment and stores and 15 million tons of petroleum products would need to be transported to Europe in 180 days in the event of mobilization, at a tempo as high as 800 sailings per month. Though the statement is ambiguous, 800 sailings per month would support the rate of reinforcement suggested in my mobilization curves and leave plenty of room for ammunition and supplies. See Adm. Wesley L. McDonald, USN, "The Critical Role of Sea Power in the Defense of Europe," *NATO's Sixteen Nations* 29 (December 1984–January 1985): 14–17. The DOD reports that the NATO allies "have committed militarily suitable ships to provide direct sealift support to the rapid reinforcement plan," with about 10 million tons of cargo capacity. See Weinberger, *Report on Allied Contributions* (1987), pp. 47–48. I have performed an independent estimate of NATO's sea and air lift capabilities that supports my deployment schedule in "Nato's Reinforcement Capability," *Defense Analysis* 5 (1990): 327–339.

projected, and given the other evidence presented above, it is likely that the projected capabilities were achieved.[40]

Thus it is reasonable to assume that NATO reserves would have arrived at rates roughly comparable to those of Pact reserves, which is reflected on figure 3.4 and in the force ratios on figure 3.3, "Pact: NATO" line.

Total Forces

I count roughly 110 Pact division equivalents in the Central Region, most of the forces usually counted in official assessments.[41]

I assume that roughly one-half of all NATO ground combat power (77 division equivalents, or 66 ADEs) would have been committed to the Central Region by M+90. This includes most French as well as most U.S. units, because I assume that the French would have fulfilled their obligations as a member of the NATO alliance.[42] Three U.S. Marine divisions, five active U.S. Army divisions, and several independent U.S. Army brigades are presumed to be held in reserve or committed elsewhere.[43]

It is possible that the popular assumption of fast buildup rates for low-readiness Soviet and East European divisions cloaked other assumptions: the Pact would in fact have taken a month or more to retrain these divisions, but Western intelligence would somehow have missed this extraordinary activity; or Western leaders would have been too frightened to take any military response to such actions; or Alliance

[40]U.S. Department of Defense, Assistant Secretary, *NATO Center Region*, pp. I-17-18, projected the arrival of 18 additional division equivalents by M+60, 24.66 by M+90. Given that there were then only 11 active divisions remaining in the United States, most of these forces had to be Army National Guard units.

[41]There were other Soviet divisions in other theaters that could ultimately be brought into the Central Region. Open-source official NATO and U.S. government accounts did not usually assume this, however, probably because the Soviets had other security problems that would have absorbed most if not all of these forces. For example, the lines of communication into and within Eastern Europe might not support a deployment of more than 120 divisions. Alternatively, the Soviets might have feared that the inherent vulnerability of their east-west line of communication created a high risk that divisions pulled from the Far East might not have made it back in the event of an emergency. Finally, they may have feared that the very act of removing these divisions to the west would have invited an attack in the east.

[42]Developments in French security policy pointing toward much greater military cooperation with the Federal Republic of Germany in the late 1980s lent additional credibility to this assumption. See James M. Markham, "French Fall in Step under a German," *New York Times*, 24 September 1987, p. A6.

[43]Active U.S. Army divisions presumed held in reserve are the 82nd, 101st, 9th, 2nd, and 25th.

Table 3.1. Estimated total NATO ADEs, 1987 (WEI/WUV I)

Country	ADEs	ADEs to Central Region
Belgium	1.86	1.5
Canada	1.35	.33
Denmark	2.00	.70
France	7.20	6.32
Germany	12.65	12.65
Greece	7.13	0.0
Italy	5.38	0.0
Luxembourg	.10	0.0
Netherlands	3.90	3.0
Norway	1.80	0.0
Portugal	1.00	0.0
Spain	5.00	0.0
Turkey	13.20	0.0
U.K.	5.85	4.00
U.S.	50.40	38.0
TOTAL	118.82	65.5

Source: Percentage distribution of NATO ADEs appears in Weinberger, *Report on Allied Contributions to the Common Defense* (1986), p. 103. No actual ADE totals are given. I have inferred the totals by estimating the ADE score of the German Army and calculating all other scores relative to the German share. Currently, attack helicopters are normally included in the ADE methodology. I exclude them and treat them as close air support assets.

consensus for mobilization would have taken too long to build. Given the tremendous publicity that attended Soviet efforts to ready some divisions for action against Poland in 1981, the amount of technical warning Western intelligence had of Soviet preparations for the invasion of Czechoslovakia in 1968 and the Afghan invasion of 1979 (both smaller affairs than that projected here), the argument that NATO leaders would not have known about Soviet preparations seems suspect.[44] If American and European planners believed that the West could have lost a war because its political leaders were likely to be too concerned with provocation to order mobilization or too militarily ill-informed to understand that NATO had to compete with Soviet partial mobilization efforts (that is, refresher training for Category IIs and IIIs), then the task was to educate the leaders, not misinform them. Finally, it might have been possible to design partial mobilization efforts for NATO that would be sufficiently unprovocative to win political approval.

[44]William W. Kaufmann, "Defense Policy," in *Setting National Priorities: Agenda for the 1980's*, ed. Joseph A. Pechman (Washington, D.C., 1980), p. 300, estimates that it takes the Soviets months, rather than weeks, even to organize a small military operation.

COMMAND, CONTROL, AND LOGISTICS

Most open-source balance assessments, even those using the WEI/WUV methodology, did not account properly for logistics or command, communications, control, and intelligence (which I refer to collectively herein as "logistics and command"). Although it is difficult to be certain, there is a good deal of circumstantial evidence to suggest that most official balance assessments conducted by the military, Pentagon officials, and Pentagon contractors shared this flaw.[45] Thus, many analyses tended to show NATO at a disadvantage, because the United States and its allies devoted disproportionately greater human and material resources to these activities than did the Pact. For example, depending on what assets one counts, and whether one compares peacetime or mobilized forces, NATO allocated 1.3 to 2 times the personnel as the Pact to generate a given unit of firepower.[46] Therefore, in the mobilization curves displayed, I multiply the NATO ADE score by 1.5 to represent this additional effort and term the result the "adjusted ADE score." See, e.g., figure 3.3, "Pact:NATO Adjusted" curve, and figure 3.4, the "Adjusted ADEs" curve.

The assignment of a substantial multiplier for command and logistics to NATO forces is probably a key determinant of more favorable combat outcomes for NATO in my analysis than those often generated in the professional military modeling community. The modeling community did not pay as much attention to these issues as it did to combat modeling, and to the extent that it did, it appears to have been remarkably unconcerned with the fact that marginal utility seldom approximated marginal cost.[47] Many of my colleagues who do this kind of work

[45]The formerly classified U.S. Department of Defense, Assistant Secretary, *NATO Center Region*, is an exception. Appendices D and E conduct the kind of analysis that I do in the paragraphs below. The text of the study develops the argument that NATO's situation is improved if credit is taken for these efforts but does not argue very strongly for this position. See pp. I-21-25.

[46]U.S. Central Intelligence Agency, *Soviet and US Defense Activities, 1970–1979*, pp. 7–10, indicates that the Soviet Union maintained a force roughly twice the size of the United States in terms of manpower in 1979, which cost nearly 50 percent more overall, but allocated virtually equal resources to "support forces." This suggests that by U.S. standards, average Soviet combat units were woefully undersupported. These different patterns of resource allocation prevail in an alliance-to-alliance comparison as well.

[47]See W. Peter Cherry, "Quantitative Analysis of Intelligence/Electronic Warfare: Vector IEW," in *Systems Analysis and Modeling in Defense: Development, Trends, and Issues*, ed. Reiner K. Huber (New York, 1984), p. 293. "Over the past ten years the military operations research community has experienced a major shift in the focus of land combat analysis. Whereas a decade ago major analysis issues dealt with armor, infantry, artillery, air defense, and air operations, emphasis is now being placed on command control, communications, intelligence, and electronic warfare. Simultaneously, efforts are being made to analyze the impact of so-called rear area processes: transportation, supply, repair, and

have informed me that they captured the effects of NATO's superior investments by assigning it higher recovery rates—that is, lost armored vehicles were estimated to be repaired or replaced by NATO at higher rates than the Pact. This is not unreasonable, but it is certainly incomplete.

Nearly ten years ago, in an essay that remains one of the more useful primers on differences between NATO and Warsaw Pact strategy, tactics, and organization, Steven Canby highlighted NATO's emphasis on the command and support areas.[48] He devised a system for comparing the total number of combat, combat support, and combat service support people, inside and outside the divisional organization, needed to generate a fighting force of a given size. Though his numbers are somewhat dated, they are good enough for our purposes here. Using an average West European division as base, Canby estimated that the NATO allies needed roughly 40,000 men to field and support a given number of individuals in front-line combat roles in wartime. Given prevailing Soviet practices, the Pact would have allocated only 21,500 people to the same task. A similar comparison was made for peacetime U.S. and Soviet divisions, which yielded 41,000 for the United States and 21,500 for the Soviets. Thus, on the average, it took NATO roughly twice as many people to field a front-line force of a given size as it did the Pact. Although divisions have grown in firepower since World War II, the British official history reports that U.S. and British divisions plus their nondivisional combat support and combat service support amounted to roughly 40,000 men by 1944—a 40,000-man slice.[49]

Because Canby's methodology is a bit opaque, it is worth looking at the current figures in several different ways as a check. Adapting figures from *The Military Balance, 1983–1984*, we see that the United States allocated roughly 34,000 men per ADE in Germany, the German Army 31,000, and the Soviet Army 24,000 per ADE deployed in Eastern Europe. This yields an average peacetime NATO superiority of 1.33:1. The wartime superiority would probably grow in the direction suggested

maintenance. While for some time the term 'force multiplier' has been applied to command control, communications and intelligence systems (and countermeasures), only recently has attention turned to issues such as contribution to combat and quantitative tradeoffs in a system performance." The author then goes on to describe in some detail the efforts of the Vector corporation to develop a corps-level command and control model. He indicates, however, that input data representing differences between U.S. and adversary forces had not been assembled as of the date of publication. (p. 306).

[48]Canby, *The Alliance and Europe*, pp. 3–4, 10, and n. 10.

[49]Maj. L. F. Ellis, *The Battle of Normandy: Victory in the West*, vol. I, *History of the Second World War*, U.K. Military Series (London, 1962), pp. 536, 541.

by Canby, since much of the American and German reserve structure was devoted to support. Given the large number of divisions that the Soviets were expected to man on mobilization, it seems unlikely that their support-to-combat ratio would grow at quite the same rate. Finally, a comparison of the organizational charts of first-class Soviet and U.S. divisions shows that within the divisional organization, the United States allocated about 1.5 times as many people to command and support per ADE as the Soviets. Soviet and Warsaw Pact divisions had only five major maneuver unit headquarters (divisional plus four regimental headquarters).[50] In contrast, a U.S. division had a divisional headquarters, three brigade headquarters, plus major headquarters for each of ten tank and infantry battalions.[51] Thus the U.S. division had fourteen major headquarters to the Soviet division's five. These numbers and ratios are all, of course, quite rough, but they are indicative of how NATO allocated its personnel and its financial resources.[52] Moreover, U.S. and NATO military commanders continued the practice throughout the 1980s. Evidence suggests that U.S. military and civilian leaders did not feel that the point of diminishing returns had been reached for logistics units.[53] Thus, we must logically assume that they were deemed to be worth more than the front-line combat power forgone to generate them.

Canby, of course, argues that whatever the difference, the west merited no special credit for these assets. Rather, by organizing their forces to achieve greater initial firepower, the Pact would have simply swamped NATO's smaller forces before these support assets became useful. In this formulation, these support assets were seen primarily as

[50]The headquarters of a Soviet battalion was quite tiny and cannot be counted as a major headquarters.

[51]For example, a three-company Soviet motorized rifle battalion based on the BMP armored fighting vehicle had roughly 150 people associated with command, logistics, and fire support. A comparable U.S. four-company mechanized infantry battalion in the new table of organization had a headquarters and headquarters company with 334 individuals engaged in similar functions. See U.S. Army, *U.S. Army Armor Reference Manual*, vol. 3, Division 86 Organizations (Fort Knox, Ky., 1981), pp. 470–482; and Defense Intelligence Agency, *Soviet Divisional Organizational Guide* (Washington, D.C., 1982), p. 30.

[52]See Kaufmann, "Nonnuclear Deterrence," pp. 55–58. On Soviet and U.S. divisions, see Defense Intelligence Agency, *Soviet Divisional Organizational Guide*; and U.S. Army, *U.S. Army Armor Reference Data*, vols. 1 and 2 (Fort Knox, Ky., 1981).

[53]For example, in the late 1980s three annual reports of the secretary of defense included plans to increase modestly the logistics support structure of the active and reserve forces: U.S. Department of Defense, *Annual Report*, FY 1988, p. 154; *Annual Report*, FY 1987, p. 156; *Annual Report*, FY 1985, p. 117. More importantly, the German Wartime Host Nation Support agreement "calls for some 93,000 military reservists in 173 units to perform wartime logistics functions for US forces." Weinberger, *Report on Allied Contributions to the Common Defense*, 1987, p. 52.

"long-war" capabilities. Others asserted that NATO's individual armies required long logistics tails because of the low level of standardization and centralization in the democratic Western alliance. And some suggested that NATO's greater efforts in the tactical command and control area were neutralized by the Pact's centralized command and control at the theater level. These observations were usually made in a general way without supporting argumentation or data.

An examination of the history of armored warfare does reveal that the command, supply, and maintenance of mechanized forces has been a consistent problem, and armies that are good at these functions have enjoyed significant advantages in the ability to generate combat power. The area of maintenance alone provides many examples. German armored formations experienced severe maintenance and supply problems in the bloodless invasion of Austria in 1937 and put these lessons to good use later in the war. Historians have commented on the excellence of the German armored recovery and repair organizations in the western desert and the Eastern Front.[54] The Soviets, by contrast, had a problem-ridden maintenance organization, so much so that at the outset of the war a relatively small percentage of the armored vehicles they owned were in running condition. This problem appeared repeatedly later in the war.[55] Finally, observers have commented on the excellence of the Israeli Defense Forces (IDF) system for armored vehicle maintenance and recovery.

It is, of course, quite difficult to glean from historical cases the "right" ratio of command and support assets to combat assets. We can, however, put the Soviet theory of command and support to the test. If the lean Soviet command and logistics apparatus reflects unity of effort and a correct theory of rapid armored offensive operations that will produce a short war, then we ought to see the Soviet structure replicated in other armies that share these Soviet political and doctrinal characteristics. If the Soviet theory is correct, it should be reflected in the IDF.

The IDF fights alone, so there are no problems of alliance coordination or standardization. Similarly, the IDF has had a good deal of experience of offensive armored operations, prefers them to the defense, and aims explicitly to produce rapid victory. Additional factors in the IDF favor a Soviet-style organization, including a relative manpower scarcity,

[54]John Erickson, *The Road to Berlin: Stalin's War with Germany* (London, 1983), pp. 112–113.

[55]Ibid., p. 53. John Erickson, *The Road to Stalingrad: Stalin's War with Germany* (New York, 1975), pp. 62–63, suggests that on the eve of the war 30 percent of Soviet tanks needed a major overhaul, 44 percent a sizable refit, but that spares and repair facilities were short. See also pp. 166, 225.

Table 3.2. Tooth-to-tail ratios

Force	Men	Tanks	Division equivalents	Men / Tanks	Men / Divisions
GSFG (peace)	380,000	6200	20.66	62	18,400
GSFG (estimated mob.)[a]	475,000	6200	20.66	77	23,000
USAREUR (peace)	200,000	1600	5.33	125	37,500
IDF[b] (mob.)	440,000	3800	18.66	116	23,600
IDF (mob.)	600,000	3850	18	156	33,000
FRG (mob.)	1,000,000	4000	21[c]	250	47,600

Note: Unless otherwise noted, the IISS *Military Balance, 1988–1989,* country entries are the source. Independent maneuver brigades and regiments are aggregated into divisions at the ratio of 3:1. U.S. and Soviet peacetime forces are used because both sides are ostensibly meant to be able to go to war on short notice, with little reinforcement from the home country. The mobilized strength of the IDF is shown because the IDF is virtually a mobilization army. The mobilized strength of the German Army is shown for the same reason, and because the distance its reservists have to travel to their units is relatively short.

[a]An estimate based on recent observations to the effect that the U.S. intelligence community believes that the Soviet divisions in the GSFG (Group of Soviet Forces Germany) are only 80 percent manned. I have generalized this to the entire force structure. The purpose of including this estimate is fairness and conservatism. Other official data suggests that the mobilized Soviet division slice is as I have described it above, roughly 20,000.

[b]Mark Heller, ed., *The Middle East Military Balance, 1985* (Boulder, Colo., 1986) pp. 121–122.

[c]I have included 15 Home Defense motorized infantry regiments, aggregated as 5 division equivalents, although these are very lightly equipped.

very short lines of communication, a general scarcity of resources in the face of a substantial threat that should strongly encourage efficient resource allocation. Unfortunately, the IDF is very secretive about its force structure. Discussions with soldiers of the IDF have convinced me, however, that in broad-brush terms it more closely resembles Western than Eastern armies. The data that are available, which also permit comparison with NATO armies, are displayed in table 3.2. They indicate that on the average the IDF, like western armies, has a people-to-tank ratio two times or more that of the Group of Soviet Forces Germany, (GSFG) presumably the best-manned and -supported divisions in the Soviet force structure. The IDF requires between 30 percent and 80 percent more people per mobilized division than the Soviet Army does for peacetime divisions in the GSFG. The higher estimate of mobilized Soviet strength and the lower estimate of Israeli mobilized strength produce equal wartime divisional slices, but even in this comparison the Israelis mobilize 50 percent more people per tank. These comparisons strongly suggest that the explanations customarily offered to explain away the differences between Pact and NATO military organization are wrong, and that NATO probably deserves sizable credit for its superior relative investments in this area.

Taking credit for support assets provides an avenue for including NATO's war reserve stocks, equipment held outside of units to replace damaged vehicles that cannot be repaired in the forward areas. NATO tries to keep its divisions in combat at full strength, in contrast to the Pact intention of pulling out and replacing the whole division. Most European allies did not have large war reserve stocks, but U.S. stocks, particularly of tanks, were quite large. The U.S. Army had 15,600 usable tanks in its inventory at the end of the decade. In 1982 the figure was about 12,000. But the U.S. Army fielded only about 100 tank battalions in 1982, which would have totaled about 5400–5800 tanks. Armored cavalry regiments would have added perhaps 450 more. Thus, in the early 1980s there were almost 6000 tanks in reserve, and by the late 1980s nearly 8000. These tanks would be worth 7–12 ADEs of combat power, which were seldom counted in balance assessments. One of the purposes of the U.S. support structure is to keep these tanks flowing into units so that they can remain near their designated strength and to keep damaged tanks flowing to the rear where they can be fixed. It is difficult to predict how long this stockpile would last in war. The average Israeli "total loss" rate in 1973 (tanks utterly destroyed) was about a half percent per day of the total original force. At this loss rate, the U.S. stockpile could keep a nominal 6000-tank operational force at full strength for more than six months of relatively serious combat.[56]

In sum, as a function of NATO's efforts in the command and support areas, a multiplier of 1.5 is applied to NATO's ADE score to take into account the increased combat effectiveness that NATO's military leaders presumably expected from their efforts. Sensitivity analysis conducted with the model (see Appendix 3) suggests there are many demanding conditions under which even a 1.25 multiplier leaves NATO in a very competitive position. (The median between Canby's U.S.-Soviet, people/division-slice ratio of 2:1, and my peacetime personnel/

[56]U.S. Department of Defense, *Annual Report*, FY 1982, then estimated about 12,000. U.S. Department of Defense, *Improvements in US Warfighting Capability FY 1980–1984* (May 1984, mimeo), p. 47, gives 100 tank battalions in 1982. The old tank battalion had 54 weapons; the new tank battalion has 58. IISS, *Military Balance, 1988–1989*, p. 20, estimates U.S. tank holdings. The DOD projected that 7400 tanks would be fielded in U.S. Active, Reserve, and Guard Units by 1992. U.S. Department of Defense, *Annual Report*, FY 1989, p. 186. The Germans also seem to have held fairly substantial war reserve stocks in the 1980s, perhaps 1000 tanks worth 1.5–1.7 ADEs. Other countries had lower war reserve stocks but often did have them. Little has been written about Soviet war reserve stocks, but they are generally not believed to be large.

ADE ratio of 1.35:1 would be 1.67:1. Thus, a 1.5 effectiveness multiplier seems a conservative way to take credit for NATO's greater support efforts.) Balance assessments that did not try to account for these factors implicitly accepted the correctness of Canby's short-war arguments. If they did, then NATO conventional force planners ought to have asked themselves whether the Alliance could afford to compete with the Soviet Union without trying to change its structure. Consistent with the respect for Soviet organization implicit in balance assessments that did not take credit for NATO's support and command efforts, NATO should have imitated its adversary. Since NATO's military professionals remained committed to doing business in their traditional fashion, then they ought to have explained and taken account of the benefits that they derived that the Soviets did not.

The Effectiveness of Tactical Air Power

Public assessments of the Central Region military balance often did not account for the possible influence of NATO's tactical air forces ("tacair") on the ground battle.[57] NATO, however, allocates substantial funds to aircraft with ground-attack capability and to special ground-attack ordnance. My analysis takes credit for NATO's tactical air investments in a simple, straightforward, and, in my judgment, very conservative way. I cannot predict how well they would do, but I can show the kinds of outcomes that might plausibly be produced if NATO tacair did as well as NATO's persistent investments in the area seem to imply.

Although public comparisons of relative NATO and Pact spending on the acquisition and operations of tactical air power are not available, one may deduce from several sources that NATO probably made a greater overall effort than did the Pact. First, in terms of the number and quality of major platforms, a rough parity existed between the two sides. An official NATO worldwide comparison of total Pact and NATO combat aircraft of all types gave the Pact 13,000 aircraft to NATO's 11,000, not the crushing quantitative superiority often implied.[58] The U.S. Department of Defense has devised a method to compare the quantity and technical quality of the combat aircraft inventories of NATO and the Warsaw Pact, and it employed this technique in a public document in 1988. In the area the Soviets call the Western Theater of

[57]See U.S. Congress, CBO, *U.S. Ground Forces*; Mako, *US Ground Forces*; and Dan Gans, "Fight Outnumbered and Win," pt. 1, *Military Review* 60 (December 1980): 31–45.

[58]Joseph Luns, *NATO and the Warsaw Pact: Force Comparisons* (Brussels, 1984), pp. 10, 13.

Military Operations (WTVD), which coincides roughly with NATO's Central Region but extends back to the Western Military Districts of the Soviet Union, the DOD judged that as of 1987 the two sides would probably have been close to parity after a month of mobilization. Depending on an unspecified range of assumptions, they suggest that the relationship could vary between 1.1 and 1.4:1 in favor of the Pact at the outset of mobilization, declining to parity after thirty days.[59] In 1980 the chart suggests a less favorable situation for NATO, with an initial ratio of between 1.4 and 1.9:1, and after thirty days a ratio between parity and 1.4:1. A formerly classified 1979 Pentagon study projected that at M+30 the two sides would be at parity in numbers in the Central Region with 4200 aircraft each and suggested that NATO still had a quality advantage at that time.[60]

Once expenditures on training and maintenance are included, it is likely that total NATO spending on tactical airpower substantially exceeded that of the Pact. Experts seem to agree that Pact efforts in the training and support of its tacair assets were significantly less than those of the United States.[61] Total American spending on tacair exceeded that of the Soviet Union during the 1970s, the last decade for which we have such information, in spite of the somewhat smaller inventory of aircraft that the United States had to operate.[62] This suggests some combination of higher quality aircraft and more intense training. The 1985 edition of the DOD's *Soviet Military Power* observes that U.S. Air Force and U.S. Navy aircrews then received about twice the flying time of their Soviet counterparts, and it notes that "US tactical air forces retain a qualitative advantage over those of the Soviet Union in aircraft and weapons and, more importantly, in personnel and training."[63] U.S. allies, who themselves spent a good deal on tacair, contributed substantially more to NATO's total defense spending than the East European states did to Pact total spending, so their inclusion should skew the effort further in NATO's favor.[64] The preceding may explain why Gen. Charles Don-

[59]U.S. Department of Defense, *Annual Report*, FY 1989, Chart I.B.3, p. 32. Although the methodology employed is unspecified, private inquiries indicate that it is called TASCFORM. A brief discussion of TASCFORM can be found in U.S. Congress, Congressional Budget Office, *Tactical Combat Forces of the US Air Force: Issues and Alternatives* prepared by Lane Pierrot and Bob Kornfeld (Washington, D.C., April 1985), pp. 70–76.

[60]U.S. Department of Defense, Assistant Secretary, *Nato Center Region*, pp. II-1, 8.

[61]Epstein, *Measuring Military Power*, pp. 96–98.

[62]U.S. Central Intelligence Agency, National Foreign Assessment Center, *Soviet and US Defense Activities, 1970–79*, p. 10.

[63]P. 88.

[64]IISS, *Military Balance, 1983–1984*, pp. 125–126; and U.S. Department of Defense, *The FY 1984 DOD Program for Research, Development and Acquisition*, statement by Richard DeLauer, undersecretary of defense for research and engineering, 2 March 1983.

nelly, former commander in chief of U.S. air forces in Europe, indicated he would not trade NATO's tactical air forces for the Pact's. "The fact of the matter is, with better airplanes, better crews, better maintenance, all of the things that make airplanes go and thus to drop bombs and other things, we are much better."[65]

None of the foregoing permits us to conclude that NATO would decisively have won an air battle in Central Europe, nor that it could have brought the bulk of its airpower to bear on the ground battle. Indeed, I know of no extant analysis in the open literature that would support such a judgment; this is a gap in the open literature that was not filled during the heyday of the debate on the conventional balance in Europe. More detailed analysis is required to support such an argument. On the basis of the observations above, however, I do believe that it is conservative to assume, for purposes of further discussion, that NATO's tactical airpower could have gotten a stalemate. That is to say that each side's air defense aircraft, fighter-bomber aircraft, and ground-based air defenses would have been occupied largely in an indecisive battle for theater air superiority (including airfield attacks), coupled with some equally effective (or ineffective) battlefield and theater interdiction of ground-force targets. Given the areas of NATO superiority in aerial warfare outlined above, its fighter-bomber aircraft would likely have done more damage against Pact ground forces than vice versa. So excluding the contributions of these aircraft to the ground battle again seems favorable to the Pact. This stalemate condition would have permitted both sides' dedicated close air support (CAS) aircraft and attack helicopters to fly the kinds of missions, with the level of effectiveness, discussed below.

NATO has made a substantial financial effort to produce aircraft and weapons devoted specifically to CAS. With the exception of the small number of "Frogfoot" aircraft deployed in the 1980s, Pact tactical fighter bombers were not well suited to this mission. Moreover, the Pact seemed more concerned with attacking NATO's tactical nuclear assets and airbases than with using tacair to affect the ground battle. Moreover, Epstein demonstrates that, even given assumptions about Soviet Frontal Aviation's performance that are relatively favorable to the Warsaw Pact (for example, three sorties per day), the Pact would probably have completed only 44 percent of its counternuclear, counterairfield

[65]Sen. Carl Levin (chairman, Senate Armed Services Subcommittee on Conventional Forces and Alliance Defense), *Beyond the Bean Count: Realistically Assessing the Conventional Military Balance in Europe*, 2d ed. (Washington, D.C., July 1988), pp. 49–50. Since there are shifts of emphasis and some changes in data from the first to the second edition, interested readers are advised to consult both.

Table 3.3. The tactical air efforts

	Initial		Reserves	
	NATO	Pact	NATO	Pact
Aircraft				
Fixed wing	660	420	230	?
Helicopter	970	805	600	525
TOTAL	1630	1225	830	525

Note: See Appendix 2 for the development of these numbers.

missions before virtually exhausting itself in the middle of the sixth day of combat. A Brookings study offers a similar estimate of the Pact's likely performance.[66]

My assessment of relative NATO–Warsaw Pact tactical air influence on the ground battle starts from the preceding discussion. Simply put, NATO and the Pact are given credit for their known CAS assets—attack helicopters and fighter aircraft specifically configured for antiarmor operations in close proximity to friendly ground forces. Effectiveness, sortie-rate, and attrition-rate values are assigned to these aircraft to produce an estimate of how many armored vehicle kills each side could achieve under conditions of intense ground combat (see tables 3.3 and 3.4).[67] Armored fighting vehicles destroyed are converted to an ADE score. The principal tactical assumption is that both sides would have allocated all their CAS assets to the breakthrough sectors. It is unlikely that this could have been fully achieved in practice, but it is a sensible way to use the aircraft.

For the initial phase of the conflict, NATO and the Pact are given credit for early reinforcing aircraft and attack helicopters.[68] The 5 percent attrition per sortie assumed here is high by historical standards for western air forces.[69] One-quarter to one-half a vehicle killed per sortie

[66]Epstein, *Measuring Military Power*, app. C, pp. 243–245, esp. table C-9, p. 245; the Brookings study is Kaufmann, "Nonnuclear Deterrence," pp. 76–77.

[67]The tacair formula is straightforward. For each sortie the total number of aircraft leaving base is multiplied by 0.95 (i.e., 5 percent attrition) and then by the kill rate to come up with a total kill per sortie. Those aircraft that have survived the sortie (i.e., 95 percent) are run through the equation for the next sortie. Second sortie survivors are run through the third, etc.

[68]I have also included my best estimate of the possible reinforcements that each side might be able to bring to bear on the battle if it wished to do so. Some of these are in units, others are in the maintenance pipeline. I have had to be quite speculative in preparing the Pact estimate. Because these numbers are quite speculative, the analysis is confined to the "Initially Available" category.

[69]U.S. Congress, Congressional Budget Office, *Navy Budget Issues for Fiscal Year 1980*, prepared by Dov S. Zackheim and Marshall Hoyler (Washington, D.C., March 1979), pp. 98, 102–103. U.S. Navy attrition over North Vietnam between 1965 and 1973 was 0.1

Table 3.4. Performance

	NATO	Pact
Attrition	5%	5%
Kills per sortie	.5	.35
Sortie rate per day	2	1

is in the historical range of performance. The west is assigned a higher kill rate primarily on the grounds of superior weaponry. The General Electric 30-mm antiarmor cannon on U.S. fixed-wing aircraft ought to be more effective than any antiarmor weapons the Pact has on its fixed-wing aircraft. Western precision-guided and antiarmor cluster ordnance for fixed-wing aircraft are also likely to be superior to their Pact counterparts, in my judgment. The relative performance of helicopter antiarmor weaponry is more difficult to gauge. Anecdotal evidence suggests that helicopter-fired Western HOT and TOW ATGMs both performed well in Middle Eastern combat. There is little such evidence on the performance of the Soviet MI-24 armed with the Swatter or Spiral missiles. These missiles were apparently radio guided, in contrast to those of NATO, which relied largely on wire guidance, and to the new U.S. Hellfire, which is laser guided. I suspect that radio guidance is less reliable than Western methods; otherwise, the West would have tried it. Moreover, Pact attack helicopters were less tactically flexible and survivable than their NATO counterparts, largely because of their limited ability to hover out of ground effect. This should either affect weapons delivery or survivability. I have chosen equal attrition rates for the two sides, so it does not seem unreasonable to extract the tactical penalty in the weapons performance assumption. For these reasons, I assign the Pact two-thirds the kill rate of NATO. This is a higher relative value than I assigned in my 1982 work; it seems conservative to assume that the Soviets have improved their relative performance in the early 1980s as newer generations of aircraft and weapons were deployed. Finally, NATO is assigned a higher sortie rate on the grounds of greater maintenance efforts and greater ruggedness of aircraft over helicopters.

Taking credit for NATO's investments in CAS aircraft and armaments as well as training and maintenance suggests that these assets could have made a substantial contribution to stopping Pact breakthrough efforts, if properly employed. NATO's CAS tacair assets destroy

---

percent. Israeli Air Force attrition during the 1973 war was 0.8 percent. Israeli A-4s, whose missions most closely approximated NATO's CAS missions, suffered 1.5 percent. Historically, U.S. air commanders were willing to accept sustained 5 percent attrition during World War II and Korea, if the mission was perceived to be important.

Figure 3.5. NATO and Pact ADEs destroyed by CAS

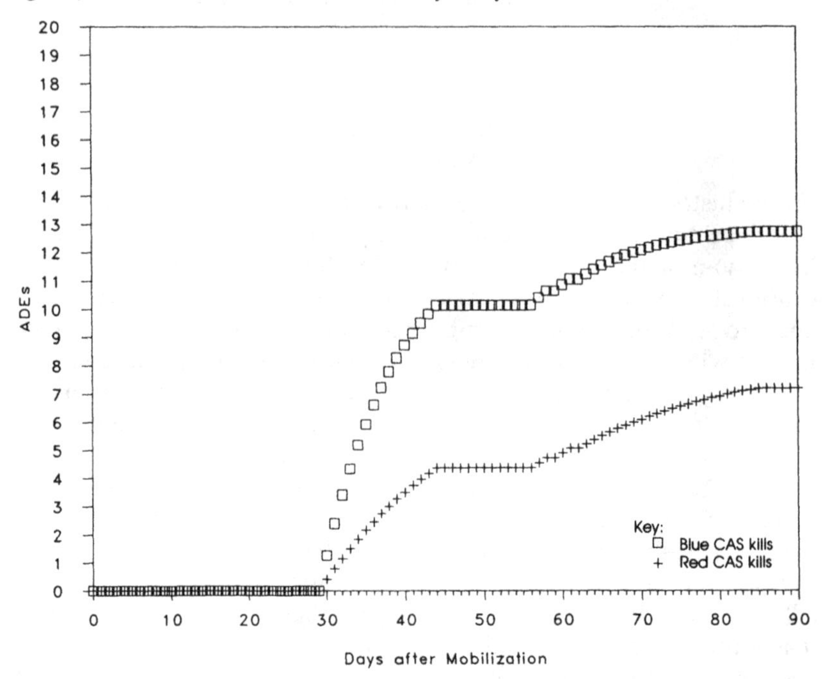

roughly thirteen Pact ADEs in six weeks of combat, while Pact tacair gets credit for destroying roughly seven NATO ADEs.[70] The initial Western air strength is virtually annihilated in this effort, with only 20 aircraft remaining, however. The Pact is left with about 170 aircraft. Put another way, NATO CAS destroys Pact ground forces equivalent to nearly all the Soviet forces stationed in East Germany in peacetime. Interested readers should consult Appendix 3 for an explanation of how these estimates were derived.[71]

[70]Neither the Pact nor NATO is permitted to fly CAS sorties on days when intense ground combat does not occur. In the "NATO favorable" scenario, between M+30, when combat begins, and M+85, when the Pact effort peters out, there are 42 days of intense combat, and thus 42 days of CAS sorties. See Appendix 3.

[71]Some skeptics may find this level of effectiveness implausible for both Soviet and Western CAS assets, even given the basic conservatism of the input values. In real life these potentials may not be realized in the form of enemy armored vehicles destroyed. Rather, ground forces will adapt their tactics to reduce the effectiveness of CAS. These adaptations would include more night attacks, more careful attention to camouflage and deception, greater presence of and coordination with air-defense assets at the FEBA, and less dense concentrations of armored vehicles in the assault. These adaptations, however,

Force-to-Space Ratios

How much force does a defender require to hold a given sector? How much force can the attacker concentrate in a given breakthrough sector? The "Soviet" and "NATO" cases illustrate different assumptions about these values. A close examination of the admittedly sparse information on these questions turns up an important insight. Simply put, given the number of forces that NATO already has, it may be extremely difficult for the Pact to achieve high offense-to-defense ratios of engaged forces in breakthrough sectors. A good deal of military experience and professional military judgment suggests that a substantial superiority of forces is necessary to achieve breakthroughs. This judgment is often codified in the "3:1" rule of thumb—at the level of a military engagement (from a small unit up to perhaps a corps-sized operation) the defender has a good chance of holding unless outweighed by the attacker by 3:1 or more in military assets, with the rule qualified by the relative quality of the two forces, the element of surprise, and the complexity of measuring the military assets brought to bear by the two sides in a particular engagement.[72]

Among those who have discussed the preferred defensive force-to-space ratio, the prevailing assumption seems to be that on average terrain roughly one ADE (WEI/WUV I) is required to hold every 25 km of front. Mako settles on this figure, although he quotes some retired U.S. officers to the effect that a U.S. armored or mechanized division armed with modern weaponry (then worth perhaps 1.1–1.3 ADEs) should have been able to hold 30 to 60 km of front (that is, as little as 0.5 or as much as 1 ADE could be needed to defend 25 km).[73] If William Kaufmann's methodology for assessing divisional firepower is con-

---

would slow down the pace of battle below the levels of intensity assumed in the model. I believe that in the net these adaptations would favor the tactical defender.

[72]The 3:1 rule has always engendered a certain informal controversy, which recently has been explicitly addressed in the academic literature. The most thorough development and defense of the rule is Mearsheimer, "Assessing the Conventional Balance," pp. 54–89. Epstein has been perhaps the most vocal critic of the rule; "The 3:1 Rule," pp. 90–127. I urge interested readers to examine their exchange with care. In my judgment, Mearsheimer's defense of the rule is successful.

[73]Mako, *US Ground Forces*, pp. 36–37, esp. n. 18. See also the most widely quoted discussion of the defender's force-to-space requirements: B. H. Liddell-Hart, *Deterrent or Defense: A Fresh Look at the West's Military Position* (New York, 1960), pp. 97–109. Liddell-Hart observed that the defender's force-to-space requirement, measured in manpower in divisions, has been dropping in this century. He also observed that the level of quantitative superiority that the attacker must enjoy if he is to achieve a successful breakthrough has been rising. Citing U.S. and British experience in World War II, he noted that superiorities between 3:1 and 5:1 were required, with some attacks failing at ratios of 10:1.

verted to ADEs, he appears to assume that between 0.75 and 1 ADE would be required to hold 25 km of front.[74] A formerly classified ten-year-old Pentagon study suggests that frontages for divisions or armored division equivalents between 15 and 30 km was then considered sufficient by U.S. army planners for the conduct of a credible defense.[75] David Isby suggests that the Soviets would assign one Motor Rifle Division (now about 0.8 ADE) to defend 25 km of front.[76] A 1984 U.S. Army publication on Soviet tactics estimates that "a tank or motorized rifle division typically defends a sector 20 to 30 km in width and 15 to 20 km in depth." This suggests that between 0.75 and 1.1 ADEs per 25 km was deemed an acceptable defensive force-to-space ratio by the Soviets.[77] Mako's one ADE per 25 km of front would then appear to be a conservative figure for analytic purposes.[78]

Because NATO had only 30 real ADEs at Pact M+14 (Pact D-day in standard planning scenarios), a literal application of this conservative planning factor plays into the hands of the Pact armored offensive, as many students of armored warfare have observed. In effect, many NATO forces would be pinned down, "conservatively" defending sectors that are not the victims of major breakthrough efforts, while those that are the victims would find themselves short of the tactical and operational reserves that might stop a breakthrough from happening or restore the situation if it occurred.

In the "NATO" case the effectiveness multiplier assigned to NATO ADEs frees some forces to act as additional operational reserves.[79] For example, if a 1.5 multiplier is assigned for command and logistics, 0.66

[74]Kaufmann, "Nonnuclear Deterrence," pp. 62, 210.

[75]U.S. Department of Defense, Assistant Secretary, *NATO Center Region*, p. I-11. "This particularly is the case in Northag, where division frontages (DEs and ADEs) are all between the 15 to 30 km range normally needed in Army planning to cover the FEBA with adequately dense forces to conduct a coordinated defense with division sized units."

[76]Isby, *Weapons and Tactics of the Soviet Army* (1981), pp. 20, 38.

[77]U.S. Army, *The Soviet Army: Operations and Tactics*, FM 100-2-1, (Washington, D.C., 1984), pp. 6-5, 6-6. As of 1989, prior to the Gorbachev cuts, a fully modernized Soviet MRD would be worth roughly 0.8 ADE of firepower, and a TD worth 1.

[78]I have not encountered a systematic explanation of how these estimates are developed. They are average estimates for average terrain. Rough terrain might require a lower density of armored vehicles and long-range antitank weapons, but a higher density of infantry and short-range antitank weapons; open terrain, a higher density of armor. To stop a heavily supported enemy offensive in its tracks, higher densities might become attractive in the course of the battle. For a discussion of some of these complexities see Paul K. Davis, Robert D. Hower, Richard L. Kugler, and William G. Wild, Jr., *Variables Affecting Central-Region Stability: The "Operational Minimum" and Other Issues at Low Force Levels* (Santa Monica, 1989).

[79]The "NATO-favorable" case also delays the initiation of hostilities until M+30. The training delay imposed on Pact Category II and III divisions leaves the Pact with too few forces to initiate combat at M+14.

of a real ADE is assigned to defend 25 km of front.[80] The command, reconnaissance, and logistics assets assigned to NATO forces should affect the amount of space that a given unit can control. The ammunition-handling capability of an average U.S. or West German division would have permitted a greater daily ammunition expenditure than that of a comparable Soviet division. Tactical command and control assets should have permitted the more rapid concentration of fire of available artillery against lucrative targets. Supply and maintenance assets should also have affected the overall attrition that NATO divisions would have suffered, since these assets should have provided NATO a superior capability to repair damaged vehicles or replace them from war reserve stocks.

The assignment of a 1.5 multiplier would still leave NATO defending within the 0.5 to 1 ADE per 25 km range cited above. Thus, in the initial stages of combat in the "NATO-favorable" case, the Alliance puts roughly one-half of its forces in the line (with each division in the line holding a small tactical reserve), and one-half of its forces in operational reserve. This is consistent with Liddell Hart's prescription that one-half of the defender's forces be held in reserve, and higher than the one-third figure suggested by Steven Canby.[81] If combat were initiated at M+14, NATO would have the same number of divisions in the line, but only about half as many in reserve (see figure 3.9).

There is even less in the open literature on the question of appropriate offensive force-to-space ratios. How much force can the attacker pack into a given segment of the front in his efforts to achieve the very high force-to-force ratios that are often thought to be the key to the successful armored breakthrough? In general, the impression has been created that the achievement of very high force-to-space ratios is relatively simple and that the adversary certainly intended to achieve very dense concentrations.

[80]This force-to-space ratio is substantially higher than that enjoyed by the Israeli 7th Armored Brigade in 1973, which successfully defended roughly 20 km of front on the Golan Heights with less than one-quarter of an ADE, no major reserves (other than the brigade's organic reserve), and virtually no CAS. This brigade was outnumbered 4:1 or worse. This was not, of course, a comfortable position, and Col. Janush Ben-gal (now Major General retired) was aided by prepared positions and Syrian unimaginativeness. Even with these advantages, the brigade was nearly exhausted after 2.5 days. Its performance, however, is exemplary of the impressive defensive potential of modern armored forces. At least 300 tanks plus other armored fighting vehicles were damaged, destroyed, or captured by the 7th Brigade. See Dupuy, *Elusive Victory*, pp. 437–461. By comparison to the 7th Brigade, the standard suggested here would leave a U.S. or West German division with two brigades forward, each on 19-km fronts, backed by one brigade in reserve. In the breakthrough sectors, such a force would receive substantial air support and could be reinforced rather quickly by reserves that are withheld in the "NATO" case.

[81]Mako, *US Ground Forces*, pp. 37–38.

Figure 3.6. NATO under severe stress: fast Pact mobilization/D at M+14

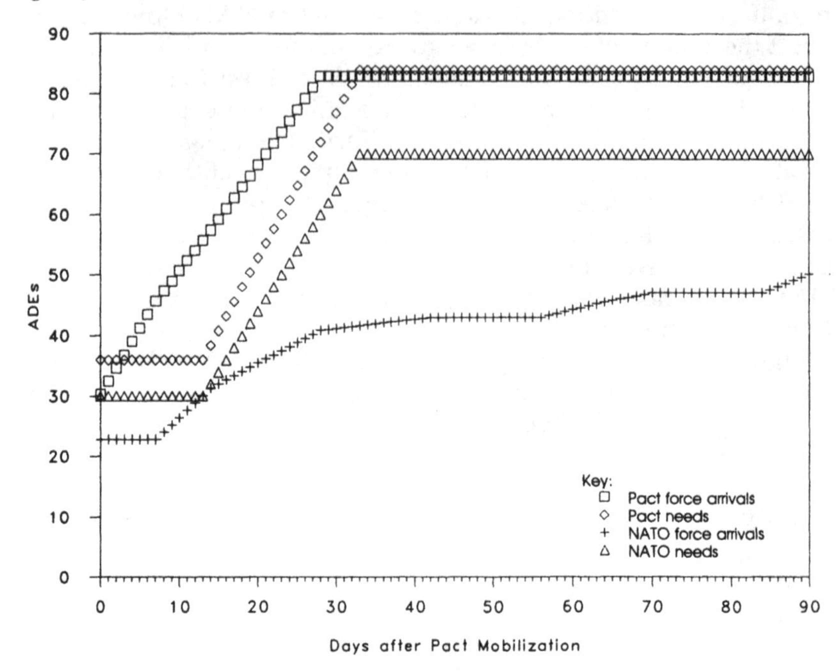

Combat assumptions: 3 Pact breakthrough efforts, 50 km wide; 4 Pact ADEs engaged in each effort; Pact accepts 10% attrition/day; NATO extracts 1.5: exchange rate; each spearhead penetrates 5 km/day; CAS neutralized by ground-based air defenses; no NATO credit for command and logistics.

The reasons for limits on the amount of force that is likely to be concentrated in a given sector of front are varied and complex. Since modern mechanized divisions contain several thousand motor vehicles, road capacity alone is a limiting factor. Readers should understand that a modern armored or mechanized division takes up a great deal of space. Even if proceeding on three parallel routes, the main body of a 1978-vintage Soviet motor rifle division on the march would have been a column occupying 60 km of road.[82] Other important considerations include: the specific nature of the terrain to be fought over, which may include ground that is simply impassable for armor; the desire to position weapons where they can exploit the terrain for cover; the desire

[82]U.S. Department of the Army, *Soviet Army Operations* (Washington, D.C., April 1978), p. 3-23.

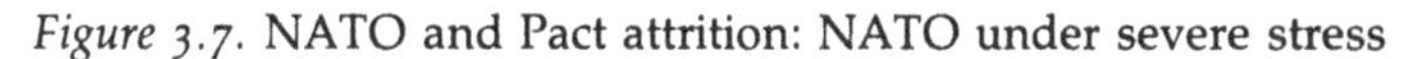

Figure 3.7. NATO and Pact attrition: NATO under severe stress

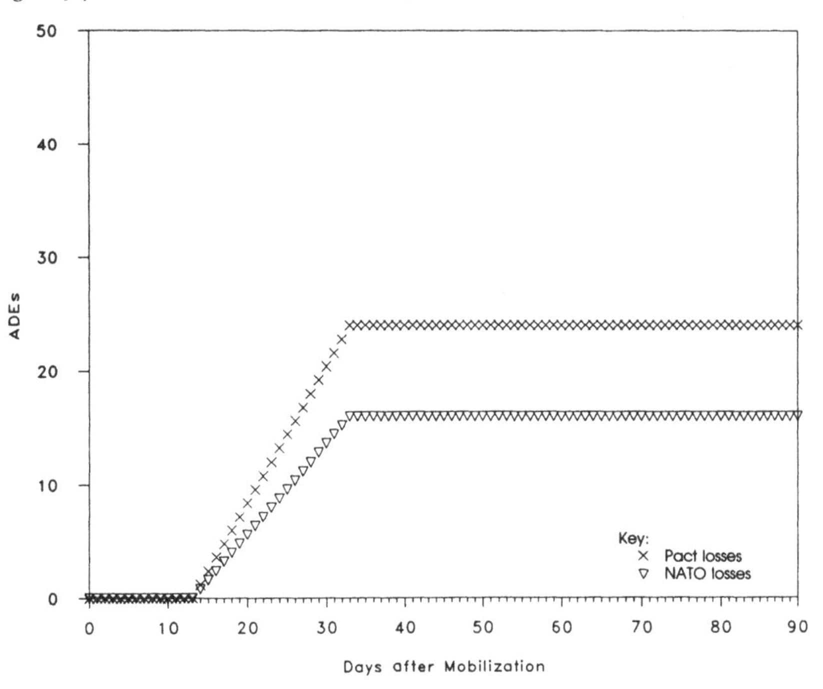

for "maneuver room," the desire to have multiple positions to which artillery and SAMs can be relocated in the event that they come under sustained fire; and the desire not to concentrate too many targets in such a small space that the adversary's air and artillery attacks become highly effective, achieving multiple kills per pass or per volley. The influence of the latter two considerations varies with the quantity and quality of artillery and airpower available to the adversary. In 1944 and 1945 high Russian and German concentrations on the Eastern Front were apparently bothered little by these considerations. Attempted German concentrations on the Western Front were bothered a great deal.[83]

Although it is true that Soviet doctrinal literature called for very high offense-to-defense ratios in breakthrough sectors, on the order of 4–6:1 in tanks and artillery, the available evidence on how the Pact would

[83]See Russell F. Weigley, *Eisenhower's Lieutenants* (Bloomington, Ind., 1981), pp. 166, 198, 338, 342.

have set up breakthrough attacks cast doubt on its ability to have achieved such ratios easily. Such favorable ratios may have been achievable, but only on a few small 4–5 km segments of the front.[84] Thus, successful attacks in these sectors would have taken the form of narrow "wedges" driven into the NATO line. Whether or not these "wedges" produce a catastrophic failure of the defense line depends upon the defending division commander's ability to bring tactical reserves quickly to bear on the engagement. A NATO division commander would normally have had these reserves available, so the question may ultimately have been one of competent leadership. In the event that division commanders fail to respond with alacrity, the corps commander may still have the opportunity to contain the damage with operational reserves.

Figure 3.8 illustrates the kinds of major efforts the Soviets envisioned. A four-division Soviet or Pact army and some attached army and front artillery would have been tasked against a 50-km breakthrough sector, like that assumed in the model. Apparently, the Soviets planned to put two divisions forward and hold two in reserve. Other estimates suggest either slightly wider army sectors—three divisions forward, and only one in reserve—or a five-division army. For example, a more recent source, the 1984 army field manual 100-2-1, *Soviet Army Operations and Tactics*, expected a four-division army tasked for a major breakthrough to be deployed in a zone 60 km wide, with three divisions each on 20 km of front, and one in reserve.[85] Two often quoted, although unofficial, open-source discussions of Soviet ground operations echoed the 20 km/division figure.[86] To capture the full potential utility attributed to the divisions in reserve, the "Soviet" case factors this entire force into the

[84]See, e.g., the diagram in David Isby, *Weapons and Tactics of the Soviet Army* (London, 1988), p. 50, which shows a division on a 15-km front, compressing its breakthrough regiments down to zones of 5–8 km, and the regimental breakthrough efforts down to pairs of battalions concentrated on 1.5–2 km of front.

[85]U.S. Army, *The Soviet Army: Operations and Tactics*; the graphic on p. 4-4 shows a main axis of advance 60 km wide. "An army offensive normally has a frontage of 60–100 km wide" (p. 4-6). "When attacking with three regiments in a single echelon, a division zone of attack is normally 15–25 km wide" (p. 5-18). See also the diagram on p. 5-19. It should be noted here that the general tone of this source is somewhat tentative, and the various observations made are not all consistent. The source concedes that higher densities are possible but doubts that the Soviets want to do this.

[86]See Isby, *Weapons and Tactics of the Soviet Army* (1988), pp. 24–25, who suggests divisions on attack sectors of 20–40 km, with main efforts within these sectors 10–15 km wide; or John Erickson, Lynn Hansen, and William Schneider, *Soviet Ground Forces: An Operational Assessment* (Boulder, Colo., 1986), fig. 4.14, p. 166, suggesting divisional frontages of 20–30 km; p. 60, 15–30 km; p. 154, a *minimum* of 9 km; p. 164, a *minimum* of 14 km, etc. The same source suggests 65 km for armies (p. 60). Isby suggests army attack sectors 60–120 km wide and main efforts within these sectors 36–72 km wide, under conditions where nuclear or chemical use is *not* expected. Wider frontages and lower concentrations are suggested when the use of such weapons is expected.

Figure 3.8. Breakthrough attack deployments (tank units). Reproduced from U.S. Army field manual FM 71-100.

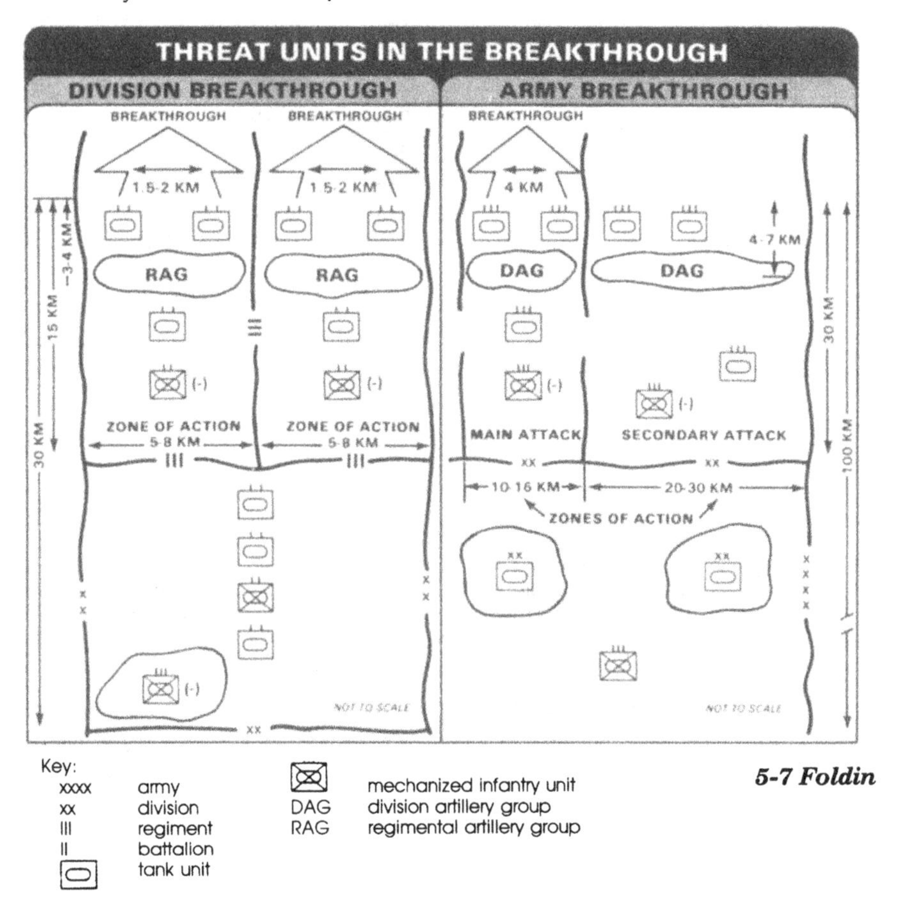

battle for every day of combat, roughly four ADEs on 50 km of front—the equivalent of four fully modernized Soviet tank divisions in the first echelon.

In the "NATO" case, the Pact is assumed to be slightly less successful at concentration than assumed above; it achieves only three ADEs in engaged combat power on any 50 km of front, the equivalent of three Soviet tank divisions fully engaged in the first echelon. This partially reflects the Soviets' apparent intention to hold a substantial part of its force in reserve. It also reflects the difficulty of managing such a high concentration of capabilities in such a small area.

For instance, during November of 1944, in its attempt to reach the

Roer River, the U.S. XIX Corps attempted a concentration similar to that assumed by the Soviet case. The commanders on the scene found their position to be very cramped, and it was necessary to withhold one-half of the armored division for several days until more space could be opened by the Corps' advance.[87] It is also worth remembering that this concentration was achieved under conditions of total air superiority and against an enemy that was short of ammunition and thus could afford little harassing artillery fire. Similar kinds of problems emerged elsewhere on the Western Front when the Allies attempted very high concentrations of forces, again in spite of the weakness of German air and artillery at this point in the war.[88]

NATO's ability to cover the front at densities that ought to permit an effective defense, coupled with real-world constraints on the ability of the Pact to concentrate large forces in small breakthrough sectors,

[87]Although one example is scarcely definitive, the XIX Corps' attempt to concentrate one armored and two infantry divisions plus fifteen-odd nondivisional artillery battalions on a 16-km front is instructive. These three divisions had, at minimum, 6500 vehicles of all types and probably more. Actual combat vehicles, however, probably added up to no more than 1500–2000, worth between one and one-and-a-half ADEs. Additionally, two infantry divisions and a cavalry group were waiting "in the wings" on the corps' left flank. The official history reports that the commanders found the situation extremely cramped. The 2nd Armored Division had to withhold half its strength from the battle for several days. This level of concentration is roughly consistent with that attributed to the Pact in the "Soviet" case, and thus one ADE per 12.5 km would seem a good theoretical maximum. On the XIX Corps assault, see Charles B. MacDonald, *The Siegfried Line Campaign* (Washington, D.C., 1963), pp. 516–544.

[88]At first glance, it appears that a higher force-to-space ratio was achieved by the British in their GOODWOOD offensive out of the Normandy perimeter. A close examination of the forces involved and the course of battle, however, suggests that the British were unable to commit their third division to the fray and were forced to engage their first two armored divisions sequentially. Once spread out and engaged, these two divisions (with roughly 1200 fighting vehicles, perhaps an ADE of combat power) took up about 12 km of front. See John Keegan, *Six Armies in Normandy* (New York, 1982), pp. 183–219, esp. p. 218. Following the narrative in Ellis, *The Battle of Normandy*, pp. 327–359, suggests that at any one time in the course of the battle, only two of the three divisions were engaged, although one engaged on the first day appears to have been pulled into reserve to be replaced by the 7th, which did not become heavily engaged on the first day. The two engaged divisions on each day may have together fought on a front as narrow as 8 km, suggesting a somewhat higher concentration than I inferred from the Keegan account when I first looked into this battle in 1984. At best, one can say that something close to an ADE was engaged on 8–12 km of front over a three-day period. Nevertheless, a high level of congestion was produced, in some places among the forward-deployed combat forces, and in other places among the support tail following behind, which appears to have held up the operation at key points. "While tanks of several regiments were milling about around the Cagny area, thousands of vehicles of the armoured divisions were crossing the river and canal and moving forward in the bridgehead. Descriptions of the resulting confusion provide unedifying reading and show that the carefully prepared traffic control plan was unable to ensure that approaches to the corridor were kept open" (p. 352). It is worth noting that the approaches suffered little from German heavy artillery or air attack. See pp. 490, 492.

suggests that the Pact would, at least initially, have had difficulty achieving high offensive-to-defensive force ratios either under assumptions rather favorable to the "Soviets" or those more favorable to "NATO."

Thus, in the "Soviet" case, a force ratio of 2:1 is produced in the breakthrough sectors. In the "NATO" case, assuming a 1.5 force multiplier, a ground-force ratio in real ADEs of 2.25:1 is produced, although in adjusted ADEs the capabilities ratio remains 1.5:1. For illustrative purposes NATO and Pact tacair should also be factored into the "NATO" case force ratio, however.[89] Using a very simple formula, one can convert NATO and Pact tacair into an ADE score and add them to the breakthrough sectors. This would produce a "real" force ratio on the order of 2:1. If this procedure was adopted for the adjusted ADE score in the "NATO" case, the ratio drops to 1.4:1. It is worth noting that none of these force-to-space ratios produce force-to-force ratios surpassing the 3:1 rule of thumb at which a defender has generally been thought to be capable of holding. Nevertheless, it should be understood that the Attrition-FEBA Expansion Model permits the Pact to push its breakthrough efforts in NATO's direction, at a specified movement rate, so long as the Pact has modest reserves of uncommitted forces available (see Appendix 3).

Attrition Rates

Attrition rates in the breakthrough sectors are a key variable in the Attrition-FEBA Expansion Model. The daily attrition rate that the Pact is willing to suffer ultimately is a key determinant of NATO's daily ground-force needs. Varying the attrition rate is a way of representing how much Pact commanders and their troops are willing to suffer on a sustained basis. Additionally, it is a way of representing the effects of "friction" on the Pact offensive. How much can the attacker suffer, even if he wants to? I have chosen two values for the sustained breakthrough-sector attrition rate: 10 percent for the "Soviet" case and 7.5 percent for the "NATO" case.

[89]For purposes of aggregation, I simply treat these aircraft as tanks, since helicopters armed with antitank guided missiles and cannon-equipped aircraft are basically just very mobile direct-fire weapons. I multiply my average-sorties-per-day figure (see table 3.4) by the ADE system's defensive weighting for tanks (55). I multiply that by a weapons effectiveness factor to come up with a weighted value that can then be converted to an ADE score. As a function of the different kill rates that I assign the two CAS fleets, NATO's effectiveness score is 1 and the Pact's is 0.5. Sorties are scored, rather than aircraft, because relative battlefield presence is the output to be measured.

Table 3.5. Historical tank attrition rates (frontwide)

Engagement	Daily rate	Sufferer	Source
Battle of the Bulge, Army[a]	2%	U.S.	U.S.
First and Third Armies, 14 days, drive for the Roer River	1%	U.S.	U.S. Army[b]
First Army, 30 days, Dec. 1944, all Europe	0.75%	U.S.	U.S. Army[c]
Yom Kippur War 20 days, one-half reparable	2%	Israel	Author's estimate[d]
Yom Kippur War	3%	Arabs	Author's estimate

Note: These are somewhat crude measurements. Generally, I have taken total tank losses for a given battle, prorated them on a daily basis over the duration of the battle, and divided by the total number of vehicles engaged at *any* time over the duration of the battle. Thus, they probably understate the attrition suffered by forces that actually engaged the enemy.

[a]Hugh Cole, *The Ardennes: Battle of the Bulge* (Washington, D.C., 1965), p. 664.

[b]Charles B. MacDonald, *The Siegfried Line Campaign* (Washington, D.C., 1963), p. 594.

[c]Roland Ruppenthal, *Logistical Support of the Armies*, Vol. 2 (Washington, D.C., 1959), p. 235.

[d]These estimates are based on Trevor N. Dupuy, *Elusive Victory: The Arab-Israeli Wars, 1947–1948* (New York, 1978), p. 609; Shlomo Gazit, "Arab Forces Two Years after the Yom Kippur War," in *Military Aspects of the Israeli-Arab Conflict*, ed. Louis Williams (Tel Aviv, 1975), pp. 188, 194.

Tank attrition rates provide a useful starting point for estimating overall ADE attrition rates. Tanks make up one-half of the ADE score for NATO divisions and one-half or more for Pact divisions. Tank attrition tends to be heavier than armored infantry fighting vehicles and artillery, since tanks are customarily sent into the most dangerous places. Four sources of data for sustained, frontwide tank attrition from real wars are shown in table 3.5.

Since these attrition rates are highly aggregated, they can function only as a rough check for the attrition rates assigned in the breakthrough sectors in the Attrition-FEBA Expansion Model. A 10-percent attrition in ADEs to Soviet forces in breakthrough sectors would amount to 1.2 ADEs lost per day, assuming that forces in the breakthrough were concentrated 1 ADE per 12.5 km, and three 50-km breakthroughs were attempted. Given that the Pact would be required to populate the rest of 600 km of the inter-German border at a 1 ADE per 25 km, a total of 36 ADEs would be engaged, yielding a daily attrition rate across the front of 3.3 percent. For NATO, at a 1.5:1 exchange rate, 0.8 ADEs would be needed to exact this Pact attrition. NATO would have 1 ADE per 25 km holding the front, for a total of 30 ADEs. Thus NATO's attrition rate on day 1 would be 2.7 percent. Thus 10 percent attrition per day in breakthrough sectors produces overall attrition in the neighborhood of my admittedly small historical sample. Nevertheless, the sample is drawn from episodes of rather intense combat sustained over a period of days.

Interestingly, a U.S. Army reserve officer, Col. Daniel Gans, has offered estimates of tank attrition in a hypothetical NATO–Pact war. Interpreting from graphs he presented, I estimate Pact attrition at 3.3 percent between D+12–32, and NATO at 2.77 percent for the same period, consistent with my estimate above.[90]

It would be useful to have some estimated attrition rates relevant to particular intense battles. Several Pentagon experts on armored vehicle attrition were skeptical that attackers would accept sustained 10 percent attrition in breakthrough sectors. Maximum breakthrough sector attrition rates in the 10 percent range are not out of line with some assumptions that have been employed in the professional military and analytic community. For example, a U.S. Army field manual from 1973, *Maneuver Control*, a guide for umpires of exercises and war games, instructs that "division casualties caused during the assault are assessed at a rate between 1 to 7 percent per day." In battalions and brigades on the offensive, "Nonnuclear casualties . . . seldom exceed 15% per day of severe combat."[91] These are *personnel* casualties, and the document is somewhat ambiguous as to whether the percentages quoted apply only to the troops directly in combat or to all the individuals associated with the unit. If the latter, given the large tail in U.S. battalions, brigades, and divisions, the actual damage to combat capability could be quite high. The document is more ambiguous an attrition to armored fighting vehicles—in one place suggesting that 10–20 percent attrition per hour for engagements of up to twenty tanks per side is plausible, and elsewhere suggesting that the loss of 40 percent of the tanks in a battalion would render the unit incapable of continuing its mission under almost all circumstances.[92] In spite of these ambiguities, the direction of the manual is clear—units in contact, for whatever reason, should not be expected either quickly to annihilate their opponents or willingly to suffer annihilation themselves. I have not encountered any subsequent field manuals that shed additional light on this issue.

James G. Taylor, a respected Military Operations Research specialist, offers some sample attrition estimates from the Atlas model expressed in terms of an aggregate firepower score. Atlas was apparently in use

[90]Gans, "Fight Outnumbered and Win," pp. 24–33, as cited by Anthony H. Cordesman, "The NATO Central Region and the Balance of Uncertainty," *Armed Forces Journal International*, July 1983, pp. 36–37.

[91]*Maneuver Control* (Washington, D.C., 1973), p. D-12.

[92]Ibid., pp. D-15, 20.

Table 3.6. Frontwide attrition rates

Case	Sufferer	Rate (%)	Unit of account
"Soviet" case	Pact	3.3	ADEs
"Soviet" case	NATO	2.7	ADEs
"NATO" case	Pact	1.2–1.7	ADEs
"NATO" case	NATO	0.5–0.6	Adjusted ADEs

in the U.S. defense community in the 1970s. Even under unfavorable conditions, an attacker-to-defender force ratio of 1:1, and a defender operating from fortified positions, the daily attrition rate of the attacking division's *firepower* was assessed at about 3.5 percent. This suggests a much lower value for breakthrough sector attrition than I have employed.

The "Soviet" case generates slightly higher frontwide attrition rates than those experienced by the Israelis or the Arabs in the 1973 war, which was viewed at the time as a very high-attrition war by historical standards. The "NATO"-favorable case employs assumptions that generate lower values to the "attacker" and the "defender" than those prevailing in the 1973 war. It seems plausible that, in the 1973 war, Arab and Israeli attrition rates were partly driven by the need for Middle East belligerents to achieve their military objectives with great speed, in order to beat the truce usually imposed by the superpowers. Neither NATO nor the Pact would be under quite so much political pressure. On the other hand, of course, weaponry has improved since that war, and some would argue that the Soviets would have pressed the pace of the war to defeat NATO conventionally before the coalition could make a decision to resort to nuclear escalation. The attrition suffered by the Alliance in the "NATO" case is a good deal lower than Gans's estimates, but it is not wildly at odds with U.S. Army experience across the front in December of 1944, while an intense battle raged in the Ardennes against a competent adversary.

Table 3.6 summarizes the range of frontwide attrition rates generated by the breakthrough rates employed in the "NATO" and "Soviet" cases in the Attrition-FEBA Expansion Model. The reader should remember that these are total loss figures—they are considered to be irreparable fighting machines. To make these figures comparable to the frontwide estimates developed above, one should include some notional estimate of attrition that each side might suffer in the "nonbreakthrough" portions of the front. I do not, however, know what this number should be, nor do I assign any value for it in my employment of the model. In the past I have used 1 percent as a plug number, for purposes of comparison, but I am no longer satisfied with that solution.

Exchange Rates

Exchange rates are an equally difficult problem to discuss. As noted earlier, given Pact superiority in numbers of weapons, NATO needed favorable exchange rates if it was not simply to be worn down into defeat. There seems to be general agreement, however, that the defender should enjoy favorable exchange rates. Table 3.7 represents a range of possible exchange rates derived from experience and from the judgments of professional defense analysts.

None of these values can be taken as definitive. Factors of troop quality, leadership, terrain, and terrain preparation would all figure in determining the exchange rate of an actual battle. Nevertheless, consistent with the view that Soviet doctrine is superior to NATO's and the view that offense is somehow a "better" posture than defense implicit in that doctrine, a relatively gentle 1.5:1 exchange rate is imposed on the Soviets in the "Soviet" case. This still assumes some advantage for the tactical defender, although not very much.

The "NATO" case assumes a more favorable exchange rate, 2:1. This is still much less than the Israelis enjoyed in 1973 and much less than many professional estimates available.

Advance Rates

Advance rates during breakthrough operations have also not received a thorough public discussion, although one analyst has compared historical advance rates after breakthroughs have occurred, that is, during exploitations, with those found in published Soviet writing. Perhaps the most definitive conclusion that can be gleaned from a quick historical survey is that sustained advances of 15–20 km per day are possible against a disorganized, erratic, and uncoordinated defense—in short, against an enemy already in retreat.[93] This estimate, however, is in sharp contrast to the 100 km or more per day found in some Soviet

[93]Jeffrey Record's dated, but still useful, examination of historical armored advance rates notes that some Soviet guidelines call for sustained advances of over 100 km per day. "Armored Advance Rates: A Historical Inquiry," *Military Review* 53 (September 1973): 63. For advance rates against scattered opposition, see pp. 65–66.

Table 3.7. Exchange rates

Example, Exchange rate, Source, Comments

ARAB-ISRAELI, 3:1, Author's estimate,[a] 1973 war, tanks, Israel outnumbered 2:1, Israel on both defense and offense

SYRIA-ISRAEL, 4.5:1, Author's estimate,[b] Golan Heights, 1973, tanks, first five days, Israel outnumbered by at least 3:1 for much of the fighting, Israel mainly on defense.

OFFENSE-DEFENSE, 2:1, U.S. Army, 1973 Field Manual,[c] tanks, offense outnumbers defense by 2:1. Exchange rate worsens as force ratio surpasses 2:1.

OFFENSE-DEFENSE, 2:1, National Defense HQ, Canada,[d] Iron Viper VIII War Games 1983, fighting vehicles, and other major weapons, combined arms.

OFFENSE-DEFENSE, 3:1 or better,[e] interviews and discussions with other defense analysts familiar with high-resolution models that attempt to simulate small-unit engagements.

OFFENSE-DEFENSE, 4–6:1, James F. Dunnigan,[f] antitank weapons against a combined arms assault, estimate derived from historical experience.

PACT–NATO, 3.2:1, Anthony Cordesman,[g] tanks, Pact outnumbers NATO 2.7:1, theater-wide.

[a]These estimates are based on Trevor N. Dupuy, *Elusive Victory: The Arab-Israeli Wars, 1947–1948* (New York, 1978), p. 609; Shlomo Gazit, "Arab Forces Two Years after the Yom Kippur War," in *Military Aspects of the Israeli-Arab Conflict*, ed. Louis Williams (Tel Aviv, 1975), pp. 188, 194.

[b]This estimate is based on Dupuy, *Elusive Victory*, pp. 437–461; and Chaim Herzog, *The War of Atonement: October 1973* (Boston, 1975), pp. 55–127. Both accounts agree that, by the end of the fourth day of combat, the two Israeli armored brigades that had withstood the initial Syrian attacks were left with fewer than two dozen operable tanks. This would imply that roughly 200 tanks had suffered enough damage to be viewed as casualties. Not all of these were seriously damaged, and some tanks from reinforcing brigades were also casualties, but 200 seems a good rough estimate of losses for this phase of the battle. Herzog reports that, for one reason or another, the Syrians left nearly 900 tanks on the Golan Heights in their retreat. Some of these had been abandoned in operable condition (p. 127). Thus, a 4.5:1 exchange rate for this phase of the battle would seem a fair estimate.

[c]U.S. Army, *Maneuver Control* (Washington, D.C., 1973), p. D-15. In 1976 a series of detailed studies conducted by the V Corps in Germany produced the conclusions that on the terrain to be defended the Soviets would require force ratios of 5:1 or greater to overcome a prepared defense. This implies that quite favorable offense-defense exchange rates were to be expected. See John L. Romjue, *From Active Defense to Airland Battle: The Development of Army Doctrine, 1973–1982*, TRADOC Historical Monograph Series (Ft. Monroe, Va., June 1984), pp. 23–24.

[d]Patrick Armstrong, "On Combined Arms," in *The Mechanized Battlefield*, ed. Lt.-Col. J. A. English (Washington, D.C., 1985), pp. 165–170.

[e]For a moderately accessible description of such a high-resolution simulation see Hans W. Hoffman, Reiner K. Huber, and Karl Steiger, "On Reactive Defense Options," in *Modeling and Analysis of Conventional Defense in Europe: Assessment and Improvement Options*, ed. Reiner K. Huber (New York, 1986). Unfortunately, the authors do not reveal the exchange rates achieved in their simulation, but they appear to have been very favorable to the defense in attacks by a Soviet motor rifle regiment against a German tank battalion cross-reinforced with infantry. James Thompson, *An Unfavorable Situation: NATO and the Conventional Balance* (Santa Monica, 1988), n. 13, p. 28, suggests that NATO exacts about a 2:1 exchange rate from the Pact in many excursions of the simulation employed by the Rand Strategic Assessment Center, including excursions where NATO loses.

[f]James F. Dunnigan, *How to Make War* (New York, 1982), pp. 39–40.

[g]Anthony H. Cordesman, "The NATO Central Region and the Balance of Uncertainty," *Armed Forces Journal International*, July 1983, pp. 36–37.

literature. Since the Attrition-FEBA Expansion Model tests NATO's ability to prevent breakthroughs during stressful assaults, the question is: What is a reasonable rate of advance for a determined breakthrough effort?

Jeffrey Record notes that during the breakthrough battle at Sedan in 1940, it took the German XIX Panzer Corps (First, Second, and Tenth Panzer divisions) some four days to crack the French defense line near Sedan for an average daily advance of about 6 km per day.[94] The "Soviet" case assumes a 5-km daily rate of advance. Such an assumption would be consistent with the hypothesis that a NATO–Pact quantitative and qualitative gap similar to that which existed between the best-armed and best-trained mechanized formations of the German army and a mixed bag of largely unmechanized, active and reserve, French infantry divisions would have prevailed in the breakthrough sectors in a war that occurred in the 1980s. This would seem a pessimistic assessment of the quality and quantity of NATO's military forces.[95]

An examination of the Cobra operation, the U.S. breakout of the Normandy beachhead in July 1944, tells a similar story. There is not much question that the German defenses in the critical VII Corps sectors were virtually eliminated in the first day of fighting. Nevertheless, the average rate of advance over the seven days of the operation was not much above 7 km per day, although individual units did better under some circumstances. The rate of advance across the 50-odd km of U.S. front was quite similar. The United States enjoyed massive superiority in men, materiel, munitions, and near complete air dominance. U.S. forces were held up by a mixture of German delaying tactics, their own bomb and shell damage to the roads, road congestion caused by their own vehicles, all combined with admittedly difficult terrain covered by a sparse road net.[96] Given these examples, and a relatively dense defense of the front by mechanized forces and some surviving air and

[94]Ibid., p. 64.

[95]An assumption that I suspect drives many professional military analyses to generate much faster movement rates for the Pact is that NATO's reserves will frequently be miscommitted and will remain miscommitted for extended periods. Models that automatically relate defense force density and offense:defense force ratio to movement will thus show accelerating movement and ultimately rupture in breakthrough sectors, since NATO's reserves are somewhere else. In breakthrough sectors under intense attack, the defender's force-to-space ratio thins, and because the attacker reinforces success, the force-to-force ratio increases. Thus movement rapidly accelerates. This strikes me as a sophisticated way of making an unsophisticated point. If NATO's commanders are comprehensively and stubbornly incompetent, they will lose the war.

[96]In the pursuit across France against a broken adversary the pace picked up considerably, but even there the high rate of 18–23 miles (29–37 km) a day was achieved for a brief eleven-day period September 1–11, 1944. MacDonald, *The Siegfried Line Campaign*, p. 4.

artillery capability, I find it unreasonable to assign the Soviets high rates of advance in breakthrough sectors.

The "NATO" case makes movement rate assumptions more consistent with the tougher defensive actions of World War II. The U.S. First and Ninth Armies' efforts to reach the Roer River, after the Siegfried Line had been partially breached, may be taken as representative of such actions. The area opposite the Ninth Army's XIX Corps was rolling, open country dotted with small villages. The Germans had taken three weeks to prepare the area with earthworks and belts of mines. This sector would be similar to the more topographically attractive breakthrough sectors along the inter-German border. Since the "Soviet" case assumes that at least a month would have been required for the Pact to train and move forward the Category II divisions needed to support a big attack, NATO would have had as much time to prepare the terrain for defense as the Germans did. Although the Allies enjoyed complete air superiority, reasonably good (though not great) flying weather, outnumbered the Germans by at least 5:1, and had a very high offensive force-to-space ratio, the advance rate for the XIX Corps was barely 1 km per day, for a three-week period.[97] Low rates of advance also prevailed in the First Army sectors, especially in the highly defensible Hurtgen forest. Similarly, low advance rates and high attrition rates were experienced by the U.S. and British forces in their efforts to break out of the Normandy bridgehead in early to mid-July 1944.[98]

[97]Ibid., pp. 397, 409–410, 520, 577, maps VII and VIII.

[98]Martin Blumenson, *Breakout and Pursuit* (Washington, D.C., 1961), pp. 175–176, 194. Extrapolation from past military engagements to possible battles between NATO and the Warsaw Pact is an exercise that requires much care. In general, I have chosen to examine recent battles in the Middle East and World War II battles on the Western Front because both involve most of the same basic kinds of ground and air forces that would be employed in a NATO-Pact war.

The Arab-Israeli wars are especially interesting because the belligerents employ virtually the same weapons and much of the same tactics and organization as are found in Central Europe today. One must, of course, be sure to account for the great qualitative disparity that seems to prevail between Israeli officers and enlisted men and those of that country's Arab adversaries. An even greater disparity of this kind prevailed between the U.S. and Iraqi militaries in Operation Desert Storm, which will complicate the derivation of lessons relevant to more comparable combatants.

Careful study of World War II battles in Western Europe between Anglo-American forces and those of Germany offers somewhat different advantages and disadvantages. Clearly, the equipment was much more primitive than that which we field today, but all the basic elements of current military forces were present. Combat in Europe in 1944 occurred on nearly as large a scale as would prevail today. By 1944, as a function of the casualties that Germany had suffered and the experience that the British and Americans had accrued, the qualitative disparity between the officers and enlisted men of the German Army and those of the Allies was probably the smallest that has prevailed between mechanized armies anywhere. Historians do seem to agree, however, that the Germans still enjoyed a meaningful degree of superior military leadership. Much of the terrain

Despite these historical examples where substantial quantitative superiority produced little forward movement, the Soviets are given credit in the "NATO" case for a sustained 2-km rate of advance in all three breakthrough sectors—this with a real force ratio, including tacair, below 2:1, and an adjusted force ratio below 1.5:1. Both of these ratios are in stark contrast to the 3:1 offense-defense superiority traditionally cited as acceptable to the defense, the 4–6:1 ratio that I have encountered among experts, and the 5:1 force ratios that U.S. and British forces usually needed to dislodge the Germans in World War II. Thus, although more favorable to NATO than the 5-km advance rate employed in the "Soviet" case, a sustained forward movement rate of 2 km per day in all three breakthrough sectors is still a conservative factor.

Lessons from the Model

In sum, using standard military judgments and historical analogies, it is possible to estimate some plausible alternative values for the seven variables discussed here. Each of these variables is, for a variety of reasons, very difficult to gauge with confidence. The analysis above describes one possible way of using these variables to model an assessment of the Warsaw Pact conventional threat to Europe. For both the "NATO favorable" and "Pact favorable" cases, I performed some sensitivity analysis, which is displayed in Appendix 3 along with the explanation of how the model works. The only "big surprise" in the sensitivity analysis is the degree of pessimism required in the assumptions about combat values needed to produce discouraging results for NATO under the "favorable" mobilization assumptions.

Using these explicit judgments for the reasons explained in the preceding sections, what do we learn about the NATO–Warsaw Pact balance during the period in question?

Figure 3.6 and 3.9 portray the results of applying "Pact" and "NATO" military doctrines respectively to assessment of NATO's ability to cope with a conflict in the Central Region in the 1980s. Figures 3.6 and 3.7 illustrate the application of Soviet doctrine and are broadly consistent with the pessimistic assessments of the balance then popular. The figure shows the rapid development of a rather dangerous situation for

---

fought over in 1944 is quite similar to that along the inter-German border. In gross terms, the Allies enjoyed a substantial material superiority over the Germans, which far exceeded the level of superiority attributed to the Pact in the 1980s. Thus, it is my judgment that German defensive successes against the Allies are quite relevant to assessing the course of conflict between NATO and Warsaw Pact.

Figure 3.9. NATO success (Pact training delay/defensive advantage)

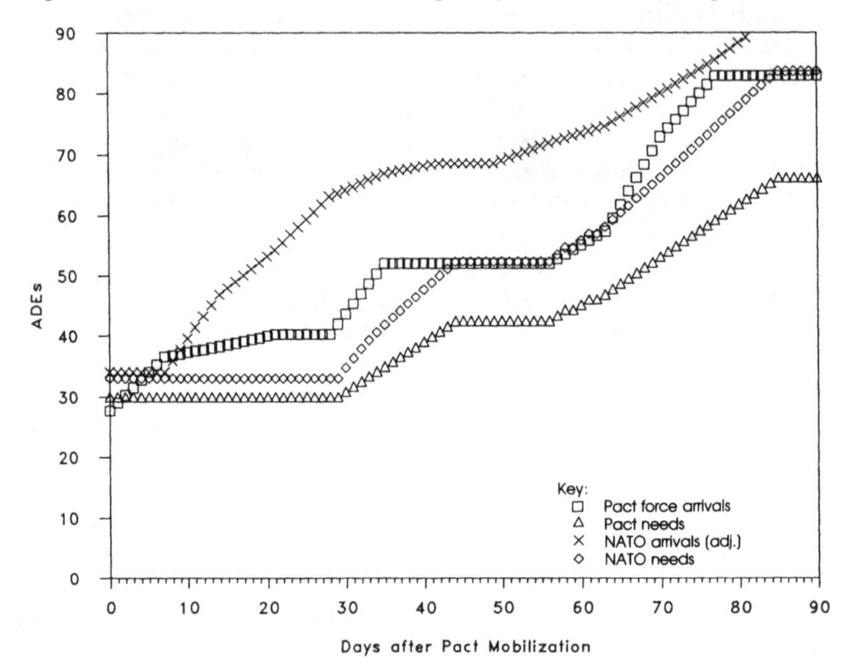

Combat assumptions: 3 Pact breakthrough efforts, 50 km wide; 3 Pact ADEs engaged in each effort; Pact accepts 7.5%/day; NATO extracts 2:1 exchange rate; each spearhead penetrates 2 km/day; 1470 Pact CAS aircraft and helicopters, 5% attrition and .35 kill per sortie, 1 sortie/day; 1630 NATO CAS aircraft and helicopters, 5% attrition and .5 kill per sortie, 2 sorties/day.

NATO, one that would ultimately have led either to the loss of Germany or to nuclear escalation. The Pact manages to move its low-readiness Category II and III divisions to the battle area in short order. They are assigned full credit for their assigned weaponry, without reference to combat readiness or supportability. I do assume, however (as did NATO planners), that the Pact would have needed at least two full weeks to ready itself for an attack of this magnitude. NATO mobilizes seven days after the Pact and receives no credit for the larger command and support apparatus with which it managed, maintained, and supplied its combat equipment. The Pact concentrates large forces and imposes a sustained, violent battle in the key breakthrough sectors, effectively neutralizes NATO tactical air capabilities, and prevents NATO from achieving a particularly favorable exchange rate. Addition-

Figure 3.10. NATO and Pact attrition: NATO success

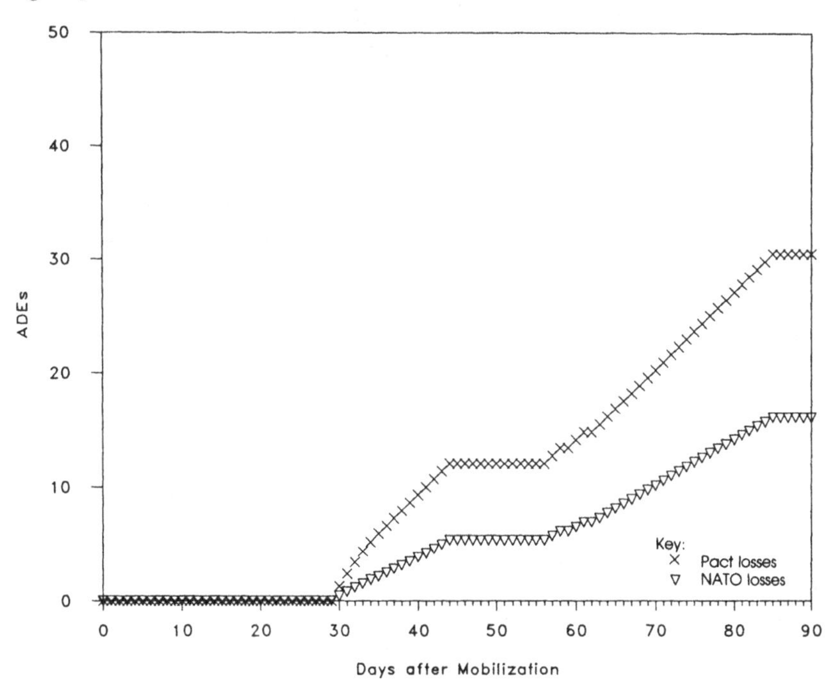

ally, the Pact achieves fairly high rates of advance in the breakthrough sectors.

Under these circumstances, after two weeks of combat NATO finds itself trying to hold 45-km sectors with each remaining ADE of firepower.[99] The Pact, on the other hand, still has enough forces left to populate the whole front and the flanks of each salient at 1 ADE per 25 km and has two ADEs per 25 km poised for a fresh effort in each breakthrough sector. Given this situation, facing 4:1 local force ratios in three breakthrough sectors, NATO is clearly in trouble. Either it will have already ordered a general withdrawal to shorten the total defense line (that is, eliminate the shoulders of the major penetrations), or it will have suffered, or be on the verge of suffering, a breach in the line. Such a breach could produce disruptive, deep blitzkrieg-style penetra-

[99]This is in sharp contrast to the 25 km per ADE that some analysts view as a conservative average strength that NATO should try to achieve along the Central Front. See, for example, Mako, *US Ground Forces,* p. 37, based on his interview with analysts in the Office of the Secretary of Defense.

tions into NATO's rear areas. More conservatively, the Pact could aim for envelopments of major NATO formations and their subsequent annihilation. In either case, NATO would face disaster. Thus, NATO would likely opt for early withdrawal across the front, allowing a general Pact advance that could ultimately result in the loss of Germany. As such a process unfolded, some NATO military leaders would no doubt request authorization for the use of nuclear weapons.

Figure 3.9 illustrates a very different outcome. In my view, this is a more accurate portrayal of the pattern of conflict than the preceding case. Here, as a consequence of the relative unreadiness of Pact Category II and III divisions, and as a function of taking some credit for NATO's efforts in the areas of command and support (that is, NATO's ADE score is multiplied by 1.5 in order to represent the increased effectiveness that should have resulted from greater efforts in these areas), the overall capabilities ratio over time looks very different from what the conventional wisdom would suggest. Figure 3.9 illustrates NATO's mobilized capabilities with the adjustment for command, control, and logistics. It also credits NATO's tactical aircraft with markedly greater success against Pact ground forces than Pact aircraft enjoy against NATO's ground forces. As a reflection of available information on Pact intentions and historical experience, the Pact is credited with a lower offensive concentration in the breakthrough sectors. A more favorable exchange rate, reflecting the advantages often credited to the defense by military planners and commentators, is also assumed. Consistent with all of the preceding assumptions, and with a good deal of American and British experience fighting the Germans in World War II, a slower advance rate in the breakthrough sectors is factored into the model.

With these assumptions, NATO appears capable of coping successfully with Pact efforts to achieve catastrophic breakthroughs. The Pact is capable of mounting a good-sized attack at M+30, which it could sustain for roughly two weeks before it would find itself short of reserves. NATO's mobilization lags the Pact's by seven days, but the Alliance would possess sufficient reserves to cope with the Pact advance without having to initiate a general withdrawal. The Pact would resume the offensive two weeks later once its Category III divisions were ready for action, but NATO forces would still be strong enough to deal with the penetrations without resorting to a general withdrawal. As a result, NATO should not be particularly vulnerable to a major rupture of the line. In this second phase of the battle, as a function of unreplaced aircraft attrition, NATO ground forces would have to work harder and take more casualties than they did in the first phase of the battle. This assumption is somewhat favorable to the Pact, because, as I argue in Appendix 2, NATO seems to have greater reserves of dedicated fixed- and rotary-wing CAS aircraft than does the Pact. Both the Pact and NATO would begin running short of forces to sustain this pace of battle after three weeks, and it seems likely that a period of reduced activity would set in. Finally, the outcome portrayed here is constrained by the limitations of the model, since NATO's reserves in some phases of the battle would probably allow it to counterattack successfully and thus hold the Pact to an even slower rate of advance than that assumed. Similarly, the "surplus" of NATO's available forces over its needs for most of the battle suggests that, even if the Pact somehow managed to convert one of its salients into a clean breakthrough, NATO would have operational reserves to throw against the Pact's exploitation effort. Several uncommitted ADEs would remain to NATO until the last week of heavy fighting, when the Pact itself would begin to run short of forces.

Conclusion

Figures 3.6 and 3.9 portray the very different implications for NATO in the Central Region that arise from a comprehensive application of assumptions consistent with Pact and NATO doctrine, respectively, to balance assessment. If assumptions consistent with the notion that most of the Pact's allocation decisions are right and most of NATO's are wrong are factored into a balance assessment, one can produce a very pessimistic portrayal of the force ratio over time. When these are combined with assumptions about the course of combat that are favorable to Pact doctrine, NATO's prospects for successful defense look bleak.

If, however, assumptions consistent with NATO's pattern of resource allocation are factored into an assessment of each side's ability to mobilize military capabilities and combined with a recognition of the constraints that would govern the employment of Pact forces, a conservative application of military rules of thumb, and some inferences from western military experience, NATO's prospects appear quite good.

Under relatively conservative assumptions, NATO's forces appear adequate to prevent the Pact from making a clean armored breakthrough. The ground forces of the Alliance seem large enough to hold the Pact to breakthrough-sector force ratios that are much lower than those that soldiers and military commentators have thought necessary to produce success. If the Pact is given credit for an ability to make

NATO withdraw at a slow pace that is consistent with the low force ratio, and Pact units are forced to pay a relatively modest price to do so (that is, a two-to-one exchange rate), NATO still appears capable of containing the penetrations and preventing breakthroughs. Moreover, as was noted earlier, NATO still would have sizable uncommitted reserves for much of the battle, which could counterattack a successful breakthrough if it occurred.

The analysis performed with the Attrition-FEBA Expansion Model thus suggests that NATO's conventional forces were quite competitive with those of the Warsaw Pact in the 1980s. It is likely that, had a war occurred during this period, early nuclear escalation would not have been forced on the West as a result of the collapse of NATO's ground forces in the Central Region. Other modes of nuclear escalation, largely unconsidered, were also possible. In the preceding chapter I discussed how NATO's tactical air operations could have created incentives for the Soviets to consider the employment of nuclear weapons. In the next chapter I discuss how U.S. naval operations could have produced such pressures.

[4]

Escalation and NATO's Northern Flank

The danger of inadvertent escalation in the 1980s arose with particular acuteness on NATO's northern flank, especially in the region comprising the Norwegian and Barents seas, northern Norway, and the Kola Peninsula in the Soviet Union. Moreover, as East-West relations improved in the late 1980s, the naval competition received less attention from senior political leadership than did the strategic nuclear competition, and the NATO–Pact ground and air conventional force relationship. Thus, the issues raised in this chapter are likely to remain important for some time.

In northern Norway NATO territory and NATO conventional capabilities are situated near a critical element of Soviet strategic nuclear power—the ballistic missile submarine force based in the Murmansk area in Kola. Conventional military operations in the region could have put this force at risk. They would also have jeopardized important segments of the Soviet early warning system for the detection of strategic nuclear attacks from missiles and aircraft. The U.S. Navy argued for early attacks against the submarines, surface vessels, and land-based support structure of the Soviet Northern Fleet based in the Kola Peninsula.[1] If such attacks had diminished Soviet confidence in their ability

[1]U.S. Congress, Congressional Budget Office, *Building a 600-Ship Navy: Costs, Timing and Alternative Approaches*, prepared by Peter T. Tarpgaard (Washington, D.C., March 1982), pp. xi–xii, xxiii, 17; Richard Halloran, "Reagan Selling Navy Budget"; John Lehman, Secretary of the Navy, "America's Growing Need for Seaborne Air Bases" (letter), *Wall Street Journal*, 30 March 1982; and U.S. Department of Defense, Annual Report, FY 1983, pp. I-15–16, 30, III–19, 21. The secretary remarks on how to deal with Soviet aircraft dedicated to antishipping missions: "Our preferred approach is to destroy enemy bombers before they can reach ASCM [air-to-surface cruise missile] launch range by striking their bases or destroying them in transit" and that "We are also studying the use of long-range strategic bombers to attack Soviet surface ships and naval targets ashore" (p. III-21). Soviet bombers are normally based in the Soviet Union. Both Secretary of Defense

to retaliate after a U.S. attack and increased their concerns that the United States might strike first, how would Soviet decision makers have reacted? They might have concluded that the employment of nuclear weapons against NATO naval assets afloat or ashore was a necessary countermeasure.

The Northern Flank: Interests and Capabilities

The possibility of inadvertent escalation in the northern flank derived primarily from the combination of the geography of the region and the character of the military forces deployed there. The key problem from the Soviet perspective was and remains that Soviet naval forces must pass through geographic "choke points" to reach open water from virtually all of their principal ports. Western antisubmarine warfare (ASW) sensors monitored these relatively narrow passages to detect the passage of the somewhat noisy Soviet submarines.[2] This constituted a particular liability for ballistic missile submarines (SSBNs) trying to reach open water undetected.

Consequently, the Soviet Union deployed most of its strategic missile submarines in the Barents Sea, adjacent to the Kola Peninsula and the major Soviet Navy base at Murmansk. Roughly two-thirds of Soviet SSBNs, protected by roughly two-thirds of their nuclear attack submarines (SSNs) and probably the best quarter of their remaining naval surface combatants, diesel submarines, and naval aviation capabilities, were based in Kola.[3] Rear Adm. John L. Butts, former U.S. Navy director of naval intelligence, stated, "The primary task is to deploy and protect the SSBN force."[4] His successor, Rear Adm. William O. Stude-

---

Weinberger and Chairman of the Joint Chiefs of Staff Admiral Crowe affirmed in congressional testimony in 1986 the U.S. intention to sink Soviet SSBNs in a conventional war. See George Wilson and Michael Weisskopf, "Pentagon Plan Coldly Received," *Washington Post*, 2 February 1986, p. A14.

[2]The bulk of the Soviet 1980s nuclear submarine force was relatively noisy. The newest boats such as the Typhoon SSBN and the Victor III, Akula, and Sierra class SSNs, etc., tend to be much quieter. Adm. Wesley McDonald, then SACLANT, wrote in 1984 that the Typhoon "is the quietest submarine they have ever built." See "The Growing Warsaw Pact Threat to NATO Maritime Forces," *NATO Review* 32 (1984): 3–8, esp. p. 5.

[3]On the strength and distribution of the Soviet SSBN force see, U.S. Department of Defense, Soviet Military Power, 1988, p. 48. On the distribution of Soviet naval assets, see Johan J. Holst, "Norway's Search for a Nordpolitik," *Foreign Affairs* 60 (Fall 1981): 66.

[4]U.S. Congress, Senate, Committee on Armed Services, Subcommittee on Sea Power and Force Projection, *DOD Authorization for Appropriations for Fiscal Year 1986, Testimony of John L. Butts . . . Part 8*, 99th Cong., 1st sess., 1985 (Washington, D.C., 1985), pp. 4367–4368. Hereafter, *SASC FY 86, Pt. 8*. The admiral speaks at length to this question, stating that the Soviet Navy has "two overarching, complementary missions to perform initially. The primary task is to deploy and protect the SSBN force. They believe that SLBMs (submarine-launched ballistic missiles), for the first time, give navies the capability to

man, reiterated this theme in 1988, noting that "Soviet SSNs, surface combatants, and antisubmarine warfare (ASW) aircraft provide echeloned defense in-depth in approaches to primary SSBN wartime operating areas (bastions)."[5] The Soviet Navy apparently decided to establish a defended wartime "sanctuary" in northern waters, especially in the Barents Sea, for SSBNs carrying long-range ballistic missiles.[6] However, its older Yankee-class SSBNs (with shorter range missiles), as well as Soviet attack submarines that might have tried to attack the Atlantic sea lines of communication (SLOC), would have had to transit the narrow passages of the North Cape–Bear Island gap (off the northern tip of Norway) and the better-known Greenland–Iceland–United Kingdom gap (GIUK), both of which would have been heavily defended by NATO forces.[7]

NATO deployed extensive naval capabilities in this area in order to protect its Atlantic SLOC (which runs south of the GIUK gap). To do so, it would have sought to bottle up and destroy Soviet naval forces (particularly submarines) in the Barents and Norwegian seas. Failing that, NATO wished to harry their southward passage to the Atlantic, exacting as high a toll as possible. NATO placed four defensive barriers between the Soviet Navy and the SLOC, including forces in the North Cape gap and the GIUK gap, ASW hunter-killer groups, and finally each convoy's own escorts.

Aside from SLOC protection, NATO would presumably also have liked to monitor the small number of Soviet SSBNs forward deployed in the Atlantic. Indeed, it is quite likely that major efforts would have

---

directly affect the course and even the outcome of the war. Because of the importance they ascribe to the SSBN force, the Soviets plan to support and protect it through an echeloned defense in depth. We believe that [deleted] would be committed initially to this mission and the overlapping task of defending the USSR and its allies from strikes by enemy sea based nuclear weapons. To accomplish these tasks, the Soviets would attempt to control all or large portions of the Norwegian and Greenland Seas and the waters to the north as well as the Sea of Japan and Okhotsk and the area off the Kamchatka Peninsula. They would also conduct sea denial operations farther to sea—about [deleted] from the Soviet homeland." Elsewhere in the testimony he states, "The primary purpose of the Soviets is on [deleted] their ballistic missile submarine force" (p. 4345). This theme pervades the admiral's entire discussion of the Soviet Navy (pp. 4344–4367).

[5]U.S. Congress, House, House Armed Services Committee on Intelligence Issues, Seapower and Strategic and Critical Materials Subcommittee, *Statement of Rear Admiral William O. Studeman*, 100th Cong., 2d sess., 1 March 1988 (mimeo). Hereafter *Statement of Studeman*.

[6]Ibid. See also Michael MccGwire, "The Rationale for the Development of Soviet Seapower," *U.S. Naval Institute Proceedings* 106 (May 1980): 155–183.

[7]Technically, the barrier actually includes the waters between Greenland, Iceland, the United Kingdom, and Norway. The term "GIN gap"—Greenland, Iceland, Norway—was briefly popular. Both terms refer to the same barrier, and I prefer the more traditional GIUK.

been made to destroy these Soviet SSBNs early in any East-West conventional conflict. Because of the short time of flight of their missiles, they posed a serious threat to U.S. strategic nuclear command and control if employed as the lead elements of a Soviet preemptive attack.[8] It is implausible that U.S. planners would simply have accepted this particular threat during intense conventional fighting. Moreover, any additional SSBNs that attempted to run the Western barriers after war had broken out were likely to have been considered fair game.[9]

In Norway, NATO's day-to-day assets in the north do not appear formidable at first glance, but they are not insignificant and could have been perceived by the Soviet military as a threat to the Soviet Northern Fleet.[10] While Norway must be defended, a consideration of how the Soviets might have perceived Norwegian, and ultimately NATO, military deployments in this area can provide valuable clues to their wartime behavior. Norwegian air bases, for example, were well situated for conducting air strikes against the Kola Peninsula. Norwegian P-3B ASW

[8]See Blair, *Strategic Command and Control*, esp. chap. 6, pp. 182–211.

[9]The actual effectiveness of Western ASW forces was said to be high, but there were few unclassified detailed estimates of the rate at which NATO expected to destroy Soviet submarines on the barriers, and none of the rate at which they might have been destroyed in the Barents Sea. The barrier defense process is largely one of attrition, with each barrier taking a modest toll of Soviet submarine forces passing through. The only hard estimate of ASW effectiveness in a SLOC defense battle that the U.S. Navy ever permitted to leak into the open literature dates from the late 1970s and is discussed in Appendix 4. More recently, navy spokesmen simply offer general assertions to the effect that "ASW is a war of attrition. Given a capability it takes time, weeks or months, to detect and localize any significant portion of a submarine force." U.S. Congress, Senate, Committee on Armed Services, *DOD Authorization for Appropriations for Fiscal Year 1986, Overview and Status of Navy Strategic Submarine and SLBM Programs, Part 7*, 99th Cong., 1st sess., 1986 (Washington, D.C., 1986), p. 3882. It is the cumulative effect of the barriers on the Soviet force, going and coming, that eventually grinds it down to a state of comparative weakness. If NATO forces go looking for Soviet submarines in the Barents Sea, finding and killing them will be more difficult than waiting for the Soviet submarines to try running the barriers. This is because the sensors and C^3 in the barriers should be more effective than anything the West could take into the Barents, either on or under the surface. I consider these points in app. 2 to my chapter "Offensive and Defensive Sea Control," in Steven Miller and Charles Glaser, eds., *The Navy and Nuclear Weapons* (book manuscript in preparation).

[10]Details on the military situation in the northern flank are drawn from Edward Hooton, "Country Portrait Norway," *NATO's Sixteen Nations* 29 (December 1984–January 1985): 53–66, esp. the map on p. 57; "Soviets' Buildup in North Exceeds Protection Level," *Aviation Week and Space Technology*, 15 June 1981, pp. 101–107; "Norway Formulating Long-Range Defense Plans," *Aviation Week and Space Technology*, 6 July 1981, pp. 42–48; R. D. M. Furlong, "The Threat to Northern Europe," *International Defense Review*, 12 April 1979, pp. 517–525; R. D. M. Furlong, "The Strategic Situation in Northern Europe," *International Defense Review*, June 1979, pp. 899–910; Gen. John Sharp, "The Northern Flank," *RUSI Journal* 121 (December 1976): 10–16; and IISS, *Military Balance 1987–1988*. No non-Norwegian NATO forces were permanently based in the country in time of peace as a matter of national policy.

aircraft flew over the Barents Sea every day helping to monitor Soviet naval activity.[11] In addition, intelligence-gathering facilities located in northern Norway allowed NATO to plot the movements of Soviet aircraft, surface vessels, and submarines. An underwater-moored sonar array (SOSUS) southwest of the Bear Island gap allowed the Norwegians to monitor the movements of Soviet submarines in some parts of the Barents Sea.[12] Data from this network was probably collected near Tromso in northern Norway and then passed to the U.S. Navy. Land-based radar helped watch the activity of the Soviet Northern Fleet's air arm and would have encouraged it, in time of war, to fly time- and fuel-consuming evasive legs to avoid Norwegian or other NATO interceptors. Electronic intelligence-gathering facilities near the Soviet border and elsewhere in Norway monitored the communications of Northern Fleet headquarters.[13]

All of these activities and capabilities would have contributed to NATO's efforts to establish a "North Cape" barrier against Soviet air, surface, and subsurface forward deployments. These intelligence assets would have provided the West with substantial early warning of Soviet preparations for general war—conventional or nuclear. If war had broken out, they could, at least initially, have provided valuable tactical warning and tactical intelligence, although they would undoubtedly soon have come under Soviet attack. Information from these sources likely would have been provided to NATO naval forces present in the Norwegian Sea and in the GIUK, presumably increasing their effectiveness and thereby increasing the threat to the Soviet Navy.

The airbase structure and intelligence-gathering facilities in northern Norway could also have been construed by the Soviets to be (and could well have been) an offensive threat to Soviet control of the Barents Sea.[14] Northern Norway's military airfields (four or five) were within

[11]Maj. Gen. Magne T. Sorensen, "Maritime Air Operations in the North," *NATO's Sixteen Nations, Special Issue*, February 1984, pp. 61–65.

[12]Discussions of U.S. ASW capabilities herein are drawn largely from Posen, "Offensive vs. Defensive Sea Control," and its app. 2, in Miller and Glaser, eds., *Navy and Nuclear Weapons*. Readers will find the following short essays useful. Norman Friedman, "SOSUS and U.S. ASW Tactics," *US Naval Institute Proceedings* 106 (March 1980): 120–123; U.S. Congress, Foreign Affairs and National Defense Division, Congressional Research Service, "Arms Control Implications of Anti-Submarine Warfare Programs," *Evaluation of Fiscal Year 1979 Arms Control Impact Statements* (Washington, D.C., 1978), pp. 103–119; Joel S. Wit, "Advances in Antisubmarine Warfare," *Scientific American* 244 (February 1981): 31–41; and Mark Sakitt, *Submarine Warfare in the Arctic: Option or Illusion*, CISAC Occasional Paper (Stanford, Calif., May 1988.)

[13]Owen Wilkes and Nils Petter Gleditsch, *Intelligence Installations in Norway: Their Number, Location, Function, and Legality*, (Oslo, February 1979, revised July 1979).

[14]Nothing in this discussion should be construed as an argument that Norway ought not to be defended. It must be defended, but with care.

tactical fighter range of the Kola Peninsula and Barents Sea. The intelligence facilities would have revealed much about Soviet operations in the area. These facilities would have aided any NATO air, surface, subsurface, or combined offensive against the Northern Fleet and its bases.

Consequently, whether the Soviet Union wished to attack NATO's SLOC in the Atlantic or simply to protect its SSBN sanctuary in the Barents Sea, elimination of NATO capabilities in northern Norway would have been attractive. To do so, the Soviet armed forces would have had to deal with Norwegian forces and substantial NATO land, sea, and air reinforcements. The Soviets would probably have liked to eliminate the North Cape barrier through aerial bombardment, special operations, and naval attack, but this would not have given high confidence of destroying the bulk of NATO capabilities in the north. Invasion and occupation of northern Norway would have been necessary to assure the permanent removal of NATO forces. Moreover, Soviet planners themselves might have seen Norwegian bases to be useful both to defend the Barents sanctuary and to attack the Atlantic SLOC. This motivation alone could have prompted a Soviet attack on Norway, even if no Norwegian or other NATO forces were present in the northern part of the country.

It is worth noting, however, that the Soviet day-to-day capability to launch a combined-arms offensive against the north Norway base structure was not especially impressive. One plausible interpretation for this uncharacteristic Soviet restraint was a desire not to provoke a more imminent NATO threat to the bastion than already existed. For much of the Cold War, all the Soviets had to contend with on a daily basis was Norwegian forces, since Norway prohibited permanent foreign bases on its soil. If the Soviets had rapidly built up their ground, air-mobile, amphibious, and tactical air forces on the Kola Peninsula, Norway might have reconsidered this policy, with results highly deleterious to Soviet interests.

It is apparent, then, even from a general examination of the interests of the two superpowers in the northern flank and of the array of forces that each deployed there that a conventional clash between the two sides in this region would have mixed strategic and conventional forces in a potentially escalatory way. The risk of inadvertent nuclear escalation in the northern flank is revealed even more clearly, however, through an examination of the operational inclinations of the U.S. Navy during the 1980s, which intended to perform its missions in ways that were likely to exacerbate a delicate situation.

Northern Flank Scenarios

Under the rubric of the "National Maritime Strategy" the U.S. Navy publicly identified three possible northern flank military operations in the 1980s:[15]

(1) forward antisubmarine warfare operations by western nuclear-powered attack submarines (SSNs) in the Norwegian and possibly the Barents seas;
(2) offensive tactical air attacks in the same region to destroy the Soviet fleet and especially its *bases* in the Kola Peninsula, attacks that would have been conducted by a combination of conventional cruise missiles launched from forward-deployed SSNs and by the tactical aircraft of later-deploying carrier battle groups; and
(3) carrier battle-group operations to help defend northern Norway from a Soviet invasion.

In varying degrees, these plans contained inherent escalatory pressures.

Forward SSN Operations

Forward operations by U.S. SSNs into the Soviet bastions were justified on the basis of two conceptually distinct strategic objectives.[16] The principal and longest lived U.S. Navy justification for these operations was (and as of publication remains) that they would quickly bottle up all Soviet naval forces, in the best case leading to their rapid destruction, but at minimum diverting them to defensive tasks—especially the defense of the SSBN bastion. Soviet attack submarines were the main

[15]The clearest and most accessible official exposition of the maritime strategy is to be found in Adm. James D. Watkins (chief of naval operations of the U.S. Navy), "The Maritime Strategy," in U.S. Naval Institute, *The Maritime Strategy* (Annapolis, Md., January 1986), pp. 4–17. A very illuminating discussion can also be found in the testimony of Secretary of the Navy John Lehman, Admiral Watkins, and Lt. Gen. Bernard E. Trainor, USMC: U.S. Congress, Senate, Committee on Armed Services, Subcommittee on Sea Power and Force Projection, DOD Authorization for Appropriations for Fiscal Year 1985, Testimony of Secretary of the Navy, John Lehman . . . Part 8, 98th Cong., 2d sess., 1984 (Washington, D.C., 1984), pp. 3851–3900.

[16]John J. Mearsheimer, "A Strategic Misstep: The Maritime Strategy and Deterrence in Europe," *International Security* 11 (Fall 1986): 3–57, offers the most thorough analysis and critique of the maritime strategy. He identifies four distinct navy arguments for these offensive operations: defense of the SLOC through "offensive sea control," counterforce coercion, direct military impact on the ground war, and horizontal escalation to attack successfully some target that the Soviets might value as much as we value Western Europe. The first two arguments were more plausible and were (perhaps not incidentally) the ones most frequently employed and forcefully argued by the navy.

objects of this strategy, which was often termed "offensive sea control." But the threat to Soviet SSBNs was necessary to fix the attention of Soviet naval commanders on the defense of northern waters.

In 1986 James Watkins, then chief of naval operations, introduced as a second explicit goal of forward SSN operations influence over Soviet willingness to continue or expand a conventional war.[17] The systematic destruction of enough Soviet SSBNs to shift the strategic nuclear balance in favor of the United States was the principal means to this end. John Mearsheimer calls this "counterforce coercion."

Both the offensive sea control and counterforce-coercion strategies, however, depended critically on the destruction of at least some Soviet SSBNs, although the second demanded a higher level and rate of practical success than the first. Offensive sea control would have destroyed SSBNs as a means to the primary end of diverting Soviet naval assets to defensive missions. The diversion of these assets to defensive missions was identified as a very high priority by the navy, and thus the Soviets would have to have suffered some real losses.[18] SSBN destruction was *instrumental* to the basic conventional war mission of SLOC defense. Counterforce coercion would have made the destruction of Soviet SSBNs the primary end of the operation. Ideally, in the first case actual SSBN destruction need not be particularly thorough or extensive, so long as enough are destroyed to attract Soviet attention; in the second, it would need to be deliberate, systematic, and quite effective. In actual practice, however, given the great difficulties of hunting and killing all kinds of Soviet submarines, I suspect that *as a practical matter* the same procedures (military operations) would probably have attended the pursuit of either objective.

Offensive Sea Control. The U.S. Navy views the Soviet Northern Fleet, particularly its nuclear-powered and diesel-electric attack submarines, as the principal threat to the Atlantic SLOC. The navy was uncomfortable with NATO's traditional barrier strategy for interdicting any at-

[17]Watkins, "Maritime Strategy," pp. 4–17; see also Linton F. Brooks, "Naval Power and National Security: The Case for the Maritime Strategy," *International Security* 11 (Fall 1986): 58–88, esp. pp. 73–74.

[18]In the next chapter I argue that NATO's defensive and offensive capabilities could have reinforced each other in this period in support of a largely defensive strategy of sea control that nevertheless retained a counterattack capability. The combination of strong defenses and a potential to counterattack if challenged would have preserved an incentive for the Soviets to withhold assets for defense of the SSBN bastion without requiring initial attacks on Soviet SSBNs. See Mearsheimer, "A Strategic Misstep," pp. 42–43. The U.S. Navy had the assets to execute this more restrained strategy had war broken out in the 1980s, but there is little evidence that they conceived of the problem in this way.

tempted southward passage of these forces and argued for reliance mainly on offensive operations against the Northern Fleet to so occupy the Soviet Navy with defending itself as to preclude attacks on the SLOC.[19] Adm. Wesley McDonald, then SACLANT and responsible for defending the SLOC to Europe, declared that *"if (Soviet) offensive operations are allowed to break out into the broad Atlantic, many more forces may be required to defeat the threat, or the time to accomplish our tasks will be excessive."*[20]

To preclude this, in the words of Vice Adm. Nils R. Thunman, former deputy chief of naval operations for submarine warfare,

> The maritime strategy calls for the majority of our nuclear attack submarines, or SSNs, as we call them, to go forward immediately at the beginning of any hostilities with the Soviets to sink his fleet, bottle up his massive submarine force, and now with advent of the Tomahawk cruise missile, to attack his land bases.[21]

The strategy attempted to exploit the Soviet concern for the possible vulnerability of their ballistic missile submarine force, their "secure second-strike capability" in Western terminology, to U.S. SSNs. As explained above, the Soviets intended to allocate most of their forces to SSBN defense anyway. The navy tried to ensure that the Soviets would

[19]It is important to note that the maritime strategy has been in process of evolution in navy circles since the time of the Carter administration, although it emerged as an explicit strategy only under the Reagan administration. Prior to 1980, the navy discussed offensive operations in a manner that suggested they would complement the barrier/convoy defense strategy, which would nevertheless remain important and effective. In the mid to late 1980s, the navy treated the offensive strategy as the main vehicle for sea control, with barriers and convoy escorts available to deal mainly with any "leakage of Soviet forces southward in the North Atlantic." See the statement of Watkins: U.S. Congress, Senate, Committee on Armed Services, *DOD Authorization for Appropriations for Fiscal Year 1986, Presentation of Annual Posture Reports, Part 2*, 99th Cong., 1st sess., 1985 (Washington, D.C., 1985) p. 989. It remains to be seen what argument the navy will make in the 1990s, but as conventional arms control in Europe achieves huge reductions in Soviet ground forces, the explicit counter-SSBN mission may remain the best servant of the navy's organizational interests. On the other hand, public discussion of such an "offensive" mission may contradict the political spirit of the times, and be suppressed.

[20]U.S. Congress, Senate, Committee on Armed Services, *DOD Authorization for Appropriations for Fiscal Year 1985, Status of the Atlantic Command, Part 2*, 98th Cong., 2d sess., 1984 (Washington, D.C., 1984), pp. 1113–1114. In the same hearings Watkins stated, "In all but the shortest of conventional conflicts, containing the Soviet Navy in home waters and forcing the Soviet allocation of resources to protect against potential attacks in other than their preferred theater of operations, is the most effective method to maintain the SLOCS with our own ground and air forces and our allies. . . . A defensive stance for direct protection of SLOCs around the world is an alternative but inefficient strategy that would require much greater force levels than currently envisioned to execute our forward, offensively oriented strategy" (p. 921).

[21]*SASC FY 86, Pt. 8*, p. 4493.

not change their minds. Judging from statements of its leaders, the U.S. Navy believed that this could not be achieved by a contingent threat to break into Soviet bastions if the Russians were foolish enough to leave them undefended. Instead, the offensive had to start at the outset of the war. In the words of Watkins,

> We have to move up north of the GIUK (Greenland, Iceland, United Kingdom) gap. We have to control the Norwegian Sea and force them back into the defensive further north, under the ice, *to use their attack subs to protect their nuclear missile submarines, to use their attack subs to protect the Kola and the Murmansk coasts, and similarly their Pacific coast as well.* If we try to draw a "cordon sanitaire" and declare that we are not going to go above the GIUK gap or we are not going to go west of such and such a parallel, then obviously they have the capability to use their attack subs offensively against our SLOCS.[22]

Soviet concern for the long-term survival of the Northern Fleet SSBN force, their "second-strike capability" or "strategic reserve force," was the glue that held this strategy together. If the Soviets had no SSBNs in the Barents Sea, or if they perceived these forces to be unimportant, or if they perceived no threat to them, it would have been difficult to argue that huge Soviet submarine forces could have been tied down defending them.[23] Thus, direct threats to the Soviet SSBN force were an important element of offensive sea control. Some Soviet SSBNs had to be sunk if the strategy was to work as intended.

From the perspective of SLOC protection, there were two additional benefits to engaging Soviet attack submarines as far north as possible. First, many potentially threatening Soviet attack submarines could simply have been destroyed before they even attempted the journey south into the Atlantic. Second, the mere presence of Western SSNs in far northern waters would have forced any Soviet submarines attempting to reach the SLOC to slow down (and thereby run more quietly) to avoid detection—thus limiting the speed with which they could reach the SLOC, and the rate at which the total Soviet force could be cycled back and forth to the mid-Atlantic. Thus, aside from diverting many Soviet submarines to defensive tasks, offensive sea control maximally would have ended, and minimally severely complicated, the activities of some Soviet attack submarines.

[22]*SASC FY 85, Pt. 8*, p. 3870.

[23]The Soviets would have defended their coastal waters in any case, however, and would also have aimed to keep U.S. aircraft carriers and cruise-missile platforms away from Soviet shores. But the importance of its SSBN force lent a special urgency to this mission, an urgency the U.S. Navy wished to exploit.

These operational preferences were evident in the public statements of navy spokesmen starting in the late 1970s. They antedate the formal enunciation of the National Maritime Strategy. One former chief of naval operations, Adm. Thomas Hayward, declared in 1979 an intention to "seek out and destroy" Soviet naval forces "wherever they may be, even in Soviet coastal waters."[24] The United States must "contain and attrite the Soviet Navy as close to their home waters in a conflict as possible. . . . Accordingly, early concepts of attack submarine employment in far forward area offensive operations, barriers, and vectored intercept roles have grown in scope and asset requirements."[25] In 1978 Vice Admiral Doyle, then deputy chief of naval operations, put "Offensive Operations in Forward Areas" at the top of his list of SSN requirements—above "Barrier Operations."[26] Because the U.S. SSN was believed to be highly survivable, he indicated, it would have been "assigned to conduct offensive operations in forward areas, particularly in the early stages of conflict."[27] Forward operations would have been conducted in areas that were "very contiguous with the home bases of an adversary."[28]

These operations could have caused inadvertent escalation in two ways: by destroying Soviet strategic submarines or by destroying the forces essential to their long-term survival. The "forward operations" of as many as thirty American attack submarines would have constituted a major attack on the Soviet SSBN sanctuary. As argued above, *some* Soviet SSBNs had to be sunk in order to scare the Soviets enough to ensure the continued diversion of large numbers of attack submarines to bastion defense, but it is unlikely that this process could have been fine-tuned. Even if offensive sea control did not require the deliberate destruction of the *bulk* of the Soviet SSBN force, once in the Barents Sea, it would have been difficult for Western SSNs to distinguish between enemy attack submarines and SSBNs. Navy spokesmen have stated that Western ASW platforms "would not be in a position of

[24]U.S. Congress, Senate, Committee on Armed Services, *Hearings on Department of Defense Appropriations for Fiscal Year 1980*, 96th Cong., 1st sess., 1979 (Washington, D.C., 1979), pt. 3, p. 1292.

[25]U.S. Congress, Senate, Committee on Armed Services, *Hearings on Department of Defense Appropriations for Fiscal Year 1981*, 96th Cong., 2d sess., 1980 (Washington, D.C., 1980), pt. 2, p. 867.

[26]U.S. Congress, House, Committee on Armed Services, *Hearings on Military Posture and Department of Defense Appropriations for Fiscal Year 1979*, 95th Cong., 2d sess., 1978 (Washington, D.C., 1978), pt. 4, p. 277.

[27]Ibid.

[28]U.S. Congress, Senate, Committee on Armed Services, *Hearings on Department of Defense Appropriations for Fiscal Year 1977*, 94th Cong., 2d sess., 1976 (Washington, D.C., 1976), pt. 12, p. 6609.

differentiating their [Soviet] attack submarines from their SSBNs."[29] Vice Admiral Kaufman, the navy's director of command, control, and communications, has declared that "in a conventional war all submarines are submarines. They are all fair game."[30] Of Soviet SSBNs it is said, "Of course the ballistic missiles are their main reason for being, but they do carry torpedoes and mines."[31] More recently Senator William Cohen queried Vice Adm. Lee Baggett, then U.S. Navy director of surface warfare, as to whether SSNs could be attacked to the exclusion of SSBNs in wartime. The admiral responded, "I don't believe you could make a distinction in a combat environment—even prehostilities—with certainty to distinguish between SSBNs and attack submarines."[32]

There was a high probability, therefore, that Soviet ballistic missile submarines would have been sunk in the conventional phase of an East-West war. The Soviet Union could have seen such sinkings as a deliberate attempt to degrade the Soviet Union's nuclear retaliatory capability rather than as accidents to be accepted with equanimity, or as reminders aimed at discouraging attacks on the SLOC.

The navy thus saw, at both the tactical and operational level, little distinction between Soviet submarine types. At the level of the individual submarine, Soviet SSBNs were a "conventional" threat to NATO submarines and surface vessels. Whenever Soviet and American subsurface conventional and nuclear forces would have been mixed together in wartime, the potential for tactical interactions that could ultimately lead to nuclear escalation existed.[33]

At the level of the theater campaign, the Soviet SSBN bastion was viewed simply as the location of the potential threat to the SLOC, to be destroyed as if it were any concentration of enemy naval forces in World

[29]Ibid., pt. 4, p. 1972.

[30]U.S. Congress, Senate, Committee on Armed Services, *Hearings on Department of Defense Appropriations for Fiscal Year 1978*, 95th Cong., 1st sess., 1977 (Washington, D.C., 1977), p. 6699.

[31]U.S. Congress, House, Committee on Armed Services, *Hearings on Military Posture and Department of Defense Appropriations for Fiscal Year 1980*, 96th Cong., 1st sess., 1979 (Washington, D.C., 1979), pp. 663, 679. Hereafter, *HASC FY 80*.

[32]*SASC FY 86, Pt. 8*, pp. 4398–4399. An extraordinarily useful survey of public statements by U.S. officials on strategic ASW is John D. Perse, *U.S. Declaratory Policy on Soviet SSBN Security: 1970 to 1985*, Center for Naval Analysis Research Memorandum 84-29 (Washington, D.C., May 1986).

[33]This discussion has ignored another kind of escalation that could have arisen from predeployment of Soviet or American SSNs or SSBNs across the barriers during periods of tension. Such predeployments might actually have caused the outbreak of hostilities by mixing Soviet and Western submarine commanders under conditions of poor communications with national command authorities. Events similar to the Libyan-American fighter clash of summer 1981 were possible.

War II. Soviet concern for the survival of its SSBN force was simply a lever to be exploited for conventional success.

Three plausible military operations could have been undertaken to sink Soviet SSBNs:

(1) The highest leverage could have been achieved by an effort to position U.S. SSNs off Soviet SSBN bases before a "surge," so that Soviet submarines could be trailed, or in the event that fighting started beforehand, destroyed, as they deployed.[34] In effect, a barrier would have been established just off Soviet harbors. For this barrier to work, either the U.S. SSN forward movement would have had to have been exceedingly stealthy, or the Soviet response extremely slow. This strategy probably would have produced the greatest initial results in terms of SSBNs destroyed, if everything went smoothly.

But on close examination, even this strategy would have been far from decisive. Only a small percentage of the Soviet SSBN force was normally at sea, so it is *plausible* that the at-sea U.S. SSN force, perhaps a maximum of sixteen boats, could have rapidly deployed to the Barents for this purpose. For the United States to deploy more SSNs, it would have needed to surge boats out of North American ports, which would likely have alerted the Soviets and prompted a preemptive surge of their own. These sixteen U.S. SSNs would have had to distinguish and track about thirteen ready Soviet SSBNs deploying along with about thirty SSNs and SSGNs (cruise missile submarines) and twenty diesel-electric submarines (SS)—a total of sixty-three submarines. The probability of perfect success in picking out and trailing, or killing, all the SSBNs during the Soviet deployment phase would seem low. On the basis of open sources, in Appendix 4, I estimate a kill probability of only .16 for a western ASW barrier farther south. Why should the West have been able to do better in the Soviet backyard, where they had more assets and the West fewer? Thus, even if the United States could have beaten the Soviets to the punch and U.S. SSNs were permitted to shoot as Soviet SSBNs deployed, it is unlikely that they could have killed more than two SSBNs, by my calculation. Efforts to trail would have been complicated by the number of attack submarine targets, the adversary's active noncooperation, and the great difficulties the U.S.

[34]Mearsheimer, "Strategic Misstep," pp. 15–17, argues that this operation was most clearly associated with counterforce coercion. Because of the assumed time pressure associated with the effort to put strategic pressure on the Soviets before NATO's widely expected early conventional defeat on the Central Front, he contends that U.S. SSNs had to deploy quickly to the Barents to catch Soviet ballistic missile submarines as they left port.

SSNs would have had coordinating their activities. Since my method is crude, the specific numbers mean little, but the implication is that very few SSBNs could have been sunk either in scenarios where the U.S. Navy was permitted to attack Soviet submarines as they deployed, or merely to trail them and attack later should war have commenced. But given the difficulties of area search, which most analysts would consider to be even more problematical, the navy would almost certainly have wished to establish this very forward barrier.[35]

(2) U.S. SSNs could have attempted a general search of Soviet SSBN operating areas after most ready Soviet submarines had deployed.[36] This "area sweep out" operation could have been launched any time after the war had commenced, but likely would have suffered from rather low effectiveness.[37]

(3) U.S. SSNs might have exploited both past and "real time" intelligence on Soviet SSBN operations, of a quality that seems implausible, that would have permitted "vectored intercept" of Soviet SSBNs in northern waters even after they had escaped their bases. Such intelligence could have arisen from a long peacetime history of Soviet SSBN operations that revealed certain exploitable patterns in their behavior, or mistakes in communications procedures that were unknown to the Soviets. I have no evidence that such high-quality intelligence existed, but it might have.[38] It is probable that the U.S. Navy sought to develop intelligence of this quality.[39] This operation could also have been

[35]In making these calculations I have assumed an at-sea rate for Soviet missile submarines of 15 percent, and all other submarines of 10 percent. U.S. Department of Defense, *Soviet Military Power, 1988*, p. 96, suggests that the Soviet Navy had "the readiness capability to deploy up to 50% on short notice." I estimate that the United States normally managed to keep about twenty SSNs at sea in the Atlantic, with four tied up in carrier escort. *Soviet Military Power, 1986*, p. 29, estimates that the Soviets had 37 SSBNs in the Northern Fleet—twenty-two Delta, eleven Yankee, and four Typhoon.

[36]This could take the form of a carefully organized offensive of large numbers of SSNs starting in the north Norwegian Sea and proceeding slowly into the Barents. I estimate that about two dozen SSNs could have been allocated to this mission. The United States had about sixty SSNs in the Atlantic area in the mid-1980s. Only about 80 percent would have been ready for immediate deployment. For analytic purposes I assume that eight would have been tied up in carrier operations, and eight would have been held in the Atlantic as a strategic reserve. I assign eight to a forward barrier off northern Norway, leaving twenty-four to actually move forward into the Barents. Submarine patrol of the GIUK gap is presumed to have been allocated to the Allies, especially the British. Given the difficulties of area search, it is unclear that this operation would have killed enough SSBNs, quickly enough, to convince Soviet naval commanders that their second-strike capability was in so much danger that the bulk of their attack submarines had to remain in the north on defensive missions. Mearsheimer, p. 12, associates this operation with offensive sea control.

[37]Sakitt, *Submarine Warfare*, pp. 59–60.

[38]I am indebted to Bruce Blair for calling this possibility to my attention.

[39]This could have been one of the purposes of submarine intelligence collection missions

launched even after a Soviet surge. Indeed, to the extent that intelligence of this quality did exist, it might simply have served to increase the effectiveness of the search operation previously discussed. When such intelligence was available, it would have been exploited; when unavailable, U.S. SSNs would have reverted to area search.

Whether the navy's primary purpose was offensive sea control or counterforce coercion, it would not have wanted to forgo the tactical leverage of trailing Soviet submarines as they left port. At the same time, given the relatively small number of U.S. SSNs normally at sea, the distance from U.S. to Soviet bases, and the plausible effectiveness of forward barrier operations off Soviet harbors, it is improbable that most or even many Soviet SSBNs could have been caught as they left port. Thus, both objectives would also have required area search. It is true, however, that neither offensive sea control nor counterforce coercion absolutely required trailing the Soviet boats as they left harbor. But the navy would probably argue that forgoing this option would have severely reduced the number of Soviet SSBNs likely to be destroyed early in a conflict and thus would have reduced the U.S. ability to achieve either objective.

These Western forward operations, though intended to defend the SLOC, might have appeared strategically offensive to the Soviets, even as Soviet deterrent forces (SSBNs) and their protecting naval forces appeared offensive to Western forces. Indeed, since Soviet SSNs protected Soviet SSBNs as a primary mission, even if an ASW campaign could have been confined to Soviet attack submarines in northern waters, if might still have been perceived by the Soviets as putting their SSBNs in jeopardy.

Counterforce Coercion and Damage Limitation. In addition to inadvertent or incidental attacks, there was the possibility that American attack submarines might deliberately and consistently have stalked and killed Soviet SSBNs during the conventional phase of an East-West war.[40] Since U.S. strategic nuclear war plans have long included plans for

close to Soviet shores conducted in the 1960s and 1970s under the rubric of "Holystone." See Desmond Ball, "Nuclear War at Sea," *International Security* 10 (Winter 1985–86), reprinted in *Naval Strategy and National Security*, ed. Steven E. Miller and Stephen Van Evera (Princeton, 1988), pp. 304–306.

[40]As noted earlier, it is not at all clear that the mechanics of this campaign would have differed very much from the preceding one. In general, however, U.S. Navy ASW capabilities were kept sufficiently secret that we cannot be sure that a deliberate campaign could not have been arranged in such a way as to increase the rate at which Soviet SSBNs were destroyed. Thus, it is worthwhile to keep the two variants of the maritime strategy conceptually distinct.

attacks on Soviet strategic nuclear capabilities, it seems plausible if not probable that steps would have been taken to keep track of Soviet SSBNs, and possibly to sink them, during the conventional phase of a war. Although for many years this mission was seldom discussed publicly, there were occasional official allusions to it.[41]

By the second half of the 1980s, forward deployment of Western attack submarines was explicitly favored by the navy because it facilitated deliberate strategic ASW against Soviet ballistic missile submarines in the Barents Sea, either during the conventional phase of an East-West war, or in the event that such a war escalated to a strategic nuclear exchange.

Admiral Watkins divided the wartime component of the maritime strategy into two phases, "Seizing the Initiative," and "Carrying the Fight to the Enemy." In the first phase, he asserted, "we will wage an aggressive campaign against all Soviet submarines, including ballistic missile submarines." In the second phase "antisubmarine warfare forces would continue to destroy Soviet submarines, including ballistic missile submarines, thus reducing the attractiveness of nuclear escalation by changing the nuclear balance in our favor."[42] The admiral expected important results from these operations. "As our maritime campaign progresses, and as the nuclear option becomes less attractive, prolonging the war also becomes unattractive, since the Soviets cannot decouple Europe from the United States and the risk of escalation is always present. Maritime forces thus provide strong pressure for war termination that can come from nowhere else."[43] In short, these forward operations were meant to induce the Soviets to "terminate the war on terms acceptable to us and to our allies through measures such as threatening direct attack against the homeland or changing the nuclear correlation of forces."[44]

One possible motive for the deliberate sinking of Soviet SSBNs even during the conventional phase of the war is that Western ASW assets would have worked better in a non-nuclear than a nuclear environment, a fact that bolstered other escalatory tendencies. As noted in the introductory chapter, counterforce operations have long played an important role in U.S. military strategy for general thermonuclear war. Counter-SSBN operations follow logically from a strategy, but the outbreak

[41]U.S. Congress, Foreign Affairs and National Defense Division, Congressional Research Service, "Arms Control Implications of Anti-Submarine Warfare Programs," prepared by Bruce Blair, in *Evaluation of Fiscal Year 1979 Arms Control Impact Statements*, p. 113.

[42]Watkins, "Maritime Strategy," pp. 11, 13.

[43]Ibid., p. 14.

[44]Ibid.

of nuclear war is probably too late to commence them. Rear Admiral Metzel, then director of ASW for the chief of naval operations, noted the extreme importance of command, control, and communications (C^3) for effective ASW; however, C^3 facilities were unlikely to survive even limited Soviet nuclear strikes.[45] As Richard Garwin has observed, "Nuclear war confined to the sea appears to degrade ASW capability far more than it degrades the survivability of the SLBM [submarine-launched ballistic missile]."[46] A relatively small number of nuclear warheads (perhaps well under fifty) directed at SOSUS data collection points, military communications facilities, and P-3 ASW aircraft bases would have significantly degraded the West's ability to conduct ASW operations.[47] Nuclear detonations generate electromagnetic pulse and other effects that would probably damage some kinds of communications equipment, even if only small numbers of lower yield weapons were employed, and even if that equipment were far enough from the detonation to survive blast effects.[48] Deliberate high-altitude, high-yield detonations would interfere with radio communications—at least for a short time. Underwater detonations could reduce the detection capability of passive sonars and might destroy moored sonar arrays (SOSUS). In short, if the West wished to reduce Soviet sea-based retaliatory capability, there was an incentive to do so during the conventional phase of an East-West war. At the same time, with the detonation of relatively few nuclear weapons against shore-based naval installations that were often located in sparsely populated areas and hence where there would have been comparatively low collateral damage to civilians, the Soviets might quickly have blocked the further progress of a Western ASW campaign.[49]

Even if U.S. political leaders were not willing to take the risk of a

[45] *HASC FY 80*, pp. 710–711; Ball, *Can Nuclear War Be Controlled?*, pp. 14–25.

[46] Richard Garwin, "The Interaction of Anti-Submarine Warfare with the Submarine-Based Deterrent," in *The Future of the Sea-Based Deterrent* ed. Kosta Tsipis, Ann H. Cahn, and Bernard T. Feld (Cambridge, Mass., 1973), p. 89.

[47] Ball, "Nuclear War at Sea," pp. 303–331. Of the Western worldwide system for supporting ASW operations, Ball observes, "The whole system could be rendered useless by attacks on fewer than 50 installations" (p. 322).

[48] I infer this from the discussion in Ashton Carter, "Communications Technologies and Vulnerabilities," in *Managing Nuclear Operations*, ed. Carter, Steinbruner, and Zraket (Washington, D.C., 1987), pp. 273–281. The two most important phenomenon associated with surface tactical nuclear weapons use would seem to be "source region electromagnetic pulse" and "transient radiation effects on electronics."

[49] Such a strike would have severely reduced the West's ability to control the SLOC and move conventional reinforcements to Europe. NATO might then have faced defeat because of growing Soviet conventional superiority in Central Europe. NATO's use of nuclear weapons in the theater, or against Soviet submarine bases on the Kola Peninsula, could then have been its only alternative to surrender.

deliberate, if conventional, counterforce campaign early in an East-West war, America's long-standing commitment to damage limitation in its strategic nuclear policy suggests that they would have wanted the capability to attack Soviet SSBNs in the Barents in the event of nuclear escalation. Thus, the National Command Authority might have been willing to permit forward deployment of SSNs to prepare in advance for deliberate strategic ASW, especially if they were persuaded by the navy's more benign offensive sea-control rationale for the forward deployment. Once in the Soviet SSBN bastions in force, however, it would have been quite difficult to fine-tune military operations in a way that would have made the second operation distinguishable from the first to a Soviet decision maker.

Summary. A deliberate conventional campaign specifically directed against Soviet SSBNs, or more generally directed at the bastion and its defending submarine forces, could have been understood by the Soviets as the beginning of a damage-limiting strategic first strike. Given the obvious importance of secure retaliatory capabilities to Soviet security, as well as the central position that nuclear weapons and nuclear war long enjoyed in Soviet open-source discussions of their military doctrine, even the appearance of such a campaign could have triggered unfortunate consequences. American leaders might have been surprised by the Soviet response, since they seem to have believed that so long as nuclear weapons were not used to destroy Soviet strategic forces, the prospect of Soviet escalation was not raised.[50]

Regardless of whether Western SSNs were in the Barents Sea or nibbling along its edges, whether they were sinking Soviet SSBNs

[50]Although I have largely relied on deduction from general principles to judge what kinds of events may suggest nuclear escalation to the Soviets, others have attempted detailed analysis of Soviet unclassified military literature. One rather extensive analysis concludes on the matter of threats to SSBNs: "The West must think through the conventional campaign against Yankee and in the bastions which might occur prior to the nuclear phase of a war. Will the Soviets view the loss of SSBNs as a continuation of the conventional war or will they regard it as initiation of nuclear warfare? This author did not uncover any themes that he felt would help answer this question, hence the decision may have to be made on very incomplete supporting analysis unless classified data can illuminate Soviet thinking. Perhaps the loss of a Yankee could serve as the warning shot prior to actual initiation of nuclear warfare." James J. Tritten, *Soviet Naval Forces and Nuclear Warfare Weapons, Employment, and Policy* (London and Boulder, Colo., 1986), p. 232. Tritten then went on to address the circumstances under which the Soviet Union might employ nuclear weapons at sea: "The author's concern was simply to analyze the literature to ascertain if the war were nuclear ashore would it be nuclear at sea (yes) and would it be initiated at and limited to the sea (inconclusive)" (p. 206). Thus, his rather extensive survey of Soviet literature did not turn up the answers to the critical questions I have raised in this chapter.

systematically or incidentally, and whether they were doing so quickly or slowly, the activity would likely have caused considerable disquiet in the Soviet Union. The more U.S. SSN activities conformed to the pattern of a deliberate operation against the Soviet SSBN bastions, the greater the disquiet would have been. Given how the U.S. Navy described its plans, it seems quite likely that U.S. naval activities in northern waters would in fact have been a dedicated military operation with this intention. But even a series of confusing accidents that appeared to be consistent with a deliberate Western strategic ASW campaign might have been interpreted as such. In wartime the combatants tend to interpret those adversary military actions that are particularly damaging as the results of a deliberate plan.[51] Had they been convinced that a successful conventional counter-SSBN operation was under way, a Soviet nuclear campaign for the purpose of saving its SSBN force would have been a plausible response.

Even if American leaders had been sensitive to these problems, preventing forward SSN operations from having some of these effects could have proven ticklish. Submarine missions are difficult to control because communications with SSNs under wartime conditions are likely to be tenuous.[52] These boats tend to operate as lone wolves; radio silence and concealment are critical to their survival—particularly in areas as heavily defended as the Barents. SSN commanders in Soviet waters are unlikely to come near the surface frequently either to send or receive messages. Once war begins, Western SSNs would presumably try to sink any Soviet submarine in their vicinity. Since submarines have little armor or defensive weapons, they survive in combat by stealth or by shooting first.[53] The SSN therefore may have an incentive to sink enemy submarines before they have a chance to detect and sink it. The SSN commander cannot afford to be particularly discriminating in his decisions to shoot or not to shoot. Extricating American SSNs from this situation before they had taken potentially escalatory actions would have been difficult, since the inclination to call them back would probably not have developed until the Soviets have suffered sufficient damage to produce a panic—exactly the situation where just a little more activity of the wrong kind could have tipped them over the edge. Carrying twenty or more torpedoes and/or sophisticated ASW mines,

[51]Robert Jervis, *Perception and Misperception in International Politics* (Princeton, 1975), pp. 319–329.

[52]I give an extended discussion in Miller and Glaser, eds., *Navy and Nuclear Weapons*, app. 2.

[53]Submarines do have devices to decoy or jam incoming torpedoes that are detected. Soviet submarines are said to have double hulls, in effect a kind of armor against enemy torpedoes.

U.S. SSNs had the potential to do a lot of damage if each was not quickly restrained. If communication problems prevented the imposition of such restraint, the continued destruction of Soviet subs could have harmed any attempted wartime negotiations. In short, putting SSNs in far-forward areas was likely to have created a situation that would have been difficult to control—whether the United States wished to fine-tune the destruction of Soviet SSBNs for its own reasons, or to stop their destruction because a grim warning had been received from the Soviet Union.

The Battle-Group Assault on the Northern Fleet

The risk of inadvertent escalation was also raised by a second type of operation advocated by some elements in the U.S. Navy: offensive-carrier battle-group operations that would have launched air attacks against the Northern Fleet and especially its bases in the Kola Peninsula. By the late 1980s limited numbers of conventional cruise missiles were becoming available that could have been fired from submarines and surface ships to assist these operations. There was always more controversy inside the navy on this issue than there was on forward SSN operations, and the ardor for this mission seems to have cooled by the end of the decade. Nevertheless, the navy conducted major training exercises in support of this mission—and its advocacy ought to be treated as an indicator of preferences. Like the forward SSN ASW operation, forward carrier task force operations would also have had two possible and interrelated purposes: pinning down Soviet forces in defensive actions (and hopefully destroying them), and altering the strategic nuclear balance.

These carrier operations would have required a minimum of four to six carriers, as well as a substantial number of American and British surface and submarine escorts.[54] As Admiral Thunman points out, the navy hoped to precede the carrier air attacks with SSN-launched conventional cruise missile attacks on critical Soviet installations ashore, attacks aimed especially at reducing the threat to carriers posed by Soviet naval attack aircraft such as the Backfire. The navy was vague as to when in a war carrier battle-group operations would have occurred and suggested that they would not have been automatic. Nevertheless, its spokesmen talked about them with great enthusiasm for several years. According to then Senator Gary Hart, Admiral Hayward, then chief of naval operations, advocated "the use of carrier attack aircraft

[54]"NATO's Sinking Feeling," *The Economist*, June 6, 1981, p. 51.

against Soviet land targets," presumably Soviet naval bases and airfields on the Kola Peninsula, as early as 1979.[55] Many public statements by the navy implied that these attacks could in fact have begun rather early in a war.[56] According to one knowledgeable observer, two large-scale U.S. naval exercises in 1984 and 1985 suggested "the desired concept of operations for a worldwide maritime campaign emphasizing prompt strikes against the Soviet fleet and targets ashore."[57]

The navy's enthusiasm for the carrier assault notwithstanding, such an operation would have been very risky for Western naval forces. An unclassified analysis by Joshua Epstein supports this judgment.[58] Some analysts privately doubted that the U.S. Navy was serious about it. Some naval officers with whom I have spoken suggest that at least some of the navy's own studies showed that carrier air sorties against Soviet bases on the Kola Peninsula were not likely to have been particularly effective.

Soviet forces were rather strong in the Barents Sea and Kola Peninsula, and could have been reinforced with a great deal of land-based defensive and offensive airpower. Of course, this would make for a

[55]U.S. Congress, Senate, Committee on Armed Services, *Hearings on Department of Defense Appropriations for Fiscal Year 1980*, 96th Cong., 1st sess., 1979 (Washington, D.C., 1979), pt. 2, p. 557.

[56]*SASC FY 1985, Pt. 8*, pp. 3871–3879, 3887, includes exchanges between Senators Nunn and Cohen, former Chief of Naval Operations Watkins, and former Secretary of the Navy Lehman which illustrate the elusiveness of the timing of carrier air strikes against Soviet naval bases. The discussion supports the proposition that air strikes would have come early if for some reason, or in some area, the Soviets failed to put together an impressive defense. If the Soviets alerted their defenses, then the battle in northern waters would probably have taken the form of an initial SSN surge to reduce the submarine and surface forces of the Soviet Navy and employ conventional cruise missiles to damage critical installations ashore. If these operations had proven successful, they would have been followed by sustained carrier air operations against the Northern Fleet base structure.

[57]Christopher Wright, "US Naval Operations in 1985," *US Naval Institute Proceedings, Naval Review Issue* 112 (May 1986): 34–40, 283–297, esp. p. 38. "Ocean Safari left a clear impression of an offensive maritime campaign conducted to defend the sea lanes by striking north rather than awaiting an enemy appearance. Ocean Safari offers an interesting parallel with the 1984 Pacific exercise FleetEx. 85-1, after which two carrier battle groups operated simultaneously in the Sea of Japan."

[58]Joshua M. Epstein, *The 1988 Defense Budget* (Washington, D.C., 1987), pp. 45–50, provides quantitative analysis suggesting that even nine carriers would have had a difficult time surviving in northern waters, much less doing serious damage to the Soviets. As Epstein points out, his analysis on the whole makes assumptions favorable to the U.S. Navy. On the other hand, the force he throws against the carriers is larger than seems plausible, and Soviet bombers, which do the bulk of the damage to U.S. carriers, do not suffer any attrition on the ground from U.S. cruise missile or aircraft strikes. A navy partisan could thus find room to quarrel with Epstein's conclusion, although I am persuaded that the thrust of his analysis is correct—carrier operations close to the Soviet Union would have been very difficult indeed.

demanding mission, one that gave the navy a strong argument for more forces in the competition for resources among the services. There is, however, a fine line between arguments employed to win more forces and beliefs about how a war should actually be fought. The navy's frequent discussion of offensive carrier operations should at minimum be taken as evidence of a strong tendency or preference. Moreover, the operation might have been attempted several weeks into a war, after additional naval power was mustered from other theaters, and after forward SSN operations and land-based air operations from northern Norway had degraded Soviet defenses. The operation could also have been supported by other NATO aircraft based in northern Norway and farther south. Thus, the operation was a serious possibility, and its implications, if successful, merit the closest attention.

The navy argued that this operation would have tied down Soviet forces that would otherwise have attacked the SLOC. With luck, the Northern Fleet would have been decisively defeated, securing command of the sea for the West and allowing easy resupply of Western Europe. In the words of the former Chief of Naval Operations Thomas Hayward:

> We must fight on the terms which are most advantageous to us. This would require taking the war to the enemy's naval forces with the objective of achieving the earliest possible destruction of his capability to interfere with our use of the sea areas essential for support of our overseas forces and allies. In this sense sea control is an offensive rather than a defensive function. The prompt destruction of opposing naval forces is the most economical and effective means to assure control of the sea areas required for successful prosecution of the war and support of the U.S. and allied war economies. Our current offensive naval capabilities, centered on the carrier battle forces and their supporting units, are well-suited for the execution of this strategy.[59]

If this operation had been ordered, it would have unfolded in close cooperation with the SSN ASW operation outlined above, although it would probably not have begun until that operation were well under way. SSNs would have defended the carriers from Soviet submarines and hunted them down, as would have surface escorts. Carrier attack aircraft would have sought out Soviet naval assets afloat and ashore. Surface vessels and maritime patrol aircraft would have been obvious targets, as would have long-range naval attack aircraft such as Backfire. Support facilities might also have been lucrative targets. A catastrophic

[59] *HASC FY 80, Pt. 1*, p. 841.

accidental explosion of much of the Northern Fleet's conventional ordnance in the spring of 1984 suggests that deliberate air attacks supported by good intelligence might have done serious damage to that fleet's ability to sustain conventional operations.[60] Aerial mining of Soviet harbors was another option the United States might have exploited.

If successful, this operation could have increased the risks of nuclear escalation in several ways. By destroying the bulk of Soviet conventional naval capabilities, the attack could have reduced, if not eliminated, the Soviet Navy's ability to protect its strategic submarines in their Barents Sea sanctuary from a concentrated attack by Western ASW forces. This would be equivalent to the United States' suddenly discovering in wartime a great new vulnerability in its SSBN forces, and one that could be expected to grow at an unpredictable rate.

This operation might also have directly destroyed Soviet SSBNs—either incidentally or deliberately. Carrier-based ASW aircraft, long-range shore-based ASW aircraft, and surface escorts would have added to the threat posed to Soviet SSBNs by Western SSNs. Conventional cruise-missile and tactical air attacks on Soviet bases might have damaged or destroyed Soviet ballistic missile submarines undergoing resupply or maintenance—as much as half of the force (although the Soviets do much of this work in hardened tunnels).

In addition, such air strikes, even with conventional ordnance, might have found critical vulnerabilities in the Soviet military system. The Soviet Navy, like the rest of the Soviet armed forces, was highly centralized and quite dependent on battle management from higher authorities.[61] Thus, destruction of naval tactical command, control, communications, and intelligence (C^3I) facilities, SSBN C^3 facilities, and Kola-based strategic early warning systems might all have had a disproportionate effect on Soviet capabilities and confidence. Destruction of any of these assets could have caused a sudden unravelling of Soviet forces, or a sudden increase in Soviet perceptions of strategic vulnerability. The navy conceded this point in discussions with the Congressional Research Service.[62]

[60]Rick Atkinson, "Soviet Arms Disaster Reported," *Washington Post*, 22 June 1984, p. A1; *SASC FY 86, Pt. 8*, p. 4365.

[61]Ball, "Can Nuclear War Be Controlled?" p. 45; "The Soviet Navy Declaratory Doctrine for Theatre Nuclear Warfare," a report prepared by the BDM Corporation, 30 September 1977, for the Defense Nuclear Agency.

[62]Ronald O'Rourke, *Nuclear Escalation, Strategic Anti-Submarine Warfare, and the Navy's Forward Maritime Strategy*, Congressional Research Service Report No. 87-138F (Washington, D.C., 27 February 1987), p. 14, notes that critics of the maritime strategy have observed "that the rate of attrition on the effectiveness of the Soviet SSBN force could be higher than expected, especially if attacks on SSBNs are combined with attacks on Soviet SSBN support facilities and command, control, and communications facilities. The Navy,

Thus, the synergistic effect of these operations might have caused, in addition to destruction of the forces defending the SSBN bastion, some quite rapid degradations of the Northern Fleet base structure, its ability to support conventional operations, and thus the security of the Soviet strategic submarine force.

Forward operations by carrier battle groups and cruise-missile-carrying submarines might also have aimed to improve the U.S. strategic nuclear position vis-à-vis the Soviet Union. Maritime strategy advocates alluded to this purpose less frequently than the others discussed above. There were two ways that the strategy could have achieved this: the deployment of special kinds of nuclear forces in close proximity to the Soviet Union; the degradation of Soviet strategic early warning capabilities.

According to Watkins, the nuclear balance would have been altered "by improving our own nuclear posture through deployment of carriers and Tomahawk platforms around the periphery of the Soviet Union."[63] Or, as Rear Adm. Stephen J. Hostettler, then director of the Joint Cruise Missile Project, put it, "The increased strike range of a larger number of surface ships operating under carrier air cover as well as independent covert forward-deployed submarines, presents the Soviets with a *formidable threat from 360 degree axis against which they have no reliable defense*"[64] (my emphasis).

But these forward deployments would have accompanied the conventional cruise missile and tactical aircraft attacks discussed above. Sustained tactical air operations would almost certainly have required

---

however, is aware of this combined effects problem and will be monitoring the situation." How the navy will "monitor" this situation ought to be a matter of some curiosity, given the U.S. C^3I problems that would have attended forward operations. What the navy would have done had their monitoring revealed extraordinary success was not addressed in the CRS study.

[63]Watkins, "The Maritime Strategy," p. 14. Secretary of the Navy Lehman's remarks, *SASC FY 1985, Pt. 8*, pp. 3876–3877, also suggest this purpose, if somewhat obliquely. Pointing to a map showing the Soviet view of the threat posed by sea-based, U.S., Tomahawk, land-attack cruise missiles, the secretary observed, "This is a Soviet view of Tomahawk. The fact is that it is not just the carriers that the Soviets have to worry about now. Because, we now have many deployed ships that, from a strike (nuclear) point of view, are a potential threat to the Soviets in a wartime situation. All of our destroyers and eventually, all of our cruisers and all of our attack subs will be potential Tomahawk shooters. This will complicate tremendously the targeting problems of the Soviets. They now have to worry as much about a destroyer as they do about a carrier from the point of view of transition to strike (nuclear) operations." This does of course complicate the Soviet targeting problem if they wish to preempt, but nuclear cruise missiles widely deployed on the Soviet periphery also complicate the Soviet early warning problem against nuclear attack.

[64]Rear Adm. Stephen J. Hostettler, "The Sea-Launched Cruise Missile," *NATO's Sixteen Nations* 29 (December 1984–January 1985): 83–88, esp. p. 84.

the systematic destruction of Soviet air defenses—including early warning radars. Moreover, U.S. Naval Intelligence believed that "Soviet naval units will also play an increasingly important role in providing air defense coverage of the Soviet Union against aircraft/cruise missile attack from seaward axes." Of particular importance was the extension of "the area of radar coverage away from Soviet coastal areas."[65] But these forces would naturally have come under attack by Western naval units.

If air attacks had succeeded for any length of time, Soviet air-defense commanders might have lost confidence in their ability to detect and stop nuclear surprise attacks by tactical fighters, strategic bombers, or cruise missiles. Repeated, undetected penetration of Soviet airspace by U.S. conventional cruise missiles or carrier-based fighters or both would have been stark evidence of the inadequacy of Soviet air defense. Indeed, the conventional carrier-aircraft and cruise-missile campaign might have been perceived by the Soviets as a deceptive operation designed to accustom them to a certain number of Western air strikes every day. How then could a nuclear surprise attack by the forward-deployed Tomahawk nuclear cruise missiles, deployed on the very same platforms that would have been responsible for the conventional cruise missile attacks, have been avoided?[66] Since most forward-deployed SSNs were undergoing modifications to provide the capability to carry both conventional and nuclear cruise missiles, their early independent operations to soften up the Soviet defenses could have produced the same Soviet nervousness before carrier operations even began.[67]

Although from a peacetime perspective submarine-launched nuclear cruise missiles appear to be quite redundant to the huge capabilities of U.S. dedicated strategic nuclear forces, their deployment near the Soviet homeland, under conditions of intense conventional combat that had degraded Soviet homeland air defenses, might have created painful choices for the Soviets. They might have perceived themselves to be highly vulnerable to surprise nuclear attacks against critical command and control installations, attacks that could have served as precursors to a full-scale U.S. strategic counterforce strike (see Chapter 2 for the way this might have occurred in Central Europe).

[65] *Statement of Studeman*, p. 7.

[66] Vasendin and Kuznetsov, "Modern Warfare and Surprise Attack," p. 45.

[67] The plan was for seventy-seven Los Angeles and Sturgeon class SSNs to have the capability to fire both conventional and nuclear cruise missiles by 1990. See the testimony of Secretary of Defense Caspar Weinberger, in U.S. Congress, House, Appropriations Committee, *DOD Appropriations for 1985*, pt. 1, p. 512. According to IISS, *Military Balance, 1989–1990*, p. 18, forty-five SSNs actually did have this capability by the fall of 1989.

For example, a map in *Soviet Military Power, 1985* shows gaps in Soviet air defenses in the northern part of the country that could have been exploited by submarine-launched nuclear cruise missiles. With their 2200-km+ range, they could easily have reached Moscow from the Barents Sea. They could have been so routed as to encounter little air defense until roughly 600–800 km from Moscow. This is 45–60 minutes' flying time for a cruise missile. If they were detected as soon as they crossed into the area of air defense coverage, this would have provided a longer interval for a decision to launch on warning than would the thirty minutes usually cited for an ICBM attack, but not much longer. Moreover, given the preceding conventional campaign, a "small" initial attack, and the general difficulties of detecting and tracking cruise missiles, this might seem to Soviet military and political leaders an uncomfortably short time for decision. Soviet commanders could have begun to fear a developing U.S. confidence in its ability to launch small precursor attacks against Soviet strategic nuclear command and control assets, thereby slowing the Soviet command system to permit successful ballistic missile attacks against the entire Soviet land-based strategic apparatus, all without triggering launch on warning or launch under attack. Such concerns admittedly seem quite far-fetched under day-to-day peacetime conditions. A month of World War III might change the way people think.

Thus, it is plausible that the air operations that the U.S. Navy justified on defensive and deterrent grounds would have threatened Soviet strategic nuclear capabilities, including SSBNs and the forces that defended them, tactical and strategic command and control installations, and early warning facilities for the detection of nuclear attacks from aircraft and cruise missiles. Since the Soviets placed a high value on these capabilities, any of these eventualities could have elicited a nuclear response. Moreover, Western naval assets, particularly the aircraft carriers, were attractive targets for a Soviet nuclear attack, both because of their relative vulnerability and because attacking them would not have required the use of nuclear weapons against the American homeland. Soviet use of nuclear weapons at sea therefore seems plausible, insofar as the purpose would have been to protect their strategic nuclear capabilities from immediate and future attack. The Soviet nuclear response could have been limited to a small number of naval and land targets in the northern flank region and still achieved its critical objectives.

Thus, the combination of military preferences for offensive operations and the difficulty both superpowers would have had distinguishing between conventional and strategic, offensive and defensive forces and operations might have lead to a potentially escalatory clash in the north

Norwegian and Barents seas. This clash would not have been easy for policymakers to control. Intelligence would have been faulty and slow; communications with the forces engaged, tenuous. Communications links would have been jammed or destroyed; commanders would have frequently observed radio silence to avoid detection. Moreover, the great firepower and range of modern conventional weaponry makes possible sudden changes in the fortunes of each side—changes that could cause panic and overreaction.[68] In such circumstances, attempts at negotiation would have been complicated and difficult.

NATO's Naval Counterattack

NATO's efforts to defend Norway against Soviet attack constitute yet a third way that inadvertent escalation could have occurred on the northern flank. Actions that might have seemed local and limited to Soviet decision makers could have created serious escalatory pressures, because a Soviet assault on northern Norway could (and probably would) have precipitated a powerful NATO naval counterattack that, unless carefully controlled, could have become a cause of escalation.

Norway's military capabilities, as well as NATO reinforcements likely to arrive early in a mobilization period or a war, might have been perceived by the Soviet Union as an offensive threat. Many of these NATO assets were essential to the defense of Norway and NATO, but this was little comfort to the Soviets. Consequently, a Soviet attempt to take northern Norway and to destroy NATO's northern ASW barriers was possible.[69]

Contrary to the then conventional wisdom, however, a quick and easy victory for Soviet forces was by no means assured, which means that NATO could well have had the time to mount its naval counterattack.[70] Although Soviet ground forces would have had an easy time crossing the Soviet-Norwegian border into Finnmark county, it would

[68]At Midway, a World War II naval battle fought with substantially less capable conventional weaponry than that deployed in the 1980s, the Japanese lost three large aircraft carriers in less than ten minutes and a fourth less than eight hours later—one-half of their entire carrier force. Samuel Eliot Morison, *The Two Ocean War* (Boston, 1963), p. 157.

[69]Kirsten Amundsen, "Soviet Submarines in Scandinavian Waters," *Washington Quarterly* 8 (Summer 1985): 111–121, esp. p. 117.

[70]For an optimistic assessment of the military balance in the "High North," see Maj. Gen. Richard C. Bowman, USAF-Ret., "Soviet Options on NATO's Northern Flank," *Armed Forces Journal International*, April 1984, pp. 88–98; for "cautiously" optimistic treatments, see Col. Joseph Alexander, USMC, "The Role of US Marines in the Defense of Northern Norway," *US Naval Institute Proceedings, Naval Review 1984*, May 1984, pp. 182–193; and Tomas Ries, "Defending the Far North," *International Defense Review* 17, no. 7 (1984): 873–880.

have been difficult for them to capture NATO's major base areas in Troms county, which lie more than 600 road miles away through difficult country. To have any hope of rapid success, the Soviets would have had to attempt a combined arms, airborne amphibious assault early in the war. Even this attack could have failed, or at least failed to produce a rapid victory, because such operations are notoriously tricky, Soviet airlift and sealift capabilities were limited, and the Norwegians were well prepared to thwart just such an attack. Free passage through northern Finland, by no means assured, would have eased the problem of providing a ground component for a Soviet invasion, but even this would not have guaranteed a quick win, because Norwegian forces were stationed close to the Finnish wedge, the likely Soviet invasion route. The road from the wedge to the main Norwegian bases runs through very mountainous terrain and is vulnerable to air interdiction, ground demolition, ambush, and other delaying and blocking tactics. Thus, a Soviet attack on northern Norway was possible, but a quick victory was not assured. It is entirely plausible that Norwegian defenders would have held on long enough to permit the arrival of NATO reinforcements.

The West would have attempted a vigorous defense of Norway, particularly because a Soviet attack there would have been seen as part of a Soviet campaign against NATO's SLOC, aiming to destroy NATO's ability to wage conventional war in Europe. (This would have been a plausible Soviet goal.) U.S. Navy carrier battle groups would probably have played an important role in any Western counterattack designed to thwart Soviet designs in Norway.

This counterattack would have been less adventurous than the offensive operations designed to attack the Kola Peninsula and the Barents Sea. However, it would have involved many of the same risks, because a great naval battle in the Norwegian Sea could, if NATO was successful, have had similar implications for the Soviets as a full-fledged attack on the Northern Fleet. U.S. Navy commanders would probably have wanted to exploit any initial success with a follow-up attack against Soviet naval units fleeing back to Kola. In short, there were other ways for the U.S. Navy to end up in a major battle with the Soviet Northern Fleet than a simple, early, all-out offensive against the Kola Peninsula.

Conclusion: Avoiding Inadvertent Escalation

These three northern flank scenarios—the forward operation of American attack submarines in the Norwegian and Barents seas, offensive carrier battle-group operations in the Barents Sea including air and cruise missile strikes on the Kola Peninsula, and a NATO naval counterattack in defense of Norway—illustrate the potential problems that might arise in trying to prevent escalation in the context of large-scale conventional conflict. Although not inevitable, the first two operations had considerable support in the navy and among some civilians. The necessity for the third rested on the restraint of the Soviet Union. If undertaken, these operations might not have been successful. Forward SSN operations probably could have been conducted without catastrophic Western submarine losses, but in the event that the Soviets deployed their forces before the outbreak of hostilities, U.S. submarines would have taken "weeks or months" to destroy significant numbers of Soviet submarines, even under the best of conditions.[71] I suspect that the carrier battle-group assault would have been both unsuccessful and disastrous for the U.S. Navy. NATO's naval counterattack would probably have been conducted with extreme caution and would at best have sunk some Soviet surface vessels. Even if fully successful, these operations might not have precipitated a nuclear response. However, insofar as such things can be thought about in advance, these northern flank operations appear to have been plausible paths to nuclear escalation in any war in the 1980s.

This is true because survivable strategic nuclear forces are critical to the security of both superpowers. States fight hardest—and may be willing to risk the most dire consequences—when assets essential to the preservation of their sovereignty are at stake. Thus, conventional operations that threaten strategic nuclear forces can be extremely provocative. Both sides were frightened of nuclear weapons and seemed in no hurry to use them. However, although it may seem paradoxical, the use of some nuclear weapons to protect the remainder of one's strategic deterrent is probably among the most plausible scenarios for nuclear escalation. As noted above, much of the Western intelligence and ASW infrastructure from the GIUK gap northward, including sensors, intelligence collection installations, and airfields, was vulnerable to tactical nuclear attacks that would not have caused great damage to civilian populations. Aircraft carrier task groups would have positively invited nuclear attack.[72] And given their inferiority in underwater detection, it seems plausible that the employment of nuclear ASW weapons would have improved the Soviet tactical position relative to Western submarines. Nuclear weapons would have improved Soviet chances of

[71]Sakitt, *Submarine Warfare*, pp. 59–60.
[72]Ball, "Nuclear War at Sea," pp. 308–310, 326–328.

a kill when a U.S. submarine was detected, and underwater nuclear detonations might have reduced the tactical effectiveness of U.S. passive sonar, reducing an important U.S. tactical advantage in submarine-to-submarine engagements.

It should be stressed that these escalation problems were not specific to the northern flank. Though it is the best example of the general escalation tendencies of an East-West conventional war, there were others. For instance, the U.S. Navy frequently argued for attacks directed against the eastern Soviet Union, especially Vladivostok and Petropavlovsk, which would have been similar to those aimed at the Kola Peninsula. Since the other one-third of Soviet SSBN assets are based in the east, such attacks could have been almost as risky as attacks against the Kola. Of course, if adequate forces were available, simultaneous attacks at both ends of the Soviet Union would have been possible, creating still greater escalation pressures because the entire Soviet strategic submarine force would then have been threatened.

Concerns of the kind outlined in this chapter were raised by a number of analysts, including myself, in the 1980s. The navy generally resisted them strongly. One consistent claim was that in the absence of forward operations, the SLOC could not have been defended, defensively. In the next chapter, I argue that it could have.

[5]

"Offensive" and "Defensive" Sea Control: A Comparative Assessment

An attack on Western Europe by the massive active and reserve ground forces and tactical air forces of the Soviet Union and its Warsaw Pact allies has been the most demanding prospective military contingency for the United States since the creation of NATO. During the late 1970s and through most of the 1980s, Soviet capabilities for such an attack were judged to be the most impressive they had been during the entire Cold War. Had such a war occurred, American military units permanently based in Europe would have played a key role in blunting the initial Pact offensive, as would those reinforcements that could have deployed rapidly by air to marry up with their prepositioned equipment. If initial resistance had proven successful, seaborne reinforcements from the United States would have been necessary to permit NATO to cope with the large number of Soviet reserve divisions that could ultimately have been brought into Central Europe and thrown against NATO.[1]

If NATO's power of conventional resistance had failed, the doctrine of flexible response called for the employment of nuclear weapons to dissuade the Pact from continuing its offensive. No western decision maker, in or out of uniform, relished this prospect. Given the forces available to the Soviet Union and to the NATO allies, seaborne reinforcements from the United States were essential for sustained conventional defense. The ability of the U.S. Navy, *in cooperation with the allied navies*, to keep open the sea line of communication (SLOC) to Europe

[1]Here I assume a comparatively short period of Pact and NATO mobilization before combat begins. If mobilization and reinforcement had arisen from a long political crisis, critical U.S. seaborne reinforcements might have deployed before the outbreak of combat. In this scenario, the battle for control of the SLOCS would have lacked much of the urgency associated with a short-warning, short-mobilization attack.

would thus have been a critical determinant of NATO's ability to thwart Warsaw Pact aggression without resort to nuclear escalation.

Civilian defense officials, analysts, and politicians have long debated the relative merits of two different strategies for keeping the SLOC open. The leadership of the U.S. Navy has, since at least the mid-1970s, favored "offensive sea control," early, large-scale attacks against the base areas and home waters of the Soviet fleet designed to destroy Soviet forces before they can reach the SLOC. Failing that, it hopes to occupy most Soviet submarines in defensive tasks, diverting them from SLOC missions and thus virtually eliminating them as threats to transport shipping, even if they are not actually destroyed.[2]

Proponents of "defensive sea control" argue that since we cannot be certain the offensive will succeed in either of its objectives, we must have the assets to defend the SLOC in the event that the Soviets attack it. NATO should set up a series of defensive barriers between those forces that most threaten the SLOC (submarines and long-range naval strike aircraft) and directly defend reinforcement convoys with escort warships.[3]

The purpose of this analysis is to assess the relative merits of each strategy for securing the sea line of communication to Europe—with particular reference to the period in question, the mid-1980s. *Which strategy would have best served the objective of moving sufficient reinforcements to Europe to permit NATO to resist successfully a Warsaw Pact conventional attack, and thus avoid recourse to nuclear escalation?*[4]

The escalatory risks of forward offensive operations discussed in the previous chapter ought to be factored into any strategic analysis of the

[2]The clearest and most accessible official exposition of this rationale is to be found in Watkins, "Maritime Strategy," pp. 4–17. A very illuminating discussion can also be found in the testimony of Secretary of the Navy John Lehman, Admiral Watkins, and Lt. Gen. Bernard E. Trainor, in *SASC FY 85, Pt. 8*, pp. 3851–3900.

[3]For a clear statement of the benefits of defensive sea control, see U.S. Congress, Senate, Budget Committee, *A Perspective on Anti-Submarine Warfare: Statement by David Schilling, Hearings on the First Concurrent Resolution for Fiscal Year 1978*, 95th Cong., 1st sess., 1977 (Washington, D.C., 1977), pp. 239–245. Although prohibited from outright advocacy, naval analysts at the Congressional Budget Office have tended to lean toward defensive sea control as the preferred strategy. See, e.g., U.S. Congress, Congressional Budget Office, *Future Budget Requirements of the 600 Ship Navy*, prepared by Peter T. Tarpgaard and Robert E. Mechanic (Washington, D.C., September 1977), pp. 3–9; *Shaping the General Purpose Navy of the Eighties: Issues for Fiscal Years 1981–1985*, prepared by Dov S. Zackheim et al. (Washington, D.C., January 1980), pp. 7–19, 127–140; *The US Sea Control Mission: Forces, Capabilities, and Requirements*, prepared by Dov S. Zackheim (Washington, D.C., June 1977).

[4]There are other scenarios in which Soviet threats to the SLOC might be important, including threats to the SLOC in the Pacific. The Atlantic SLOC defense mission is sufficiently difficult, and sufficiently important, however, that it ought to serve as a good indicator of the relative merits of offensive and defensive sea control in other scenarios.

relative merits of offensive versus defensive sea-control strategies. For example, if one agrees that these risks are real and sizable, and if analysis were to suggest that both strategies were equally likely to defend the SLOC successfully, then the risks of nuclear escalation associated with the offensive strategy might be the determining factor in deciding which strategy to adopt.

Plan of the Chapter

This chapter has three main sections and one appendix. First, I summarize the NATO sea control problem. This entails a brief description of the threat and a short discussion of the reinforcement issue. Second, I discuss the fundamentals of defensive sea control. (The preceding chapter outlined the fundamentals of offensive sea control.) Third, I assess the absolute effectiveness of each of the two strategies as methods of SLOC defense and suggest which of the two makes more sense for the United States and its NATO allies.[5] A brief discussion of how *capabilities* for both offensive and defensive sea control reinforce each other is also included.

Appendix 4 offers a brief discussion of a simple standard arithmetic model for assessing the contribution of ASW barriers and choke points to a defensive sea control campaign.

The Atlantic SLOC and the Potential Threat

NATO's Reinforcement Effort

The NATO worst-case planning assumption for conventional war in the 1980s was a relatively short-warning, short-mobilization Soviet

[5]In Miller and Glaser, eds., *Navy and Nuclear Weapons,* I present a lengthy analysis that compares the two strategies in terms of their tactical advantages and disadvantages. This addresses the traditional arguments the navy has made for a forward strategy—that it is simply a better way to kill submarines than a defensive strategy. Although this argument has fallen into disuse to be supplanted by the "diversion" argument, it nevertheless merits systematic attention. The navy abandoned the "effectiveness" argument during the early years of the Reagan administration when conventional attacks on SSBNs became legitimate in public discourse. In some future administration this gambit might be considered unduly escalatory. If so, the navy can be expected to revert to a simple tactical effectiveness argument. Additionally, a simple comparison of the tactical strengths and weaknesses of the two strategies provides a vehicle for developing sufficient understanding of both to assess the probability that either will successfully defend the SLOC. Killing submarines is one means to that end, but as the navy correctly points out, diverting them to other activities would be another means. Such diversion cannot occur, however, unless that strategy possesses a modicum of tactical effectiveness narrowly defined, i.e., it must do or threaten to do some meaningful damage.

attack. In most NATO planning scenarios, NATO's mobilization order was expected to lag the Pact's by roughly four days, with war starting ten days after that at NATO M + 14. According to official estimates, some reinforcements were expected to move to Europe by sea very quickly. "The Army depends upon airlift to deploy and sustain units until sealift takes effect which may range from about 15–20 days in Europe."[6] This assumption is consistent with reported shortfalls in prepositioned equipment for U.S. units scheduled for rapid reinforcement, the sheer tonnage associated with ground-force units for which no prepositioning has been planned, and limitations in NATO ammunition stocks.

Adm. Wesley McDonald suggested that the necessary military equipment and munitions might amount to 8.5 million tons, plus 15 million tons of petroleum, all to be delivered within six months.[7] Given average cargo capacities of about 5000 tons per ship, this implies 1700 shiploads of military dry cargo and perhaps 250 tankers, or an average of 325 ships per month if six months were indeed allotted to this effort. Elsewhere, I have developed my own estimates of the cargo to be delivered and NATO's ability to move it, which suggest that the total reinforcement could probably have been completed in roughly four months rather than six.[8]

Although world economic activity would no doubt diminish during the initial period of war, it has been suggested that as many as 1500 shiploads of economic cargo per month might be needed to keep the European economies functioning. By my estimate, only about 450 of these could be accommodated in military equipment convoys. If another 1000 economic cargoes per month were considered truly critical, then NATO might have had an escort shortfall, although my own estimated allocation of escort vessels to convoy duty and their monthly activity rate is conservative, suggesting that more convoys could have been

[6]Lt. Gen. Fred K. Mahaffey, Deputy Chief of Staff for Operations and Plans, Department of the Army, "Prepared Statement," in *SASC FY 85, Pt. 8*, p. 3954.

[7]McDonald, "The Critical Role of Sea Power," pp. 14–17. "The volume of military shipping needed is 8.5 million tons of equipment and stores and 15 million tons of petroleum products. All of this has to be transported within 180 days at a tempo of up to 800 sailings per month." The NATO allies agreed to make available 600 ships, "the majority of the sealift capacity needed for a Nato reinforcement." *U.S. Department of Defense, Annual Report*, FY 1986, pp. 196–197. These would have been provided "during preconflict period of increased readiness." Roughly 1200 additional militarily useful ships could have been provided once the war began. *SASC FY 86, Pt. 8*, p. 4661.

[8]Posen, "Nato's Reinforcement Capability," pp. 327–339. I estimate the military cargo to be moved, the rate at which transport shipping could have become available, and the escort vessels that could have been allocated to convoy duty. I argue that fifteen sixty-ship convoys, each accompanied by seven escort vessels, with one-half of the ships loaded with military cargo, could have been dispatched monthly.

organized if necessary. Thus, in the first sixty days of the war, as many as 4000 shiploads of material would have needed to find their way to Europe, although only the military equipment and munitions, roughly a quarter, would have been considered truly irreplaceable.[9]

Comparisons with World War II

The SLOC battle in an East-West war would probably have taken a rather different form from that of World War II. Atlantic sea control forces were seldom if ever called upon to deliver such a large quantity of scarce, critical resources, against a relatively fresh adversary, under such severe time pressure, over such a great distance in World War II. German U-boats were seldom called upon to destroy particular military convoys in particular time frames. The principal exception to these two observations seems to be the North Africa landings of November 1942 (TORCH), when several large convoys from England and the United States had to reach North Africa at the same time in the face of substantial *potential* resistance from German and Italian submarines. A combination of good intelligence, intense air cover from Gibralter, and a very high density of escorts held losses to U-boats to a low-level—84,000 tons of merchant shipping (twelve to fourteen ships) and six naval vessels—in spite of initial orders to the German Navy to commit its U-boats to throw back the invasion. Moreover, in November operations in the Mediterranean, fifteen U-boats may have been sunk, a high price to pay for so little success.[10]

The Battle of the Atlantic, on the other hand, was a protracted war of attrition in which hundreds of ships loaded with both finished military equipment and economic cargoes of all kinds had to cross the Atlantic every month. The German submarine effort was mainly directed at the Anglo-Saxon war economy; it was analogous to Allied strategic bombing.

[9]See McDonald, "The Critical Role of Seapower"; Robert King, "Are NATO's Navies Shipshape?" *Armed Forces Journal International*, March 1986, p. 38; see Paul H. Nitze and Leonard Sullivan, eds., *Securing the Seas: The Soviet Naval Challenge and Western Alliance Options*, (Boulder, Colo., 1979), pp. 345–347, 359, 371.

[10]Patrick Beesley, *Very Special Intelligence* (New York, 1981), pp. 153–156; and Sternhell and Thorndike, *Antisubmarine Warfare*, pp. 34–35, 100–112. Good intelligence did *not* include German Navy message decrypts, since Bletchley Park had not yet broken the Atlantic U-boat Triton cipher used in the German Navy's Enigma machines. There was no magic involved, just hard work, careful planning, and massed forces. The six British Mediterranean assault convoys held 158 transports and 52 escorts, while six other convoys contained 84 ships and 40 escorts. Thus, escort-to-transport ratios of 1:2–1:3 prevailed, versus my assumed ratio for current convoys of roughly 1:9. World War II convoys in the North Atlantic during 1942–43 seem to have averaged about 1:6.

Given the apparent "short-war" focus of Soviet continental military strategy, the limited size of the Soviet submarine force, and the relatively small target set critical to NATO's reinforcement, a Soviet effort against the SLOC could not have followed the German pattern in World War II. The Soviets would have needed to destroy specific ships, in large numbers, at a particular time. It had to find those ships against a possible backdrop of many more unimportant ships. Moreover, since the target set was small, NATO had the option to "super-protect" these ships in fast, well-escorted convoys that were somewhat analogous to the amphibious invasion forces of World War II.

These distinctions are relevant to understanding the debate on the relative merits of offensive and defensive sea control, since the Soviet Navy seems to have had greater potential for an early, intense campaign to slow initial U.S. reinforcements, and greater incentives to engage in it. The Soviets were widely believed to posture their ground and air forces, and plan their operations, in pursuit of a quick victory on land. Although it is difficult to define "quick," an operation that promised a possibility of denying NATO ground forces operational reserves in the second month of conflict might have appeared very attractive to the Soviets. Thus, the U.S. Navy was motivated to seek a sea-control strategy that could have been effective in a short, intense campaign.

If the early phase of a future sea-war could have been successfully negotiated by NATO, then the SLOC battle might have developed into a campaign like the World War II Battle of the Atlantic. But given the geographical disadvantages of the modern Soviet Navy in comparison with the position of the Nazis in 1942, the liabilities of diesel-electric submarines (the easiest to mass produce and man) in attacks against convoys of modern merchant ships, and the production and manning difficulties that would have attended any effort to mass produce nuclear-powered submarines, an ASW attrition war against the Soviet Union would likely have been less problematical than the campaign of World War II.[11] This point would be moot, however, if the initial battle to control the SLOC was lost and U.S. reinforcement failed to reach Europe in time to forestall a Soviet victory on the ground.

The Threat

The primary threat to the Atlantic SLOC was the Soviet Northern Fleet's force of 136 diesel-electric and nuclear-powered submarines

[11]Shilling, in U.S. Congress, Senate, Budget Committee, *A Perspective*. This assumes the United States and its allies manage to hold on to the geographic choke points that currently limit Soviet access to the high seas.

armed with torpedoes, cruise missiles, or both.[12] Fifty long-range cruise-missile-carrying, Badger C naval bombers were reported to be permanently attached to the Soviet Northern Fleet. Some forty of the much more capable Tu-22M Backfire B, then assumed to be based in the Baltic, were also apparently available for Northern Fleet operations.[13] These, however, were more often viewed as threats to carrier task forces operating in the Norwegian Sea than to convoys operating in the Atlantic.[14] Thus, this chapter mainly discusses the submarine problem.

Although possession of this large number of submarines and long-range bombers gave the Soviets substantial raw capability to attack the SLOC, there was little evidence that Soviet naval strategists envisioned this role for these forces. Rather, their purpose was mainly to set up and protect a defended bastion for the Soviet SSBN force.[15] This was the view of the U.S. Navy, and it was shared by most naval analysts and commentators. Because of the comparative noisiness of most Soviet SSBNs, the high quality of Western antisubmarine warfare equipment, and Western control of the fleet's access to the open ocean, the Soviets seemed intent on operating most of their SSBNs close to home, and protecting them and their crucial bases with the majority of the submarine, surface ship, and land-based aircraft of the Northern Fleet. Indeed, this Soviet concern was the glue that held the maritime strategy together. Rear Adm. John L. Butts, then U.S. Navy director of naval intelligence, stated that "the primary task [of the Soviet Navy] is to deploy and protect the SSBN force."[16] In the same testimony the admiral listed SLOC interdiction as the fourth of five Soviet missions, just before support of state interests. Though he did not state clearly that the

[12]See table 5.1 for a breakdown of Soviet submarine assets.

[13]Information on the organization and distribution of Soviet naval Backfires is not good. IISS, *Military Balance, 1987–1988*, pp. 38, 45, offers some rough estimates of Soviet naval Backfire strength (130) and their distribution. Two Backfire Regiments totaling forty aircraft were said to be based in the Baltic, two in the Black Sea and one in the Pacific. A sixth was unaccounted for. Given that the Baltic is too small a sea to require the great range of these aircraft, I hypothesize that they were available for duty with the Northern Fleet. Although a bit vague, public accounts of Backfire activities in the Soviet naval maneuvers support this hypothesis. See also Donald Daniel and Gael Donelan-Tarleton, "The Soviet Navy in 1985," *US Naval Institute Proceedings Naval Review Issue*, May 1986, p. 99.

[14]Most published reports of Soviet use of Backfires in exercises suggest a carrier focus for these aircraft. See Donald C. Daniel and Gael Donelan-Tarleton, "The Soviet Navy in 1984," *US Naval Institute Proceedings, Naval Review Issue*, May 1985, pp. 91, 361–363; Daniel and Donelan-Tarleton, "Soviet Navy 1985," pp. 99, 104–105; and the testimony of Rear Adm. John L. Butts, in *SASC FY 86, Pt. 8*, pp. 4358, 4366.

[15]There were thirty-eight ballistic missile submarines based in the Northern Fleet (60 percent of the total Soviet modern SSBN force). On the strength and distribution of the Soviet SSBN force, see U.S. Department of Defense, *Soviet Military Power, 1988*, p. 48.

[16]*SASC FY 86, Pt. 8*, p. 4367.

Table 5.1. Soviet submarine order of battle: Major fleets, estimated distribution (1988)

Type	Northern	Pacific
SSBN		
Typhoon	5	—
Delta	24	16
Yankee	9	8
Diesel attack		
Tango	9	9
Kilo	4	7
Foxtrot	40	20
SSGN		
Echo II	15	14
Charlie I	6	6
Charlie II	6	—
Oscar	3	—
Yankee	1	—
SSG-SSB		
Juliet	10	6
Golf	—	6
SSN		
Alfa	7	—
Victor (all)	24	16
Sierra/Akula	3	2
Yankee (convert)	2	—
November	6	7
Echo I (convert)	—	5
Total (attack)	136	92
TOTAL	174	122

Note: This estimate is prepared from diverse sources. In many cases the distribution of specific submarine classes is little more than a hunch. For SSBN distribution, see U.S. Department of Defense, *Soviet Military Power, 1988* (Washington, D.C., 1986), p. 48; for submarine force totals in the Northern, Baltic, Black Sea, and Pacific fleets, see ibid., pp. 14–15; see also IISS, *Military Balance, 1985–86* (London, 1985), pp. 26–30; *Jane's Fighting Ships, 1985–1986* (London, 1985), p. 511; Rear Adm. J. R. Hill (RNR), *Anti-Submarine Warfare* (Annapolis, Md., 1985), pp. 18–36; U.S. Navy, *Navy Fact File*, 7th ed. (Washington, D.C., 1984), p. 63; Office of Naval Intelligence, *Current Naval Intelligence Issues* (March 1987, mimeo), pp. 4–6; U.S. Congress, House, House Armed Services Committee on Intelligence Issues, *Statement of RADM Studeman* (Washington, D.C., 1 March 1988, mimeo).

missions were listed in order of priority, his main comment on SLOC interdiction was to the effect that the mission was becoming "more practicable . . . with the growing number of ships and aircraft that the Soviets have."[17] In March of 1988 his successor, Rear Adm. William O. Studeman, offered a very similar characterization of Soviet missions, although with a subtle shift of emphasis; he stressed that the primary mission of the Soviet Navy was to gain control of waters proximate to the Soviet Union and deny enemy naval operations out to 2000–3000 km from Soviet territory.[18] This strategy would both help protect the Soviet SSBN force and extend the radius of Soviet strategic air defenses.

Given the consensus that SLOC interdiction was not a primary, or apparently even a secondary, Soviet mission, why be so concerned about it? The answer lies in the potential damage that Soviet submarines might have done had they been committed against the SLOC. So long as the Soviets had the potential to attack the SLOC, NATO had to have the capability to defend it.[19]

The Two Strategies

Offensive Sea Control

To briefly remind the reader of the discussion of the preceding chapter, offensive sea control, as practiced in the U.S. Navy's maritime strategy required large-scale attacks into the contiguous waters around the Soviet Union and against Soviet naval bases *early* in a conflict. At least in the Atlantic, it appears that the offensive would have occurred in two phases. If permitted by the National Command Authority, a relatively large number of SSNs would have surged into the north Norwegian and Barents seas in a crisis, even before the initiation of hostilities.[20] If fighting commenced, their mission would have been to

[17]Ibid., p. 4345.

[18]*Statement of Studeman*, p. 3. "SLOCs outside the sea denial perimeter will initially be threatened by relatively few forces, so long as higher priority CVBGs and other nuclear capable units constitute a threat or until resupply SLOCs become of strategic importance to the outcome of the conflict" (p. 12).

[19]U.S. Congress, CBO, *Shaping the General Purpose Navy*, p. 51, "Regardless of Soviet priorities, the NATO allies would nevertheless have to conduct defensive sea control missions in the North Atlantic to deter or defeat any Soviet attacks on the sea lanes and to hedge against shifts in Soviet plans."

[20]Some U.S. SSNs operated regularly in these areas. I have been unable to discover whether or not a presidential authorization was required substantially to increase their numbers. Authorization from higher authority would definitely have been required to change the "rules of engagement" in a more permissive direction.

sink as many Soviet submarines and surface vessels as possible and to employ land-attack conventional cruise missiles to whittle down Soviet land-based naval aviation, especially Badger and Backfire aircraft that could threaten carrier task forces. If predeployment was prohibited or simply was too slow, then the United States would have marshaled its SSN force in the southern Norwegian Sea and fought its way northward, ultimately breaking into the Barents Sea. Once SSNs had reduced Soviet naval defenses, U.S. carrier task forces could have moved into northern waters to bring Soviet bases under more sustained air attack.

Before discussing defensive sea control, it is important to note that the navy's interest in offensive sea control may have been driven by fears of one particular option open to the Soviets, at least in principle, had the Soviets believed that early SLOC attacks were militarily significant. Since NATO was unlikely to have started a war, the Soviets would have chosen when combat began. Thus, they could have safely deployed some of their submarines across NATO's defensive barriers in time of crisis, avoiding the attrition that those barriers could otherwise have exacted. These submarines would have then been positioned astride the sea lanes at the outset of the war. There is some evidence that this "pre-hostilities" deployment option frightened the U.S. Navy and helped stimulate its interest in trying to convince the Soviets that they would find themselves under significant pressure in their home waters very early in any war. Thus, they would keep their attack submarines at home to defend their SSBNs. In supporting the forward strategy, Adm. Wesley McDonald, a former commander in chief of the U.S. Atlantic Command, asserted,

> In the event that we are forced into a conflict with the Soviet Union and Warsaw Pact countries establishing sea control quickly is of utmost importance. We must put at risk as many of the Soviet naval forces as possible early in any conflict. The majority of Soviet naval forces must be contained as far north as possible. This can be accomplished by offensive actions that keep the Soviet Navy focused on the threat to their own force in the Norwegian and Barents Seas. *If offensive operations are allowed to break out into the broad Atlantic, many more forces may be required to defeat the threat, or the time to accomplish our tasks will be excessive.*[21]

The Fundamentals of Defensive Sea Control

Defensive sea control starts from the premise that finding and killing submarines is not easy. Yet the vital seaborne traffic to Europe in the

[21] *SASC FY 85, Pt. 2*, pp. 1113–1114.

event of large-scale conventional war must somehow be secured against these dangerous foes. The best way to do so is to follow the tried and true methods of two great wars. Indeed, the debate about the relative merits of offensive and defensive sea control arose in both those wars and was largely resolved in favor of the more defensive approach.[22]

Defensive sea control first tries to exploit every technological and geographical advantage available to make it difficult for the submarine to reach the sea lanes, and difficult to return home after a patrol. Opportunities for leverage on the enemy submarine may be offered by nature—constricted passages and long distances, or by the submarine's mission—it ultimately must reveal itself if it wishes to attack.

Every possible advantage of surprise, stealth, and deception must be exploited to hide the convoy's route from the adversary. The convoy should be surrounded with escorts of ships and planes to inhibit final approach and attack. If the adversary does attack, they try to ensure that he does not have a second opportunity. If available, mobile hunter-killer groups should be kept at sea so that if an organized attack by several enemy submarines is mounted against a convoy, a task force of heavily armed, well-trained, experienced, professional submarine killers can break it up before it gets under way, or counterattack to limit its effectiveness. The primary objective is to get convoys through successfully. The means to that end is making the enemy submariners' life as complicated, unpleasant, and short as possible. *Because of the submarine's stealth, the process is one of attrition.*

NATO would have been particularly blessed in such a contest. Roughly a 2200-nm voyage is required for Soviet submarines to reach the southwestern approaches to the United Kingdom. Along the way, the Soviet Northern Fleet must traverse two geographical choke points to reach the Atlantic SLOC. The Germans suffered no such disadvantage in World War II.[23] The first barrier runs from the North Cape to

[22]On the campaign against German U-boats in World War I, see the excellent brief accounts in C. R. M. F. Cruttwell, *A History of the Great War, 1914–1918*, 2d ed. (London, 1934), pp. 376–389; Bernadotte E. Schmitt and Harold C. Vedeler, *The World in the Crucible* (New York, 1984), pp. 238–243, esp. the authors' observation that "the Admiralty under Jellicoe's professional leadership, however, resisted the strategy of convoy mainly because it had concentrated so long, in the tradition of naval activism, on fighting the U-boat rather than protecting the merchantmen. The Admiralty was thus not ready to transfer many ships from antisubmarine work to service as convoy escorts" (p. 240). Although there was little resistance to the concept of convoy at the outset of World War II, assets useful to a convoy protection strategy were not always provided as a matter of priority. Theodore Ropp, *War in the Modern World* (New York, 1962), pp. 325–328.

[23]The possible exception is the moderately constricted approaches to the Bay of Biscay, where most U-boats were based during the height of the Battle of the Atlantic. The "Bay Offensive" exploited this choke point with some success, although its proximity to German air and sea bases coupled with the limitations of existing technology made it a

Svalbard to Greenland. It was seeded with underwater listening devices and would have been defended with mines and SSNs, and to a limited extent by ASW patrol aircraft. The second, the GIUK gap, runs from Greenland to Iceland to Scotland to Norway. It was seeded with listening devices and could have been supported by the full panoply of sea-based and land-based ASW forces. Once past the barriers, Soviet submarines would still not have been in an entirely hospitable environment; the only friendly shore was Cuba. The North Atlantic Treaty Organization came by its name honestly.

Defensive sea control had few "boosters" but many friends. Anyone who has studied the antisubmarine campaigns of World Wars I and II is unlikely to view a repetition as anything other than the least bad of a number of bad alternatives. Although they ultimately won the SLOC battle, the Allies lost 2753 ships to Axis submarines from September of 1939 to August of 1945.[24]

Included among the friends of defensive sea control, first and foremost has been the U.S. Navy itself. Although the navy most enthusiastically supported the offensive strategy, it did not leave the rear unprotected. The navy understood that the Soviets did not need to follow the script written for them.[25] A huge infrastructure and substantial supporting forces for a defensive SLOC battle was acquired.

Adm. Wesley McDonald, then SACLANT, reflected the navy's preference for offensive operations, as well as its more conservative intention to exploit choke points for barrier ASW:

> The method of control most likely to be effective against SACLANT's major threat, the submarine, will be a mixture of forward ASW barriers to control the choke points, attrition warfare against targets of opportunity that have escaped into the open sea, and offensive strikes against the enemy's ports and bases. Geography has not been kind to Russia, and this liability must be exploited. The Soviets are seriously disadvantaged by the remoteness

---

less impressive barrier than the one that NATO ought to be able to deploy in the GIUK gap. The barrier off northern Norway, however, may suffer many of the tactical difficulties suffered by the Allies in the Bay Offensive. See Samuel Eliot Morison, *The Atlantic Battle Won, May 1943–May 1945*, vol. X: *History of United States Naval Operations in World War II* (Boston, 1975), pp. 85–107; see also Sternhell and Thorndike, *Antisubmarine Warfare*, pp. 143–145.

[24]Sternhell and Thorndike, *Antisubmarine Warfare*, p. 86.

[25]*SASC FY 86, Pt. 2*, p. 989. Admiral Watkins argued that the navy was prepared to deal with "the leakage of Soviet forces southward in the North Atlantic." "We are ready to go both ways, but we can match their strategy as it changes. We have built a navy based on a range of options that does not require a single strategy to be carried out. We are ready to deal with that kind of problem." (He refers to Soviet submarine predeployment.) Nevertheless, these problems were treated in his testimony as secondary.

> of their seaports and the fact that their fleets must pass through relatively narrow areas they do not control. It will be imperative that as many of their forces as possible be stopped at the natural bottlenecks.[26]

Although the navy seldom made this point explicitly, it is clear that the offensive maritime strategy worked only in conjunction with substantial defensive capabilities. It was the historical noisiness of Soviet SSBNs, and *their consequent fear of NATO's defensive barriers* and large ASW infrastructure in the Norwegian Sea and Atlantic Ocean, that encouraged the Soviets to keep their SSBNs close to home under protection of other naval forces. If these boats were very quiet, or if they had had the safe run of the open seas, the Soviets would have had little reason to keep them at home and defend them directly. The former proposition, however, started to become tenuous in the late 1980s as the Soviets began to deploy new and presumably much quieter SSBNs.[27] Nevertheless, NATO's barriers remained strong, and even a quiet boat would not have wanted to run them if doing so was not essential. Moreover, it is far easier for barrier ASW to remain competitive with Soviet quieting efforts than it is for offensive ASW to do so. Hence, the forward offensive strategy depended (and will continue to depend) on the competence of NATO's defensive barriers to achieve any effectiveness at all.

Potent defensive barriers also aided the offensive strategy in another way; they discouraged the Soviets from risking their best SSNs and SSGNs on SLOC attacks. Even by the mid-1990s perhaps 60 percent of Soviet submarine-based warheads will still be on older or less technically sophisticated platforms, although perhaps 40 percent will be on newer quiet boats.[28] Given overall Soviet naval priorities in the 1980s, one of the main purposes of the aggressive Soviet program to produce a fleet of quiet SSNs was probably to better ensure the protection of the SSBN bastion. The Soviet Navy had about twenty-two Victor IIIs, three Akulas, and two Sierras, for a total of twenty-seven relatively quiet,

[26] McDonald, "The Critical Role of Seapower," p. 16.

[27] *Statement of Studeman*, p. 35. "Newer generations of quieter Soviet submarines are most difficult to detect, classify, and prosecute than their antecedents. This, combined with their normal operation in or near the periphery of the Soviet Union in peacetime, presents a new ASW challenge to the U.S. Navy. Nevertheless, where these submarines are encountered, the U.S. has maintained a distinct tactical advantage over the Soviets by virtue of superior knowledge, sensors, and quieting." See also p. 31.

[28] See U.S. Department of Defense, *Soviet Military Power, 1987* pp. 27, 33–35. Soviet SSBNs will ultimately become quiet enough to survive on their own, but this change will be gradual. The Soviets were introducing relatively quiet Typhoon SSBNs at the rate of roughly one boat every two years during the second half of the 1980s.

modern SSNs by 1988—a small number.[29] It would have been quite illogical for the Soviets to have exerted such an effort, only to squander the force on a long and harrowing trip to the Atlantic from which many would not have returned, thus weakening the defenses of the bastion and facilitating the entry of U.S. SSNs and the destruction of Soviet SSBNs at a later date.

Those outside the navy who favored defensive sea control did so as much by default as by conviction. In mounting a rhetorical counterattack against those who have opposed the Maritime Strategy, Maj. Hugh O'Donnel, U.S. Marine Corps, divided the opponents into three classes—those such as retired Vice Adm. Stansfield Turner who simply felt it could not be executed without serious damage to our own forces; those (particularly this author) who argued that the strategy would have increased the risks of precipitate nuclear escalation; and those such as Robert Komer who felt that the strategy diverted resources from higher priority missions—especially direct defense of the central front.[30] Although opponents of the maritime strategy either explicitly or implicitly settled on defensive sea control as the likely alternative, none of them straightforwardly argued that defensive sea control was an effective way to deal with the Soviet submarine threat to the SLOC, or that it was equal or superior to offensive sea control as a way to protect NATO shipping. To these tasks I now turn.

Defensive Sea Control: Absolute Effectiveness

The prospects for defensive sea control may profitably be measured against two "model" contingencies, the classical, World War I and II style attrition campaign against economic cargoes, and an early intense campaign by predeployed Soviet submarines aimed specifically at military cargoes. In combination, the two provide insight into the intermediate case, possible Soviet efforts to interfere with NATO's military reinforcement and resupply in a war that lasts several months.[31]

[29] *Statement of Studeman*, pp. 30, 34. At best, they were completing two or three SSNs per year. Even by the mid-1990s they will thus only have about forty high-quality SSNs, split between the Northern and Pacific fleets.

[30] Maj. Hugh K. O'Donnell, Jr., USMC, "Northern Flank Maritime Offensive," *US Naval Institute Proceedings* 111 (September 1985): 42–57. In fairness to Admiral Turner, he opposed only the carrier portion of the maritime strategy.

[31] A quite different interdiction campaign from that discussed below is often suggested. It is argued that the Soviets would—through a combination of aerial bombing, aerial minelaying, and submarine minelaying—have damaged NATO's ports so badly that even if convoys arrived with few losses, they would have been unable to unload their vital equipment. This campaign merits a thorough analysis in its own right, which is beyond the scope of this essay. The navy's proposed offensive maritime strategy could not have dissuaded the Soviets from striking NATO's ports from the air, nor was it likely to have

Economic War of Attrition

The first contingency is the easiest to assess. As argued earlier, the Soviet Union did not have many reasonably modern SSNs/SSGNs to commit against the Atlantic SLOC—roughly fifty boats. (Of these, no more than twenty were likely to have been boats that the U.S. Navy would consider to be "quiet.") Reasonably modern diesel-electrics could have provided perhaps fifty more platforms. *Soviet Military Power, 1987* suggests that about 50 percent of the Soviet submarine force could have deployed on short notice.[32] (The Soviet attack submarine commissioning rate in the late 1980s was about three and a half per year. This would barely sustain a force of 105 attack submarines worldwide, presuming a thirty-year service life, a 60 percent cut from current levels. Thus, the number of potential Atlantic SLOC attackers will drop.)[33]

Nuclear-powered submarines do not lend themselves to an attrition commerce campaign. In the normal order of tactical operations, the submarine must provide the defender with many opportunities to engage. In fact, given that merchant ships are now able to reach speeds of 15 knots or more, and even "quiet" nuclear submarines seem to generate an uncomfortably exploitable acoustic signature at these speeds, operations against convoys, over time, may be a risky activity for SSNs.[34] Repeated convoy attacks would make it very likely that the force would suffer significant attrition. As discussed in Appendix 4, any submarine dispatched from the Northern Fleet to attack convoys in the Atlantic would have had to traverse two major, geographically

---

discouraged the Soviets from risking older diesel-electric or nuclear-powered submarines on offensive mining missions. Given the very large throughput capacities of NATO ports demonstrated in peacetime trade and the relatively small amount of military cargo that had to be delivered, the Soviet port destruction campaign would have to have been very effective to stop NATO's reinforcements.

[32]U.S. Department of Defense, *Soviet Military Power, 1987*, p. 96.

[33]Ibid., p. 122, estimates that the Soviet Union built eight submarines in 1985, and eight in 1986. Testimony in 1988 by the director of naval intelligence suggests that eight boats were launched in 1987, including an SSBN, but three were SSs sold abroad. One Oscar SSGN, one Akula SSN, one Victor III SSN, and one Kilo diesel-electric were delivered to the Soviet Navy. (see n. 29 above). On the basis of the forgoing and an examination of data presented in the 1985–1987 editions of *Soviet Military Power*, plus data presented in testimony by the navy before the Senate Armed Services Committee for the FY 1986 budget, I estimate that the Soviet Navy took delivery of a small number of submarines annually in the mid-1980s, perhaps one SSBN, a half an SSGN, two SSNs, and one SS. There were twenty-two Victor III deliveries between its 1979 appearance and 1987, two and a half boats per year. It seems unlikely that SSN deliveries will exceed three per year in the 1990s. See *SASC FY 86, Pt. 8*, pp. 4345–4365. Assuming a thirty-year submarine life, this would permit a ninety-SSN force to be sustained.

[34]Although at 15 knots the convoy itself generates quite a bit of noise, which may serve to partially mask the signature of the SSN.

determined defensive barriers, plus the various escorts and maritime patrol aircraft operating in direct support of convoys. Patrols are of limited duration because of limits on food and torpedoes. The Soviets were not well placed to resupply themselves anywhere in the Atlantic and thus would have had to regularly cycle through NATO's barriers. If we assume that the SSN had been able to mount two convoy attacks per patrol, it would have been exposed to six possible NATO attacks per complete patrol.[35] At a plausible .1 pk (probability of kill) per barrier, the Soviets would have lost 47 percent of their force on its first patrol. If only half the force was ready for the first patrol, this means a loss of twelve SSNs. At then Soviet commissioning rates, this loss would have taken four to five years to replace.

To mount a sustained SLOC campaign in World War II, the Germans had to build 1162 boats; they lost 785, sank 2600 ships, and although the campaign diverted many resources, it failed to prevent the Allied buildup for the invasions of North Africa, Italy, Normandy, and the south of France, and only intermittently disrupted the flow of Lend-Lease material to the Soviet Union.[36] Nuclear submarines and their crews cannot be cranked out at anything remotely like this rate.[37] Even if Soviet nuclear submarines were several times more effective in comparison with Allied defensive measures than were German boats in World War II, the Soviets would have needed to produce several dozen nuclear submarines per year (as well as trained crews) in an attrition war.

The alternative, of course, is to revert to World War II practice and produce an updated diesel-electric submarine in large numbers. The

[35]Most open-source analyses assume one to two convoy attacks per patrol (see n. 55 below). Nobody explains the source of this number. I have been unable to turn up an average number of attacks per patrol for German submarines in World War II, but an examination of various data suggests to me a combination of the following: average torpedo kill probabilities were low; many submarines fired few, if any, torpedoes per patrol; some submarines did most of the killing with the rest doing comparatively little. The latter two phenomena are consistent with the hypothesis that, on the average, only one or two convoy attacks per patrol would actually occur under combat conditions. Barriers at geographical choke points would exact attrition both on the outward and homeward legs of the journey, for a total of four encounters. I treat each convoy encounter as one killing opportunity for the defender, although some analysts also treat convoy defenses as a barrier that must be traversed once on ingress and once on egress. This seems too stylized to me.

[36]James L. Stokesbury, *A Short History of World War II* (New York, 1980), p. 131; Shilling, in U.S. Congress, Senate, Budget Committee, *A Perspective. . .*, pp. 240–241.

[37]Schilling, in U.S. Congress, Senate, Budget Committee, *A Perspective . . .*, p. 239, observes that "nuclear submarine represent the expenditure of much more time, money and skilled manpower than do diesel submarines. This means that wartime losses cannot be replaced from new construction." See also pp. 240, 242–243.

Soviets built the Kilo diesel-electric submarine in three yards in the 1980s, with roughly twenty completed between its introduction in 1980 and 1987.[38] It seems quite plausible that the construction rate of these boats could have been increased. Given German production in World War II, the Soviets, with a far larger economy, ought to have been able to produce sizable numbers of non-nuclear boats. Diesel-electrics are unlikely to have fared well in a SLOC battle, however.

In 1977, on the basis of calculations presented in Appendix 1, a notional barrier was expected to have a pk of roughly .18 against a diesel electric submarine (SS). There is no reason to believe that NATO's ability has worsened or diesel-electric technology has improved to change this factor very much. Thus, if the Soviet Union had dispatched half of its available SSs against the SLOC, twenty-five boats, and these had been able to mount two convoy attacks per patrol, it might have expected to lose 70 percent of them, seventeen boats in the first deployment of the war. From the outset of World War II, it took the Germans nearly a year and a half to bring their submarine commissioning rate to twenty per month.[39] For the first year and a half of the war only sixty boats were constructed.[40] At 500–700 tons displacement, these boats were much smaller and presumably less technically advanced, and hence difficult to build, than the 3000-ton Kilo. Unless a war is preceded by a long period of political tension and mobilization, it would take some time for the Soviets to bring SS construction to a rate that could sustain an intense SLOC battle.

The diesel-electric is probably not as useful a high-seas convoy attack weapon as German U-boats were in the first half of World War II. Proceeding under water, on battery, at the 15-knot speed that current transport shipping can achieve, a modern diesel-electric submarine would probably exhaust its batteries in seven or eight hours.[41] Running on diesel with snorkel exposed, necessary to recharge batteries, provides the defenders with five exploitable signatures—acoustical, optical, radar, infra-red, and exhaust fume. This situation is dangerous for the submariner, especially if an ASW aircraft is in the vicinity. Thus, just intercepting and keeping contact with a convoy would currently

[38] *Statement of Studeman,* p. 34. Nine were sold abroad.

[39] Sternhell and Thorndike, *Anti-Submarine Warfare,* p. 81. (This is the summary report of Division 6, vol. 3, of the National Defense Research Committee. It offers a brief history of the Atlantic ASW campaign, as well as a sample of data collected while the campaign was under way and examples of how the data was used to better Allied performance.)

[40] Ibid., p. 83.

[41] U.S. Congress, CBO, *Shaping the General Purpose Navy,* p. 133. For short periods, of an hour or two, a modern diesel-electric on battery could proceed at 25 knots.

be much more difficult for an SS than it was in World War II.[42] In that war, merchant ships were quite slow, so that during the period before radar was widely deployed on escort vessels and aircraft, submarines could outrun convoys on the surface, at night. It was possible to keep contact for extended periods.[43] This is probably no longer possible. A 1979 study concluded that, relative to World War II, "conventionally powered submarines are perhaps somewhat more vulnerable—at least when they are in motion."[44] Adm. Wesley McDonald was skeptical that diesel-electric boats were a major problem, noting that "Soviet nuclear attack submarines offer the main threat to our reinforcement shipping."[45]

The position of the NATO alliance regarding merchant tonnage was far superior in the 1980s to that of the Alliance at the outset of World War II. The NATO alliance proper had about 115 million gross tons of shipping (6700 vessels) available. Roughly another 100 million tons (5500 vessels) was registered in Liberia and Panama, much of which was actually owned by nationals of Alliance countries.[46] If Soviet diesel-electric submarines were able to sink ships at the highest rate achieved by the Germans in World War II, eighty-seven ships per month from January to September of 1942, it would have taken them eleven years to sink all these ships. At the World War II average sinking rate of thirty-six ships per month, it would have taken twenty-eight years. At the best German U-boat/merchant ship exchange rate (22:1 from July 1940 to March 1941), 554 Soviet subs would have been needed to sink all of these ships. At the average World War II exchange rate (3.8:1), 3200 would have been required. At the beginning of World War II 40 million gross tons of shipping (about 7500 vessels) was available. In the course of the war all Axis U-boats sank 2753 ships, of 14,557,000 gross tons.[47]

[42]If Soviet satellite reconnaissance and Command and Control had worked well, however, it might have been possible to maneuver diesel-electric submarines or SSNs into barrier positions astride the convoy's course to permit an intercept without necessarily alerting NATO's defenses. This is not as simple as it sounds since NATO commanders responsible for convoy security would have been looking for this gambit. And diesel-electrics would still have had a difficult time maintaining contact with the convoy.

[43]F. H. Hinsley, *British Intelligence in the Second World War: Its Influence on Strategy and Operations*, vol. 2 (New York, 1981), p. 562, reports that the worst convoy losses of March 1943 occurred in battles of at least four days' duration. It is improbable that diesel-electric submarines could accomplish this against current transport ships capable of at least 15 knots sustained speed.

[44]Nitze and Sullivan, eds., *Securing the Seas*, p. 344.

[45]McDonald, "The Critical Role of Seapower," p. 15.

[46]These figures are extracted from U.S. Department of Transportation, Maritime Administration, *Merchant Fleets of the World* (Washington, D.C., December 1986), pp. 6–7.

[47]All World War II statistics are drawn from Sternhell and Thorndike, *Antisubmarine Warfare*, pp. 80, 84. The same data are available in Willem Hackmann, *Seek and Strike* London, 1984), pp. 233–240.

It is true, of course, that the economies of the NATO allies are larger and more intensively involved in international trade than were those of the late 1930s. But had a conventional war lasted a long time, NATO's GNP superiority over the Warsaw Pact should have translated into a net advantage, as superior economic resources did in the wars against Germany. The amount of shipping available ought to have been sufficient cushion to permit NATO to increase its rate of transport ship, escort, and maritime patrol aircraft construction, in step with any increase in Soviet diesel-electric submarine construction.

Finally, as outlined in the previous section, much of the ASW infrastructure laboriously built up in World War II was already in place in the 1980s. For example, during the period of greatest German success in World War II, convoys had to proceed for long periods without air cover because of the absence of sufficient long-range aircraft and air bases. This situation was very favorable to the submarine. Students of the battle against the German U-boats agree that convoys with adequate surface escorts and constant air cover *lost virtually no ships to U-boats.*[48] Thus, the high loss rates that prevailed during the early phases of the Battle of the Atlantic are probably unrealistically pessimistic for application to the course of a NATO–Pact SLOC battle.

In sum, a World War II style attrition campaign against NATO's SLOCs would be unlikely to produce decisive results. Indeed, it would appear to have been unsustainable for the Soviets. Moreover, barrier calculations suggest that two complete patrols would have annihilated the Soviet diesel-electric submarine force and severely depleted the Soviet SSN force—suggesting that the Soviet submarine force was not well placed even for a campaign lasting longer than six months.[49] Indeed, its ability to maintain a large number of submarines deployed in the Atlantic sea lanes would have dropped substantially after the first patrol, within roughly two and a half months, assuming Soviet submarines were deployed in two successive waves.

This is not to say that the Soviets could not have put great pressure

[48]Cmdr. E. Cameron Williams, USNR, "The Four 'Iron Laws' of Merchant Shipping," *Naval War College Review* 39 (May–June 1986): 39–40, notes that "World War II convoys which had both an adequate, continuous surface escort and continuous air cover lost not one ship to enemy action." The British official historian is in virtual agreement: "during the entire war, in the Atlantic, British home waters, the Caribbean and the Arctic, only twenty-five ships (one per cent of our total losses) were sunk by U-boats when both air and surface escorts were present." Capt. S. W. Roskill, *The War at Sea, 1939–1945*, vol. 3: *The Offensive, Part I* (London, 1960), p. 264.

[49]At the end of its second patrol, the force would have traversed twelve barriers, each with a kill probability of .18, leaving only 10 percent of the force. At a kill probability of .1 per barrier versus Soviet nuclear submarines, about 30 percent of the force would remain after two complete patrols.

on the Allies, given the commitment of large resources. And, if the Soviets had found a way substantially to degrade NATO's barriers by conquering Norway, than a SLOC war would have been very much more difficult. But if Western SSN operations in the North Cape gap could have been sustained and the GIUK gap made secure, and if both were fully exploited, and if convoys were adequately protected, NATO ought to have been able to sustain intense conventional combat on the Eurasian land mass. The caveat, of course, is that NATO would have had to stalemate the initial Soviet ground onslaught. Given that the Soviets seem to have preferred a "short" war, the question arises as to whether a campaign focused against U.S. reinforcements required in the first two months of combat could have exerted a decisive impact on the ground battle.

Direct Support of the Initial Ground Offensive

Some four hundred shiploads of military cargo per month would need to reach Europe during the first two to three months of a war.[50] They would have to begin arriving about three weeks after a decision to mobilize. In addition, modest shipments of general cargo probably would have been required to preserve the morale of European populations and to sustain some minimal level of economic activity. The principal objective of a submarine campaign in this period would have been the scarce military equipment associated with U.S. Army reinforcements, and ammunition and parts to permit U.S. and European divisions and air wings to sustain combat beyond the agreed thirty-day NATO stockage requirement. Some Western analysts argue that Soviet naval commentary indicates disdain for a World War II style "tonnage war" and a belief that reinforcements and military resupply were in fact the most appropriate targets for submarine operations.[51]

The Soviets have two options in this campaign: wait until the outbreak of combat to dispatch their submarines to the SLOC, or surge their submarines across NATO's barriers before the initiation of combat. The second strategem would have permitted the avoidance of two barriers' worth of attrition—the North Cape barrier and the GIUK gap. Put another way, a quarter of the Soviet force that could have expected to

[50]Posen, "NATO's Reinforcement Capability," pp. 328–330.

[51]Robert S. Wood and John T. Hanley, "The Maritime Role in the North Atlantic," *Naval War College Review* 38 (November–December 1985): 8. One encounters this observation frequently in conversations with U.S. Navy strategists and military and civilian students of Soviet naval strategy.

Table 5.2. The Soviet gain from pre-war deployment

	Nuclear submarine patrol	
	Post D-Day Sortie	Predeployment
Number	25	25
Barriers	2	0
Barrier pk	.1	.1
Losses %	19	0
Losses (*N*)	5	0
	Diesel-electric submarine patrol	
	Post D-day sortie	Predeployment
Number	25	25
Barriers	2	0
Barrier pk	.18	.18
Losses %	33	0
Losses (*N*)	8	0
Deployed Force	37	50

die on the way to the SLOC would not (see Table 5.2). This would appear to be quite a bargain, and fear of this stratagem was one of the many motives for the U.S. Navy's maritime strategy.[52]

There were two reasons why the Soviets might have found this strategy less attractive than it appears at first glance. First, a Soviet submarine surge, especially of fifty-odd SSNs, SSGNs, and SSs, into the Atlantic would have been so unprecedented that alarm bells would have gone off all over NATO. The action risks any hope of Soviet surprise in a ground offensive. The Soviets respected the element of surprise during this period and would surely have liked to have it working for them in Central Europe in their quest for a quick victory. The only reason to predeploy attack submarines would be to inhibit the arrival of U.S. reserves that could thwart the Soviet ground offensive. Thus, the Soviets at the very least would face a dilemma: attack submarine predeployment could have helped the ground war, or hurt it.

The second reason the Soviets might have chosen not to predeploy arises from the *combined* effects of NATO's offensive and defensive capabilities. NATO's defensive barriers were sufficiently strong that forward-deployed Soviet attack submarines would likely have suffered serious casualties before reaching home. The weaker the Soviet attack submarine force, the greater the probability of success of a subsequent

[52]*SASC FY 85, Pt.* 2, pp. 1113–1114.

U.S. offensive move into the Barents Sea, and the greater the risk to the long-term survival of the Soviet SSBN force.

The foregoing arguments do not mean that the Soviets would not have ventured a large-scale predeployment. The Soviets could still have determined that the benefits would exceed the costs. If so, NATO would have faced a tough ASW campaign replete with difficult choices. The departure of reinforcement convoys could have been delayed until decision makers were satisfied that the threat was under control; or reinforcements could have crossed the Atlantic under the threat of significant submarine attack, hoping to control losses through aggressive escort and hunter-killer tactics. Given the importance of relatively early arrival of U.S. reinforcements, the second decision was more likely.

Prospects for Success Against a Predeployed Soviet Submarine Force

It is difficult to estimate the rate at which Soviet submarines could have destroyed NATO transports in the initial two or three months of the war.[53] Clearly, *they* would have tried to sink transports while NATO ASW forces tried to sink *them*.[54] Here I will employ two methods to bound the damage that predeployed submarines might have done during the first month of the war. One method simply estimates the number of antishipping weapons available to the Soviets in the Atlantic, assum-

[53]In general, open-source estimates of possible transport losses are not very satisfying. One is forced to fall back on the generally repeated assertion that they will be "high." Shilling, in U.S. Congress, Senate, Budget Committee, *A Perspective*, p. 243, concludes, "While it is true that a sizeable submarine force can sink *a large number of ships* in the first few weeks of conflict, in a few months a vigorous ASW campaign will destroy a major portion of the enemy submarines." Writing in 1977, he observed, "The assessments of the last three Annual Defense Department Reports (FY 78, 77, 76) support this view. They conclude that while a major Soviet effort to interdict the Atlantic sea lanes would likely *sink a significant number* of ships in the first few weeks, 'the Soviets would lose many of their attack submarines and (NATO's) naval force would ultimately maintain sea control' " (p. 244). One looks in vain for any kind of similar overall assessments in the DOD *Annual Reports* during the 1980s. The closest thing to an official assessment of NATO's naval situation is to be found in Office of the Chairman, Joint Chiefs of Staff, *1989 Joint Military Net Assessment* (Washington, D.C., 18 May 1989), p. 5–15, paragraph (b), "With sufficient warning and time to deploy naval assets, US and allied forces could probably achieve stated objectives, although not without cost."

[54]Nitze and Sullivan, eds., *Securing the Seas*, chap. 13, p. 346, cite a chart that they claim represents the results of a 1975 DOD study. The source they cite for the study is incorrect, and some of the results displayed are physically impossible. They show 300–400 Soviet submarines destroyed on the Atlantic SLOC in the first ninety days of the war. Maximally, the Russians had 350 torpedo and cruise missile submarines worldwide in 1975, so 300–400 Soviet submarines could not have been sunk in the Atlantic. The study estimated that in the first month of the war, out of roughly 900 transport ships put to sea, more than 300 would have been sunk. This is twice the cost of the worst month of World War II in terms of numbers of ships lost, June 1942, when 80 percent of the losses were

ing a certain degree of submarine attrition.[55] A second employs inferences from World War II, the Battle of the Atlantic experience. Neither makes particularly complex tactical assumptions. For example, there is no distinction between cruise-missile and torpedo attacks.[56] Neither estimate should be taken as a prediction of the exact number of ships likely to have been lost; rather, they are estimates that support judgments about the potential decisiveness of a Soviet anti-SLOC campaign.

Antishipping Weapons Present. As noted earlier, maximally the Soviets had about fifty reasonably modern nuclear-powered submarines and about fifty diesel-electrics that could have been committed to a SLOC battle in the North Atlantic. If the Soviets had been sufficiently persuaded of the merits of early SLOC interdiction to predeploy their force, then they probably would also have been sufficiently committed to send diesel-electrics in spite of their tactical limitations. As noted above, roughly one-half would likely have been available for predeployment. Even if more were ready, which apparently they were not, it would still have been wise for the Soviets to hold a second wave in reserve, to cover the Atlantic during the second month of a war. Otherwise, the Atlantic would have been free of Soviet submarines after a month, and transit would have become easy. If NATO figured out that most Soviet submarines were predeployed, it might have withheld part of its reinforcement package until the force was compelled to return home. On the average, modern submarines are usually assumed to have space for about twenty-four torpedoes. (The Oscar cruise-missile submarine carries twenty-four missiles plus torpedoes; the Charlie class SSGNs carry fewer.) Presumably,

---

independents. (November was the worst from a tonnage perspective.) Hinsley, *British Intelligence*, pp. 679–680. At 33 percent of the sailings, it is 47 times the overall convoy ship loss rate for the entire war of .7 percent. Lindsey, "Tactical ASW," p. 31. No explanation was presented for this high degree of pessimism. The authors of this study offered their own base case estimate of 180 lost merchantmen in the first month of the war, and a range of higher and lower alternative values, based on varying assumptions.

[55]This basic method is employed by Nitze and Sullivan, eds. *Securing the Seas*, pp. 351–360; Christopher C. Wright, "Developing Maritime Force Structure Options for the US Defense Program" (Masters thesis, MIT, 1976), pp. 50–62, and table A-1, p. 165; and probably first appeared in the open literature in Enthoven and Smith, *How Much Is Enough?* pp. 225–234.

[56]Comparatively few antishipping cruise-missile submarines were likely to have been present on the SLOC; in the future this could change as the Soviets deploy antishipping cruise missiles that can be fired from torpedo tubes. Given that my analysis is quite abstract and that the use of cruise missiles introduces a new set of problems and vulnerabilities for both attacker and defender, I do not believe that lumping all antishipping weapons together unduly biases this discussion in favor of the defender. Similarly, I have not tried to examine the potential for deliberate escort attacks designed either to strip away a particular convoy's defenses or simply to reduce NATO's overall escort force over time. Nitze and Sullivan discuss this option, in *Securing the Seas*, p. 359.

a submarine would hold some torpedoes in reserve for self-protection on the journey home. Let us assume four. This means that the Soviets would have had about 1000 antishipping weapons available in the Atlantic, most of them torpedoes, if they surged fifty submarines into the Atlantic.

How much damage might fifty submarines armed with 1000 weapons achieve? To simplify the calculation, let us assume that each submarine must on the average penetrate convoy defenses twice to fire its full load of weapons and that convoy escorts exact attrition before the submarine can shoot. Let us also assume that convoy defenses exact 10 percent attrition against all attackers, the rate developed for nuclear submarines above. Thus, forty-five boats survive to launch ten weapons each in the first attack, and forty-one boats survive to launch ten weapons each in the second attack, for a total of 860 weapons launched. A recent SLOC study employing this basic methodology seems to have assumed a torpedo pk of roughly .25, which is consistent with the most devastating German convoy attacks with nonhoming torpedoes in World War II.[57] This implies 215 potential sinkings.[58]

[57]See Nitze and Sullivan, eds., *Securing the Seas*, p. 362, suggesting five kills per convoy attack for their base case, although it is difficult to tell how many torpedoes they presume are fired. Their n. 14 indicates that the authors believe as many as ten kills are plausible, assuming twenty-torpedo weapons load. The ambiguity of the discussion and the range of the estimates presented suggest a minimal pk of .1, a best guess of .25, and a worst-case pk of .5 (see p. 372); p. 364 suggests a pk of .3 for a Captor mine, firing the basic Mk-46 lightweight ASW acoustic homing torpedo over a very short range at an enemy submarine. Elsewhere the authors suggest a pk of .1–.2 for this weapon, when launched with a crude fire control solution off a merchant vessel after attack by an enemy submarine (pp. 362–364). Jurgen Rohwer, *The Critical Convoy Battles of March 1943* (London, 1977), pp. 197–198, offers figures suggesting an overall pk against merchant ships of .26 per torpedo launched in two particularly effective convoy attacks. A total of eighty-five torpedoes were fired against merchant ships; thirty-five hits were obtained; twenty-two ships were sunk. Eighteen of the torpedoes fired, and nine of the hits obtained were against damaged ships. None of these were homing torpedoes, but some were "pattern runners." The attacks on these two convoys were among the most devastating, if not the most devastating, German convoy attacks of the war against the Atlantic SLOC, so for nonhoming torpedoes .25 would seem a conservative estimate of Soviet effectiveness. The average effectiveness of unguided U.S. torpedoes in the Pacific submarine campaign of World War II was much lower. Some 14,748 torpedoes were fired by submarines in the course of the war for 1314 confirmed sinkings, a pk of .09. Clay Blair, *Silent Victory* (New York, 1975), pp. 877–879. Estimates of homing torpedo effectiveness against surface vessels are harder to make. The Germans are said to have fired 640 relatively primitive T-5 acoustic homing torpedoes during World War II, sinking twenty-five ASW vessels and twenty merchant ships, for a pk of .07. See Hackmann, *Seek and Strike*, p. 311. It is worth noting that a variety of tactical and technical countermeasures to this torpedo were quickly developed. Modern homing torpedoes are presumably much more effective, although it is noteworthy that the Argentine cruiser *General Belgrano*, sunk by the British SSN *Conqueror* during the Falklands War, was attacked with a salvo of conventional torpedoes rather than a homing or wire-guided torpedo, suggesting that homing torpedoes may still have some limitations in antisurface warfare.

[58]Since the second wave of Soviet submarines would have to traverse NATO's barriers,

Since NATO would have tried to move some four hundred shiploads of military assets across the Atlantic, the fifty-submarine force would seem to have had great promise. Some 50 percent of the ships could have been sunk. But, as observed earlier, NATO had many ships. Let us suppose that for each ship in a convoy containing military cargo there was one that did not.[59] Thus, on the average every target attacked would have had only a 50 percent probability of being militarily important ship. NATO's expected important losses would drop to 107 ships, less than a quarter of the cargoes. This loss is not trivial, but it is considerably better from NATO's perspective than the alternative. This technique can be continued until the convoy gets too large or there get to be more convoys than available escorts. By my estimate, NATO's available escort forces could have easily supported a ratio of one decoy-economic cargo to one military cargo, for a total of 900 ships per month, sailing in fifteen sixty-ship convoys.[60]

These figures are probably optimistic from the attacker's perspective, since finding, tracking, attacking, and reattacking a convoy are all difficult tasks in and of themselves. For example, the assumption is that submarines have little difficulty making multiple torpedo attacks once contact with a convoy has been established. But this assumption is very favorable to the attacker. World War II data suggests that in 1941–42, in wolfpack attacks of five to eight boats, versus convoys of fifteen to fifty-five ships, covered by six to eight escorts, each U-boat on the average achieved about one kill.[61] In the preceding calculation, they achieve 2.5 kills.

The World War II Analogy. World War II experience can provide a useful perspective on the SLOC defense problem. The major issue is where on the curve of changing relative intelligence capabilities, skill,

---

the force initially available to the Soviets in the second month of the war would be thirty-seven boats, and thus convoy losses would drop from the first month. By sometime in the third month of the war, the initial wave of Soviet submarines would return to the Atlantic, having rearmed at their bases. Having fought two convoy engagements during their first deployment, and then having twice traversed two geographical choke points on their round trip to base, they would have suffered very high attrition, as high as 70 percent. Thus, by the third month of the war, NATO convoy losses should be quite low.

[59]This gambit is suggested in Nitze and Sullivan, eds., *Securing the Seas*, p. 360.

[60]Posen, "NATO's Reinforcement Capability," pp. 334–335.

[61]Sternhell and Thorndike, *Antisubmarine Warfare*, pp. 106, 108. By the last quarter of 1942 "about two ships were torpedoed in each successful attack" (p. 39). I can find no data suggesting how long this level of success prevailed, but in the famous March 1943 battles against convoys SC.122 and HX.229 each U-boat that mounted attacks scored about 1.3 sinkings. Only about half the U-boats involved in the four-day battle actually engaged. Rohwer, *Critical Convoy Battles*, pp. 198, 228.

organization, and strength that prevailed in that war between the German submarine force and the Anglo-American ASW force did the Soviets and the NATO alliance stand in the mid-1980s? One must be careful in one's inferences from this experience because the situation that would have prevailed in the opening days of a SLOC war differs in many ways from most of World War II. The kind of defensive infrastructure NATO had in the Atlantic in the 1980s was not really in place until mid-1943.[62] From that time, the U-boats performed very poorly against the convoys. On the other hand, the U-boats of 1943 had to spend a good deal of time on the surface, whereas modern Soviet nuclear- and diesel-powered submarines would not have to spend any time on the surface at all.

Nevertheless, one period of the Atlantic SLOC battle of World War II, October 1942–June 1943, provides some suggestive statistics. During this period the Germans averaged their largest forward deployments of the war, 104 boats. Allied escort forces had grown to a substantial size, yet it still was not possible to provide complete air cover during the entire Atlantic transit, and the weather was even worse than usual that year, which exacerbated the air-cover problem. German and Allied intelligence roughly balanced each other out. German naval intelligence had cracked the convoy code; between the data it provided and the sheer presence established by 100 U-boats, the Germans were able to intercept a large percentage of the convoys dispatched. (For example, from 1 January 1943 to 31 May 1943, thirty-eight out of eighty-six convoys were contacted by U-boats.)[63] Moreover, the Allies tried to pass an increasing number of convoys across the Atlantic as the effort to build up forces to invade North Africa, and ultimately Europe, intensified.

[62]A relatively dense land-based network of Radio Direction Finding Stations and a dedicated communications system for transmitting their data to a central location was apparently not in place until early 1942 (Beesley, *Very Special Intelligence*, p. 115). The Allies were heavily reliant on decoding German naval radio transmissions (Ultra) for tracking the long-range movements of German submarines, and the availability of this intelligence varied with German changes in the employment of their Enigma machines (ibid., esp. pp. 106–121, pp. 179–191). NATO had an entire wide-area surveillance system in place in the mid-1980s, which exploited overhead intelligence on Soviet submarine bases, long-range radio direction finding, and most of all fixed passive sonar arrays. This would have provided from the outset of the war a practiced system for submarine tracking that would not have been dependent on Soviet encryption mistakes. The Allies did not have sufficient long-range aircraft to provide continuous air coverage for U.S.–U.K. convoys until April of 1943. The Allies only began to deploy ASW carriers in late March of 1943. These two deployments were of critical importance, since until then the German U-boats were relatively free of air threats in the mid-Atlantic, directly astride a key convoy route. In the mid-1980s NATO controlled hundreds of land-based and sea-based ASW aircraft and helicopters that could provide air cover virtually anywhere it was necessary.

[63]Hinsley, *British Intelligence*, p. 680.

Table 5.3. World War II worldwide U-boat war, October 1942–June 1943

Average number of U-boats at sea	104
Vessels sunk per month	57
U-boats sunk per month	14.3
Vessels sunk per month per U-boat month at sea	.5
Average life of U-boat at sea (months)	7
Vessels sunk per U-boat sunk	4

Source: D.M. Sternhell and A. M. Thorndike, *Antisubmarine Warfare in World War II* (Washington, D.C., 1946), p. 84.

Nevertheless, the German interception record was far from perfect, since from the end of 1942 the Allies were reading the German naval Enigma codes (although not always in real time) and thus were able to evade many German wolf packs. In a very crude sense, then, we have a representation of what Soviet maritime reconnaissance satellites might achieve relative to NATO's elaborate acoustic and electronic intelligence network.

Crediting for the moment the average Soviet boat with twice the effectiveness relative to NATO's convoy defense effort as U-boats sustained to Allied efforts in 1942–43, we will treat this as a plausible performance for the predeployed Soviet force of fifty attack submarines (half nuclear). Since these are worldwide statistics, they include losses outside the Atlantic SLOC. Moreover, roughly 50 percent of the losses occurred to ships sailing independently.[64] Thus, the statistics are not fully comparable to a NATO SLOC campaign. But the incomparability makes inferences from the loss rate conservative, since NATO would presumably have had sense enough to escort or otherwise protect its high-value military reinforcement shipping in the first months of the war.[65]

[64]George R. Lindsey, "Tactical Anti-Submarine Warfare: The Past and the Future," in *Power At Sea*, Adelphi Paper, 122 (London: International Institute for Strategic Studies, 1976), p. 31. The loss rate of independents for the entire war was at least twice as high as the loss rate for escorted ships. Williams, "Four Iron Laws," pp. 39–40, puts it at 28 percent.

[65]Williams, "Four Iron Laws," argues that NATO planners probably would not have had sense enough to organize the resupply effort into convoys, and in conversations on this matter with civil servants, policy analysts, and naval officers I have encountered scattered evidence that the professional naval bias against the convoy has resurfaced. Whether the bias would have proven powerful enough in wartime to divert NATO from this proven method of shipping protection is difficult to determine. There is one reasonable argument against the wholesale employment of convoy. Since convoys take much time to assemble and unload, and involve evasive routing, the average ship spends less time at sea moving goods than it would if simply dispatched independently. Thus, convoying inevitably implies a "virtual" loss of some shipping capacity which makes

A more focused analysis on some specific Atlantic convoy battles also suggests limitations on the plausible effectiveness of Soviet attacks. For example, in March of 1943, generally considered to be the turning point of the Atlantic campaign, several very violent convoy battles occurred in the North Atlantic. These battles are generally considered to have been stunning German successes. The Germans had some sixty-six U-boats in the north Atlantic, a record for the war.[66] Thirty-three ships were lost in convoy, from four convoys, plus ten stragglers.[67] Forty-three out of the worldwide total of 102 merchant ships lost to all causes were thus sunk on the Atlantic convoy run, or 0.65 ship per submarine present.[68] This amounted to about 5 percent of the ships that sailed in convoy that month.[69]

Given that the diesel-electric submarine's effectiveness relative to ASW measures is probably no better, and perhaps worse, than it was in World War II, let us hold its effectiveness equal to the German performance and credit the Soviet nuclear submarine with a threefold qualitative improvement. Thus, twenty-five Soviet SSs each sink 0.65 ships per month, and twenty-five Soviet SSNs each sink 2 transport ships per month. This would yield sixty-six merchant ships destroyed, or an average of 1.3 ships lost for every Soviet submarine at sea, rather than the 1942–43 average of 0.5 per U-boat.[70] Thus, the 1943 experience suggests that a total loss of sixty-six ships in the first month of the war would be a fair estimate. (This amounts to 7.3 percent of the sailings, a rate of 50 percent higher than that suffered in March 1943, a bad month.) Doubling this figure, however, substantially increasing yet again the conservatism of our inferences from World War II data, would still only yield 130 transport ships destroyed. (This would be 14.5 per-

sense only if the expected real losses associated with independent sailings exceed the virtual losses of convoy. This calculation applies more to a "tonnage" war against economic cargoes than it does to a focused campaign against scarce military cargoes early in a war. NATO would have faced no scarcity of shipping for moving military cargoes—rather, it would have faced a scarcity of military equipment. Thus, it would have been prudent to treat military equipment the same way invasion shipping was treated in World War II, and to organize it into escorted, indeed super-escorted convoys. But there may have been a case for dispatching civilian cargoes independently in the early phases of a war. See Sternhell and Thorndike, *Antisubmarine Warfare*, pp. 111–112.

[66] Hinsley, *British Intelligence*, p. 562.

[67] Ibid., p. 680.

[68] Ibid., p. 679.

[69] Sternhell and Thorndike, *Antisubmarine Warfare*, p. 38.

[70] Coincidentally, two convoy attacks, at the barrier pk's I have developed in Appendix 1, would produce roughly fourteen submarines destroyed, the 1942–43 rate. I have no explanation for this, although one suspects that this particular month of the U-boat war has assumed a special salience for all subsequent analysts of convoy attack and defense. In 1943 four merchant ships were lost for every submarine destroyed, which is very close to the wartime average.

cent of the sailings, nearly three times the March 1943 loss rate.) Assuming each convoy contains a fifty-fifty mix of military and economic cargoes (see above), we would still only see about sixty-five military cargo sinkings, 14 percent of the military cargoes dispatched.

Even at March 1943 exchange rates, which were still rather favorable to the Nazis, the Soviets would have to pay something for these kills in lost submarines. According to one reliable source, some seventy-two ships were sunk in convoy, by the Germans, worldwide, for a loss of six U-boats "at the hands of the convoys sea and air escorts."[71] At this 12:1 exchange rate, we would expect eleven Soviet submarines to suffer destruction in convoy attacks. (This is coincidentally quite close to the casualties suffered in the preceding barrier attrition analysis.) Doubling the exchange rate to provide yet additional credit to the nuclear-powered component of the Soviet submarine force would still imply the loss of five or six boats.[72]

Clearly, this simple method of estimating plausible losses depends on a critical assumption: the basic structure of convoy attack and defense in the mid-1980s was not much changed from *this phase* of World War II; only the relative effectiveness of particular platforms had changed—particularly nuclear-powered submarines. This assumption may not be correct. I have attempted to buffer the estimate against this possibility by drawing inferences from particularly stressful World War II episodes and assigning Soviet SSNs improvements in platform effectiveness relative to NATO defenses that seem to me to be very favorable to them. As convoy attackers, Soviet nuclear submarines in the mid-1980s are credited with six times the productivity of German U-boats in the North Atlantic in March of 1943. Diesel-electrics are presumed to be twice as productive.

In spite of the conservatism of this methodology, it produces lower expected NATO losses than our first estimate, based on torpedo availability and lethality. The reasons for this probably lie in the greater operational realism buried in the estimates based on World War II. In contrast to the assumptions of our first method, not all submarines find convoys in real life; when they do, they do not necessarily press home

[71]Beesley, *Very Special Intelligence*, p. 179. A total of fifteen German U-boats were sunk that month.

[72]A 22:1 overall exchange rate prevailed between July of 1940 and March of 1941 and was the highest achieved by the Germans in World War II; the average for the war was 3.8:1; the 1942–43 average was 4:1. Since these figures include all transport losses in and out of convoy, and all U-boat casualties, they are not strictly comparable, but they do give an indication of how conservative a 24:1 exchange rate would be. See Hackmann, *Seek and Strike*, p. 236, which reproduces figures from Sternhell and Thorndike, *Antisubmarine Warfare*, p. 84.

attacks successfully; when they press home attacks, they do not often succeed in making multiple kills. World War II data reflect these constraints. Since I believe these are factors that would have prevailed in actual military operations, I find the "World War II inferences" to be more plausible.

If half of NATO's cargo in the first thirty days of conflict had been munitions, parts, and replacement equipment to sustain all NATO forces for the next thirty days, NATO forces would have lost, on the basis of the preceding calculation, about 14 percent of the supplies required. This would have forced each division to reduce its planned daily activity by 14 percent, thus reducing the effectiveness of NATO divisions in combat. Of course, the process would have been both less and more rational than this. Individual units cannot calculate and plan an exact 14 percent reduction in activity. On the other hand, not all units are in contact with the enemy, and corps and army logistics commanders direct the available supplies to the neediest units. This is their job. The rationing of supplies and restraints on activity are common practices in wartime.

The remaining ships lost would have been loaded with the equipment for reinforcing U.S. divisions. By my calculations, each ship might contain roughly 0.05 ADE's worth of equipment.[73] Thus, NATO would have lost 1.5 ADEs. This represents about 2 percent of the fully mobilized NATO force. Moreover, it seems likely that the losses would have been distributed over many reinforcing divisions, so no actual unit would have been rendered totally unfit for combat. The people for these units travel by air, so the actual degradation in the combat capability of individual divisions would have been even less than it appears. There were limited stocks of war reserve replacement equipment available in Europe that could have been tapped to some extent to compensate for the equipment lost at sea. Although not pleasant, then, the ammunition and equipment losses associated with the sinking of sixty military resupply ships was unlikely to have been the cause of any catastrophe on the Central Front. This is, however, an "average" kind of judgment. One can certainly imagine a combination of military circumstances and bad luck that could produce the destruction of several dozen critical cargoes exactly when they are most needed.

At the end of this month of combat, Soviet submarines would then have to begin their dangerous voyage home. The second wave of Soviet submarines would have arrived, less some 25 percent casualties suffered on the barriers. Thus, a smaller force would have been available

[73]This is a simplification.

to attack the convoys in the second month of the war, and casualties would likely have diminished.

Before we leave this discussion, one final caution is in order. The preceding analysis is, in my judgment, rather conservative. It is, in many ways, very favorable to the Soviet Union. It assumes that the West would not have undertaken extraordinary measures for the protection of its reinforcement effort. Particularly, most of the U.S. Navy surface ship and submarine force is presumed to be occupied elsewhere—*but not on barrier or convoy defense missions.* The diversion of some of these assets from then planned forward "offensive" operations could have substantially increased the protection of these initial convoys. The high concentration of defensive assets to protect the amphibious assault forces for the North African invasion in World War II was tremendously successful. There is no reason why the initial reinforcement effort for NATO should have been considered any less important than the North African campaign was for U.S. strategy in World War II. If extraordinary protective measures were taken, it is very plausible that convoy losses could be a great deal lower than those discussed above. Thus, the convoy losses suggested in the preceding analysis makes *offensive sea control,* discussed next, appear in a better light than it probably should.

Offensive Sea Control

Assessing the potential absolute effectiveness of the offensive sea control strategy is very difficult. It promises to pin down most Soviet attack submarines on defensive missions. At most, some "leakage" to the sea lanes is expected, although it is not clear how much leakage the navy expected in this period.[74] The presumed overriding Soviet concern for the protection of their SSBN force, as well as a more generalized concern to protect the oceanic approaches to the Soviet homeland, including the extension of Soviet homeland air defenses out to sea, was the foundation for the strategy. The assumption, based in large measure on intelligence analysis of Soviet naval literature and operating practices, was that U.S. threats to the SSBN force were taken very seriously, and that most Soviet naval resources would have been committed to defense against U.S. offensive sea control efforts as soon as they became evident. If we argue this way, the implication is that offensive sea

[74]"Leakage" is Admiral Watkins's term. See *SASC FY 86, Pt. 2,* p. 989.

control could have reduced the losses of military transport shipping virtually to zero. There could have been no better outcome than this.

The question, then, is how do we assess the strategy's potential for achieving the wholesale diversion of Soviet submarines? There were three ways that the strategy could have failed on its own terms, and one additional way. First, U.S. submarines might have failed to do sufficient damage to the Soviet attack and ballistic missile submarine force to convince the Soviets that there was indeed a major threat to be defended against. A sophisticated technical analysis of forward ASW operations by Mark Sakitt suggests a relatively low rate of SSBN destruction.[75] The relatively unimpressive results are confirmed by navy statements, and they are consistent with general historical experience.

The navy stated on several occasions that Soviet SSBNs could not have been killed at a high rate in forward operations. A Congressional Research Service report on the maritime strategy, which claimed to be "the first time . . . that the Navy's arguments have appeared at length in the public record," observed that "the Navy is not talking about eliminating the Soviet SSBN force in a short period of time. Quite the contrary: Strategic ASW is a difficult task, and Soviet SSBNs will be destroyed individually over an extended period of time."[76]

Indeed, in World War II offensive area search, exactly the type of operation envisioned in offensive sea control, was found to be the least effective strategy. The British official historian concludes that in the matter of the employment of ASW aircraft, "we seem to have been slow to realise that to escort and support our convoys was a far more effective strategy than to send out patrols to seek the enemy."[77]

[75]For a comprehensive analysis, see Sakitt, *Submarine Warfare in the Arctic*. I have devised a simple spreadsheet model of SSN offensive sweeps of the Barents Sea that suggests similar conclusions. My own model uses a very basic sweep-out equation and effectiveness parameters inferred from open-source estimates of the plausible effectiveness of NATO's ASW barriers (see Appendix 4), suitably derated for the difficulties of offensive sweep. For the basic sweep equation, see Clayton J. Thomas, "Models and Wartime Operations Research," in Wayne P. Hughes, ed., *Military Modeling*, 2d ed. (Alexandria, Va.: Military Operations Research Society, 1989), p. 75.

[76]See O'Rourke, *Nuclear Escalation*, pp. 9–10, 12–14. This report quotes similar statements by Lehman, *SASC FY 85, Pt. 8*, p. 3877; and Watkins, *SASC FY 86, Pt. 7*, p. 3882, on the difficulties of finding and destroying a submarine force of any kind. Both speak in terms of weeks or months.

[77]Roskill, *The War at Sea*, vol. 3, Pt. 2, p. 397. Indeed, with the exception of one brief period of war during which the Germans made a fatal error in judgment, aircraft were roughly four times as effective during convoy escort than they were trying to catch German U-boats in transit from the Bay of Biscay. See Lindsey, "Tactical ASW," p. 38. He also observes after a brief survey of developments since World War II, that "the arguments against the employment of anti-submarine units in open ocean hunter killer sweeps appear to have been strengthened by recent changes" (p. 39).

Similarly, Robert Hallex, an expert on modeling naval campaigns, observes, "ASW naval campaigns, on the other hand, tend to proceed at a much slower pace because operating areas are vast and surveillance coverage is poor (especially underwater surveillance)."[78] "*It is difficult for an area ASW commander to force a decisive engagement with a deployed submarine force that chooses to be evasive.*" ASW operations are characterized by "search and attrition operations over extensive operating areas. Operating areas may exceed a million square miles, while limited search areas covered by single units (such as patrol aircraft or a submarine) may consist of several thousands of square miles of ocean. Detection of individual enemy units within an operating area may require weeks of search. Localization of an underwater target may consume several hours or several days, before attack criteria are achieved."[79] Lt. Comdr. Ralph Chatham, an experienced U.S. Navy submarine officer, notes that "we currently have serious trouble detecting our own nuclear submarines that were designed almost twenty years ago. We have greater difficulty detecting anyone's diesel submarines."[80]

As the campaign unfolded, the Soviets might have concluded that they had less to fear than they had imagined. If so, they might have perceived themselves to be free to begin the diversion of assets to the SLOC. This may seem a bit paradoxical, but there is precedent. Before World War II, statesmen feared that strategic bombing of cities would produce wholesale destruction and civilian panic. This was a cause of some restraint at the outset of the war. As such attacks developed and the long-feared chaos failed to materialize, statesmen began to lose their fear and behaved in a less restrained fashion when considering their own counterattacks on cities. The strategy of offensive sea control might have been more effective in prospect than had it actually been implemented.

Second, there was a modest but real potential for a U.S. catastrophe. The Soviets have many tactical advantages in their home waters, most notably, the tremendous military presence they can establish to develop and prosecute contacts with U.S. submarines, the minefields they can

[78]Robert Hallex, "Sea Battle Models," in *Military Modeling*, ed. Wayne P. Hughes (Alexandria, Va.: Military Operations Research Society, 1984), pp. 165–186. "The combination of high mobility, complex surveillance, large operating areas, and small numbers of units included in sea battle models tends to cause concentration of attention on restricted ocean passages or 'funnels' through which enemy forces must transit to or from operating areas" (pp. 172–173).

[79]Ibid., pp. 171–172.

[80]Lt. Cmndr. Ralph E. Chatham, USN, "A Quiet Revolution," *US Naval Institute Proceedings* 110 (January 1984): 42.

deploy for relatively cheap kills, and the land-based command and control infrastructure available to support their ASW battle.[81] Even if Western SSNs were qualitatively superior to a significant degree, these Soviet advantages might have resulted in serious U.S. SSN attrition. Such losses could have had two effects. First, NATO could have lost assets that would have strengthened its ability to defend the SLOC—particularly SSNs that could have strengthened the North Cape and GIUK barriers. Second, the Russians could have caught a touch of the victory disease. If they had found themselves sinking more than a few U.S. SSNs and suffering relatively small losses of SSBNs themselves, they might have become more confident of their ability to divert resources to the SLOC battle.

A third possibility was that the Soviets would simply have "called and raised." Since they had the initiative in the war, they could have reasoned that a good-sized predeployment against the SLOC would have exerted the same influence on U.S. behavior as the U.S. Navy expected its predeployment to the Barents to exert on Soviet behavior. Indeed, the Soviets could have exerted a double effect by increasing the nuclear threat to U.S. strategic nuclear command and control with a combination of forward-deployed nuclear cruise missile submarines and Yankee Class SSBNs, which could not have reached U.S. targets from the Barents in any case. This might have forced the United States to change its strategy and withhold SSNs from the forward offensive campaign to deal with the Soviet predeployed threats to the SLOC and to U.S. strategic nuclear command and control.

The fourth way that the strategy could have failed is that it could have *succeeded too well.* As outlined in the previous chapter, there were several different ways that initial U.S. forward operations might have done better than the basic facts of the case suggest. Political and military development of whatever crisis precipitated the war might have permitted the U.S. SSNs to move forward in strength prior to the outbreak of hostilities. Deployed Soviet SSBNs might have made mistakes in communications procedures that rendered them more vulnerable. Or the synergistic effects of attacks on SSBNs proper, their supporting forces, and the infrastructure ashore might have produced rapid degradation in the Soviet perceived ability to keep the bastion safe and protects its SSBN force for very long.

Thus, it is not inconceivable that the Soviet defensive effort could simply have failed to protect Soviet SSBNs. Under these circumstances the Soviet Navy might indeed have retained all its attack submarines

[81]See esp. Sakitt, *Submarine Warfare,* pp. 40–60.

at home. The SLOC would have remained secure. But events might have taken the dangerous course outlined in the previous chapter, as the Soviet Union struggled to save its second-strike capability.

Relative Effectiveness—Offensive versus Defensive Sea Control

I have argued that in the worst case, Soviet attack submarine predeployment, NATO ought to have been able to move sufficient resources across the Atlantic to meet its then current reinforcement plan. Heavy losses might have been incurred in this scenario, but successful reinforcement was nevertheless probable.

The offensive sea-control strategy offers more ambiguous conclusions. This ambiguity arises in part from the fact that there are no historical examples of campaigns pitting many submarines against each other from which we can make inferences about the course of such a battle. The more general historical record of antisubmarine warfare, navy commentary, and an examination of the basic facts of the case, all suggest that Soviet submarines would probably not have been speedily killed in large numbers in forward offensive operations. The strategy relied largely on influence over Soviet behavior, not destruction of Soviet capabilities. Although the U.S. Navy apparently had good reason on the basis of Soviet statements and operating practices to attempt this strategem, it was still a gamble. Had a pure either-or choice been necessary, from the perspective of SLOC security, the defensive strategy would be the safest given Soviet capabilities. That the navy realized this was evidenced by its sustained interest in keeping the defensive ASW barriers intact. In fact, the offensive sea control strategy could not have worked without effective ASW barriers and the well-developed ASW support infrastructure on the Atlantic littoral. U.S. SSBNs wander the oceans and rely on stealth for their survivability. NATO's defensive barriers and infrastructure made this a risky strategy for Soviet SSBNs even had they been much quieter than they were. These barriers made it unattractive for the Soviet SSBNs to leave their sanctuaries, and the inferior quality of Soviet SSBNs made them vulnerable in their own waters if they were not protected. Although they hardly represented a concentrated target set in their home waters, they would have been even less vulnerable if the world's oceans were available for their dispersal. In the absence of the barriers that NATO (and Japanese) territory permitted worldwide, searching for Soviet SSBNs would have been even more difficult. Thus, offensive sea control in the absence of a well-organized system of defensive sea-control barriers could not have been very effective. The only aspect of defensive sea control not essential to offensive sea control was direct defense of convoys. Interestingly, this probably received the least U.S. Navy attention in the 1980s.[82]

Similarly, offensive sea control would have complemented defensive sea control. There could have been no better outcome than the nearly complete absence of Soviet submarines from the SLOC. The Soviets gave the impression of being so concerned with the survivability of their SSBN force and the security of their coastal waters that they intended to commit most of their resources to defense. It would have been unwise for the West to completely forgo the leverage over the Soviet attack-submarine force that the U.S. Navy's threat to the Soviet SSBN force and home waters provided. An offensive ASW *capability* created the *possibility* that the Soviet SSBN force would have suffered attrition if left undefended. Had the Soviets risked their attack submarines against the SLOC, NATO's strong defensive sea-control capabilities would have degraded these very assets that the Soviets would have needed to defend their bastions if they were attacked later in the war. It was not essential to exercise this capability at the outset of a war for the offensive capability, *in combination with a strong defensive capability,* to dissuade the Soviets from predeployment of their submarines against the SLOC. Clausewitz calls this the effect of the "possible engagement."[83] NATO's possible defensive engagements and possible offensive engagements would have given pause to any Soviet planner responsible for protection of Soviet SSBNs. This was the navy's strongest argument for maintenance of an offensive ASW capability, but given

[82]Aside from the rarity and brevity of convoy defense discussions in most official navy public documents, the navy paid much less material attention to the mission in the 1980s than it did to others. Production of the FFG-7 frigate, specifically designed for convoy escort, was terminated in FY 1984. The first eighteen ships of this class were transferred to the reserves. Full equipment of the FFG-7 escort frigate force with first-class ASW helicopters was slow. Each was designed to operate with two Lamps III ASW helicopters aboard. The Lamps III was a very sophisticated $20-million machine. The FFG-7 force alone had a requirement for 102 Lamps III, and fifty other surface ships were also expected to have this helicopter aboard. The navy had a stated requirement for 209, yet as of 1986 there were only about 60 in inventory of a total of 114 authorized. By 1988 they were procured at only six per year. Meanwhile, the more austere version of the helicopter designed for inner-zone aircraft carrier defense was procured at three times this rate. For a discussion of this system see, *SASC FY 86, Pt. 8*, pp. 4502–4511. Eighteen U.S. Naval Reserve FFG-7s were outfitted with a single Lamps I helicopter, an earlier less effective ASW helicopter than the Lamps III. Navy plans did not call for the acquisition of a sufficient number of ASW helicopters force-wide to permit a second ASW helicopter to be embarked on these frigates until as late as 1995. Ibid., pp. 4577–4578. See also *U.S. Department of Defense, Annual Report*, FY 87, p. 190.

[83]Carl Von Clausewitz, *On War* (Princeton, 1984), p. 181, the section titled, "Possible Engagements Are To Be Regarded as Real Ones Because of Their Consequences."

strong defenses, it did not provide support for an initial forward surge into the Barents Sea (or the other marginal seas) where the Soviets based their SSBNs.

Thus, the navy had a case for maintaining an offensive capability to convince the Soviets to keep as many attack submarines at home as possible. The argument for using this capability at the outset of the war was less powerful—given strong defensive barriers and convoy defenses. Moreover, if the purpose of the offensive capability had been to create a contingent threat to *counter-attack*, then the navy's stress on rapid construction of Los Angeles–class nuclear-attack submarines and on a range of high-cost items to defend carriers in forward operations need not have been so pronounced.[84]

Conclusions

The preceding analysis leads to a simple conclusion. The U.S. Navy's claim that only early offensives into the Barents Sea to threaten Soviet SSBNs could have ensured the defense of the SLOC was exaggerated. Even given the resources that existed, it ought to have been possible to assure the successful reinforcement of U.S. forces in Europe in a plausible worst-case scenario—the predeployment of one-half of the best attack submarines in the Soviet Navy. Moreover, in terms of its actual procurement during the 1980s, the navy did surprisingly little to improve its ability to protect directly the transport shipping that would have carried these reinforcements. Instead, the navy bemoaned the threat to the SLOC and proposed enhanced emphasis on an offensive strategy that required very expensive forces to address the threat.

As discussed above, offense and defense in this period did not need to be an either-or question from a strategic point of view. Offensive and defensive capabilities supported each other, although the defensive capabilities were clearly the most essential ones from the perspective of American strategy. Bureaucratic politics and the navy's quest for the largest number of the most capable weapons that money could buy seem to have been the big drivers in the navy's rhetoric. It is

[84]Of roughly sixty U.S. submarines based in the Atlantic in the mid-1980s, as many as twenty-four could plausibly have been allocated to forward operations in the Barents Sea. More explicit reliance on a defensive strategy, supported by the threat of counterattack, might have required fewer boats. Similarly, the design criteria that made the SSN 21 Seawolf, the navy's next generation attack submarine, so expensive, could have been relaxed. The navy justified this boat almost exclusively on the basis of its ability to go into the defended bastions proximate to the Soviet Union.

difficult to say in retrospect how much the navy actually believed its own declarations on the strategic necessity of early large-scale forward deployments in the event of crisis or war. Not only open-source statements but the naval professional literature was characterized by tremendous stress on the offensive strategy in the mid-1980s. Navy exercises seem to have been consistent with the strategy, and in conversations naval officers defended the strategy aggressively. Finally, civilian leadership, especially the president and the secretary of defense, did not distinguish themselves during their time in office by their interest in controlling the details of military strategy.[85] In retrospect, a direct confrontation between the United States and the Soviet Union in this period seems likely to have generated escalatory pressures in the naval sphere that were unacknowledged by, or unknown to, the likely decision makers.

[85]Secretary of the Navy John Lehman showed an interest in doing so, but he was not in the chain of command, and moreover he was a big booster of the maritime strategy.

[6]

Conclusion

What Has Been Demonstrated?

Can we conclude that it would have been impossible to confine a NATO–Pact war to conventional weaponry had such a war occurred in the 1980s? Indeed, ought we to conclude that U.S. military planning since the birth of flexible response in the early 1960s, which has focused precisely on such a scenario, has been futile? We cannot do so. Nuclear escalation is an extremely dangerous step, and statesmen have thus far not proven themselves cavalier in taking it. It may be that during an intense conventional conflict among states with large nuclear arsenals, statesmen and soldiers will be more impressed by the few hundred adversary long-range nuclear weapons that would survive even the most successful surprise attack than by the thousands that might be destroyed in such an attack. On the other hand, it may be that the elaborate plans, weapons, and doctrines that support damage-limiting nuclear strategies will come to the fore during an intense conventional war. Our present state of theoretical knowledge does not permit a high-confidence judgment on this question.

What I have done is establish a theoretical link between conventional military operations and superpower decision making about escalation to the use of nuclear weapons. Two "cases" of conventional operations that illustrate these theoretical linkages have been examined. These operations are not the stuff of Cold War adventure fiction; in the context of an East-West conventional war, they were likely to occur, and they were likely to produce at least some of the effects I have identified. Although political changes in the Soviet Union and Eastern Europe have taken much of the political heat out of the East-West security competition, the force structures, strategies, and organizational predispositions discussed in the text are likely to remain with us for many years to come. Finally, I have shown that at least in these two cases alternative military operations existed that would plausibly have achieved the West's basic conventional war objectives at much lower risk of nuclear escalation—options that remain open to us today as we try to recast the superpower military relationship. The West has real choices about how to fight this war, in the unhappy event that it should occur.

Were these the only plausible cases of this kind? They were not. At least two other mid-1980s issues lend themselves to this kind of treatment: U.S. naval strategy in the Pacific, and the ability of U.S. and Soviet strategic nuclear forces to sustain very high levels of alert for long periods of conventional conflict.

Moreover, there are a number of issues currently on the horizon that also lend themselves to this type of analysis. First, the emergence of Soviet mobile ICBMs, as well as mobile strategic command and control installations, suggests that in all probability the U.S. Air Force will give considerable thought to intelligence capabilities necessary to find these so-called relocatable targets, or RTs. The advent of the stealth bomber provides one vehicle to attack these targets during the conventional phase of a war, and it may be more attractive to attempt this in a non-nuclear environment. Arguments will be made that resemble those advanced by the navy concerning the dissuasive (or coercive) effects of altering "the nuclear correlation of forces" or tying down various Soviet assets on defensive tasks.

Second, a good deal of work is currently under way in the U.S. research and development community on very accurate, long-range conventional weapons, perhaps a new generation of stealthy cruise missiles. Such weapons would be usable against the Soviet homeland during conventional combat. Many stationary targets might be vulnerable, such as railroad facilities, early warning and air defense radars, command centers, intelligence installations, and air bases. Many of these installations would be relevant to both conventional and nuclear warfare. The United States might target them for conventional warfare reasons, only to produce effects on Soviet nuclear forces. (These would also be vulnerable to stealth bombers and, to a lesser extent, stealth fighters.) Depending on U.S. intelligence and command capabilities, mobile Soviet targets might also be vulnerable to stealthy, conventional cruise missiles.

Third, it seems plausible that antisatellite operations, launched to improve one's conventional warfighting capability, would reduce the adversary's intelligence and command and control assets for strategic nuclear war.

The Effects of Political Change

Extensive political changes in Eastern Europe and progress in conventional and nuclear arms control will not necessarily eliminate the risk of inadvertent escalation. The dissolution of the Warsaw Pact means that the Soviets have lost their ability to push their air defense network outward from the Soviet border—reducing their warning of air attack and their ability to do anything about it. The reunification of Germany may, ultimately, bring NATO forces—particularly NATO air forces—even closer to the Soviet border. The loss of the East German and Polish coasts, not to mention the possible loss of the Baltic states, is likely to reduce the ability of the Soviet Navy to defend the Baltic sea and air approaches to the Soviet heartland. That the Soviets seem willing to accept these new vulnerabilities may be a good sign. It provides hard evidence that their military doctrine has embraced the deterrent power of nuclear retaliation and that they judge Western intentions to be sufficiently benign to rely on this power to close any theoretical "windows" of vulnerability. But a new political equilibrium inside the Soviet Union and in Eastern Europe as a whole has not quite emerged, and we must remain alert to the underlying military relationships that could affect any future crises.

Although the real cuts in the size of strategic nuclear forces currently under discussion in 1990 do not much reduce either side's nuclear retaliatory capability, we should understand that, at some point, deep cuts in strategic nuclear forces may enhance the damage-limiting potential of conventional counterforce operations by reducing the number of targets that they have to work on to a level that may seem manageable. Deep cuts in major conventional warfare forces in Central Europe may, if carefully conceived, reduce the incentives of either side to initiate conventional conflict under any circumstances. But they may also free military resources for more exotic programs, such as those outlined above.

In sum, there is much evidence that suggests that the causal patterns I have identified would have made themselves felt in a large-scale East-West conventional war during the 1980s. The two specific scenarios I have outlined are likely to remain plausible paths to escalation for some time to come. The U.S. Navy has, admittedly, abandoned the more extreme rhetoric of the maritime strategy—but there is no reason to believe that the emphasis on early forward deployment of SSNs has been reduced. NATO's possible air operations have been affected by the evaporation of Soviet military control over the Eastern European former members of the Warsaw Pact and the likely withdrawal of Soviet forces from virtually all these countries. These changes, combined with reductions in the sheer mass of Soviet forces associated with the Conventional Armed Forces in Europe Treaty, signed on November 19, 1990, should reduce the pressures on NATO air forces to mount early interdiction operations. But, as outlined above, such operations are probably easier now than formerly.

Political events under way have, at least for now, substantially reduced the prospects of a major East-West clash. But this should not blind us to the importance of keeping our military and conceptual arsenals in good working order in the event that politics takes a different turn. Iraq's conquest of Kuwait in August 1990, and the UN counterattack of January 1991, illustrates both the unpredictable nature of international politics and the continued importance of military power in relations among states. Given the unhappy history of the species—especially in this century—security matters ought not to be left to take care of themselves.

Inferences for Medium- and Small-Power Competitions

The analysis presented in this book also has implications for conflicts outside the superpower arena.

Political tensions in some parts of the world currently run at least as high as the superpower competition ever did. The disputes between the Arab coalition and Israel, India and Pakistan, and Iraq and Iran have often been distinguished by an elemental quality of nationalism and religion that lends an intensity to the dispute that equals or surpasses the ideological intensity of the Cold War. The rivalry between North and South Korea has that special intensity associated with civil wars. Substantial outright, large-scale, non-nuclear violence has marked these disputes. The recent Iraq-Iran war also saw the introduction of chemical weapons, including their use against civilians. The UN coalition's war to liberate Kuwait saw a series of Iraqi rocket attacks upon Israeli cities.

The specter of the nuclearization of these conflicts has already emerged. India has tested a nuclear device; North Korea and Pakistan are believed to be building a weapons production capability; Israel is believed to have nuclear weapons. Iraq had a nuclear weapons program, which the UN has tried to eliminate. India, Israel, and North Korea have short- to medium-range ballistic missiles. Iraq has such weapons, but the UN proposes to take them away. All of these countries own long-range, high payload fighter-bomber aircraft. And given the coming contraction in demand for weaponry in the West, it seems likely that more military technology of even greater capabilities will flow to these regional competitors.

But these countries are unlikely to deploy nuclear weapons in ways that enhance stability. They are unlikely to be able to afford the numbers, basing modes, or early-warning capabilities that helped the superpowers to develop survivable retaliatory forces. The conventional forces with which these countries have conducted their competition have all regularly engaged in offensive military operations. The Israeli Defense Force is probably as committed to the offensive as any military force in history. The nuclear capabilities that these countries deploy, if they have done so or do so in the future, are likely to be grafted onto the existing conventional forces—institutions with strong offensive traditions. The likelihood that these forces will embrace assured-destruction nuclear doctrines or abandon the kinds of conventional strategies and capabilities that they have had in the past is low. Instead, it seems more likely that these countries would drift into military relationships that manifest the kinds of possibilities for inadvertent escalation that I have outlined above. Indeed, they may have these problems to a greater degree than did the superpowers in the period I have analyzed.

The advanced military powers, East and West, may not be particularly well placed to restrain these developments. In the past, nonproliferation policy has stressed exactly that—preventing the emergence of new nuclear powers. In the future a more important policy question may be what to do if this fails? The fallback position probably ought to be to help new nuclear powers acquire second-strike capabilities—delivery systems, command and control capabilities, and early warning systems. This would be a foreign policy revolution on the proliferation issue and seems an unlikely outcome.

Conventional arms sales policy has not paid much attention to qualitative issues—especially the inherent offensive potential of weapons offered for sale. Rather, advanced military powers have sold weapons largely in pursuit of specific political interests. The United States has not tried to limit Israeli or Pakistani offensive conventional capabilities. Instead, they are sold top-of-the-line multipurpose aircraft such as the F-15 and F-16. Neither does it appear that the Soviet Union has exercised much restraint over exports to India, Libya, and Iraq. French and British arms sales have not shown much discrimination either. Thus the arms sales policies of the advanced military countries, if the past is any guide, will exacerbate the potential for the kinds of conventional-to-nuclear interactions I have outlined in this book.

Finally, military research and development and production capabilities have spread. Israel and India have well-developed military industries and scientific establishments that are likely to grow quickly in the next decade. In spite of the physical damage done to Iraq by the UN coalition, many of its scientists and engineers undoubtedly survived the bombing. The possibility of a resurgence exists.

The advanced military powers have had some influence on medium- and small-power military competitions, but it has not been great. Their ability to fine-tune regional competitions in the future to help avoid the kinds of problems outlined in this book is likely to be low. Nuclear weapons technology has proven difficult to deny to states who are motivated to get it. Advanced conventional technologies are often sold for reasons of narrow political or economic interest. To enhance their autonomy from superpower interference, states involved in intense regional competitions have tried to develop their own military scientific, engineering, and production capabilities, and have enjoyed considerable success in doing so.

Military Strategy, Deterrence, and Escalation

The military strategy that a nation or alliance chooses is partly a function of the perspective that its leaders have on the roots of international conflict. A strategy developed on the basis of one perspective will look quite different from an alternative perspective. U.S. strategy is largely based on what one might call a "second image" theory of international conflict. Kenneth Waltz coined the term for the family of theories of international conflict that locates causes at the level of the state or society. Among U.S. policymakers during the Cold War second-image theories were very popular. They grew out of the experience of the 1930s and were consistent with the idealist tradition in U.S. foreign policy. Wars are assumed to be started by greedy aggressor states who come to believe that their victims are militarily, politically, or psychologically weak. Greed arises from something endemic to the adversary country that demands expansion—such as autocracy, militarism, fascism, or communism. The United States requires military strength to "deter" such adversaries from starting wars and to fight the enemy, indeed to annihilate the enemy, if a challenge occurs. The adversary could not misperceive U.S. military power as implying U.S. aggressive intentions; he surely knows it is acquired only because of his bad behavior. Besides which, the very nature of the adversary means that all he respects is power.[1] The military prescription for dealing with an adversary of this kind is to buy plenty of offensive capability, and in the event of war to use it.

An alternative perspective might be that of the "third image," again a term coined by Kenneth Waltz, which locates the roots of conflict in the international system.[2] The "third image" sees that the anarchical condition of international politics makes all states fearful—including states whose social system we may not like. Third-image theorists are drawn to the competition among the great powers before World War I, including the competitive mobilization of the July crisis, as a particularly apt example of the impact of fear on the political and military behavior of states.

Because there is no sovereign in international politics to protect those who fail to look to their own security, states eye one another warily. Thus, third-image strategists are keenly aware of the security dilemma, discussed in the introductory chapter. Political or military preparations that improve one state's capability for aggression will be strongly resisted by its neighbors, whether or not those preparations owe their origin to a will toward aggression or simply to accidents of geography, technology, or human eccentricity that make it seem that offensively capable forces are the only way to defend oneself.

Third-image theorists also understand that the anarchical condition of international politics permits aggression, and that states will from time to time be tempted to expand their power or wealth by the sword. Military preparations must be made to deal with this possibility. At the same time, attention must be paid to the fact that others are also affected by the anarchical condition and will eye any military preparations warily. Thus, overtly offensive preparations should be avoided unless careful political and military analysis shows them to be absolutely essential.[3] A military strategy designed with an eye toward mitigating the effects of the security dilemma would look rather different from one

[1]Second-image theories were prominently represented in the Reagan administration. I would include such people as Paul Nitze, Richard Pipes, and Richard Perle. See also my review essay "Competing Images of the Soviet Union," *World Politics* 39 (July 1987): 579–597.

[2]Third-image strategic ideas tend to be better represented in academia. I would classify Robert Jervis and Thomas Schelling, and more recently Jack Snyder and Stephen Van Evera, as among the best known strategists of this school. For a more elaborate discussion of second- and third-image theories, see Kenneth N. Waltz, *Man, the State, and War: A Theoretical Analysis* (New York, 1954, 1959).

[3]The most insightful and thorough discussion of the general considerations that should guide such a careful analysis is to be found in an unpublished paper by Stephen Van Evera, "Offense, Defense, and Strategy: When Is Offense Best?" delivered at the annual meeting of the American Political Science Association, Chicago, Ill., September 1987.

that concerned itself primarily with convincing ferocious expansionists not to make any aggressive moves.[4]

Second-image and third-image thinkers exhibit contrasting perspectives on the political implications of nuclear weapons. Fundamentally, second-image thinkers believe that nuclear weapons give the aggressor the advantage. They are concerned mainly with the credibility of the U.S. commitment to use nuclear weapons to secure interests abroad. However, it often seems that they doubt the willingness of the United States to employ nuclear weapons in response to attacks on its own soil.[5] The basic assumption is that the horrors of nuclear war are so great that the advantage in a contest of wills goes to the most ruthless, who is by definition the aggressor, driven to expansion by the very nature of his political system. U.S. strategists have been particularly fearful of nondemocratic countries, the governing elites of which can be portrayed as caring little for the suffering of their own people. The task for Western nuclear strategy is to increase the adversary's belief that nuclear weapons will be used.

Third-image theorists, while sharing the view that nuclear war is horrible, assume that even a modest prospect of retaliation deters even ambitious powers from most challenges. Given the consequences of nuclear war, which would leave even cold-blooded expansionist leaders with little to lead and few conquests to enjoy, they suspect that should a challenge come, it will arise more from fear than greed. The problem in a very abstract sense is not that one's own nuclear weapons might prove insufficiently frightening to the adversary to deter adventurism, but that through a thoughtlessly chosen offensive nuclear posture, one might, in an intense political dispute, provoke the adversary to make a preemptive attack. If there were a political challenge, or a conventional military attack, the risks of nuclear escalation are so great for all dispu-

[4]What I term "second-image theory" has some similarity with Robert Jervis's "deterrence model." Third-image theory has much in common with his "spiral model." See Jervis, *Perception and Misperception*, pp. 58–113. His discussion of the "deterrence model" does not stress the beliefs about the nature of the adversary held by those who consistently advocate policies of firmness and strength in foreign and defense policy.

[5]For example, many strategists expressed doubts that the United States would mount any retaliation against the Soviet Union even after a full-scale counterforce attack of several thousand warheads against the North American continent, if that attack had successfully destroyed the U.S. ICBM force. Thousands of surviving bomber and submarine ballistic missile warheads would not be used, since their ability promptly to destroy hard Soviet targets would be low. Their use would simply precipitate another Soviet nuclear attack. This scenario, popularized by Paul Nitze, "Assuring Strategic Stability in the Age of Detente," *Foreign Affairs* 54 (January 1976): 207–232, was a favorite among second-image strategists. Indeed, the intellectual foundations of the Reagan administration defense buildup, both in quantity and quality, are to be found in second-image theorizing.

tants that a common interest remains in the avoidance of escalation. Military restraint accompanied by firm diplomacy and threats to use nuclear weapons for punishment are viewed as a reasonable way to terminate hostilities and secure vital interests.[6]

Western military strategy since the late 1940s has been driven largely by the second image. As Ernest May has pointed out, Hitler continues to exert his baleful influence on international politics.[7] The third image, though far from having been totally ignored, has on the other hand had a relatively more limited influence on Western military strategy. This book has looked at Western military strategy from the perspective of the third image and its allied concept—the security dilemma—to discern what pitfalls we may have unintendedly generated for ourselves that may jeopardize our ability to avoid nuclear escalation should conflict begin. There are some powerful ones, as Chapters 1, 2, and 4 indicate. For the sake of prudence alone, a look at U.S. military strategy from an alternative perspective is warranted. Moreover, in my judgment, the Soviet Union has for most of its history, in its foreign relations, behaved more like a classical great power than a ferocious, cost-insensitive, high-rolling aggressor state. The Soviet Union has not fit the description of the second-image strategists. Today, political changes in the Soviet Union provide still further impetus to consider U.S. strategy from an alternative perspective.

A Dis-Integrated Nuclear-Conventional Military Strategy

The primary message of this book is that confusion about the relationship between conventional and nuclear war can lead to situations in which Western conventional and nuclear forces work at cross-purposes. The United States has bought counterforce nuclear weapons to enhance the credibility of its threat to escalate a conflict. At the same time, it has trumpeted its desire for more sustainable conventional forces to postpone the prospect of nuclear escalation indefinitely. Did we wish the adversary to believe or to disbelieve our threats to escalate?

Tensions also arise between the objectives of various elements of Western conventional forces. U.S. naval strategy has for many years planned operations that would have destroyed Soviet ballistic missile submarines from the outset of any conventional or nuclear conflict, an activity sure to be perceived as a strategic nuclear threat by the Soviets

[6] Thus second-image theorists tend to subscribe to military strategies that would likely lead to "total war" and tend to be skeptical of limited war strategies. Third-image theorists believe in the possibility of limited war, even between superpowers.

[7] *"Lessons" of the Past* (New York: Oxford University Press, 1973), esp. pp. 19–51.

and that might be responded to accordingly. Meanwhile, in NATO's Central Region, the United States badgered its allies to build up stocks of conventional munitions to permit the West to wage conventional war for as long as necessary. Although they refused to admit it, the navy was in effect creating pressures for nuclear escalation, "lowering the nuclear threshold," even as the allies in the Central Region were asked to buy conventional ammunition to "raise the nuclear threshold." Did the United States want its conventional military operations to force the pace of escalation or slow it down?

The costs of such internal inconsistency can be more than monetary. U.S. flexible response strategy made sustained large-scale conventional warfare seem plausible to our principal adversary, who, following our lead, energetically expanded conventional forces in the 1970s. The likelihood of a conventional challenge went up. At the same time U.S. leaders, as far as I have been able to discern, were unaware of the hidden tripwires to nuclear escalation that were buried in the nation's conventional and nuclear force postures and operational plans.

In Chapters 2 and 4 I argue that U.S. and NATO planning for the conduct of "conventional" naval and air war on the Soviet periphery, coupled with the theater and strategic nuclear capabilities that the United States and its NATO allies command, may have created powerful pressures for escalation from conventional to nuclear war. Even if the Soviets (or some other power for that matter) had chosen to begin a war with conventional weapons, they might shortly have found themselves in a position where the initiation of nuclear operations would begin to appear as the "best" of a number of bad alternatives.

Paths to an "Integrated" Nuclear-Conventional Strategy

U.S. and NATO military strategy was "disintegrated." It was—and to some extent remains—shot through with contradictions between its conventional and nuclear components. These contradictions neither serve the goal of deterring a highly aggressive, motivated adversary, nor that of escalation control. In principle, one could design a strategy that best serves one or the other of these two objectives. Below I offer two "ideal" military strategies that the West might have developed to deal with the Soviet threat during the height of the cold war competition.

"Ideal" Second-Image Strategy

An "ideal" military strategy for devotees of second-image theories of aggression would respond to its two main interrelated assumptions about the sources of conflict and the implications of nuclear weapons. The fundamental Cold War problem for U.S. and NATO defense policy is to make the Alliance's willingness to fight, with nuclear weapons if necessary, appear very strong to a committed, ferocious, aggressor state. How is this to be accomplished? Aside from political and diplomatic activity such as formal alliances, and the like, some specific nuclear and conventional military efforts would seem to follow.

First, at the level of intercontinental strategic forces, an effort to build a "counterforce," plausibly "warfighting," maximally "war-winning," capability is to be expected. An aggressive adversary will expect the United States to run nuclear risks only if it can be convinced that the United States sees the risks and costs as bearable. Hard-target killing ICBMs, real-time battle management, and strategic defense would be consistent with this position. One would also expect to see a good deal of strategic antisubmarine warfare activity in the navy. The incentives for speed of reaction, and preemption, imposed by these nuclear capabilities are a good thing for the second-image model theorist. As things currently stand, if a state is to have any hope of limiting the damage it would suffer in a nuclear war, offensive operations offer the greatest leverage. Political challenges over vital issues are better deterred if the adversary fears rapid nuclear escalation as a consequence of mutual offensive incentives.

At the level of "theater-nuclear" forces a similar pattern of military deployments is to be expected. The purpose is to make the forces seem "usable," in some discriminate way. From this perspective, one would expect theater forces to appear connected to the warfighting purposes of the strategic nuclear forces. They would, if possible, improve the West's overall ability to wage nuclear war. One would expect to see short-time-of-flight, highly accurate, medium-range ballistic missiles deployed in theater.

At the conventional level, a rather unusual looking force would make sense. It would not be an especially *sustainable* force. From the perspective of frightening an aggressive adversary and convincing him that the West would use nuclear weapons, huge stocks of ammunition and weapons, and large numbers of trained reserves would be a mistake. They would counteract the impression of inevitable escalation that the nuclear forces were trying to create. These conventional forces would have the role assigned to them by the early Cold War advocates of enhanced conventional forces such as Bernard Brodie. They would be used to reinforce nuclear deterrence. One way they do so is by being sufficiently large that "thin-slice" salami tactics are not attractive to the aggressor. If he wants to mount a challenge, he ought to have to mount a fairly big one, big enough to make nuclear escalation by the West plausible. There is no magic number here, but one would have thought that once NATO's conventional forces were large enough to require substantial reinforcement from Central Russia to guarantee their defeat, this purpose would have been achieved.

Another way that these forces would reinforce nuclear deterrence is by doing some of the things that theater nuclear forces are customarily expected to do, creating a substantial "gray area" between conventional and nuclear war. This would further enhance deterrence by convincing the adversary that NATO's military operations might incrementally develop important nuclear implications. Therefore, conventional forces should be armed with a variety of the most exotic, lethal, and long-range weaponry that money could buy. For example, NATO would want fighter bombers able to reach Soviet air space with a meaningful load of conventional ordnance and successfully to penetrate a dense air-defense system. Nuclear attack submarines and naval surface forces capable of operations in close proximity to Soviet naval bases would further cloud the distinction between conventional and nuclear war. Rather than purchasing huge quantities of the basic munitions needed to sustain conventional conflict, such as artillery shells and antitank weapons, one would purchase expensive, theoretically highly lethal ordnance. This kind of ordnance would have the capability to force the pace of conventional conflict in unpredictable ways. Even in the ground forces, a preference for very high quality weapons and formations in modest numbers might make sense. Such forces inevitably appear to have some, not easy to predict, counteroffensive potential. The adversary's expectations of his prospects in the war would be one of either a high-cost, incredibly violent, but relatively quick conventional victory (shortly followed by nuclear escalation), or a more modest probability of sudden, unexpected, but potentially catastrophic NATO counterattack.

Clearly, many elements of this strategy were present in NATO's forces, but not all. Some elements were present that did not belong. In general, however, the United States and NATO were closer to this strategy and force posture than to a posture that suited the third-image theorist's view of conflict, although Western political leaders seemed unaware of it.

"Ideal" Third-Image Strategy

The third-image military strategist is as concerned with the possibility of an adversary who initiates war out of fear as out of greed. The image of the adversary does not assume benign intent, but it does make fear an important motive. States are pictured more as "limited aims" security seekers than insatiable power seekers. Power is simply the means to the end. The view of nuclear weapons is that they are so scary that the smallest probability of retaliation deters all but the most insane aggressor. Indeed, the assumption is that although nuclear weapons cannot make individuals sane, they encourage the sane individuals in every state to be very careful that sane leaders are chosen. Given these assumptions, and given the technical fact that for advanced industrial powers, secure punitive nuclear retaliatory capabilities seem to be achievable with astonishingly small commitments of national resources, premeditated aggression of the size and importance to produce meaningful declines in national security is most unlikely. Nevertheless, the possibility exists and must be confronted. It is, however, essential that the act of preparing for this very remote possibility not make it less remote. The third-image theorist would look at the strategy outlined above with horror.

What constellation of military forces would the third-image theorist prefer? At the strategic level, he would prefer an impressive, survivable retaliatory capability, but little more. The third-image theorist would want to be very sure that putative adversaries understood this capability, so substantial redundancy, indeed "overkill," would be desirable. The preference for initial use of the force, should that unlikely event ever arise, would be for demonstrative strikes at nonmilitary targets. An ability to engage in large-scale counterforce attacks would be deliberately and emphatically forsworn. Strategic defense, and strategic ASW would have no place in this strategy. In the view of the third-image theorist, these kinds of capabilities can easily be perceived by putative adversaries to imply malign political and military intent, making it more likely that the opposing state could come to see the initiation of war to be the least bad alternative. They increase the adversary's fear that we are coming after him, perhaps causing him to engage in preemptive war, or preemptive escalation.

The third-image theorist would probably not be overly concerned with theater nuclear capabilities. The deterrence problem is primarily one of will and commitment, and the institution of the NATO alliance, plus a good deal of diplomatic reinforcement, could be counted upon to convey the appropriate message. If theater nuclear weapons were perceived as necessary, a relatively limited number of weapons of modest range and accuracy—more appropriate for demonstration than for waging an all-out nuclear war—would be sufficient. The theater forces preferred by the second-image advocate would be needlessly provocative.

The third-image theorist is sensitive to the charge that these measures could reduce the risks that the adversary would perceive to be associated with aggression. The nature of the nuclear forces deployed would turn nuclear war into a pure "slow motion" competition in the willingness to suffer; the risks of rapid escalation to large-scale use of nuclear weapons would be reduced since large-scale use would serve no military purpose. An aggressor might employ "salami" tactics to make each individual act of aggression seem too small to warrant any use of nuclear weapons. Thus, the third-image theorist would be in favor of strengthened conventional forces.

Conventional aggression should require major military preparations by the adversary. At the same time, the adversary should have low confidence of success at the level of conventional war. The third-image theorist does, however, fear that conventional forces and operations can make war more likely. Against the backdrop of a very stable strategic nuclear relationship, traditional conventional logic might come to dominate thinking about theater war. Offensively postured conventional forces may create the kind of threat that could make the adversary preempt. Too much offensive capability and striking power might make the war difficult to control. Because the third-image theorist's image of war is that it arises as often from fear as from greed, he or she is willing to bet that the war may be settled by diplomacy rather than victory or catastrophic escalation. So the third-image theorist wants to slow the pace of the war. Appropriate ground forces might include a mix of large numbers of defensively postured light forces (mechanized or unmechanized as the terrain requires), backed by a small number of heavy mechanized forces for counterattack. A substantial portion of the force could be based on reserves. At sea, a convoy escort and barrier ASW capability would be sufficient. A mix of air defense, close air support, and shallow interdiction aircraft would constitute an acceptable air capability. To provide the time for diplomacy to work, the third-image theorist would probably favor large stocks of munitions and parts necessary to sustain lengthy conventional conflict. As long as a substantial secure second-strike capability exists, a reasonable adversary's overall temptation to engage in *any* war is low. If conventional war does break out, such a capability probably exerts a healthy, diplomatically exploitable tendency toward restraint on both sides. As long as a volatile mix of offensively capable conventional and nuclear forces do not drive the pace of crisis or war, there is hope for a settlement that preserves fundamental security interests.

The one problem with this strategy is that it depends very substantially on political will—for deterrence and war fighting. Thus, a second-image theorist would fear that it lacked deterrent power against an especially motivated adversary. The third-image theorist would try to address this concern through a clear and consistent public and private diplomacy to clarify his country's commitment to defend certain interests.

Real-World Constraints

The preceding are, of course, ideal types. Real-life military strategy varies substantially from these ideal types for a host of reasons. In general, states are more likely to adopt military strategies that reflect second-image theories of conflict than strategies that reflect third-image theories.

As noted in the introduction, there are cases where one has no choice but to defend oneself with assets that permit offensive operations. NATO's ground forces have been heavily mechanized and have had a certain inherent offensive capability. I doubt that they could have looked otherwise and still constituted a credible defense against a Pact mechanized ground assault. Some advocates of "defensive defense" argue differently, but I do not find their arguments persuasive. In my judgment, NATO needed armor to defend successfully, and only radical restructuring of Pact forces could have changed that. As long as Soviet ground forces retain their armor, NATO will need some too.

International politics is not subject to fine-grained predictions. Particularly, the motivations and the behavior of possible opponents can change. Recently, Soviet behavior has changed markedly for the better, and indeed Soviet statements and actions quite explicitly show a heightened awareness of the third image and the security dilemma, and the extent to which they have gotten themselves into spirals with the West. Just as their behavior has changed for the better, however, it can change for the worse. Statesmen will generally want to have sufficient flexibility in their military capabilities to cope with such changes if they occur.

Finally, and of critical importance, for a host of reasons military organizations prefer offensive military strategies. They have a high degree of functional autonomy within the modern state that permits them to develop offensive strategies and force postures.

Today U.S. and NATO strategy and force posture are more consistent with a second-image than a third-image theory of conflict, but nevertheless there has been some modest awareness of the risks of uncontrollable escalation spirals in Western and Eastern military decisions. Although both sides have deployed a lot of counterforce weaponry in their strategic nuclear forces, they have also tried to harden, hide, and disperse their own weapons to make them harder for the adversary to target. The United States has not pursued a strategic defense capability with much dedication; the Alliance's counteroffensive capabilities on the ground are modest; some of the allies in the more exposed geographic positions (for example, Norway) have tried to limit military deployments so that they do not unduly threaten the Soviet Union. But most important, the United States and NATO have deployed very extensive conventional ground and air capabilities, and defensive ASW capabilities, to permit the waging of a lengthy conventional war. The Soviet Union has been even more committed to a pure second-image strategy, but it, too, has moved strongly in the direction of very impressive conventional capabilities. In the late 1980s the rhetoric of defensive specialization for conventional forces crept into Soviet political and military writings—although there have thus far been only modest reductions in the offensive military capability of Soviet forces. Thus, both Eastern and Western strategies contain these fundamental tensions. Each deploys a mix of military capabilities organized by incoherent strategies that aim both to create risks of unlimited war and the possibility of limited war. Political and military leaders seem unaware of the peculiar dangers buried in these incoherent strategies and force postures, potential energy that could prove surprisingly explosive in crisis and war.

Policy Recommendations

In my judgment, U.S. strategy and force posture have paid too little attention to the third image and the security dilemma. I would prefer that most of the nuclear counterforce programs, navy forward ASW programs, and air force and navy deep-attack aircraft and cruise missile programs be removed from the U.S. and NATO force posture and doctrine.[8] For the first time, it seems plausible that the Soviets might cooperate in such a venture.[9] I do not, however, believe that this is a likely turn of events. Statesmen's fears of an uncertain environment and military preferences for offensive military strategies, both, will

[8]In brief, my own preferences run to a very strong assured destruction capability in the strategic nuclear forces, accompanied by quite modest capabilities for limited strategic nuclear attacks; in the air force a stress on air defense, close air support, and battlefield air interdiction; in the navy a strong defensive sea control and convoy escort capability, with modest capabilities for forward operations for harassment, reconnaissance, and the threat of counterattack; and for ground forces I continue to favor mechanized forces of the kind we have today—wherever we face a mechanized opposition.

[9]Until recently, the Soviet Union paid even less attention to the third-image model and paid for its mistakes by encircling itself.

make it very difficult to move U.S. and NATO military doctrine and force posture in the direction specified, much less coordinate a simultaneous doctrinal transformation with the Soviet Union. Given a continuation of political good will, some movement is possible, but progress is likely to fall short of my own force posture preferences, and far short of the "ideal type" third-image posture outlined above.

Regional conflicts are likely to prove even less tractable. The regional competitions discussed above are characterized by high levels of political hostility and, in many cases, mutually exclusive political objectives. The disputants probably have less reason than did the superpowers to integrate awareness of the security dilemma into their military postures. The superpowers have established a number of arms control venues to try to coordinate such reforms if they wish to do so; the parties to regional disputes have little reason to initiate arms control negotiations, simply because they still expect to fight over their irreconcilable political objectives. And, as discussed above, both resource constraints and the recent experience of their military organizations will make it hard for them to replicate in any nuclear force they deploy the extensive measures the superpowers have taken to ensure the survivability of their strategic nuclear forces. On the other hand, it seems quite plausible that as weapons of mass destruction intrude into these regional conflicts, states will exhibit the superpower pattern of sustained interest in large non-nuclear forces for limited war. Thus, I expect that the military strategies and force postures of the principal regional competitors will, if they deploy nuclear weapons, exhibit the same kinds of tensions exhibited by the superpowers.

Structures of Political-Military Integration

If strategies and force postures are unlikely to be channeled in directions that consistently serve either the goal of keeping states back from the brink or providing them with the tools to navigate a crisis or a war should it occur, then what other mechanisms are available to better integrate political-military strategy? If the constellation of capabilities currently deployed by NATO and the Soviet Union today are to deter during a political crisis, however unlikely such a crisis may now seem, then their hidden potential for escalation must be clearly understood. If precipitate and/or unintended nuclear escalation is to be avoided during a conventional conflict, then statesmen on both sides will require a keener sense of the military potential and vulnerability of their conventional and nuclear forces than currently seems the case. They will also require a greater understanding of the implications of the military operations they or their adversaries may launch. These requirements will be even more pressing in regional competitions where nuclear weapons make their appearance.

In an earlier work I discussed at length both the importance of and obstacles to the close connection of military means and political ends in national strategy.[10] As a consequence of the division of labor, of functional specialization within the structure of the modern state, responsibility for the conduct of foreign policy and the conduct of war falls into the hands of different professions—statesmen and soldiers. It is important to remember that this process occurred because it made the state a more efficient competitor in international politics. But once this separation occurs, powerful barriers arise to the effective integration of the entire chain of military and political means and ends of national strategy.

These disjunctions are not merely aesthetically unappealing. They have real effects on the security of states. Such disjunctions were fundamental to the failure of French security policy in the late 1930s. Although disagreements persist on the specific causes of World War I, at least some analysts agree that a major problem of Wilhelmine Germany during the July crisis is that it lacked the military posture to support its foreign policy. Bethmann pursued a policy of coercive diplomacy, but he tried to do so with a military instrument that had programmed itself for one major option—mobilization followed closely by large-scale assault in the West. Moreover, he did not understand this at the outset of the crisis—discovering only on the eve of mobilization that for the German Army, the order for mobilization was an order for attacks on Belgium.[11] A more flexible military policy might have achieved his apparent objective, a localized Austro-Hungarian and Serbian war in the east. Failing that, it might have permitted Germany to wage a limited war on both frontiers.

If political-military integration is to be achieved, then a certain degree of civilian intervention in military affairs is essential. Military organizations must specialize in warfare if they are to be truly competitive with their putative adversaries.[12] Thus, the civil power must be dominant in warfare states because, where the professional military usurps all civil-

[10]Posen, *Sources of Military Doctrine*.

[11]See L. C. F. Turner, "The Schlieffen Plan," in *War Plans of the Great Powers*, ed. Paul Kennedy (Boston: Allen and Unwin, 1979), p. 213; John Moses, *The Politics of Illusion* (London: George Prior, 1975), pp. 86–87.

[12]The huge disparity in military professionalism was an important factor in the British victory over Argentina in the Falklands war.

ian functions, it loses its professional focus on combat and therefore its fighting power. Military organizations themselves increasingly consist of powerful suborganizations—whether services or service branches. They cannot set priorities among themselves, according to strategic criteria, without the intervention of higher authority, usually civilian authority. But if a degree of civilian intervention is required, how is it to occur? What structures facilitate civilian intervention? How can the necessary intervention be achieved without at the same time usurping the military's professional function to the extent that irresponsible amateurs begin to demand of military forces things alien to their nature?

There is no easy answer to these questions. In the past century two broad strategies have been attempted in the West. The first may be termed "autocratic." It is best exemplified by Hitler and Stalin (and Napoleon Bonaparte, for that matter.) All civil and military power is concentrated in the hands of a warlord. The warlord either has, or fancies himself to have, such genius that he can manage all the state's affairs and run the war out of his own head. Of course, both Hitler and Stalin benefited from very efficient, bureaucratized political and military staffs, without which their feats would have been impossible. And given the military catastrophes produced by these two warlords, one doubts that the system has much to commend it. The principal problem is that a single individual with great authority and power can defy rationality criteria on a whim—as Stalin did in the spring of 1941, and as Hitler did for the latter part of the war.

The other method of political-military integration parallels developments in large bureaucracies and corporations in the twentieth century. This method might be termed the "Anglo-Saxon," or "pluralist" approach; it was first institutionalized in Britain in the Committee for Imperial Defense (CID) at the turn of the century. Here a civil-military "boundary spanning unit" is created, staffed by soldiers and civilians. It provides an institutional bridge across the functional specialties essential to the modern warfare state—the raising of money, the conduct of diplomacy, the collection of intelligence, the waging of war, and the mobilization of domestic political support. This method is not foolproof—it does not guarantee textbook efficiency and effectiveness. It sets a bureaucracy, albeit a small one, to catch a bureaucracy, albeit a large one. Thus, it is subject to the foibles of bureaucracy. The solution is less than perfect. The pulling and hauling that characterizes bureaucratic politics within the modern state cannot be eliminated. Change is slow. Decisions are muddled, and priorities only intermittently set. Nevertheless, the regular commitment to rationality criteria, the vetting of options, the consideration of cost and benefit, and the systematic inclusion of all relevant technical expertise do (I believe) buffer the state against the worst excesses of the autocratic system.

Today, this pluralist system of national security management has been brought to a relatively high state of development in the United States of America. The National Security Council provides a top-level boundary-spanning unit. The Office of the Secretary of Defense in the Pentagon centralizes tremendous authority in the hands of the civilian secretary, who legally controls the field commanders for the president, through the chairman of the Joint Chiefs of Staff. At lower levels of the government horizontal relationships include quasi-independent civilian organizations in the development of military hardware, the assessment of the military balance, and the consideration of military strategies. A large number of independent university centers for research, and for training civilian and military strategists, provide sources of trained expertise and policy analysis. Similarly, there exist several completely independent civilian organizations dedicated to critical evaluation of U.S. strategy and force posture.

Since the death of Stalin, the Soviet Union has relied on what appears to have been a more ad hoc approach to the fundamental issue of political-military integration. Partly, they have relied on the reservoir of military expertise created in the party as a function of the close participation of political officials in military operations during the civil war and World War II. Partly, they satisfied themselves that essential control was maintained through the medium of the "Main Political Administration" of the armed forces, which ensured against the rise of Bonapartism. But as the generation that lead the Soviet Union through World War II began to age and die, these expedients seemed to outside observers to be less and less reliable. And one suspects that the very large resources that flowed to the Soviet military in the latter Brezhnev period had something to do with the military's corner on the market for military expertise. Since Mikhail Gorbachev came to power, however, there has been increasing evidence of a nascent civilian community of defense experts concentrated in the political and economic research institutes. If true, this would put the Soviet Union on the path that other Western states have trod over the past century.

Among the most active regional competitors in the world today institutional arrangements for civil control of the military vary widely. The highest degree of integration is probably found in Israel—but even here the system broke down during the 1982 Lebanon War.[13] India probably

[13]Schiff and Ya'ari, *Israel's Lebanon War*, presents this argument, summarized on pp. 301–308.

approaches the Anglo-Saxon model of civilian control. Syria and Iraq probably approach a "warlord" model. Pakistan and Iran are at this point mysteries.

The development of an elaborate system linking political and military considerations, statesmen and soldiers, in the United States, has not, however, reached the level appropriate for the military capabilities that we possess. Many civilians who have participated in the U.S. national security apparatus have observed that some critical aspects of military activity remain rather exclusively controlled by the uniformed services—particularly, operational planning and execution. Where civilians try to involve themselves in these matters, they are strenuously opposed. This opposition is to be expected since it cuts to the core of the military's professional identity. It also cuts to the core of the requirement for effective fighting power. It is implausible that civilians who have not been responsible for a series of career military tasks can episodically become great commanders.

In spite of these obstacles, however, the thrust of the analysis in this book suggests that the military capabilities that modern states have developed require some subtle political management if they are not to precipitate a catastrophe that we all wish to avoid. This means that civilian strategists must educate themselves much more fully than they have been accustomed to doing in the detail of military operations and planning—both conventional and nuclear. Equally if not more important, however, an institutionalized system for the review of military plans for their more esoteric political implications is essential. Just as the Office of the Secretary of Defense has specialist civilian-led organizations for the review of military budgets, such as the office of Program Analysis and Evaluation, and the assessment of the military balance, such as the Office of Net Assessment, an organization is needed to review military operational plans. It is worth noting that military men and women serve in both of the aforementioned organizations, providing a core of expertise as well as cautionary restraint. But a civilian-led and -dominated organization for the *review* of operational plans is essential. That organization must function in peace and in war. Its relations with the military will be problematic, and considerable diplomacy and self-restraint will be necessary. It will need to resist the temptation to try to plan military operations itself. Instead, it must focus on the more limited but more practical role of auditor and adviser. I would strongly advise the leaders of the Soviet Union to create a similar organization. The superpower competition is at a unique point, which facilitates these developments. How to encourage such developments elsewhere in the world is a question for which I have no answer. But insofar as we invite professional soldiers from all over the world to participate in our military education system, as does the Soviet Union, it seems possible that such institutional reforms could at least be introduced to other countries. Whether they adopt them or not is a development over which the United States will have little influence.

A suggestion for educational and organizational reform may seem an odd conclusion. But the suggestion I make, however much it is resisted politically, is consistent with a century of institutional development in the modern state. It permits some common ground between third-image and second-image model theorists—in which each can hope to have some of his or her concerns met. And it is more likely to be adopted than a suggestion that U.S. (or any other country's) military strategy be firmly anchored at one end or the other of the second-image–third-image spectrum. Indeed, given the uncertainties of international politics, structural reform better suits the security requirements of modern states for the long haul.

APPENDIX 1

The Suppression of Enemy Air Defenses (SEAD) Model

SEAD is a simple model that captures a few of the essential aspects of the effort NATO's forces would have made to suppress or destroy the Warsaw Pact air defense network in East Germany, Poland, and Czechoslovakia in the event of war in the 1980s. SEAD was developed with a Lotus 1-2-3 or Symphony spreadsheet package. A sample "run" is included below.

SEAD simply tracks the radar-killing potential of a given force of dedicated aircraft over many sorties on the basis of certain assumptions. It keeps a running count of the share of the adversary's radars in Eastern Europe that these expected kills represent. SEAD examines the interrelationships among six variables, although sensitivity analysis is conducted with only three of them. These six variables are the number and type of available NATO defense suppression aircraft; the number of "shots" fired per sortie; the probability of kill of each shot; the share of the surviving NATO force in flying condition for each sortie; the level of attrition exacted by Pact air defenses on each sortie; and the number of major Pact radars deployed in the theater of operations. Sensitivity analysis is performed for a range of attrition rates (Pact defensive effectiveness) and kill probabilities (NATO offensive effectiveness), the variables about which there is the greatest uncertainty. Excursions were run with 180 current-generation aircraft, 50 stealth aircraft, and a combination of the two. The results of model runs should be treated cautiously, as indicators of plausible combat potential. There are reasons why the model may understate NATO's plausible success, since it does not attempt to account for jamming or attacks on missile launchers, especially launch control vehicles. On the other hand, the model may overstate the extent of NATO's plausible success: the actual destruction of radar antennae has not proven simple in practice. Although easily damaged by fragments and blast, these antennae are apparently not that difficult to repair. They seem not to stay dead. On balance, I believe that the model I have developed, combined with the relatively conservative values I have employed, does offer insight into plausible trends in NATO's air-defense-suppression effort over time.

One variable, NATO's sortie rate, is not directly included in the model. The reader can, however, easily include it. As noted in the text, one's assessment of how many sorties NATO can fly within the plausible range of one to three per day is a function of one's assessment of the damage NATO's airfields are likely to suffer. This would require an analysis in its own right. Epstein has done part of such an analysis, showing the potential number of weapons the Pact might deliver against NATO by air.[1] Unfortunately, the subject of airfield attack and repair is quite arcane, and information about the quality of Pact airfield-attack munitions is very sparse. One must, therefore, perform one's own assessment.

Finally, one rather complicated relationship is greatly simplified in the model, which will be discussed below. This is the relationship between the number of surviving Pact radars and the attrition that the Pact air defense can continue to exact. In simplest terms, that attrition rate is reduced as NATO aircraft destroy an ever-increasing share of the Pact's radars.

Aircraft Numbers. While open-source information on the numbers of F-111s, Tornados, F-4Gs and F-4Es, and F-16s in NATO's inventory is easy to derive from sources such as *The Military Balance*, the actual allocation of these forces worldwide, and theater-wide, is a secret. Here I have assumed that 60 percent of the U.S. F-4G Weasel force (60 aircraft), with 60 accompanying F-4Es or F-16s, is allocated to the Central Region.[2] This assumption does not seem implausible since this is, after all, where the ground-based air defense threat is toughest. Indeed, as is evident below, more than half of Soviet tactical air defense missiles are probably captured in my estimate of the radar target set. As of 1988, roughly 140 U.S. F-111s were based in Europe. Germany and the United Kingdom had about 290 Tornados in air force and navy attack units. In the model runs for this analysis, 60 F-111s and/or Tornados are allocated

[1] Epstein, *Measuring Military Power*.

[2] As of 1983 there were 102 F-4G Weasels "combat coded and permanently assigned." Statement of Lt. Gen. Lawrence Skantze, in U.S. Congress, House, House Armed Services Committee, *Department of Defense Authorization of Appropriations for Fiscal Year 1984*, p. 1264.

to the suppression mission.[3] They would be quite useful for low-altitude attacks against fixed or semimobile radar installations.[4] In the course of the campaign NATO is not permitted to reinforce these assets. Of course, if it wished to, NATO could allocate more aircraft to the suppression mission, but it would do so at the cost of leaving other missions uncovered. In the Central Region, 180 aircraft is only a fraction of NATO's total air attack capability. By my count, after reinforcement NATO would have about 1000 high-quality aircraft (F-4s, F-16s, F-111s, and Tornados) available for attacks into Eastern Europe during the period in question.

As noted in the text, the U.S. F-117 stealth fighter aircraft is useful for air-defense suppression. Therefore, an excursion that adds 50 stealth fighters to the basic force was developed. Consistent with the hypothesized characteristics of the aircraft, they are assigned higher effectiveness (.25 pk/shot) than other planes and suffer lower initial attrition (2 percent).[5]

"Shots" per Sortie. All of my SEAD runs give each aircraft credit for four shots per sortie. For the sake of conservatism, aircraft destroyed are assumed not to have an opportunity to deliver any ordnance. Four shots per sortie is consistent with the average Weasel load of four Shrike antiradiation missiles (ARMs). F-4Es or F-16s are assumed to have enough munitions of different kinds to mount four attacks. For example, F-4s have been known to carry as much as four tons of bombs per sortie. This would permit a weapons load of 16 Mk-82 500-pound bombs. (If maneuverability is essential, a smaller bomb load is preferred, perhaps two tons; thus 8 Mk-82s, or 4 large cluster bombs, or 4 or more precision guided weapons, is a more likely configuration for a defense suppression F-4E or F-16.) Notionally, these could be delivered in four passes. F-4Es in air-defense-suppression missions have practiced the use of the Mk-82 with a "proximity" fuse, which permits an airburst. The widely dispersed shrapnel and the blast overpressure are quite damaging to the relatively sensitive components of radar antennae. The new Imaging Infrared Maverick antitank weapon would also be useful in defense-suppression attacks. SAM guidance and control units radiate

[3]This is a simplification. F-111s would probably be employed only against particularly lucrative targets associated with Soviet air defenses, not against the average SAM site.

[4]The German Air Force ordered 35–40 ECR versions of the Tornado. These were specially modified both for reconnaissance and air-defense-suppression missions. Peter Pletschacher, "German Air Force to Buy Tornado ECR," *International Defense Review* 19 (January 1986): 88–89.

[5]Bill Sweetman, *Stealth Aircraft: Secrets of Future Air Power* (Osceola, Wis.: Motorbooks International, 1986), pp. 59–70.

quite a bit of heat that would permit these missiles to lock on to them. Since the warhead is designed to penetrate heavy tank armor, air-defense vehicles are likely to be obliterated.

For both F-4G and F-4E/F-16 sorties I assume that the adversary is operating his radars with sufficient frequency and duration to permit the Weasels to acquire them and then either to lock on an antiradiation missile or to direct an attack by an accompanying aircraft. A canny defender might employ clever radar tactics to reduce the Weasel's effectiveness. For example, he could leave his radars off most of the time to inhibit detection; he could turn his radars off whenever he believed an ARM attack to be under way and thus inhibit its guidance. This would, however, also inevitably reduce his effectiveness against attacking aircraft. In the sensitivity analysis presented, the reader can pair plausible attrition rates with plausible NATO kill probabilities. If the adversary did exact 5 percent attrition from early NATO sorties, his radars would probably have to be on much of the time, which also means that NATO would be getting more information and its missiles would be acquiring the target more effectively. Thus a kill probability in the .1–.15 range might be plausible. On the other hand, if the adversary could impose only 3 percent attrition, it might be because he had chosen to behave in a more tactically canny fashion, and therefore NATO would do less well against him. A .05 pk might be more plausible under such conditions. Finally, F-111s and Tornados probably would not release their ordnance in four passes, although some F-111s are capable of nighttime, low-altitude, precision-guided ordnance delivery. Rather, given the kinds of targets they would attack (medium and large, fixed or semimobile, early warning and ground control intercept or GCI radars), a low-altitude release of an entire bomb load might be the optimal tactic. For the sake of simplicity, a single attack with a probability of kill of .4 is treated in the model as four attacks, each with a probability of kill of .1.

Attrition. The attrition that an air-defense system can exact from an attacking force is a function not only of the effectiveness of the system itself but of the efforts that the attacker makes to suppress that system and to avoid its effects. Historically, attrition rates as low as a tenth of a percent have prevailed over rather long periods of air attack, but attrition rates as high as 10 percent (perhaps higher) have prevailed over short periods.[6] It is thus quite difficult to guess what the attrition

[6]U.S. Navy attrition over North Vietnam between 1965 and 1973 was .1 percent (one suspects that this figure involved some creative accounting); average Israeli air force attrition during the 1973 war was .8 percent. Israeli A-4s in the same war, flying the most

rates might be in a NATO–Pact war. My starting point for these assumptions is based on U.S. experience during the 1965–68 bombing campaign over North Vietnam. Gen. William Momyer, USAF ret., reports that the U.S. Air Force's worst losses in the heavily defended Hanoi area during this period rarely exceeded 4 percent, and that the "overall loss rate for attack sorties from 1965–1968" was about 4.1 percent. At the beginning of this campaign the air force was not well prepared for a sustained conventional effort against modern ground defenses, since it was just emerging from the period of tactical nuclear-weapon emphasis associated with the Eisenhower massive-retaliation doctrine. Attack sorties, in which planes must expose themselves to ground fire to deliver ordnance, tend to suffer the highest attrition.[7] Interestingly, Israeli attack sorties during the second day of the 1973 war, the worst day of the war for the Israeli Air Force, suffered nearly 4.7 percent attrition. Following a dedicated campaign of defense suppression, as well as tactical changes that admittedly lowered its effectiveness, this attrition rate dropped so that the average attrition for the whole war for attack sorties was about 1.5 percent.[8] A year earlier over North Vietnam a somewhat more sophisticated defense-suppression effort forced the average attrition rate down to 2 percent. But it must be remembered that large, slow B-52 strategic bombers were permitted to operate over the north at this low average rate. An all-fighter-bomber force would have done even better. Interestingly, the U.S. Air Force predicted that its newest attack aircraft, the F-15 Strike Eagle, might expect to suffer 1.5 percent per sortie in a NATO–Pact war, flying at very low altitudes and at night, a capability that the F-111 and Tornado had in the mid-1980s.

I believe that a 5 percent attrition rate is a conservative estimate of what the Soviets might be able to exact against dedicated defense-suppression aircraft at the war's outset. Consistent with lower values

---

dangerous attack sorties, suffered about 1.5 percent average attrition, according to the Congressional Budget Office, *Navy Budget Issues*, pp. 98, 102–103. The U.S. Air Force suffered an average attrition rate of about 2 percent during the lengthy strategic bombing campaign of World War II but suffered the same 2 percent attrition during the 1972 Christmas bombing of Hanoi. The Argentinian Air Force appears to have suffered nearly 10 percent attrition per sortie during the most intense combat of the South Atlantic war. Alberts, *Deterrence*, n. 27, p. 50. Guenter Lewy, *America in Vietnam* (New York: Oxford University Press, 1978), p. 411, quotes several U.S. government sources to the effect that losses for all sorties flown in 1967 were about .024 percent, and in Linebacker I, April–October 1972, .018 percent. This includes all sorties flown, however, including reconnaissance.

[7]Momyer, *Air Power in Three Wars*, p. 119.

[8]Historical Evaluation and Research Service, *The Development of Soviet Air Defense Doctrine and Practice* (Dunn Loring, Va.: T. N. Dupuy Associates, 1981), chap. 6, pp. 31–32.

experienced elsewhere, 4 percent and 3 percent attrition rates are tested. The attrition rate is degraded over time, however, again consistent with much Western experience. The simplifying, and again conservative, assumption is made that there is some lower boundary on attrition. The wear and tear caused by intense operations, anti-aircraft gunfire, and simple heat-seeking missiles are assumed to cause roughly 1 percent attrition no matter what the attacker does. On the basis of overall historical experience, this number may be too conservative. The remaining attrition rate is then degraded proportionally in relation to the number of Pact radars destroyed. For example, if the initial attrition rate is set at 5 percent, by the time one-half of the Pact's radars are destroyed the rate should drop to 3.5 percent. This rate of change may also be conservative since it assumes that every air-defense radar is worth as much as every other and that NATO enjoys no ability to target the more valuable radars first. It seems quite likely that if early warning radars are destroyed first (perhaps 25 percent of the total), the local acquisition and missile tracking radars will work much less effectively. NATO planners know this and will plan their attacks accordingly.

The Probability of Kill per Radar Attack. Regrettably, information on this variable is remarkably sparse in the open literature. For precision-guided (laser-illuminated or electro-optical) glide bombs, hit probabilities in the 0.5 range have been recorded in combat.[9] Indeed, it is quite common in "back of the envelope" analysis to assume .5 as the pk for precision-guided ordnance. Unfortunately, these numbers can provide only an upward boundary on potential effectiveness, especially since these weapons are delivered by different principles than antiradiation missiles, or "dumb-bombs."[10] They simply suggest that very high accuracies are plausible. Similarly, although it appears that U.S. Shrike and

[9]For example, in 1967 the U.S. Navy reportedly dropped 68 Walleye electro-optical (television-guided) bombs over North Vietnam for 65 hits. In attacks on the Thanh Hoa bridge the U.S. Air Force delivered a mix of laser-guided and electro-optical weapons in several different attacks. While it is difficult to be precise, pk's of .4 or better seem to have been achieved. See Maj. A. J. C. Lavalle, ed., *The Tale of Two Bridges and the Battle for the Skies over North Vietnam*, USAF Southeast Asia Monograph Series, vol. I, monographs 1 and 2 (Washington, D.C.: Government Printing Office, 1976), pp. 59, 84–92.

[10]The term "dumb-bomb" should now be used with caution. The electronic systems for accurately delivering dumb bombs have become quite effective, as the Israeli success against the Osirak reactor illustrates. I have had pilots say to me, "You don't have to put a 'smart bomb' on a 'smart' airplane." The airplanes have gotten quite smart. Many of the F-4E's that operated with the F-4G's had been retrofitted with America's most sophisticated bomb-delivery systems. The bomb-delivery system of the F-16 is known worldwide for its accuracy.

Standard ARM antiradiation missiles played an important role in the successful Israeli strikes on Syrian air defenses in the Bekaa Valley in 1982, little specific information has leaked to the press. Indeed, uncertainty remains as to whether the majority of kills were achieved by these weapons, by "dumb" weapons, or by a specially designed Israeli surface-to-surface antiradiation missile.[11] Again, the example only serves to show that high effectiveness is achievable. Mixed but still positive results were apparently achieved in U.S. Navy carrier air operations against Libya in April of 1986. According to journalistic accounts, a dozen Shrikes and three dozen HARMs were fired for a total of at least five radar antennae destroyed.[12] If true, this translates into an average probability of kill of .1 per shot, although we cannot tell how much of the effectiveness was generated by the new, and still relatively scarce, HARM.

Unfortunately, there is also evidence to the effect that SAM radars are not necessarily easy to engage successfully, and that the West's most numerous antiradiation missile, the Shrike, enjoyed uneven effectiveness in Vietnam. This information is largely anecdotal; there is very little by way of recorded hit or kill probabilities with Shrike. General Momyer summarizes Wild Weasel operations in North Vietnam this way:

> The Iron Hand (Weasel) missions and tactics remained about the same during the 1965–1968 campaign and the 1972 offensive, though the effectiveness of the flights was often debated. It was particularly difficult to confirm the destruction of a SAM, and some critics claimed that the Weasels were not effective since a relatively small number of destroyed SAM sites could be attributed with certainty to these flights. However, as much as we wanted to destroy the sites, the effectiveness of the Iron Hand flights must be measured against the criteria of suppression as well as one of destruction. If a SAM site could be suppressed so that it couldn't fire against strike aircraft, the mission of the Iron Hand flight was a complete success. With better air to ground missiles, the Weasels could probably have destroyed, rather than merely suppressed, more of the SAMs.[13]

In spite of these observations, one should not jump to the conclusion that antiradiation missiles were useless then, or are useless now. In its

[11]On this operation, see Clarence Robinson, "Surveillance Integration Pivotal in Israeli Successes," *Aviation Week and Space Technology*, 5 July 1982, pp. 16–17; Maj. Charles Mayo, "Lebanon: An Air Defense Analysis," *Air Defense Artillery*, Winter 1983, pp. 22–24.

[12]"Jet Believed Lost," *Washington Post*, 16 April 1986, and "Military Believes Stray Bomb Struck Civilian Neighborhood," *Washington Post*, 17 April 1986.

[13]Momyer, *Air Power in Three Wars*, pp. 131–132.

initial employment, the Standard Arm missile was apparently quite effective in Vietnam, one report suggesting a .6 pk against SAM missile guidance radars.[14] In spite of its seeming initial superiority over the Shrike, few Standard Arms were actually produced. Instead, Shrike appears to have been modified to correct its deficiencies, and several thousand additional Shrikes were purchased after the end of the Vietnam war.[15]

The effectiveness of an antiradiation missile is in part a function of the detection and weapons control system on the launching aircraft. The mid-1980s F-4G Weasel was a fourth-generation system, which itself had been continuously upgraded, making it much more capable than its Vietnam-era predecessors, even when firing Vietnam-era Shrike and Standard Arm munitions. The combination of HARM with the F-4G was predicted to increase the aircraft's destructiveness "by an order of magnitude," that is, tenfold.[16] HARMs fired from the F-4G should be more lethal than the same missile fired from U.S. Navy F-18 and A-7 aircraft, since these navy systems lack the F-4G's sensors.

On the basis of the above information, my suspicion is that the improvements in the missile, and the platform that delivers it, brought overall performance to an acceptable standard. Even so, it seems unlikely that this standard equalled the nominal .5 pk often attributed to precision-guided weapons. Moreover, a good many of SEAD's suppression "shots" against the Pact air defenses are "dumb" bomb, or other types of non-ARM shots. Thus, it would be unwise to attribute very high probabilities of kill to the *average* attempted engagement. Hence, I decided to test a range of relatively low effectiveness values: .05, .1, and .15 for standard aircraft, .25 for stealth aircraft. The sample runs below show the substantial damage that can be done assuming even these low effectiveness values. Finally, it is worth mentioning that the new HARM costs about four times as much in constant dollars as the

[14] *Washington Post*, 1 April 1968, p. 17: "New US Rocket Is Successful against N. Vietnam Missile Sites."

[15] Altogether, the U.S. Air Force purchased about 13,000 Shrikes. Bill Gunston, *Modern Airborne Missiles* (London: Salamander, 1983), pp. 134–135. This figure reappears in many discussions of the weapon and is not controversial. Estimates of what remains in air force inventory are harder to find. I estimate that perhaps as many as 9000 missiles remained in the mid-1980s. My methodology is simple. The production rate for the air force *averaged* about 1000 missiles per year over the lifetime of the program. During Vietnam there were about four years of intense bombing of the North. I assume that in those years production was set to equal expected use, plus a cushion to build up stocks against the future. Thus, it seems unlikely that more than 4000 missiles were used. This would have left about 9000 for training and war reserve stocks.

[16] U.S. Department of Defense, *Improvements in U.S. Warfighting Capability, FY 1980–1984* (Washington, D.C., May 1984, mimeo), p. 57.

Shrike it replaced. If one believes that effectiveness increases at least somewhat with investment (not always true) and one believes that Shrike puts NATO only in the .05 pk range, then HARM deployments, combined with the F-4G, should move the West in the direction of .15 pk and the high level of overall effectiveness illustrated by model runs with this value.

Readiness. The share of aircraft on hand and ready to fly is also an area of uncertainty. Joshua Epstein has developed an elaborate model of Soviet maintenance practices in an effort to estimate the impact on aircraft availability of the high tempos and maintenance deferrals associated with very intense combat. Epstein persuasively argues that the deferral of essential maintenance can quickly cause major, possibly irreparable, equipment failures.[17] I allude to this study to provide some support for the assumption that at any given time an important share of aircraft on hand will be unavailable for combat because of a requirement either for major maintenance or battle-damage repair. Gen. Charles Donnelly, then commander in chief of U.S. Air Forces Europe and commander of Allied Air Forces Central Europe, suggested that some 80 percent of his aircraft were "in commission" and that he could generate several sorties a day with each of them.[18] This number may have a history. General Momyer reports that this was the readiness rate of U.S. Air Force fighters flying out of Thailand in the 1965–68 period, although these aircraft apparently flew only a single sortie per day. Momyer notes that "this rate of operation was derived from planning factors based on fighter-bomber experience in World War II and Korea."[19] Since this 80 percent readiness figure tends to recur, and I have found no other estimates, I do not bother to vary it in these SEAD excursions. One might do so, however, if one were inclined to be pessimistic about the overall sortie rate that could be supported under conditions of airfield attack. It seems plausible that if airplanes were flying only a sortie per day due to *runway* damage, then they would suffer less wear and tear, and maintenance personnel would have more time to do their jobs. Thus, the readiness rate might actually rise. Similarly, although battle damage and intense operations would put considerable wear and tear on the aircraft, high losses would free maintenance personnel to work on the survivors. Again, the readiness of the survivors might actually go up.

[17]Epstein, *Measuring Military Power.*
[18]Interview, *Armed Forces Journal International,* June 1985, p. 98.
[19]Momyer, *Air Power in Three Wars,* p. 220.

Threat Radars. Estimating the number of major threat radars in East Germany, Poland, and Czechoslovakia under mobilization conditions demands a good bit of detective work. Most official open-source estimates are vague. Three groups of radars were identified.

First, there are some fixed or semimobile radars performing general early warning functions and GCI functions. GCI radars control Pact air defense aircraft in their efforts to intercept enemy penetrators. The Soviet Union and the Pact have long been said to depend far more heavily on this procedure than does the West. Historically, the West has permitted more latitude to the pilot and has put more technology in the aircraft to permit him to run the intercepts for himself. (This is not to say that the West does not also use GCI radars. Ground controllers simply have much less to do with the final engagement than they do in the East.) Estimates *are* available of the number of radars of all kinds defending the Soviet Union. Although these numbers are probably exaggerated, they do provide a place to start. *Soviet Military Power 1985* estimates 7000 radars in Soviet territory.[20] Using maps provided in that publication, I estimate that only about one-half of Soviet territory is well defended. Thus, a density of Soviet radars can be developed by dividing 7000 by one-half the land area of the Soviet Union. This factor can be multiplied by the land area of East Germany, Czechoslovakia, and Poland. The result is 343. This figure, however, includes both general early warning and GCI radars *and* those directly associated with surface-to-air missile units. To split the latter out from the former, I have estimated the strength of East European SAM units (see below) and subtracted their associated radars, yielding a figure of 120.

Another group of radars that must be attacked are those associated with the "strategic" missile defenses of the three Warsaw Pact countries. *Military Balance 1984–85* figures for Sa-2 and Sa-3 holdings in the three countries are the basis for these estimates. It is necessary to make a few simplifying assumptions, but when IISS totals are allocated to notional batteries and radars are allocated to those batteries according to open-source estimates of how Soviet batteries of different kinds are organized, a figure can be developed.[21] Proceeding in this fashion, I estimate

[20]U.S. Department of Defense, *Soviet Military Power, 1985* p. 45; Jones, "Air Defense Forces," pp. 132–195.

[21]This kind of information must be pieced together from a variety of sources. Occasionally, one must simply infer the relationships. The various weapon entries in *Jane's Weapons Systems* are a good place to start. Michael Crutcher, *Soviet Tactical Air Defense* (Washington, D.C.: Defense Intelligence Agency, 1980) (unclassified) offers a great many useful details. The discussions of Soviet air defense found in the various editions of *Soviet Armed Forces Review Annual*, ed. David Jones, are also very useful. There are also many "enthusiasts' "

that there were 70 acquisition radars and some 150 engagement radars associated with the Eastern European Sa-2 and Sa-3 force.

The final category of radars is the largest. These consist of the air-defense systems directly associated with the ground forces. Here, I have endeavored to capture those air-defense systems that would have guarded the notional "90 division" Warsaw Pact threat, a reinforced attack. For ease of accounting, these divisions are allotted to four-division armies, more or less the way that the Pact would actually deploy them. Two notional "army" air-defense systems were developed: that of the Soviet, fully modernized, all Category I division army equipped largely with SA-8s; and that of the Soviet or Eastern European, partially modernized (Category II and III division) army equipped largely with Sa-6s.[22] The first type includes Sa-4 and Sa-8 acquisition and missile engagement radars, and early warning radars, for a total of 104 radars per army; the second includes Sa-4 and Sa-6 radars for a total of 44 per army. Every army is assumed to have one Sa-4 brigade, but a dozen additional Sa-4 brigades are assumed to be scattered throughout Eastern Europe. (The Sa-11 and Sa-12a were beginning to replace Sa-4s in the mid-1980s, but since there is little information on how these missiles are organized, I employ the Sa-4 organization as a surrogate.) On the basis of open-source breakdowns of the numbers of Soviet and East European Category I, II, and III divisions, I assume eight armies of the first type and sixteen of the second with a total of roughly 1728 radars to be present. I omit ZSU-23 and other anti-aircraft artillery radars. Overall, the methodology outlined above yields a target set of 2200 radars. Of this total, perhaps 600 radars are search, acquisition, height-finding, or GCI units that can plausibly be assumed to be netted together to greater or lesser extent into an early warning system. The rest are fire control radars—with limited search capability—whose purpose is to control the actual surface-to-air missile engagement. I have omitted a very small number of radars that might be associated with the "front" and have made no special allowance for a small number of

---

books on Soviet weaponry, written by individuals of apparently substantial technical competence. Finally, the military professional and technical press has many essays.

[22]These estimates are consistent with standard, open-source estimates of available divisions of Category I, II, and III readiness, and their geographical distribution. Estimates of the total number of air-defense missiles and air-defense units were devised based on a variety of sources. Most helpful were IISS, *Military Balance, 1986–87*, p. 38; Richard Kaufman, "Causes of the Slowdown in Soviet Defense," *Soviet Economy* 1 (January–March 1985): 19, 21, 25; and John M. Collins, *American and Soviet Military Trends since the Cuban Missile Crisis* (Washington, D.C.: CSIS, 1978), p. 194. On the basis of these sources, as well as available information on the organization of Soviet SAM units (see n. 18), I estimate that there are 59 Sa-4 brigades, 45 Sa-6 Regiments, and 45 Sa-8 regiments.

Sa-5 units said to have been forward deployed in Germany. I believe this total to be favorable to the Pact.[23]

Basic Relationships

To facilitate the work of those who might like to set up this model on a spreadsheet for themselves, I briefly discuss here the basic relationships. I refer to the columns in the exemplary model output provided, by the alphabetic labels I have assigned them. Initial force strengths and effectiveness values are listed at the top of the output, and I refer to them by descriptive labels I have assigned them. The model is extremely simple. A person unacquainted with spreadsheet programs should be able to learn enough about a given program and develop sufficient understanding of the model to have it up and running with a day's work. Below I display the state of the campaign at every seventh sortie. The appearance of several decimal places ought not to be taken to indicate precision, but rather "slow change."

The number of aircraft that manage to launch weapons (D) on a given sortie (A) is given by the number of aircraft remaining in inventory (B), multiplied by a readiness rate ("readiness") multiplied by the average share that survive Pact air defenses (that is, the attrition rate "Attrition" subtracted from one). On the following sortie, the number of aircraft

[23]It is difficult to tell how many air-defense missile units might have remained in Soviet units in other theaters. If there were any left, they could have been brought into the theater to replace assets lost to NATO's attacks, but my accounting system generates a total that is so high that few mobile Soviet radars would have been left. U.S. Department of Defense, *Soviet Military Power, 1987*, p. 48, offers an estimate of 4800 Soviet mobile surface-to-air missile-launcher vehicles. By my calculations the total of 2200 radars advanced in the text includes 70 percent of all Soviet Sa-8 and Sa-6 radars, 50 percent of all Sa-4 radars, and 65 percent of all mobile radars then associated with the surface-to-air missiles of the Soviet Army. This is roughly consistent with the peacetime allocation of all Soviet missile and gun air-defense assets suggested by *Soviet Military Power, 1985*, p. 69. It estimated that roughly 47 percent of major Soviet air-defense systems were allocated against *all* of European NATO, with another 17 percent retained in the strategic reserve, for a total of 64 percent available in the West. Thus the DOD publication provides some support for my assessment. I have assumed in my calculation that the strategic reserve is committed to the Central Region battle, and that virtually all Soviet mobile air-defense assets in the West are committed in the same area. Thus, for the sake of analytic conservatism, Soviet forces opposite Northern and Southern Europe are in effect already stripped of air defense assets. If this force suffered the kind of attrition illustrated by my SEAD runs, then the Soviets would face the choice of bringing in radars and SAMs from other theaters of operation such as the Far East or Central Asia, probably not a simple expedient, and depending on the level of combat in those theaters, perhaps not a safe one. Alternatively, they could move forward radars and missiles associated with homeland air defense. This would also be a tough choice.

remaining in inventory is the number of successful penetrators from the previous sortie, plus the aircraft in inventory that did not fly that sortie because they were unready.

The number of radars expected to be killed on a given sortie is given by the number of successful penetrators (D) multiplied by the number of weapons carried ("munitions"), multiplied by the individual kill probability (pk) of the weapons. It is assumed that all weapons carried are employed. This is not unreasonable given the high density of Soviet air defenses usually posited for Eastern Europe and the low kill probabilities assumed for NATO's antiradar weapons. It is further assumed that radars are not "overkilled." Weapons are on the average not wasted on radars that cease to be a threat. This is a simplification. In general, I would expect the average engaged emitting radar to be subjected to one antiradiation missile (ARM) shot, and one non-ARM shot (dumb bombs or other precision guided munitions) for a total of two shots. If the radar ceases to emit, no further weapons would be fired against the target. If it continues to emit, it would be engaged again, probably by two shots. If it has temporarily ceased to emit for tactical reasons, it will be engaged again once it resumes, even if by a later sortie. As noted in the text, real sorties by F-111s and Tornados against fixed radars would probably involve a single attack by a pair of aircraft, each of which would drop an entire load of "dumb" ordnance on the target in a single pass. For ease of calculation, however, I simply lump these sorties into the overall effort. These simplifications do not, in my judgment, undermine the purpose of the exercise—which is to get a rough idea of how NATO's SEAD effort could proceed. Indeed, I suspect that these and other simplifications I have introduced drive the analysis in a conservative direction from NATO's perspective.

Attrition on any given sortie is somewhat complicated. I introduce this complexity to capture the basic proposition that the effectiveness of the adversary's air-defense system should drop as its radars are destroyed. I do not know the precise pattern of this effectiveness degradation. The relationship I propose here is a conservative *surrogate* for a very complex process. I posit two attrition rates going into the analysis. The first is the overall attrition rate initially suffered by NATO attackers ("Attrition"). I vary this rate in the sensitivity analysis. The other is a much lower rate that represents the attrition NATO would suffer even if all radars were successfully destroyed—call it a "basic loss rate" ("basiclr")—that is, attrition exacted by anti-aircraft artillery, heat-seeking missiles, Pact air-defense fighters flying defensive sweeps without ground control, NATO pilot error, and the like. I set this at 1 per cent and do not vary it in sensitivity analyses. This is a rather conservative floor by historical experience. The attrition NATO suffers on any given sortie is given by the difference between the initial attrition rate and the "floor attrition rate" multiplied by the surviving share of the Pact's initial radar inventory, plus the "floor attrition rate." For any given sortie, this is calculated at the end of the previous sortie (J). For example, with an initial attrition rate of 5 percent, once 25 percent of the Pact's radars were destroyed, NATO attackers would suffer 4 percent attrition on that sortie—3 percent arising from radar-directed air defenses, 1 percent arising from flak, fighter sweeps, and the like.

In cases where NATO's attacks are very effective, after many sorties are flown the expected number of radars destroyed exceeds the radars present in theater. This occurs because I simply permit the model to run even when all Pact radars are gone, illustrating the "surplus" capability present under the chosen assumptions. This indicates how many additional radars the adversary could bring into the theater from elsewhere to replace his losses and yet not succeed in maintaining the integrity of the air-defense system.

To capture the potential impact of the stealth fighter, if it is employed as an air-defense-suppression aircraft, I simply run two sets of sorties simultaneously, one with conventional aircraft at given effectiveness and attrition rates, and the second with stealth aircraft at higher effectiveness and lower attrition rates. The successes of each aircraft type are summed to give the total kills for the combined force for the given sortie.

Brief Discussion of Columns

A. "Sorties" is simply a sortie counter.

B. "Aircraft" is the number of aircraft in the attacker's inventory before the sortie is launched.

C. "Ready" is the product of remaining aircraft and the readiness rate, in this case 80 percent.

D. "Penetrate" gives the number of ready aircraft that survive Pact air defenses to deliver ordnance. It is "Ready" × (1 − "New Attrition"). See column J below.

E. "Cum.S" simply tracks the cumulative successful aircraft penetrations that have occurred as of the given sortie. Two other columns like this (F, H) are displayed for informational purposes. Access to these totals permits judgment as to whether the radar destruction achieved as of the given sortie seems plausible to the analyst.

F. "Cum.shot" tracks the number of shots fired as of a given sortie.

G. "K/sortie" is radar kills for the sortie; it is the product of column D, shots, and the constant effectiveness pk.

H. "Cum.k" tracks the total radar kills as of the sortie.

I. "%Threat/k" is the share of the total radar threat destroyed as of the completion of the sortie. It is given by H/"Radars."

J. "NewAttr." is the attrition that the next sortie will suffer. It is given by (100% − I) × ("attrition" − "basiclr") + ("basiclr").

Table A1.1. Sample SEAD output

A Sorties	B Aircraft	C Ready	D Penetrate	E Cum.S	F Cum.shot	G k/sortie	H Cum.k	I %Threat/k	J NewAttr.
1	180	144	137	137	547	27	27	1%	5%
7	142	113	108	853	3,411	22	171	8%	5%
14	109	87	83	1,505	6,021	17	301	14%	4%
21	85	68	65	2,011	8,046	13	402	18%	4%
28	67	53	51	2,408	9,633	10	482	22%	4%
35	53	42	41	2,722	10,888	8	544	25%	4%
42	42	34	32	2,972	11,887	6	594	27%	4%
49	34	27	26	3,172	12,687	5	634	29%	4%
56	27	22	21	3,332	13,329	4	666	30%	4%

Input values: Aircraft = 180; attrition = 5%; readiness = 0.8; basiclr = 1%; shots = 4; pk = 0.05; radars = 2,200.

APPENDIX 2

Central Region Close Air Support Aircraft and Attack Helicopters (1988)

This appendix briefly discusses the method by which I have estimated NATO and Pact close air support (CAS) assets. The tables that follow list aircraft and attack helicopters. Most of the sources are circa 1988 and thus represent a 1987–88 force structure.

The German Alpha-Jet is not ideally suited for CAS but that seems the most plausible way to use the aircraft. RAF Harriers seem a likely candidate for CAS missions. I have allocated roughly 380 of the 500 A-10s then in U.S. active and reserve units to early reinforcement of NATO. I assume that one squadron would have remained in Korea, the Alaska squadron would have gone to Norway, and three reserve squadrons would have been withheld against the possibility of another contingency. Perhaps another 140 aircraft were available in storage or the maintenance pipeline, which could have been tapped as replacements for attrition suffered by combat squadrons. The U.S. Air National

Table A2.1. NATO CAS aircraft—initial reinforcements

Country	Aircraft	Number	Remarks
FRG	Alpha-Jet	153	
U.K.	Harrier	36	
U.S.	A-10	144	U.K., 6 sqdrns
	A-10	234	U.S.-based, 13 sqdrns, active & reserve
	A-7	90	U.S.-based, 5 sqdrns, reserve, 30-mm gun pod
TOTAL		657	

Source: IISS, *Military Balance, 1988–1989* (London, 1989), country entries, and author's estimates.

Table A2.2. NATO attack helicopters

Country	Number	Type	Formation	Source
Peacetime				
FRG	210	PAH-1	7 sqdrns	IISS/FRG
France	24	Gazelle	1 (?)	IISS
U.S.	54	AH-64	3 batt.	DOD
	168	AH-1S	8 batt.	
	84	Misc.	CAV	
TOTAL	540			
Rapid reinforcements				
U.S.	210	Misc.	10 batt.	est.
	74	Misc.	CAV	est.
France	124	Gazelle		IISS
U.K.	25	Lynx		UKMOD
TOTAL	433			
Initial total	973			
Long-term reinforcements				
U.S.	415			

Sources: IISS—*Military Balance, 1988–1989* (London, 1989); FRG—Federal Republic of Germany, Federal Minister of Defense, *White Paper 1985: The Situation and the Development of the Federal Armed Forces* (Bonn, 19 June 1985), p. 197; UKMOD—United Kingdom, Ministry of Defence, *Statement on the Defense Estimates 1988*, vol. 1 (London: HMSO, 1988), p. 48.

Guard had thirteen combat squadrons of A-7s. I assume that three would have been withheld for other contingencies and ten would ultimately have deployed to Europe. Roughly 260 30-mm gun pods were purchased to outfit A-7s and F-4s for close support missions. I allocate one-half of the A-7s, 90 aircraft, (five squadrons) with two gun pods each to early reinforcement of Europe. The then current strength of U.S. A-10 and A-7 active and reserve units can be read from graphs provided in U.S. Department of Defense, *Annual Report* FY 1990, p. 155, Chart III.C.1. The IISS provides estimates of the number of squadrons. U.S. fighter squadrons vary in size between 18 and 24 aircraft. I have assumed that forward-deployed squadrons in Korea, Alaska, and Europe had 24 aircraft each, and all the rest had 18. I count the 140 A-10s in storage, and one-half of the ANG A-7 squadrons as "reserves," for a total of 230 aircraft available for reinforcement.

U.S. Department of Defense, *Soviet Military Power, 1988*, gives NATO 600 attack helicopters then deployed in Western Europe.[1] Seven hundred reinforcing attack helicopters would have ultimately been available. Although the counting rules are opaque, it appears that all 700 of

[1]P. 114.

the reinforcements were U.S. Although 180 French and Spanish attack helicopters are excluded, nearly all other European attack helicopters are probably included in the "In-Place and Rapidly Deployable" category. Figures from the country entries in the IISS *Military Balance, 1988–1989* yield a total for NATO Europe of about 300 attack helicopters—210 German, 25 British, and 66 Italian. Subtracting this from the *Soviet Military Power* total suggests that about 300 U.S. attack helicopters were forward deployed in Germany. This tracks roughly with other sources, as well as deductions one would make from the basic U.S. force structure.[2] In the rapid-reinforcement category I have included all British and French attack helicopters (perhaps a bit optimistic) and those U.S. attack helicopter units that would plausibly have been associated with U.S. units that had prepositioned sets of ground equipment—six divisions and one armored cavalry regiment. The United States did not, to my knowledge, preposition attack helicopters, so these are unlikely to have been included in the *Soviet Military Power* estimate of initially available forces. But they ought to be assumed to arrive rather quickly. In total, roughly 1000 U.S. attack helicopters in units were likely to have been deployed to Europe in a full mobilization. This would have left roughly 150 other attack helicopters in units elsewhere, and perhaps 200 attack helicopters in the training base and maintenance pipeline. I

[2]IISS, *Military Balance, 1984–85*, p. 237. Formerly, attack helicopter battalions were intended to have 42 attack helicopters, divided into two companies of 21, although some battalions had only one company. As of 1986 the Pentagon planned to have some 32 active and reserve companies of AH-1S Cobras distributed among 19 battalions. See U.S. Department of Defense, *Improvements in US Warfighting Capability, FY 1980–1984* (mimeo, May 1984), p. 47. Additional Cobras would have been assigned to divisional and corps cavalry units. The U.S. Department of Defense, *Annual Report*, FY 1990, p. 133, indicates a change in organization. Attack helicopter battalions fielding the new AH-64 were planned to have 18 aircraft, while battalions retaining the Cobra would have 21, the strength of the former company. It reports that 15 of the new AH-64 battalions were then fielded, and that three were stationed in Western Europe. As of 1988, between 100 and 200 AH-64s were deployed by the U.S. Army in a total of five battalions, presumably of the old table of organization. Organization of the Joint Chiefs of Staff, *Military Posture FY 1988*, p. 53. I have assumed that some of these were already in Europe. The divisional cavalry units of each heavy division were also theoretically assigned 8 helicopters each. Each of the three corps-level armored cavalry regiments should have fielded about 26 attack helicopters. This gives a fielded U.S. 1988 total of about 1100 machines—880 Cobras and 210 AH-64s. The U.S. Department of Defense, *Annual Report*, FY 1988, p. 155, suggests the United States owned 1087 Cobras, so this accounting leaves 200 in training units and the maintenance pipeline. Also useful in making these calculations is U.S. Army, *Armor Reference Data*, vols. 1, 2, 3, which has Tables of Organization and Equipment both for past attack helicopter units, and those then projected. In making my estimate of U.S. forward deployments in Europe, I have included AH-64s equivalent to three battalions of the new structure and assumed that they were associated with one heavy division, 26 Cobras each for the two armored cavalry regiments, one battalion of 21 Cobras each for the two independent brigades, and two battalions for each of three heavy divisions. I have also assumed 8 attack helicopters for each divisional cavalry unit.

Table A2.3. Warsaw Pact fixed-wing CAS aircraft

Country	Type	Number
Soviet Union	SU-25 Frogfoot	270
Czechoslovakia	SU-25 Frogfoot	40
GDR	SU-22	35
Poland	SU-22	75
TOTAL		420

Source: IISS, *Military Balance, 1988–1989* (London, 1989), country entries.

count these attack helicopters, plus the last 400 U.S. reinforcing attack helicopters in the "reserve" category.

There is no source that explicitly estimates the Soviet allocation of aircraft to CAS missions. Although the SU-25 most closely resembles a purpose-built CAS aircraft and is often identified as such, it is less clearly specialized for tank killing close to front than the U.S. A-10. Any other Soviet aircraft with ground-attack capabilities, like any NATO aircraft with ground-attack capabilities, could have been allocated to CAS missions, but there were many other attack missions for these aircraft. Thus, I have tried to bound the problem by assigning all known SU-25s in the Soviet inventory, as well as those in the Czech inventory, to early CAS missions in the Central Region. I have assumed that Czechoslovakia and Poland had some need for CAS missions and have arbitrarily assigned some of their most austere attack aircraft (SU-22) to this mission. This is about one-half of GDR and Polish attack aircraft, a conservative allocation. The Soviet Union owned many older fighter aircraft that could have been allocated to CAS missions, but I have no way of estimating how many might ultimately have been committed, so I have declined to estimate Soviet "reserves" in this category.

U.S. Department of Defense, *Soviet Military Power, 1988,* gives the Warsaw Pact a total of 1250 attack helicopters west of the Urals. Of these, 1000 were deemed to be in place or rapidly deployable, and another 250 were expected to be available at full mobilization, whenever that was achieved.[3] I have worked backward from this figure with the aid of more detailed estimates of formations and strengths offered by the IISS, *Military Balance, 1988–1989.* The IISS offers figures on East European attack helicopter holdings, as well as the holdings of forward-deployed Soviet forces. By totaling the last two categories and subtracting from 1000, I get my estimated total of ready attack helicopters in the Western Military District—115. This number just happens to nearly equal what one would find in two Soviet attack helicopter regi-

[3] P. 114.

Table A2.4. Warsaw Pack attack helicopters (estimated breakdown—initial strength, potential reinforcements)

Category	Number	Type	Formation	Source
E. Europe	140	Mi-24	4 regt.	IISS
	35	Mi-8		
Soviet Union (forward)	370	Mi-24	7 regt.	IISS, SMP 1987
	140	Mi-8		
Soviet Union (w. district)	80	Mi-24	2 regt.	Author, SMP 1988
	40	Mi-8		
INITIAL + RAPID REINFORCE	805			
Other w. Soviet Union	160	Mi-24	4 regt.	Author, SMP 1988
	80	Mi-8		
TOTAL	1045		13 regt. (SU), 4 regt. (E. Eur.)	

Sources: IISS—*Military Balance, 1988–1989* (London, 1989); SMP—*Soviet Military Power.*

ments.[4] Judging from the counting rules explained in *Soviet Military Power, 1988*, all 250 reinforcing helicopters available after full mobilization must also have been Soviet. The figure 250 is quite close to the total one would expect to find in four Soviet attack helicopter regiments, so I deduce that they were in such formations. Presumably, *Soviet Military Power* estimates that these arrive late in a mobilization either because they were reserve units or because they were from more distant military districts. Thus, I estimate that fifteen of the twenty regiments credited to the Soviet Union were probably in the west, and that thirteen of these would have been thrown into the Western Theater of Operations (TVD). (It is not unreasonable to allocate one regiment each to the Arctic TVD, opposite Scandinavia, and one to the Southwestern TVD, opposite Turkey.) There were probably some other Soviet attack helicopters that I have omitted—but I have conservatively assigned to the Central Region 1045 of the 1250 total estimated by *Soviet Military Power, 1988* to have been present west of the Urals.

[4]U.S. Department of Defense, *Soviet Military Power, 1987*, gives the following information on Soviet attack helicopters. The Soviets were estimated to have "20 attack regiments," "with up to 60 HIP and HIND attack helicopters in each." "More than half are deployed opposite NATO forces." It also notes that some attack helicopters can be found in Soviet Army divisions but it does not say how many, and the *Soviet Military Power, 1988* estimate of total attack helicopter strength in the western Soviet Union and Eastern Europe suggests that there could not have been many Soviet divisions with attack helicopters of their own. An unclassified DIA manual from the early 1980s suggests that Soviet attack helicopter regiments had 40–50 Mi-24 and 20–25 Mi-8, 60–75 machines. Defense Intelligence Agency, *Soviet Front Fire Support* (Washington, D.C., 1982), p. 121.

APPENDIX 3

The Attrition-FEBA Expansion Model: Symphony Version

The purpose of this appendix is to provide the reader with sufficient information to enable him or her to program the model on a spreadsheet package. I employ Symphony, and users of that package will recognize the output displayed below. The conceptual underpinnings of the model are described in Chapter 3.

The model employs the input variables listed below. The abbreviations employed on the spreadsheet are given first. The cell occupied by the value of the variable in this version of the spreadsheet is given second. When cell addresses are preceded by $ signs, it signifies the specific value in the specific cell, not the cell location relative to another cell. This is an important Symphony convention.

initial front length. The length of the line that NATO must defend. A straight-line measurement of the former inter-German and Czech-German border yields 750 km, a figure commonly used among analysts. (B9, represented in the printout as $B$9)

breakthrough width. This is the width of each attempted breakthrough effort. I use 50 km, for reasons explained in the text (B10, $B$10)

breakthru#. The number of Pact breakthrough efforts. (B8, $B$11)

offense ade sector. This is the width of front occupied by a Pact ADE at the front of a breakthrough effort. The higher the number, the fewer the ADEs in the breakthrough. (B12, $B$12)

offense non-breakthru. This is the width of front occupied by a Pact ADE either defending the flanks of a Pact breakthrough effort or engaging in offensive or defensive operations in areas of the frontier not slated for breakthrough efforts. (B13, $B$13)

defense ade sector. This is the width of front occupied by a NATO ADE. This is the same defending against major Pact efforts, covering the flanks of such penetrations, or occupying the remainder of the border. This parameter introduces a strong degree of conservatism into the model, in my judgment, since it requires NATO to defend everywhere at a relatively high density, sufficient to cope with the initial stages of a major attack. If one wished, one could introduce separate variables for required NATO densities on breakthrough sectors and nonbreakthrough sectors. One could then employ the density requirement on nonbreakthrough sectors as an indicator of one's best guess about the ability of NATO intelligence to make relatively high-confidence judgments as to where new breakthrough efforts might suddenly materialize. (B14, $B$14)

Pactattrition. This is the rate of attrition taken each day by the divisions at the front of each Pact breakthrough effort. (D9, $D$9)

Pact advance rate. The daily rate at which every breakthrough effort (piston) moves in NATO's direction. The piston moves only when the Pact fights intensively, and the Pact fights intensively only when it has a surplus of force available at the FEBA over and above what it needs to populate the front and flanks of its pistons, and the remainder of the front. The Pact is permitted to fight even if this surplus is very small. (D10, $D$10)

Nato c3,log.multiplier. This is the factor by which NATO's basic ADE score should be multiplied to fairly represent the combat capability it presumably expects from its relatively greater propensity to invest in command and logistics. (D12, $D$12)

Pact D at M+ This is the day after mobilization that the Pact is permitted to initiate combat, assuming that it also has sufficient forces to meet its requirements for covering the front. When this number is set at 0, the Pact can initiate combat as soon as it meets these requirements. If set at 14, it means that the Pact can initiate combat at M+14. In the NATO-favorable case, I permit combat to begin at M+30; in the Pact-favorable case, M+14.

Pact ac. The number of Pact CAS helicopters and aircraft. The Pact gets a fixed number at the outset, and no reinforcements are counted. It would not be complicated to develop a "mobilization curve" for these assets, but I simply use a single figure representing each side's initial force with early reinforcement. (F9, $F$9)

Pact attr. The attrition suffered on each sortie of the Pact CAS force. (F10, $F$10)

Pact k. Pact kills per sortie. (F11, $F$11)

Pactsr. The number of sorties, on the average, each Pact aircraft flies per day. Pact and NATO CAS assets are permitted to fly only on the days that the Pact engages in intensive combat. (F12, $F$12)

Nato ac. NATO CAS aircraft and attack helicopters. (H9, $H$9)

Nato attr. The attrition suffered on each NATO CAS sortie. (H10, $H$10)

Nato k. The average number of kills per sortie. (H12, $H$11)

Nato sr. NATO's sortie rate per aircraft per day. (H12, $H$12)

breakthruforceratioifdensitiesachieved. This is simply a convenience. It calculates the capabilities ratio in the breakthrough sectors, assuming that NATO meets its FEBA density requirement. The ratio is the same in real or adjusted ADEs, depending on whether the analyst believes that one or the other is the best criteria for assessing the adequacy of NATO's forces. It is displayed for one purpose, to permit some judgment by the analyst as to the plausibility of the input values chosen for any particular excursion. For many analysts, force ratio is considered to be a handy back-of-the-envelope way of judging prospects for successful attack or defense. To many analysts, breakthrough force ratios less than 3:1 suggest low prospects for offensive success. Thus a 5 km movement rate and a 1.25:1 exchange rate at "high" defensive force densities would seem favorable to the Pact and thus a quite demanding test of NATO's force structure. See chapter 3. ($B$14/$B$12)

worstcaseaderatioifdensityachievedinadjades. This calculates the force ratio in real ADEs if NATO populates the front with adjusted ADEs. For example, in the excursion displayed NATO's ADE multiplier is 1.25.

Thus, if one adjusted ADE is placed every 25 km, this means that 0.8 of a real ADE is every 25 km. The ratio here is calculated against that factor. ($B$14 × $D$12/$B$12)

The output displayed contains thirty-three columns. Each one of them is not essential to generate the main products of the model, which are the "supply" and "demand" curves illustrated in the graphs in the text. Many of them, however, are useful to sustain a complete picture of the course of combat and to permit one to form judgments as to whether the values selected for specific variables, and the processes and relationships represented by specific equations, produce results that seem reasonable in common-sense terms. They help one get the feel of the model.

I run the model for 120 days, starting with Pact mobilization. A day of combat is represented by one line in the spreadsheet. For brevity, the attached output displays only every seventh day of combat, for ninety-one days.

Below I discuss each column of the displayed output. I provide the equations governing each column using abbreviated words to represent all variables. Most of the equations are quite simple and require little explanation. Others are more complex. Symphony printout in Symphony symbology that provides the equations governing each column is provided below. The symbols refer to cell addresses. Columns are represented by letters, rows by numbers. Many of the equations employ the input values outlined above. The columns often refer to each other as well. Throughout, rather than employing the conventional arithmetical notation of T for the value of a particular variable at a given time, and $T-1$ as the value at a preceding unit of time, I employ the words "today" and "yesterday." Finally, because the first row of the column is day 0 of Pact mobilization, several columns have zero as their initial value at $M+0$. The stated equations kick in at $M+1$. These will be noted.

Pact Mob+, column A. This is simply a day counter, marking each consecutive day after the Pact decision to mobilize.

Pact ADEs, column B. This is the Pact mobilization schedule. This schedule is not generated by any simple assumptions that can be captured in a single equation. I have estimated the Pact buildup schedule and load it as data into this column.[1]

[1]This is the same Pact mobilization schedule I developed in "Is Nato Decisively Outnumbered?" *International Security* 12 (Spring 1988): 186–202, graph 2.

NATO ADEs, column C. This is the NATO mobilization schedule. In the output displayed, NATO's force does not grow during the first seven days after Pact mobilization, which represents a lag for analysis of intelligence and political decision. The schedule is also loaded as data into the column. Mobilization schedules with shorter or longer delays could be loaded.[2]

Pactcoverforce, column D. This is the calculation of what the Pact needs to populate the sectors of the front where breakthrough efforts are not mounted. It is given by: initial front length − (breakthrough width × breakthru#)/offense non-breakthru.

Pactassaultforce, column E. Calculates what the Pact needs at the front of its breakthrough efforts. (breakthrough width × breakthru#)/Offense ADE sector.

dailyflank, column F. Calculates the additional forces the Pact needs to populate the flanks of the pistons if they drive forward that day. The pistons move forward only if the Pact has more forces than it needed the preceding day. But this surplus can be tiny and still drive the piston forward. This is a very important aspect of the model. Readers are encouraged to examine the sensitivity analysis included below to see some of the implications of this assumption. In many cases, the introduction of input values that intuitively seem unfavorable to NATO produce favorable results. The reason is that the Pact, under the mobilization assumptions included in this excursion, often lacks the forces to participate in sustained, high-intensity combat. I do not consider this to be artificial but, rather, central to an assessment of *the relative competitiveness of the two sides.* In the excursion displayed combat is permitted to begin thirty days after Pact mobilization, if the Pact has the necessary forces (and it does). The model contains a parameter that permits the user to specify the earliest day that combat can begin, if the Pact has the necessary forces. In many of the sensitivity analyses I have run, the Pact lacks sufficient forces to sustain high-intensity combat after a few days of mobilization, even if it has just enough to get started. This is represented by a symphony IF/THEN function. If today's PactADEs > yesterday's Pactforceneeds (see column O below), and if PactMob+ > = PactDatM+, then (breakthru# × Pact advance rate × 2)/offense non-breakthru, otherwise 0. (Each piston has two flanks.) At M+0 the value is 0.

[2]Ibid.

Pactflankforce, column G. This displays the cumulative Pact force committed to flank defense. It is given by its own value for the preceding day + today's dailyflank (column F). At M+0 the value is 0.

nrmldailyloss, column H. This gives the forces the Pact would normally be expected to lose in the breakthrough sectors that day, assuming that combat occurred. If today's PactADEs > yesterday's Pactforceneeds, and if PactMob+ >= PactDatM+, then Pactassaultforce × Pactattrition, otherwise 0. At M+0 the value is 0.

combatdaycount, column I. This keeps track of the number of days of intense combat that occur under the specified values of the input variables. If today's PactADEs > yesterday's Pactforceneeds, and if PactMob+ >= PactDatM+, then yesterday's combat day count + 1, otherwise yesterday's count + 0. At M+0 the value is 0.

bluCASkilled, column J. This gives the ADE score of the number of Pact combat vehicles killed by NATO's CAS sorties that day. NATO CAS is credited with kills only during the days that the Pact engages in intense ground action; otherwise, no sorties are flown. The same assumption applies to Pact CAS sorties. If today's PactADEs > yesterday's Pactforceneeds, and if PactMob+ >= PactDatM+, yesterday's bluCASac × Natok × $[\{1-(1-\text{Natoattr})^{\text{Natosr}+1}/\text{Natoattr}\} - 1] \times 1/1200$.[3] I assume that the destruction of 1200 armored vehicles close to the FEBA will approximately equal 1 ADE, which accounts for the last factor.

bluCASac, column K. This gives the number of NATO CAS aircraft surviving in theater after the day's sorties are flown. They become the input for the next day's calculation of CAS kills (see previous paragraph). If today's PactADEs > yesterday's Pactforceneeds, and if PactMob+ >= PactDatM+, then yesterday's blucasac × $(1-\text{Natoattr})^{\text{Natosr}}$, otherwise yesterday's blucasac. Again, NATO flies no sorties unless there is ground combat, and if NATO flies no sorties, it loses no aircraft.

CumCASkill, column L. This keeps track of the total kills that accrue to the NATO CAS effort. This gives the user of the model a chance to check the plausibility of his or her assumptions about CAS effectiveness against the total damage that the model credits to the CAS effort. This is given by the previous day's CUMCASkill + today's bluCASkilled.

[3] I did not devise this equation. It is taken from Epstein, *Strategy and Force Planning*, p. 121.

groundcbt, column M. This gives the share of the Pact ground force losses that arise from actual ground combat, rather than from NATO CAS kills. During the first couple of days of combat in most excursions I have run, this number ends up close to zero. Even at the relatively low effectiveness parameters I have specified for CAS performance, NATO CAS often kills Pact forces somewhat faster than the specified Pact attrition rate. This peculiarity quickly evaporates as NATO suffers attrition to its CAS assets. If nrmldailyloss > bluCASkilled, then nrmlsdailyloss − bluCASkilled gives the extent of ground-combat-induced attrition; otherwise 0 is displayed here.

Pactattrition, column N. This gives total Pact attrition as of today. This is given by yesterday's attrition plus one of two factors. If today's bluCASkills > today's nrmldailyloss, then add bluCASkills to yesterday's Pactattrition; otherwise, add nrmldailyloss to yesterday's attrition. In general, nrmldailyloss governs the attrition the Pact takes on any given day. But when large numbers of CAS sorties are flown, even at a half a kill per sortie and 5 percent attrition, more kills will be generated than nrmldailyloss. I was faced with two choices in how to deal with this problem. I could ignore all CAS kills over and above the nrmldailyloss factor, in effect throwing some capabilities away; or I could credit NATO with the kills associated with this capability, even though it means that for a few days the Pact ends up suffering a little more attrition than it "intends" to, and NATO ends up suffering no ground force casualties to Pact ground forces, although it does suffer from Pact CAS. At M+0 the value is 0.

Pactforceneeds, column O. This indicates the cumulative requirement for forces for the Pact on any given day. It is the sum of Pactcoverforce, Pactassaultforce, Pactflankforce, and Pactattrition for the given day.

Pactliveade, column P. This keeps track of the number of surviving forces the Pact has available for combat on any given day. It is given by PactADEs − Pactattrition. A subsequent column AB, keeps track of surviving NATO ADEs, permitting a record of a running theaterwide force ratio. This helps in the interpretation of the results of any given model run. For example, if the model shows a modest NATO shortfall at M+75, but the theater-wide ratio of surviving forces is close to 1:1, then one is disinclined to leap to the conclusion that NATO's front is in danger of snapping as a consequence of material inadequacy.

Pactamsur/def, column Q. This tracks the surplus or deficit of forces faced by the Pact on the morning of a given day of combat. It is given by that day's PactADEs − yesterday's Pactforceneeds.

NatoDefForce, column R. This is the quantity of forces that NATO would need to populate the front at the outset of combat at the densities specified in the input values. It is given by InitialFrontLength / defenseADE.

Ndailyflank, column S. This gives the NATO forces that must be committed to the flanks of the penetrating pistons. NATO is required to hold these flanks at the same density it is required to hold elsewhere along the front, and at the front of the pistons. If Pact ADEs today > yesterday's Pactforceneeds, and if PactMob+ >= PactDatM+, then breakthru# × Pactadvancerate × 2 / defenseadesector, otherwise 0. To remind the reader, the pistons do not move every day; if they do not move, there is no additional flank to defend. At M+0 the value is 0.

Natoflankforce, column T. This tracks the total NATO forces committed to flank defense on any given day. Yesterday's Natoflankforce + today's Ndailyflank. At M+0 the value is 0.

dailylossgrnd, column U. NATO's losses to ground combat for the day. If Pact ADEs today > yesterday's Pactforceneeds, and if PactMob+ >= PactDatM+, then Pgroundcbt / Pact:Natoexchangerate, otherwise 0. In English, if there is combat today, and if NATO's CAS did not do all the necessary killing, then NATO's ground forces must exact the Pact's ground combat losses at the designated Pact:NATO exchange rate. If there is no combat today, then NATO's ground forces lose nothing. At M+0 the value is 0.

dailylossredair, column V. This calculates NATO's losses to Red CAS. These losses occur only on days that intense combat occurs. These losses are always added to whatever losses NATO sustained in ground combat, if any. If Pact ADEs today > yesterday's Pactforceneeds, and if PactMob+ > = PactDatM+, then Yesterday's RedCASac × Pactk × $[\{1 - (1 - \text{Pactattr})^{\text{Pactsr}+1}/\text{Pactattr}\} - 1] \times 1/1200$, otherwise 0.[4]

RedCASac, column W. This tracks surviving Red CAS helicopters and aircraft. If Pact ADEs today (column B) > yesterday's Pactforceneeds

[4]Ibid.

(column o), and if PactMob+ >= PactDatM+, yesterday's RedCASac × (1 − Pactattr)^{Pactsr}, otherwise yesterday's redCASac.

CumRCASkill, column X. Accumulated Pact CAS kills in ADEs. Yesterday's CumRCASkill + today's dailylossredair. At M+o the value is o.

totaldailyloss, column Y. This is NATO's total losses to ground and air action for the day, assuming intense combat occurred. dailylossgrnd + dailylossredair.

Natoattrition, column Z. This is simply the total attrition NATO has suffered as of a given day. It is yesterday's Natoattrition + totaldailyloss. At M+o the value is o.

Natoforceneeds, column AA. This gives the total forces that NATO needs in theater as of a given day. This includes the forces needed to populate a 750-km front, plus the forces needed to populate the flanks of the penetrating pistons, plus cumulative attrition from all sources. Thus NatoDefForce + Natoflankforce + Natoattrition.

Natoliveades, column AB. This tracks the total *real* NATO ADEs available in theater as of a given day after attrition, assuming that NATO deserves no credit for superior relative investments in command and logistics. The purpose of displaying this column is to have immediate access to a somewhat more pessimistic picture of NATO's situation. Nato ADEs − Natoattrition.

Natodivisionfront, column AC. This tracks the average sector that would be defended as of a given day by a real NATO ADE, again assuming no bonus for command-and-logistics efforts. This also serves the purpose of providing immediate access to a somewhat more pessimistic picture of NATO's situation. The total frontage NATO needs to defend is divided by its surviving ADEs in theater. The former includes the initial 750 km plus the flanks of the penetrating pistons. [Initial Front Length + (Pactflankforce × nonbreakthru)] / NATO live ADEs.

adjarrivs, column AD. This applies the NATO command and logistics multiplier to the NATO mobilization schedule from column C. Nato ADEs × Nato c3, log. multiplier.

natoadjdivfrnt, column AE. This tracks the frontage defended by each adjusted ADE in theater—that is, it assumes that the command-and-logistics multiplier specified in the input values is a fair estimate of the real combat power NATO derives from its disproportionate investments in this area. [Initial Front Length + (Pactflankforce × nonbreakthru)] / [NATO live ADEs × NATO c3, log. multiplier].

adj am sur/def, column AF. This tracks NATO's surplus or deficit of cumulative force arrivals in theater (adjusted for command and logistics), to cope with the cumulative demands of combat as of a given day. This is the most obvious Measure of Effectiveness for the model, and much of the sensitivity analysis displayed tests various input values against this variable at Pact M+75. Adjusted arrivals − Natoforceneeds.

real am surdef, column AG. This does the same as the preceding but on the assumption NATO warrants no special credit for command-and-logistics efforts. NatoADEs − Natoforceneeds.

Sensitivity Analysis: NATO-Favorable Case

The following tables are a sample of the sensitivity checks I conducted both to better understand the inner workings of the model and to determine whether there were plausible values for certain variables that would radically alter the basic conclusion I have drawn from this excursion—that is, NATO was quite competitive with the Warsaw Pact in the mid-1980s. All center on M+75. This day was chosen because in many of the combinations of values I tested, this turned out to be the most common period of stress on NATO's forces. I conducted tests of one variable against another until I felt comfortable with the workings of the model. I did not encounter any results that I regarded as unreasonable. Nevertheless, it is entirely possible that a relationship is buried in the model, of which I am unaware, that could produce peculiar results. Readers are encouraged to conduct their own analysis.

The Lotus or Symphony package has a built-in sensitivity generator called "What-If." I let its capabilities govern the pattern of the sensitivity analysis. Two kinds are possible. One may test combinations of two input variables against one output cell, in this case, the state of a particular output variable on a given day. Or one may vary one input variable to test many output variables on a given day. Of course, one could simply do a lot of runs, draw a lot of graphs, and compare them.

I have done this as well, but the display of many graphs and many alternative combinations of assumptions would consume a great deal of space.

I tested several pairs of variables, for several values each, against NATO's surplus or deficit (preceded by a minus sign) as of M+75 in *adjusted ADEs*. There is one sensitivity check that addresses variations in the number of days of intense combat. Two variables were tested over several values for four output variables—combat days, NATO's surplus or deficit, Pactlosses, and Natolosses. The descriptors on the output should be sufficient to indicate what was done in each sensitivity. Output values are rounded to the first decimal place.

Some relationships appear odd at first glance, but upon reflection they make sense, at least to me. The assumption embedded in the model that Red cannot sustain intense combat if he cannot meet his own demands for attrition and FEBA-population produces many important results. This assumption does not produce notable results if one assumes that Pact reinforcements arrive very quickly. But if one uses mobilization schedules that delay Pact divisions for postmobilization training, the Pact frequently finds itself with insufficient forces to sustain intense combat. Thus, combat has an erratic quality. (CAS is also slaved to the pace of the ground battle; it is not permitted to grind out kills if the pace of the ground war slackens.)

One might assume that a larger number of Pact breakthrough efforts would automatically put greater strain on NATO, but this is not so. The reason is that the Pact must find more forces to sustain such an effort, and if it cannot, combat stops. When combat stops, both attrition and movement stop, so less strain is placed on NATO's forces.

Similarly, higher densities of Pact forces within breakthrough sectors may kill NATO forces faster, but since the demands on the Pact also grow, again combat stops on days when the Pact has too few forces to populate the pistons at the appropriate densities. When combat stops, pistons do not move forward and NATO is not forced to populate their deepening flanks. This highlights another aspect of the model—the double stress that it imposes on NATO. Red "consumes" Blue forces by killing them, at the selected exchange rate. Red ties down Blue forces on the flanks of his salients at virtually a one-to-one ratio, since each side in this run is obliged to populate the flanks of the piston at one ADE per 25 km. Because even in the NATO-favorable case all Pact pistons move forward at 2 km/day so long as the Pact has sufficient forces to keep up with the attrition and populate the deepening flanks, NATO is always subjected to two sources of stress—one associated with killing, the other associated with movement. For example, in the

NATO-favorable run displayed, each of the three Pact pistons has penetrated to a depth of 84 km when the Pact "runs out" of forces to stay the course.[5]

Perhaps the most striking sensitivity test is that varying the command-and-logistics multiplier and the exchange rate. Under the more favorable mobilization assumptions of the NATO-favorable scenario, NATO can cope with exchange rates as low as 1.25:1 and will remain competitive at this exchange rate if a command-and-logistics multiplier of 1.25 is applied. These are quite conservative assumptions, in my judgment. Similarly, with a 1.25:1 exchange rate and a 10-km-per-day movement rate, NATO still has a surplus of a dozen adjusted ADEs at M+75.

[5]Each side is also obliged permanently to populate the rest of the front at these designated force-to-space ratios. Red cannot thin these forces to keep up his strength in the breakthrough salients, and Blue cannot thin his forces to sustain higher densities in the breakthrough sectors. This is another way that even the NATO-favorable case remains conservative, since Red is permitted to fix blue forces at capabilities ratios of roughly 1:1.

Table A3.1. NATO surplus or deficit at M+75 adjusted ADEs

	Exchange rate			
Advance rate	1.25	1.5	2.0	2.0
2.0	24.2	26.0	27.4	29.1
5.0	16.1	17.0	17.9	18.9
7.5	14.1	14.6	15.1	15.7
10.0	12.1	12.4	12.7	13.0

	Pact attrition			
C^2 multiplier	.08	.1	.15	.2
1.25	13.4	13.4	11.0	12.7
1.5	27.4	27.4	25.0	26.7
1.75	41.4	41.4	39.0	40.7
2.0	55.4	55.4	53.0	54.7

	Breakthrough sectors				
Offense breakthrough – density (km)	2	3	4	5	6
8.5	33	31.6	33.5	35.9	36.7
12.5	31.3	29.5	27.0	28.3	28.7
16.5	30.0	27.4	25.2	22.7	23.3
20.5	29.7	26.5	23.9	21.0	19.4

	Attrition			
Exchange rate	.08	.1	.15	.2
1.25	24.2	23.2	18.4	19.1
1.5	25.6	25.0	21.4	22.5
2.0	27.4	27.4	25.0	26.7
2.0	29.1	29.7	28.8	30.9

	C^2 multiplier			
Exchange rate	1	1.25	1.5	2
1.25	−3.8	10.0	24.2	52.0
1.5	−2.4	11.6	25.6	53.6
2.0	−0.6	13.4	27.4	55.4
3.0	1.1	15.1	29.1	57.2

Table A3.2. Combat days by M+75

Offensive concentrations (km) – nonbreakthrough sectors	Offensive attrition – breakthrough sectors			
	.08	.1	.15	.2
25	32	29	26	21
30	37	34	29	23
35	41	37	31	25
40	45	39	33	27

Table A3.3. Single-variable influence on conditions at M+75

	cbt days	sur/def	Pact losses	NATO losses
Breakthru sectors				
2	40	30.1	21.9	13.6
3	32	27.4	23.7	12.2
4	27	25.2	25.3	12.7
5	24	22.7	27.4	13.6
6	19	23.3	25.9	12.5
Offense breakthrough density (km/ADE)				
8.5	21	31.6	27.8	13.6
12.5	27	29.5	25.0	12.6
16.5	32	27.4	23.7	12.2
20.5	35	26.5	22.0	11.5

Table A3.4. Attrition-FEBA Expansion Model input value cell addresses

A8: DIMENSIONS	
A9: Initial Front Length	B9: 750
A10: Breakthroughwidth	B10: 50
A11: breakthrough#	B11: 3
A12: offenseadesector	B12: 16.5
A13: offense non-breakthrough	B13: 25
A14: defense ade sector	B14: 25
C8: DYNAMICS	
C9: Pact attrition	D9: .075
C10: Pact advance rate	D10: 2
C11: Pact:Nato exchange rate	D11: 2
C12: Nato c3,log.multiplier	D12: 1.5
C14: PactDatM+	D14: 30
E8: CLOSEAIR	
E9: Pact ac	F9: 1470
E10: Pact attr.	F10: .05
E11: Pact k	F11: .35
E12: Pact sr	F12: 1
G9: Nato ac	H9: 1630
G10: Nato attr	H10: .05
G11: Nato k	H11: .5
G12: Nato sr	H12: 2

Table A3.5. Equations for Attrition-FEBA Expansion Model

Cell	Label	Cell	Formula
A17:	Pact Mob+	A19:	+A18+1
B17:	Pact ADEs	B19:	29.0
C17:	NATO ADEs(7-day lag)	C19:	22.8
D17:	Pactcoverforce	D19:	($B$9−($B$10*$B$11))/$B$13
E17:	Pactassaultforce	E19:	+$B$10*$B$11/$B$12
F17:	Pdailyflnk	F19:	@IF(B19>018#AND#A19>=$D$14,+$B$11*$D$10*2/$B$13,0)
G17:	Pactflankforce	G19:	+G18+F19
H17:	nrmldailyloss	H19:	@IF(B19>018#AND#A19>=$D$14,+E19*$D$9,0)
I17:	combatdaycount	I19:	@IF(B19>018#AND#A19>=$D$14,I18+1,I18+0)
J17:	bluCAS killed	J19:	@IF(B19>018#AND#A19>=$D$14,K18*$H$11*((1−(1−$H$10)^($H$12+1))/$H$10−1)/1200,0)
K17:	bluCASac	K19:	@IF(B19>018#AND#A19>=$D$14,K18*(1−$H$10)^$H$12,K18)
L17:	CumCaskill	L19:	+L18+J19
M17:	Pgroundcbt	M19:	@IF(H19>J19,H19−J19,0)
N17:	Pactattrition	N19:	@IF(J19>H19,N18+J19,N18+H19)
O17:	Pactforceneeds	O19:	+D19+E19+G19+N19
P17:	Pactliveade	P19:	+B19−N19
Q17:	Pact am sur/def	Q19:	+B19−O18
R17:	NatoDefForce	R19:	+$B$9/$B$14
S17:	Ndailyflank	S19:	@IF(B19>018#AND#A19>=$D$14,+$B$11*$D$10*2/$B$14,0)
T17:	Natoflankforce	T19:	+T18+S19
U17:	dailylossgrnd	U19:	@IF(B19>018#AND#A19>=$D$14,+M19/$D$11,0)
V17:	dailylossredair	V19:	@IF(B19>018#AND#A19>=$D$14,W18*$F$11*((1−(1−$F$10)^($F$12+1))/$F$10−1)/1200,0)
W17:	redCASac	W19:	@IF(B19>018#AND#A19>=$D$14,W18*(1-$F$10)^$F$12,W18)
X17:	CumRedCasKill	X19:	+X18+V19
Y17:	totaldailyloss	Y19:	+U19+V19
Z17:	Natoattrition	Z19:	+Z18+Y19
AA17:	Natoforceneeds	AA19:	+R19+T19+Z19
AB17:	Natoliveades	AB19:	+C19−Z19
AC17:	Natodivisionfront	AC19:	($B$9+(G19*$B$13))/AB19
AD17:	adjarrivs	AD19:	+C19*$D$12
AE17:	Natoadjdivfrnt	AE19:	($B$9+(G19*$B$13))/($D$12*AB19)
AF17:	adj am sur/def	AF19:	+AD19−AA18
AG17:	real am sur/def	AG19:	+C19−AA18

Table A3.6. Attrition-FEBA Expansion Model—NATO favorable case

Pact Mob+ (A)	Pact ADEs (B)	NATO ADEs (C)	Pactcover (D)	Pactassaul (E)	Pdailyflnk (F)	Pactflankforce (G)	nrmldailyloss (H)	combatdaycount (I)
0.0	27.8	22.8	24.0	9.1	0.0	0.0	0.0	0.0
7.0	36.6	22.8	24.0	9.1	0.0	0.0	0.0	0.0
14.0	38.3	31.3	24.0	9.1	0.0	0.0	0.0	0.0
21.0	40.3	36.2	24.0	9.1	0.0	0.0	0.0	0.0
28.0	40.3	42.1	24.0	9.1	0.0	0.0	0.0	0.0
35.0	52.1	44.7	24.0	9.1	0.5	2.9	0.7	6.0
42.0	52.1	45.8	24.0	9.1	0.5	6.2	0.7	13.0
49.0	52.1	45.8	24.0	9.1	0.0	7.2	0.0	15.0
56.0	52.1	48.0	24.0	9.1	0.0	7.2	0.0	15.0
63.0	57.4	49.8	24.0	9.1	0.5	9.6	0.7	20.0
70.0	73.0	53.4	24.0	9.1	0.5	13.0	0.7	27.0
77.0	83.0	57.1	24.0	9.1	0.5	16.3	0.7	34.0
84.0	83.0	61.4	24.0	9.1	0.5	19.7	0.7	41.0
91.0	83.0	65.8	24.0	9.1	0.0	20.2	0.0	42.0

(continued)

Table A3.6. (cont.) Attrition-FEBA Expansion Model—NATO favorable case

bluCAS killed (J)	bluCASac (K)	CumCaskill (L)	Pgroundcbt (M)	Pactattrition (N)	Pactforceneeds (O)	Pactliveade (P)	Pact am sur/def (Q)	NatoDefForce (R)
0.0	1630.0	0.0	0.0	0.0	33.1	27.8	−5.3	30.0
0.0	1630.0	0.0	0.0	0.0	33.1	36.6	3.5	30.0
0.0	1630.0	0.0	0.0	0.0	33.1	38.3	5.2	30.0
0.0	1630.0	0.0	0.0	0.0	33.1	40.3	7.2	30.0
0.0	1630.0	0.0	0.0	0.0	33.1	40.3	7.2	30.0
0.8	880.8	5.9	0.0	5.9	41.9	46.1	11.4	30.0
0.4	429.5	9.5	0.3	10.7	50.0	41.4	3.2	30.0
0.0	349.9	10.1	0.0	12.1	52.4	40.0	−0.3	30.0
0.0	349.9	10.1	0.0	12.1	52.4	40.0	−0.3	30.0
0.2	209.5	11.2	0.5	15.5	58.2	41.9	0.4	30.0
0.1	102.2	12.1	0.6	20.2	66.3	52.7	7.8	30.0
0.0	49.8	12.5	0.6	25.0	74.4	57.9	9.7	30.0
0.0	24.3	12.7	0.7	29.8	82.6	53.2	1.5	30.0
0.0	21.9	12.7	0.0	30.5	83.7	52.5	−0.8	30.0

Table A3.6. (cont.) Attrition-FEBA Expansion Model—NATO favorable case

Ndailyflank (S)	Natoflankforce (T)	dailylossgrnd (U)	dailylossredair (V)	redCASac (W)	CumRedCasKill (X)	totaldailyloss (Y)	Natoattrition (Z)
0.0	0.0	0.0	0.0	1470.0	0.0	0.0	0.0
0.0	0.0	0.0	0.0	1470.0	0.0	0.0	0.0
0.0	0.0	0.0	0.0	1470.0	0.0	0.0	0.0
0.0	0.0	0.0	0.0	1470.0	0.0	0.0	0.0
0.0	0.0	0.0	0.0	1470.0	0.0	0.0	0.0
0.5	2.9	0.0	0.3	1080.6	2.2	0.3	2.2
0.5	6.2	0.2	0.2	754.6	4.0	0.4	4.6
0.0	7.2	0.0	0.0	681.0	4.4	0.0	5.3
0.0	7.2	0.0	0.0	681.0	4.4	0.0	5.3
0.5	9.6	0.3	0.2	527.0	5.2	0.4	7.3
0.5	13.0	0.3	0.1	368.0	6.1	0.4	10.2
0.5	16.3	0.3	0.1	257.0	6.7	0.4	13.0
0.5	19.7	0.3	0.1	179.5	7.2	0.4	15.7
0.0	20.2	0.0	0.0	170.5	7.2	0.0	16.1

(continued)

Table A3.6. (cont.) Attrition-FEBA Expansion Model—NATO favorable case

Natoforceneeds (AA)	Natoliveades (AB)	Natodivisionfront (AC)	adjarrivs (AD)	Natoadjdivfrnt (AE)	adj am sur/def (AF)	real am sur/def (AG)
30.0	22.8	32.9	34.2	22.0	4.2	−7.2
30.0	22.8	32.9	34.2	22.0	4.2	−7.2
30.0	31.3	24.0	46.9	16.0	16.9	1.3
30.0	36.2	20.7	54.3	13.8	24.3	6.2
30.0	42.1	17.8	63.2	11.9	33.1	12.1
35.0	42.5	19.3	67.0	12.9	32.8	10.4
40.8	41.2	22.0	68.7	14.7	28.7	5.8
42.5	40.4	23.0	68.7	15.3	26.1	3.2
42.5	42.7	21.8	72.0	14.5	29.5	5.5
46.9	42.4	23.3	74.7	15.6	28.6	3.7
53.1	43.2	24.8	80.1	16.6	27.9	1.2
59.3	44.1	26.3	85.6	17.5	27.2	−1.4
65.4	45.7	27.2	92.1	18.1	27.6	−3.1
66.2	49.7	25.2	98.7	16.8	32.4	−0.5

APPENDIX 4

A Barrier Defense Model

The purpose of this discussion is to describe a notional NATO ASW barrier defense system, review the effectiveness estimates of such barriers available in the expert literature, and adjust those estimates for changes in the Soviet submarine force and NATO ASW capabilities.

Dave Shilling offered an estimate of cumulative barrier effectiveness in a 1977 report for the Senate Budget Committee.[1] There, he repeated an estimate of ASW effectiveness that first surfaced in a 1973 newspaper account of a classified OSD study.[2] It concluded that in ninety days of combat NATO's ASW barriers could destroy between 70 percent and 90 percent of the Soviet attack submarine force, if that force were thrown through the barriers against the SLOC.

Assumptions about the number of barriers that this force would plausibly have crossed in ninety days permits an estimate of the effectiveness of each barrier. First, I assume a sixty-day submarine patrol.[3] In that sixty days, the average Soviet submarine (then a diesel-electric boat) is expected to spend fifteen days in transit to the mid-Atlantic sea lanes, thirty days on station, and fifteen days in transit to home base. It rests for fifteen days and then begins the cycle anew. In this period it could be expected to pass through eight notional barriers:

Day 1–15: A North-Cape-Svalbard barrier of SSNs and mines; a GIUK gap barrier of submarines, mines, and land-based aircraft;

[1]U.S. Congress, Senate, Budget Committee, *A Perspective*, p. 242.

[2]Michael Getler, "Study Insists NATO Can Defend Itself." *Washington Post*, 7 June 1973, p. 20

[3]See app. B, prepared by Peter Tarpgaard, in Zackheim, *General Purpose Navy*, p. 130, for estimates of modern diesel-electric patrol durations. The bulk of the Soviet submarine fleet in 1973 was diesel-electric, although probably less capable than Tarpgaard's model submarines.

Day 15–45: two convoy escort forces during two convoy attacks; close escorts would be supported by proximate "open ocean" search conducted by carrier task forces and land-based ASW aircraft that could also reinforce convoy escorts in the event that they found themselves overwhelmed; some NATO submarines might also have been present;
Day 45–60: the same two barriers as Day 1–15;
Day 60–75: rest and refit;
Day 75–90: the same two barriers as Day 1–15.

If one takes the average of 70-percent and 90-percent destruction, 80-percent destruction will be the working figure, which yields 20 percent of the Soviet submarine force surviving eight barriers. This means that the eighth root of .2 yields the share of the force that survives each barrier encounter, which is .82, or 82 percent. Thus the pk of each barrier is 1 − .82, which is .18.[4]

There was, however, a shift in the qualitative relationship of the two forces between 1973 and the mid-1980s. In response to a question on how much of a shift against the United States has occurred, how much our qualitative advantage has "depreciated," Adm. Wesley McDonald replied, "That would be very difficult, because we have at the same time upgraded our capabilities to meet that threat. But I would say we have probably lost about half. And that would be a rough estimate."[5] From the text of the exchange it appears that the admiral did not refer to U.S. capability versus the entire Soviet submarine force, much of which was old, but versus its newest combatants. If we assume that this included everything deployed after 1975, and if we further assume that the newest assets went to the two major Soviet naval commands, the Northern and the Pacific fleets, then roughly 25 percent of those

[4]This is within the range of "illustrative" barrier pks that others have chosen for their analysis. Enthoven and Smith, *How Much Is Enough?*, pp. 225–234, use .2 and assume ten barriers per submarine roundtrip. Wright, "Developing Maritime Force Structure Options for the US Defense Program," p. 58, tests barrier kill probabilities of .05 and .1 but assumes eleven barriers per roundtrip, rather than eight as I do; the authors of chap. 13, "Quantifying the Sealane Defense Problem," in Nitze and Sullivan, eds., *Securing the Seas*, assume a .1 barrier pk in their base case, with a total of ten barriers, but test barrier pks of .05 and .2 (pp. 352, 372). Although it may be unfair to point this out, all of these "illustrative" numbers were offered by experts who had reason to know how illustrative they might be. In the only intensive, real-life barrier ASW campaign, the Bay Offensive of 1 May–31 December 1943 in the Bay of Biscay, the Allies sank 32 U-boats of 258 entering and 247 departing submarines, for an overall pk of .063. During the first three months of the period, however, the Germans made a serious blunder by trying to travel on the surface by day and shoot it out with flak against Allied patrol aircraft. From 1 June 1942 to 31 May 1944 the average pk of the Bay barrier was only about .03. See Morison, *The Atlantic Battle Won*, p. 105; and Lindsey, "Tactical ASW," p. 38.

[5]*SASC, FY 86, Pt. 3*, p. 1315.

fleets were modern.[6] Thus, the best Soviet SSNs would have suffered 9 percent attrition per barrier.

One can then use a weighted average to derate the overall effectiveness of NATO's mid-1980s ASW barriers. Three-quarters of the force would have suffered as much as in the mid-1970s; one-quarter of the force, the newest quarter, would have suffered half as much. The former assumption is probably pessimistic, since the improvements the United States made to deal with the evolving threat should have increased ASW effectiveness versus earlier submarines. Thus,

$$\frac{(.18 \times 3) + (.09 \times 1)}{4} = .1575.$$

These are, of course, only rough estimates of the average effectiveness of each barrier against old and new Soviet submarines over many trials over many weeks. They are based on sparse information that has trickled out from the professional military, analytic, and intelligence community over many years. On the basis of my own open-source research on ASW in the 1980s, as well as my own assessment of World War II experience, I find these values plausible.

[6] U.S. Department of Defense, *The FY 1987 DOD Program for Research and Development, Statement by the Under Secretary of Defense for Research and Engineering to the 99th Congress, 2d session* (Washington, D.C., 1986), pp. iv–17.

Selected Bibliography

Books, Monographs, and Articles in Books

Alberts, D. J. *Deterrence in the 1980's: Part II, The Role of Conventional Air Power. Adelphi Paper,* 193. London: International Institute for Strategic Studies, 1984.

Allison, Graham. *Essence of Decision.* Boston: Little, Brown, 1971.

Arkin, William, and Richard W. Fieldhouse. *Nuclear Battlefields: Global Links in the Nuclear Arms Race.* Cambridge, Mass.: Ballinger, 1985.

Armstrong, Patrick. "On Combined Arms." In *The Mechanized Battlefield,* ed. Lt. Col. J. A. English. Washington, D.C.: Pergamon, 1985.

Ball, Desmond, *Can Nuclear War Be Controlled?* Adelphi Paper, 169. London: International Institute for Strategic Studies, 1981.

——. "Nuclear War at Sea." In *Naval Strategy and National Security,* ed. Steven E. Miller and Stephen Van Evera. Princeton: Princeton University Press, 1988.

Beesley, Patrick. *Very Special Intelligence.* New York: Ballantine, 1981.

Betts, Richard K. *Soldiers, Statesmen, and Cold War Crises.* Cambridge: Harvard University Press, 1977.

——. *Surprise Attack: Lessons for Defense Planning.* Washington, D.C.: Brookings Institution, 1983.

Birnbaum, Karl E. *Peace Moves and U-Boat Warfare.* Hamden, Conn.: Archon, 1970.

Blair, Bruce. *Strategic Command and Control: Redefining the Nuclear Threat.* Washington, D.C.: Brookings Institution, 1985.

Blair, Clay. *The Forgotten War: America in Korea, 1950–1953.* New York: Times Books, 1987.

——. *Silent Victory.* New York: Bantam, 1975.

Blumenson, Martin. *Breakout and Pursuit.* Washington, D.C.: Government Printing Office, 1961.

Bracken, Paul. *The Command and Control of Nuclear Forces.* New Haven: Yale University Press, 1983.

Brodie, Bernard. *Strategy in the Missile Age.* 1959. Reprint. Princeton: Princeton University Press, 1965.

Builder, Carl. *Strategic Conflict without Nuclear Weapons*. Santa Monica: Rand Corporation, April 1983.

Builder, Carl, et al. *The Rand Winter Study on Nonnuclear Strategic Weapons: Executive Summary*. Santa Monica: Rand Corporation, December 1984.

Canby, Steven. *The Alliance and Europe: Part IV, Military Doctrine and Technology*. Adelphi Paper 109. London: International Institute for Strategic Studies, 1978.

Carter, Ashton B., John D. Steinbruner, and Charles A. Zraket, eds. *Managing Nuclear Operations*. Washington, D.C.: Brookings Institution, 1987.

Charles, Dan. *Nuclear Planning in NATO: Pitfalls of First Use*. Cambridge: Ballinger, 1987.

Cherry, Peter W. "Quantitative Analysis of Intelligence/Electronic Warfare: Vector IEW." In *Systems Analysis and Modeling in Defense: Development, Trends, and Issues*. ed. Reiner, K. Huber. New York: Plenum Press, 1984.

Clausewitz, Carl Von. *On War*. Princeton: Princeton University Press, 1984, 1976.

Craig, Gordon. *The Politics of the Prussian Army, 1640–1945*. London: Oxford University Press, 1955.

Crutwell, C. R. M. F. *A History of the Great War, 1914–1918*. 2d ed. London: Oxford, Clarendon, 1934.

Davis, Paul K. *The Role of Uncertainty in Assessing the NATO–Pact Central-Region Balance*. Santa Monica: Rand Corporation, 1988.

Dixon, Norman. *On The Psychology of Military Incompetence*. London: Jonathan Cape, 1976.

Douglas, Joseph, and Amoretta Hoeber. *Conventional War and Escalation: The Soviet View*. New York: Crane, Russak, 1981.

Dunnigan, James F. *How to Make War*. New York: William Morrow, 1982.

Dupuy, Trevor N. *Elusive Victory: The Arab-Israeli Wars, 1947–74*. New York: Harper and Row, 1978.

Durch, William, and Peter Almquist. "East-West Military Balance." In *International Security Year Book, 1984–1985*, ed. Barry M. Blechman and Edward N. Luttwak. Boulder, Colo.: Westview Press, 1985.

Ellis, Major L. F. *The Battle of Normandy, Victory in the West*, vol. 1: *History of the Second World War*. U.K. Military Series. London: HMSO, 1962.

Enthoven, Alain C., and Wayne K. Smith. *How Much Is Enough?* New York: Harper and Row, 1971.

Epstein, Joshua. *Measuring Military Power: The Soviet Air Threat to Europe*. Princeton: Princeton University Press, 1984.

——. *The 1987 Defense Budget*. Washington, D.C.: Brookings Institution, 1986.

——. *The 1988 Defense Budget*. Washington, D.C.: Brookings Institution, 1987.

——. *Strategy and Force Planning: The Case of the Persian Gulf*. Washington, D.C.: Brookings Institution, 1987.

Erickson, John. *Road to Berlin: Stalin's War with Germany*. London: Weidenfeld and Nicolson, 1983.

——. *The Road to Stalingrad: Stalin's War with Germany*. New York: Harper and Row, 1975.

——. *The Soviet High Command: A Military-Political History, 1918–1941*. Boulder and London: Westview, 1984. (First published in 1962.)

Erickson, John, Lynn Hansen, and William Schneider. *Soviet Ground Forces: An Operational Assessment*. Boulder, Colo.: Westview Press, 1986.

Foot, Rosemary. *The Wrong War: American Policy and the Dimensions of the Korean Conflict, 1950–1953*. Ithaca: Cornell University Press, 1985.

Garwin, Richard. "The Interaction of Anti-Submarine Warfare with the Submarine-Based Deterrent." In *The Future of the Sea-Based Deterrent*, ed. Kosta Tsipis, Ann H. Cahn, and Bernard T. Feld. Cambridge: MIT Press, 1973.

Gazit, Shlomo. "Arab Forces Two Years after the Yom Kippur War." In *Military Aspects of the Israeli-Arab Conflict*, ed. Louis Williams. Tel Aviv: University Publishing Projects, 1975.

Hackman, Willem. *Seek and Strike.* London: HMSO, 1984.

Hallex, Robert. "Sea Battle Models." In *Military Modeling*, ed. Wayne P. Hughes. Alexandria, Va.: Military Operations Research Society, 1984.

Halperin, Morton. *Limited War in the Nuclear Age.* New York: John Wiley, 1963.

Hersh, Seymour M. *The Target Is Destroyed.* New York: Random House, 1986.

Herzog, Chaim. *The Arab-Israeli Wars: War and Peace in the Middle East.* New York: Vintage, 1984.

——. *The War of Atonement: October 1973.* Boston: Little, Brown, 1975.

Hinsley, F. H. *British Intelligence in the Second World War: Its Influence on Strategy and Operations*, vol. 2. New York: Cambridge University Press, 1981.

Hoffman, Hans W., Reiner K. Huber, and Karl Steiger. "On Reactive Defense Options." In *Modeling and Analysis of Conventional Defense in Europe: Assessment and Improvement Options.* New York: Plenum Press, 1986.

Holloway, David. *The Soviet Union and the Arms Race.* New Haven: Yale University Press, 1983.

Hosmer, Stephen T., and Glenn Kent. *The Military and Political Potential of Conventionally Armed Heavy Bombers.* Santa Monica: Rand Corporation, August 1987.

International Institute for Strategic Studies. *The Military Balance.* London: International Institute for Strategic Studies, 1983–1989 editions.

Isby, David C. *Weapons and Tactics of the Soviet Army.* London: Jane's, 1981.

——. *Weapons and Tactics of the Soviet Army.* London: Jane's, 1988.

Jane's World Railways, 1984–85. London: Jane's, 1984.

Jervis, Robert. *Perception and Misperception in International Politics.* Princeton: Princeton University Press, 1975.

Jones, David R. "Air Defense Forces." In *Soviet Armed Forces Review Annual, Vol. 6*, ed. David R. Jones. Gulf Breeze, Fla.: Academic International Press, 1982.

——. "National Air Defense Forces." In *Soviet Armed Forces Review Annual, Vol. 4*, ed. David R. Jones. Gulf Breeze, Fla.: Academic International Press, 1980.

Kaufmann, William W. "The Arithmetic of Force Planning." In *Alliance Security: NATO and the No-First-Use Question*, ed. John D. Steinbruner and Leon V. Sigal. Washington, D.C.: Brookings Institution, 1983.

——. "Defense Policy." In *Setting National Priorities: Agenda for the 1980's*, ed. Joseph A. Pechman. Washington, D.C.: Brookings Institution, 1980.

——. "Limited Warfare." In *Military Policy and National Security*, ed. William W. Kaufmann. Princeton: Princeton University Press, 1956.

——. "Nonnuclear Deterrence." In *Alliance Security: NATO and the No-First-Use Question*, ed. John D. Steinbruner and Leon V. Sigal. Washington, D.C.: Brookings Institution, 1983.

——. "Nuclear Deterrence in Central Europe." In *Alliance Security: NATO and the No-First-Use Question*, ed. John D. Steinbruner and Leon V. Sigal. Washington, D.C.: Brookings Institution, 1983.

Keegan, John. *Six Armies in Normandy.* New York: Viking, 1982.

Legge, Michael P. *Theater Nuclear Weapons and the NATO Strategy of Flexible Response.* Santa Monica: Rand Corporation, 1983.

Liddel-Hart, B. H. *Deterrent or Defense: A Fresh Look at the West's Military Position.* New York: Praeger, 1960.
Longstreth, Thomas K., John E. Pike, and John B. Rhinelander. *The Impact of US and Soviet Ballistic Missile Defense Programs on the ABM Treaty.* 3d ed. Washington, D.C.: National Campaign to Save the ABM Treaty, 1985.
McCarthy, James R., Brig. Gen., and Robert E. Rayfield, Lt. Col. *Linebacker Two: A View from the Rock.* USAF Southeast Asia Monograph Series, vol. VI, No. 8. Maxwell Air Force Base, 1979.
MccGwire, Michael. *Military Objectives in Soviet Foreign Policy.* Washington, D.C.: Brookings Institution, 1987.
MacDonald, Charles B. *The Siegfried Line Campaign.* Washington, D.C.: Government Printing Office, 1963.
MacDonald, Gordon, Jack Ruina, and Mark Balaschak. "Soviet Strategic Air Defense." In *Cruise Missiles: Technology, Strategy, Politics,* ed. Richard K. Betts. Washington, D.C.: Brookings Institution, 1981.
Mako, William. *US Ground Forces and the Defense of Central Europe.* Washington, D.C.: Brookings Institution, 1983.
May, Ernest R. *The World War and American Isolation, 1914–1917.* Cambridge: Harvard University Press, 1966.
Mearsheimer, John J. *Conventional Deterrence.* Ithaca: Cornell University Press, 1983.
Meyer, Stephen M. "Soviet Nuclear Operations." In *Managing Nuclear Operations,* ed. Ashton B. Carter, John D. Steinbruner, and Charles A. Zraket. Washington, D.C.: Brookings Institution, 1987.
——. *Soviet Theatre Nuclear Forces,* pts. 1 and 2. Adelphi Papers 187 and 188. London: International Institute for Strategic Studies, 1984.
Miller, Steven E., ed. *Military Strategy and the Origins of the First World War.* Princeton: Princeton University Press, 1985.
Miller, Steven, and Charles Glaser, eds. *The Navy and Nuclear Weapons.* Book manuscript in preparation.
Momyer, William, Gen. *Airpower in Three Wars.* Washington, D.C.: Government Printing Office, 1978.
Morison, Samuel Elliott. *The Atlantic Battle Won, May 1943–May 1945,* vol. X: *History of United States Naval Operations in World War II.* Boston: Little, Brown, 1975.
——. *The Two Ocean War.* Boston: Little, Brown, 1963.
Nitze, Paul H. and Leonard Sullivan, eds. (with the Atlantic Council Working Group on Securing the Seas). *Securing the Seas: The Soviet Naval Challenge and Western Alliance Options.* Boulder, Colo.: Westview Press, 1979.
Osgood, Robert. *Limited War: The Challenge to American Strategy.* Chicago: University of Chicago Press, 1957.
Perse, John D. *U.S. Declaratory Policy on Soviet SSBN Security: 1970 to 1985.* Center for Naval Analysis Research Memorandum 84-29. Washington, D.C.: Center for Naval Analysis, May 1986.
Posen, Barry R. "The Defense Resource Riddle." In *European Assertiveness: Is There a New Role for Europe in International Relations?* ed. Beverly Crawford. Berkeley: Institute for International Studies, 1990.
——. *The Sources of Military Doctrine: France, Britain, and Germany between the World Wars.* Ithaca: Cornell University Press, 1984.
Quester, George. *Deterrence before Hiroshima.* New York: John Wiley, 1955.

Record, Jeffrey. *Sizing Up the Soviet Army*. Washington, D.C.: Brookings Institution, 1975.

Rohwer, Jurgen. *The Critical Convoy Battles of March 1943*. London: Ian Allen, 1977.

Ropp, Theodore. *War in the Modern World*. New York: Collier Books, 1962.

Roskill, S. W. *The War at Sea, 1939–1945*, vol. III: *The Offensive, Part I*. London: HMSO, 1960.

Sakitt, Mark. *Submarine Warfare in the Arctic: Option or Illusion?* CISAC Occasional Paper. Stanford, Calif.: Stanford University Center for International Security and Arms Control, May 1988.

Sallagar, F. M. *The Road to Total War: Escalation in World War II*. Santa Monica: Rand Corporation, 1969.

Salman, Michael, Stephen Van Evera, and Kevin Sullivan. "Analysis or Propaganda? Measuring American Strategic Nuclear Capabilities, 1969–1988." In *Nuclear Arguments: Understanding the Strategic Nuclear Arms and Arms Control Debates*, ed. Lynn Eden and Steven E. Miller. Ithaca: Cornell University Press, 1989.

Schelling, Thomas. *Arms and Influence*. New Haven: Yale University Press, 1966.

Schelling, Thomas, and Morton Halperin. *Strategy and Arms Control*. Washington, D.C.: Pergamon-Brassey's, 1985.

Schiff, Ze'ev, and Ehud Ya'ari. *Israel's Lebanon War*, ed. and trans. Ina Friedman. New York: Simon and Schuster, 1984.

Schmitt, Bernadotte E., and Harold C. Vedeler. *The World in the Crucible*. New York: Harper and Row, 1984.

Schnabel, James F. *United States Army in the Korean War, Policy and Direction: The First Year*. Washington, D.C.: Office of the Chief of Military History, United States Army, 1972.

Schwartz, David. *NATO's Nuclear Dilemmas*. Washington, D.C.: Brookings Institution, 1983.

Sigal, Leon. "No First Use and NATO's Nuclear Posture." In *Alliance Security and the No-First-Use Question*, ed. John Steinbruner and Leon V. Sigal. Washington, D.C.: Brookings Institution, 1983.

Snyder, Jack. "Civil-Military Relations and the Cult of the Offensive, 1914 and 1984." In *Military Strategy and the Origins of the First World War*, ed. Steven E. Miller. Princeton: Princeton University Press, 1985.

Steinbruner, John D. "Choices and Trade-offs." In *Managing Nuclear Operations*, ed. Ashton B. Carter, John D. Steinbruner, and Charles A. Zraket. Washington, D.C.: Brookings Institution, 1987.

Stokesbury, James L. *A Short History of World War II*. New York: William Morrow, 1980.

Streetly, Martin. *World Electronic Warfare Aircraft*. London: Jane's, 1983.

Sutton, Boyd, et al. "Strategic and Doctrinal Implications of Deep Attack Concepts for the Defense of Central Europe." In *Military Strategy in Transition: Defense and Deterrence in the 1980's*, ed. Keith J. Dunn and William O. Staudenmaier. Boulder, Colo.: Westview Press, 1984.

Thomas, Clayton P. "Models and Wartime Operations Research." In *Military Modeling*, ed. Wayne P. Hughes. Alexandria, Va.: Military Operations Research Society, 1989.

Thompson, James. *An Unfavorable Situation: NATO and the Conventional Balance*. Santa Monica: Rand Corporation, 1988.

Tritten, James J. *Soviet Naval Forces and Nuclear Warfare. Weapons, Employment, and Policy.* London and Boulder, Colo.: Westview Press, 1986.

Van Evera, Stephen. "The Cult of the Offensive and the Origins of the First World War." In *Military Strategy and the Origins of the First World War*, ed. Steven E. Miller. Princeton: Princeton University Press, 1985.

Van Evera, Stephen, et al. "Appendix: How Our Simulations Were Performed." In *Nuclear Arguments*, ed. Lynn Eden and Stephen E. Miller. Ithaca: Cornell University Press, 1989.

Vasendin, N., Maj. Gen., and Kuznetsov, N., Col. "Modern Warfare and Surprise Attack," *Voyennaya Mysl* 6 (1968). Reprinted and translated in *Selected Readings from Military Thought 1963–1973, USAF Studies in Communist Affairs* 5, pt. 1. Washington, D.C.: Government Printing Office, 1982.

Waltz, Kenneth. *Man, the State, and War: A Theoretical Analysis.* 1954. Reprint. New York: Columbia University Press, 1959.

Watkins, James. "The Maritime Strategy." In U.S. Naval Institute, *The Maritime Strategy.* Annapolis, Md.: U.S. Naval Institute, January 1986.

Weigley, Russell. *Eisenhower's Lieutenants.* Bloomington: Indiana University Press, 1981.

Wilkes, Owen, and Nils Petter Gleditsch. *Intelligence Installations in Norway: Their Number, Location, Function, and Legality.* Oslo: International Peace Research Institute, February 1979, revised July 1979 (photocopy).

Wright, Christopher C. "Developing Maritime Force Structure Options for the US Defense Program." Masters thesis, Massachusetts Institute of Technology, 1976.

Articles in Journals and Magazines

Alexander, Joseph. "The Role of US Marines in the Defense of Northern Norway." *US Naval Institute Proceedings, Naval Review 1984*, May 1984.

Amundsen, Kirsten. "Soviet Submarines in Scandinavian Waters." *Washington Quarterly* 8 (Summer 1985).

Ball, Desmond. "Nuclear War at Sea." *International Security* 10 (Winter, 1985–86).

Blechman, Barry M., and Mark R. Moore. "A Nuclear Weapon Free Zone in Europe." *Scientific American*, April 1983.

Bowman, Richard C. "Soviet Options on NATO's Northern Flank." *Armed Forces Journal International*, April 1984.

Brooks, Linton. "Naval Power and National Security: The Case for the Maritime Strategy." *International Security* 11 (Fall 1986).

Chalmers, Malcolm, and Lutz Unterseher. "Is There a Tank Gap? Comparing NATO and Warsaw Pact Tank Fleets." *International Security* 13 (Summer 1988).

Cordesman, Anthony H. "The NATO Central Region and the Balance of Uncertainty." *Armed Forces Journal International*, July 1983.

Daugherty, William, Barbara Levi, and Frank Von Hippel. "The Consequences of 'Limited' Nuclear Attacks on the United States." *International Security* 10 (Spring 1986).

Davis, Gen. Bennie, USAF. "Indivisible Airpower." *Air Force Magazine* 67 (March 1984).

Donald, Daniel C. and Gael Donelan-Tarleton. "The Soviet Navy in 1984." *US Naval Institute Proceedings, Naval Review Issue,* May 1985.
——. "The Soviet Navy in 1985." *US Naval Institute Proceedings, Naval Review Issue,* May 1986.
Ermarth, Fritz. "Contrasts in American and Soviet Strategic Thought." *International Security* 3 (Fall 1978).
Epstein, Joshua. "The 3:1 Rule, the Adaptive Dynamic Model and the Future of Security Studies." *International Security* 13 (Spring 1989).
"An Exclusive AFJI Interview with General Wilbur L. Creech." *Armed Forces Journal International,* January 1983.
Ford, Daniel. "The Button," pts. 1 and 2. *New Yorker,* 1 and 8 April 1985.
Friedberg, Aaron L. "A History of the US Strategic Doctrine, 1945–1980." *Journal of Strategic Studies* 3 (December 1980).
Friedman, Norman. "SOSUS and US ASW Tactics." *US Naval Institute Proceedings* 106 (March 1980).
Furlong, R. D. M. "The Strategic Situation in Northern Europe." *International Defense Review,* June 1979.
——. "The Threat to Northern Europe." *International Defense Review,* April 1979.
Gans, Dan. "Fight Outnumbered and Win," pt. 1. *Military Review* 60 (December 1980).
Garthoff, Raymond L. "Mutual Deterrence and Strategic Arms Limitation in Soviet Policy." *International Security* 3 (Summer 1978).
Gormley, Dennis. "Understanding Soviet Motivations for Deploying Long-Range Theater Nuclear Forces." *Military Review* 61 (September 1981).
Heymont, Irving, and Melvin Rosen. "Foreign Army Reserve Systems." *Military Review* 53 (March 1973).
Holst, Johan J. "Norway's Search for a Nordpolitik." *Foreign Affairs* 60 (Fall 1981).
Homer-Dixon, Thomas F. "A Common Misapplication of the Lanchester Square Law, A Research Note." *International Security* 12 (Summer 1987).
Hooton, Edward. "Country Portrait Norway." *NATO's Sixteen Nations* 29 (December 1984–January 1985).
Hostettler, Stephen J. "The Sea-Launched Cruise Missile." *NATO's Sixteen Nations* 29 (December 1984–January 1985).
Jervis, Robert. "Cooperation under the Security Dilemma." *World Politics* 30 (January 1978).
King, Robert. "Are NATO's Navies Shipshape?" *Armed Forces Journal International,* March 1986.
Lebow, Ned. "The Soviet Offensive in Europe: The Schlieffen Plan Revisited?" *International Security* 9 (Summer 1985).
Lepingwell, John W. R. "The Laws of Combat? Lanchester Reexamined." *International Security* 12 (Summer 1987).
Libbey, Miles III. "Tomahawk." *US Naval Institute Proceedings, Naval Review,* 1984.
MccGwire, Michael. "The Rationale for the Development of Soviet Seapower." *US Naval Institute Proceedings,* 106 (May 1980).
McDonald, Wesley L. "The Critical Role of Sea Power in the Defense of Europe." *NATO's Sixteen Nations* 29 (December 1984–January 1985).
——. "The Growing Warsaw Pact Threat to NATO Maritime Forces." *NATO Review* 32 (1984).

Mearsheimer, John J. "Assessing the Conventional Balance: The 3:1 Rule and Its Critics." *International Security* 13 (Spring 1989).
——. "A Strategic Misstep: The Maritime Strategy and Deterrence in Europe." *International Security* 11 (Fall 1986).
——. "Why the Soviets Can't Win Quickly in Central Europe." *International Security* 7 (Summer 1982).
"NATO's Sinking Feeling." *The Economist*, 6 June 1981.
"Norway Formulating Long-Range Defense Plans." *Aviation Week and Space Technology*, 6 July 1981, pp. 42–48.
O'Donnell, Hugh. "Northern Flank Maritime Offensive." *US Naval Institute Proceedings* 111 (September 1985).
Peterson, Phillip A., and John G. Hines. "The Conventional Offensive in Soviet Theater Strategy." *Orbis* 27 (Fall 1983).
Posen, Barry R. "Competing Images of the Soviet Union." *World Politics* 39 (July 1987).
——. "Is NATO Decisively Outnumbered?" *International Security* 12 (Spring 1988).
——. "Measuring the European Conventional Balance." *International Security* 9 (Winter 1984–85).
——. "NATO's Reinforcement Capability." *Defense Analysis* 5 (Winter 1990).
Record, Jeffrey. "Armored Advance Rates: A Historical Inquiry." *Military Review* 53 (September 1973).
Ries, Tomas. "Defending the Far North." *International Defense Review* 17, no. 7 (1984).
Robinson, Clarence A., Jr. "US Says Soviets Knew Korean Air Lines 747 Was Commercial Flight." *Aviation Week and Space Technology*, 12 September 1983.
Sagan, Scott D. "Nuclear Alerts and Crisis Management." *International Security* 9 (Spring 1985).
Sharp, John. "The Northern Flank." *RUSI Journal* 121 (December 1976).
Smoke, Richard. "Extended Deterrence: Some Observations." *Naval War College Review* 36 (September–October 1983).
Sorensen, Magne T. "Maritime Air Operations in the North." *NATO's Sixteen Nations, Special Issue*, February 1984.
"Soviets Order Sa-8s into Action in Bekaa after Israeli Successes." *Aviation Week and Space Technology*, 9 August 1982, pp. 18–19.
Steinbruner, John. "Launch under Attack." *Scientific American* 250 (January 1984).
Ulsamer, Edgar. "Bombers for the Battlefield." *Air Force Magazine* 70 (January 1987).
"USAF Planning Stealth Cruise Missile." *Aviation Week and Space Technology*, 8 November 1982.
"US Says Soviets Knew Korean Air Lines 747 Was Commercial Flight." *Aviation Week and Space Technology*, 12 September 1983, pp. 18–21.
Wit, Joel, S. "Advances in Antisubmarine Warfare." *Scientific American* 244 (February 1981).
Wood, Robert S., and John T. Hanley. "The Maritime Role in the North Atlantic." *Naval War College Review* 38 (November–December 1985).
Wright, Christopher. "US Naval Operations in 1985." *US Naval Institute Proceedings, Naval Review Issue*, May 1986.

Government Documents

Aspin, Les. "The World After Zero INF." News release, House Armed Services Committee, 29 September 1987.
Carlucci, Frank C. *Report on Allied Contributions to the Common Defense*. Washington, D.C.: Department of Defense, April 1988.
Commission on Integrated Long-Term Strategy. *Discriminate Deterrence, Report of the Commission on Integrated Long-Term Strategy*. Washington, D.C.: Government Printing Office, January 1988.
Defense Intelligence Agency. *Soviet Divisional Organizational Guide*. Washington, D.C.: 1982.
DeLauer, Richard. "Estimated Dollar Cost of NATO and Warsaw Pact Defense Activities, 1965–1985." In *The FY 1987 DOD Program for Research and Development*, 99th Cong., 2d sess., 18 February 1986. Washington, D.C.: Government Printing Office, 1986.
Federal Republic of Germany. Federal Minister of Defense. *White Paper 1985, The Situation and Development of the Federal Armed Forces*. Bonn, 1985.
Future Security Environment Working Group. *Sources of Change in the Future Security Environment*. Report to the Commission on Integrated Long-Term Strategy. Washington, D.C.: Department of Defense, April 1988.
Levin, Carl. *Beyond the Bean Count, Realistically Assessing the Conventional Military Balance in Europe*, 2d ed. Washington, D.C.: Senate Armed Services Subcommittee on Conventional Forces and Alliance Defense, July 1988 (mimeographed).
Luns, Joseph. *NATO and the Warsaw Pact: Force Comparisons*. Brussels: NATO Information Service, 1984.
NATO. "Conventional Arms Control: The Way Ahead," statement issued under the authority of the heads of state and government participating in the meeting of the North Atlantic Council in Brussels. In *Conventional Forces in Europe: The Facts*. Brussels: NATO, 25 November 1988.
NATO Information Service. *NATO and the Warsaw Pact: Force Comparisons*. Brussels: NATO Information Service, 1984.
Organization of the Joint Chiefs of Staff. *United States Military Posture, FY 1986*. Washington, D.C.: Joint Chiefs of Staff, 1985.
O'Rourke, Ronald. *Nuclear Escalation, Strategic Anti-Submarine Warfare, and the Navy's Forward Maritime Strategy*. Congressional Research Service Report No. 87-138F. Washington, D.C., 27 February 1987.
Romjue, John L. *From Active Defense to Airland Battle: The Development of Army Doctrine, 1973–1982*. TRADOC Historical Monograph Series. Ft. Monroe, Va.: Historical Office, U.S. Army Training and Doctrine Command, June 1984.
Sternhell, D. M., and A. M. Thorndike. *Antisubmarine Warfare in World War II*. Operations Evaluation Group Report No. 51. Washington, D.C., 1946.
U.S. Army. *Maneuver Control*. Washington, D.C.: Headquarters Department of the Army, 1973.
——. *Operations*. Field Manual 100-5. U.S. Army, 1976.
——. *Operations*. Field Manual 100-5. U.S. Army, 1982.
——. *The Soviet Army: Operations and Tactics*. Washington, D.C.: Headquarters, Department of the Army, 1984.

——. *U.S. Army Armor Reference Data*, vols. 1 and 2. Fort Knox, Ky.: U.S. Army Armor School, 1981.

——. *U.S. Army Armor Reference Manual*, vol. 3. Fort Knox, Ky.: U.S. Army Armor School, 1981.

——. *Weapon Effectiveness Index/Weighted Unit Values (WEI/WUV), Executive Summary*. U.S. Army War Gaming Directorate Concepts Analysis Agency, Study Report CAA-SR-73-18. April 1974 (mimeographed).

U.S. Central Intelligence Agency. Directorate of Intelligence. *The Soviet Weapons Industry: An Overview*. Washington, D.C.: Central Intelligence Agency, September 1986.

——. National Foreign Assessment Center. *Soviet and US Defense Activities, 1970–79: A Dollar Cost Comparison*. Washington, D.C.: Central Intelligence Agency, 1980.

U.S. Congress. Congressional Budget Office. *Army Ground Combat Modernization for the 1980's: Potential Costs and Effects for NATO*. Prepared by Nora Slatkin. Washington, D.C., November 1982.

——. *Building a 600-Ship Navy: Costs, Timing and Alternative Approaches*. Prepared by Peter T. Tarpgaard. Washington, D.C., March 1982.

——. *Future Budget Requirements of the 600-Ship Navy*. Prepared by Peter T. Tarpgaard and Robert E. Mechanic. Washington, D.C., September 1977.

——. *Improving the Army Reserves*. Prepared by John Enns. Washington, D.C., November 1985.

——. *Modernizing US Strategic Offensive Forces*. Prepared by Bonita Dombey. Washington, D.C., November 1987.

——. *Navy Budget Issues for Fiscal Year 1980*. Prepared by Dov S. Zackheim and Marshall Hoyler. Washington, D.C., March 1979.

——. *Shaping the General Purpose Navy of the Eighties: Issues for Fiscal Years 1981–1985*. Prepared by Dov S. Zackheim et al. Washington, D.C., January 1980.

——. *Tactical Combat Forces of the US Air Force: Issues and Alternatives*. Prepared by Lane Pierrot and Bob Kornfeld. Washington, D.C., April 1985.

——. *U.S. Ground Forces: Design and Cost Alternatives for NATO and Non-NATO Contingencies*. Prepared by Pat Hillier and Nora Slatkin. Washington, D.C., December 1980.

——. *US Ground Forces and the Conventional Balance in Europe*. Prepared by Frances M. Lussier. Washington, D.C., June 1988.

——. *The US Sea Control Mission: Forces, Capabilities, and Requirements*. Prepared by Dov S. Zackheim. Washington, D.C., June 1977.

U.S. Congress. Foreign Affairs and National Defense Division. Congressional Research Service. "Arms Control Implications of Anti-Submarine Warfare Programs." Prepared by Bruce Blair. In *Evaluation of Fiscal Year 1979 Arms Control Impact Statements*. Washington, D.C.: Government Printing Office, 1978.

U.S. Congress. House. Appropriations Committee. Subcommittee on the Department of Defense. *DOD Appropriations for 1985, Part 1, Secretary of Defense and Chairman, Joint Chiefs of Staff*, 98th Cong., 2d sess., 1984. Washington, D.C.: Government Printing Office, 1984.

——. Committee on Armed Services. *Hearings on Military Posture and Department of Defense Appropriations for Fiscal Year 1980*, 96th Cong., 1st sess., 1979. Washington, D.C.: Government Printing Office, 1979.

——. Committee on Armed Services. *Hearings on Military Posture and Department of Defense Appropriations for Fiscal Year 1979*, 95th Cong., 2d sess., 1978. Washington, D.C.: Government Printing Office, 1978.

——. Committee on Armed Services. *Soviet Readiness for War: Assessing One of the Major Sources of East-West Instability. Report of the Defense Policy Panel*, 100th Cong., 2d sess., 5 December 1988. Washington, D.C.: Government Printing Office, 1988.

——. Committee on Armed Services. Subcommittee on Research and Development. *Statement on Nuclear Force Modernization.* 100th Cong., 2d sess., 1 March 1988 (mimeographed).

——. House Armed Services Committee. *Department of Defense Authorization of Appropriations for Fiscal Year 1984, Part 3, Statement of General Lawrence Skantze*, 98th Cong., 1st sess., 1983. Washington, D.C.: Government Printing Office, 1983.

——. House Armed Services Committee on Intelligence Issues. Seapower and Strategic and Critical Materials Subcommittee. *Statement of Rear Admiral William O. Studeman.* 100th Cong., 2d sess., 1 March 1988 (mimeographed).

U.S. Congress. Joint Economic Committee. *Allocation of Resources in the Soviet Union and China—1985*, 99th Cong., 2d sess., Part 11, 1986. Washington, D.C.: Government Printing Office, 1986.

——. Subcommittee on International Trade, Finance, and Security Economics. *Allocation of Resources in the Soviet Union and China—1981*, 97th Cong., 1st sess., pt. 7, 1982. Washington, D.C.: Government Printing Office, 1982.

U.S. Congress. Office of Technology Assessment. *New Technology for NATO: Implementing Follow-On Forces Attack.* Washington, D.C.: Government Printing Office, June 1987.

——. *Technologies for NATO's Follow-On Forces Attack Concept.* Washington, D.C.: Government Printing Office, July 1986.

U.S. Congress. Senate. Budget Committee. *A Perspective on Anti-Submarine Warfare: Statement by David Shilling. Hearings on the first concurrent resolution for Fiscal Year 1978*, 95th Cong., 1st sess., 1977. Washington, D.C.: Government Printing Office, 1977.

——. Committee on Armed Services. *DOD Authorization for Appropriations for Fiscal Year 1985, Status of the Atlantic Command, Part 2*, 98th Cong., 2d sess., 1984. Washington, D.C.: Government Printing Office, 1984.

——. Committee on Armed Services. *DOD Authorization for Appropriations for Fiscal Year 1985, Maritime Strategy, Part 8*, 98th Cong., 2d sess., 1984. Washington, D.C.: Government Printing Office, 1984.

——. Committee on Armed Services. *Hearings on Department of Defense Appropriations for Fiscal Year 1981*, 96th Cong., 1st sess., 1980. Washington, D.C.: Government Printing Office, 1980.

——. Committtee on Armed Services. *Hearings on Department of Defense Appropriations for Fiscal Year 1978*, 95th Cong., 1st sess., 1977. Washington, D.C.: Government Printing Office, 1977.

——. Committee on Armed Services. *Hearings on Department of Defense Appropriations for Fiscal Year 1977*, 94th Cong., 2d sess., 1976. Washington, D.C.: Government Printing Office, 1976.

——. Committee on Armed Services. Subcommittee on Sea Power and Force Projection. *DOD Authorization for Appropriations for Fiscal Year 1986. Testimony of John L. Butts, Rear Admiral, US Navy Director for Naval Intelligence, Part 8,* 99th Cong., 1st sess., 1985. Washington, D.C.: Government Printing Office, 1986.

——. Committee on Armed Services. Subcommittee on Sea Power and Force Projection. *DOD Authorization for Appropriations for Fiscal Year 1985. Testimony of Secretary of the Navy, John Lehman, Admiral James D. Watkins, Chief of Naval Operations and Lt. Gen. Bernard E. Trainor on Seapower and Force Projection, Part 8,* 98th Cong., 2d sess., 1984. Washington, D.C.: Government Printing Office, 1984.

——. Subcommittee on Strategic and Theater Nuclear Forces of the Senate Armed Services Committee and the Defense Subcommittee of the Senate Committee on Appropriations. *Soviet Strategic Force Developments, Testimony by Robert M. Gates and Lawrence K. Gershwin,* 99th Cong., 1st sess., 1985. Washington, D.C.: Government Printing Office, 1985.

U.S. Department of the Army. *Soviet Army Operations.* Washington, D.C.: U.S. Department of the Army, April 1978.

U.S. Department of Defense. *Annual Report to the Congress.* Washington, D.C.: Government Printing Office, annual, for the fiscal year.

——. *The FY 1984 DOD Program for Research, Development and Acquisitions.* Washington, D.C.: Department of Defense, 1983.

——. *A Report to Congress on U.S. Conventional Reinforcements to NATO.* Washington, D.C.: Government Printing Office, 1976.

——. *Soviet Military Power, 1988.* Washington, D.C.: Government Printing Office, 1988.

——. *Soviet Military Power, 1987.* Washington, D.C.: Government Printing Office, 1987.

——. *Soviet Military Power, 1986.* Washington, D.C.: Government Printing Office, 1986.

——. *Soviet Military Power, 1985.* Washington, D.C.: Government Printing Office, 1985.

——. *Soviet Strategic Defense Programs.* Washington, D.C.: Government Printing Office, October 1985.

——. Assistant Secretary of Defense for Program Analysis and Evaluation. *NATO Center Region Military Balance Study 1978–84* (declassified). Office of the Secretary of Defense, 13 July 1979 (photocopy).

U.S. Department of State. *Foreign Relations of the United States, 1950.* Vol. VII: *Korea,* September 9, 1950. Washington, D.C.: Government Printing Office, 1976.

U.S. Department of Transportation, Maritime Administration. *Merchant Fleets of the World.* Washington, D.C.: U.S. Department of Transportation, December 1986.

Voigt, Karsten. *Interim Report of the Sub-Committee on Conventional Defense in Europe.* Brussels: North Atlantic Assembly, 1984.

Weinberger, Caspar W. *Report on Allied Contributions to the Common Defense.* Washington, D.C.: Government Printing Office, 1983–(annual).

Index

Library of Congress Cataloging-in-Publication Data

Posen, Barry R.
Inadvertent escalation : conventional war and nuclear risks/ Barry R. Posen.
p. cm.—(Cornell studies in security affairs)
Includes bibliographical references and index.
ISBN: 978-0-8014-7885-7
1. Escalation (Military science) 2. Nuclear threshold (Strategy) 3. Limited war.
4. Europe—Defenses. 5. United States—Military policy. I. Title. II. Series.
U11.P83 1991
355.02'15—dc20 91-55055

Printed in the USA
CPSIA information can be obtained
at www.ICGtesting.com
LVHW030420100923
757650LV00002B/158